War By Other Means

WAR BY
OTHER MEANS
Soviet Power, West German
Resistance, and the Battle of
the Euromissiles

Jeffrey Herf

THE FREE PRESS
A Division of Macmillan, Inc.
NEW YORK

Collier Macmillan Canada
TORONTO

Maxwell Macmillan International
NEW YORK   OXFORD   SINGAPORE   SYDNEY

The Free Press
A Division of Macmillan, Inc.
866 Third Avenue, New York, N.Y. 10022

Collier Macmillan Canada, Inc.
1200 Eglinton Avenue East
Suite 200
Don Mills, Ontario M3C 3N1

Printed in the United States of America

printing number
1 2 3 4 5 6 7 8 9 10

Library of Congress Cataloging-in-Publication Data

Herf, Jeffrey
    War by other means : Soviet power, West German resistance, and
the battle of the Euromissiles / Jeffrey Herf.
        p.   cm.
    Includes bibliographical references.
    ISBN 0-02-915030-2
    1. Germany—Politics and government—1982- 2. Europe—Politics
and government—1945- 3. Germany (West)—Foreign relations.
4. Nuclear weapons—Europe—History. 5. Nuclear weapons—Germany
(West)—History. 6. North Atlantic Treaty Organization—Armed
Forces —Weapons systems—History. 7. Intermediate-range ballistic
missiles—History. 8. SS-20 Missile—History. I. Title.
DD262.H47 1991
940.55—dc20   90-43201
                                                                      CIP

For Sonya

CONTENTS

PREFACE

THE BATTLE OF EUROMISSILES of the early 1980s was the last great political conflict of the Cold War in Europe. In the summer of 1990, communism has collapsed in Eastern Europe, the Berlin Wall is gone, Germany's political unification is soon to follow its economic unification, former dissidents serve as heads of state of emergent democracies in Czechoslovakia, Poland, and Hungary, and the Soviet Union has agreed to membership of a unified Germany in the NATO alliance. None of these events is the direct consequence of the battle of the euromissiles. However, it is hard to imagine their coming without the reversal in the momentum of global politics which it represented. Less than a decade ago, respected commentators of the European scene asked if democracies would perish because of their political virtues, and if dictatorships would triumph because of their political vices. Knowledgeable Western observers worried that the Soviet Union would be able to drive the United States out of Western Europe by playing on internal divisions in Western Europe, especially on neutralist and pacifist sentiment in West Germany.

As the following study seeks to show, fears of democratic vulnerability were not without some foundation. However, they underestimated the moral and political resources of liberal democracy in Western Europe. To the surprise of Soviet leaders, and even of many Western leaders, West Germany's leaders successfully resisted Soviet pressures. The following study seeks to account for both vulnerability and resilience in West Germany by looking closely at its political culture, that is, at the political beliefs, moral convictions, and public language of the leading personalities of West German political life, as well as of those journalists and intellectuals who tried to influence the decisions of these leading individuals. The causes of the collapse of communism in Eastern Europe and the first steps towards the democratization of the whole of Europe are multiple and complex. The following study examines one of the historical preconditions of the events of 1989, the reversal of the momentum of global politics from 1977 to 1983 which took place in the course of the political battle over nuclear weapons, or euromissiles, in Europe.

Though the battle of the euromissiles raged in all of the countries of Western Europe, especially the five NATO countries where American missiles were to be deployed, it was most intense in West Germany. The most remarkable and historically unprecedented aspect of the turning point of 1983 was that it was accomplished without war. The intensity and the political stakes of the battle of the euromissiles merit paraphrasing Clausewitz to describe it as a war by other means. Given the nuclear stalemate war was unthinkable as an instrument of policy. Fear of nuclear war remained a potent political force. Though this fear of war was equally distributed in the hearts and minds of all people, its capacity to influence the policies of the contending governments varied dramatically. This was a direct result of Eruope's division between dictatorships and democracies, and the absence of political freedom in the then intact Warsaw Pact. All of the public debate took place in Western Europe and the United States, while the Soviet Union and its Warsaw Pact allies remained immune from domestic criticism. A study of the battle of the euromissiles illuminates the instability of the juxtaposition of dictatorship and democracy in Europe, while reminding us that peace in Europe and freedom in its Eastern half are mutually reinforcing.

Although the European political landscape has been transformed by the revolution of 1989, the issues discussed in West Germany during the battle of the euromissiles have continuing significance. The author stands by his view that a neutral Germany will either be too strong, tempted to have its own nuclear arsenal, or too weak, tempting a Soviet Union which will be anything but stable for some time to come. What Thomas Mann called a European Germany in place of a German Europe is most likely to continue to emerge if the United States continues to remain engaged in Europe. A redefined Atlanticism with a united Germany still firmly anchored in the West, continued European economic integration, and a United States still engaged in Europe are all key to a peaceful Europe composed of free democratic states. Faced with the possibility of a Europe in which liberal democratic values and institutions are predominant, it is important to reflect on a turning point of the recent past, a past which seems more distant than seemed possible to imagine only a year ago. In so doing, we recall the actors, and acts of human freedom and decision, that helped to bring dictatorship in Europe to an end.

ACKNOWLEDGMENTS

I WISH TO ACKNOWLEDGE the following institutions and individuals for their support. A postdoctoral fellowship in the Ford Foundation Program on Western Society and European Security at the Center for International Affairs at Harvard in 1983–84 made possible partial release from teaching responsibilities. A summer travel grant in the Ford program in 1984 made possible research in West Germany. A Fellowship for Independent Study and Research from the National Endowment for the Humanities in 1985–86 made possible a second year of research and writing at the Center for International Affairs. A grant from the Lynde and Harry Bradley Foundation for 1988–89 made possible completion of the manuscript.

I benefited greatly from the interaction of historians, political scientists, and sociologists at Harvard's Committee on Degrees in Social Studies, at the Center for European Studies, and at the Center for International Affairs. David Landes, Stanley Hoffmann, and Samuel P. Huntington, respectively, have directed these three institutions in ways that aided many scholars. I am grateful for Robert Putnam's able administration of the Ford program, his determination to combine the study of international relations and comparative politics, and his encouragement to do open-ended interviews. Thanks are due to Robert Blackwill, formerly of the John F. Kennedy School at Harvard, later with the National Security Council, and now back at Harvard. I am also indebted to Daniel Bell for his very broad conception of sociology and his continuing encouragement over the years.

Many West German politicians, intellectuals, journalists, and government officials took time from busy schedules to grant interviews in summer 1984 and 1985 or respond to my written inquiries. In particular, I want to thank then former West German Chancellor Helmut Schmidt for agreeing to an interview. I note with regret the passing of Kurt Becker, one of West Germany's finest journalists writing on international affairs, and Alois Mertes, Christian Democratic speaker in the Bundestag and Staatssekretär in the Foreign Ministry in 1982–84, whose passionate intelligence was appreciated by political allies and adversaries. Michael Hereth, Günther Hoffmann, Douglas Stanglin, and Victoria Pope facilitated my research in West Germany with their insight and hospitality.

Elizabeth Nölle-Neumann, director of the Allensbach Institute for Demoskopie, and her staff were most gracious in making the Allensbach archives accessible to me. The staff of the Zentralarchiv für Empirische Sozialforschung in Cologne helped me to find appropriate survey materials. Hans Witt, director of the marketing department of *Der Spiegel*, made available that magazine's very informative annual market research reports. Bernhard Rosenblatt, directory of *Infratest Sozialforschung* in Munich, the staff of the Information and Press Staff at the West German Defense Ministry, and the Emid Institute made surveys results available. Members of the staff of the European Branch, Office of Research, at the International Communication Agency in Washington, as well as the staff of the National Archives, Machine Readable Division, made available the results of American government surveys of European public opinion, as did the staff of the Roper Center for Public Opinion Research at the University of Connecticut, where a wealth of surveys on postwar Europe are held.

I am grateful to librarians at the *Abteilung Wissenschaftlich Dokumentation* of West German Bundestag's archive, and at the press archives of the Bundestag, the *Frankfurter Allgemeine Zeitung*, the Fredrich Ebert Foundation, and the Foundation for Science and Politics at Ebenhausen. The staff of the library of the *Westdeutsche Rektorenkonferenz* was particularly helpful in advancing my examination of the documents of West German university life in the 1970s. The staff of the Government Documents Division of Widener Library at Harvard guided me through the vast sources at their disposal. Thanks are also due to the staff of Harvard's Office of Information Technology and to Robert Ross, for assistance while I was performing secondary analysis of quantitative data.

Many conversations contributed to my thinking. Thanks are due to my colleagues and students in the Committee on Degrees in Social Studies at Harvard, and in the department of political science at the College of the Holy Cross, where David Schaeffer shared my enthusiasm for Raymond Aron. Conversations with Alvin Bernstein, chair of the department, and with colleagues in the strategy department of the United States Naval War College in 1987–88 were a source of considerable stimulation.

Allan Bloom and Nathan Tarcov, co-directors, and Judy Chernick, administrative coordinator, of the John M. Olin Center for Inquiry into the Theory and Practice of Democracy at the University of Chicago, welcomed me to the Center in 1988–89, and provided rich intellectual stimulation and practical assistance for a year of writing. I enjoyed conversations with members of the Committee on Social Thought at the University of Chicago during a year at that university.

Conversations about German politics with Walter Laqueur and Josef Joffe have been most helpful. Michael Zöller, of the University of Bayreuth, read and commented on my analysis of developments in the 1970s in the universities. Robert S. Leiken commented on several chapters and shared his insights on the interaction of democracy and dictatorship drawn from recent Central American history. Karl Dietrich Bracher graciously read and commented on the entire manuscript.

Several steadfast friends and fine scholars added greatly to this book. Jerry Z. Muller has generously shared his clear insight into modern German history as well as his good humor and common sense. He read and commented on several chapters. Liah Greenfeld also read and commented on several chapters, published an essay drawn from this project dealing with "center and periphery" and German nationalism, and offered moral support throughout. Many conversations with Mark Osiel about liberal democracy and intellectuals were of great help.

Brief portions have previously appeared in *International Security, The National Interest, Partisan Review*, and *Telos*. I am grateful to editors and readers of those journals. In particular, I want to thank William Phillips and Edith Kurzweil of *Partisan Review*. Their friendship and their belief that civility and partisanship go hand in hand made this a better book. I appreciate comments and criticisms I received when I spoke about research in progress at the Center for European Studies and at the Center for International Affairs at Harvard, at the College of the Holy Cross, the Naval War College, the Committee on Social Thought at the University of Chicago, and the University of Illinois at Urbana-Champaign. Robert and Jana Kiely, masters of Adams House, Harvard University, helped to make the two years of 1984–86 which my wife and I spent as resident tutors pleasant and productive ones.

Thanks are due to loyal friends, and to my parents who communicated a love of learning and passion for truth which were the beginning of my commitment to scholarship. Nadja, my daughter, arrived in 1982, and has been a source of immense joy ever since. In the same period, my wife, Sonya Michel, completed her doctorate, and has begun to make her mark as an American historian. I am much indebted to her encouragement, support, and insight. I dedicate this book to her.

1

WAR BY OTHER MEANS

THIS BOOK IS ABOUT the battle of the euromissiles, one of the major turning points of postwar German, European, and international history. In 1975, in the European areas of its territory, the Soviet Union began to deploy the SS–20, a new missile with three nuclear warheads capable of striking all of Western Europe. The West's dispute with the Soviet Union over these intermediate-range nuclear weapons began in 1977 with a speech by the West German chancellor, took political shape in the form of NATO's two-track decision of December 1979, was tested in a four-year period of negotiations and public debate, and ended in November 1983 with a vote by the West German parliament to deploy in West Germany the cruise and Pershing II missiles, capable of striking Soviet territory. From 1979 to 1983, a public debate raged in the parliaments, media, and streets of Belgium, England, France, Holland, and Italy. In 1987, the United States and the Soviet Union signed an INF treaty that abolished both American and Soviet medium-range missiles. That treaty was based on principles first articulated by the United States in November 1981. The blunting of Soviet pressure on Western Europe in the early 1980s represented a victory for Western policy. It was one of the many preconditions for the emergence of efforts at reform in the Soviet Union and the collapse of communism in Eastern Europe in 1989.

To understand how the Soviet Union's political offensive was blunted, we will look at German and West German intellectual and political history and at how it influenced and was influenced by power politics between states and alliances. For the intellectual historian of modern Germany and the theorist of international relations, the fascination of the battle of the euromissiles lies both in the clarity with which it underscored the impact of ideas on politics in West Germany and in the example it offered of interaction of democratic and dictatorial regimes in relations between states.

The Western alliance entered the battle over the euromissiles with some strategic liabilities rooted in the political virtues of democracy, while the Warsaw Pact possessed some strategic advantages due to the political vices of dictatorship. The Soviet Union could use its dictatorial rule to prevent domestic dissent while taking advantage of Western pluralism and freedom to advance its policy. Hence all of the battle of the euromissiles took place in Western Europe. But democratic political virtues did not become disabling strategic vices. A common theme of historical and political commentary of the early 1980s concerned the vulnerability and coming crisis of Western democracies. In this study of the battle over the euromissiles, we turn to trends in political culture and the nature of democratic institutions to account for the unexpected resilience of West German democracy from 1977 to 1983.

The battle of the euromissiles convulsed the entire Atlantic Alliance, but the focal point of this international dispute lay in West Germany, where all of the major crises of the Cold War in Europe have been centered. A nonnuclear power, the Federal Republic was also the most exposed of NATO countries to Soviet military pressure. A West German leader, Chancellor Helmut Schmidt, first raised the question of the balance of intermediate-range nuclear forces. West German politicians, intellectuals, journalists, and antinuclear activists were the primary focus of Soviet efforts to gain a veto over the NATO decision. While all the other countries of Western Europe, especially Britain, Italy, and France, played important roles and while an indispensable precondition for implementing the NATO decision was the determination of President Reagan to carry through with the decision initiated by President Carter, it was in West Germany that the stakes and the temperature of the dispute were highest. Inability to implement the NATO decision in Belgium, Britain, Italy, or the Netherlands would have been a serious blow for the NATO decision. Had the West German electorate chosen leaders in 1983 who opposed the NATO deployments, the NATO decision would have been cancelled. In its intensity, high stakes, and peaceful character the battle of the euromissiles in West Germany merits the description of a war by other means.

This is a study of what Clausewitz called strategic interaction, that is, of the contest of wills between the Soviet Union and the Western alliance in West Germany during the euromissile dispute. Hence, I examine trends in West German political culture in light of their impact on the competition between NATO and the Warsaw Pact in West Germany. In my view, the history of the euromissile dispute supports the hypothesis that the Soviet Union had a political, military, and diplomatic policy whose goal was to weaken the link between Western Europe and the United States and to

expand Soviet influence in Western Europe. An American exit as a result
of political defeat would have left the Soviet Union as the dominant power
in Europe. Such an outcome would have been the most important change
in world politics since 1945. While the war in Afghanistan contributed to
more dissatisfaction among citizens of the Soviet Union with their own
government than did the euromissile dispute, no other defeat of Soviet
policy in the early and mid-1980s—in Afghanistan, Poland, or Central
America—had so significant an impact on preserving or changing the global
balance of forces as the euromissile dispute. None of these conflicts, taken
by themselves, had so great an immediate impact on the balance of forces
between the United States and the Soviet Union as a dispute in the center
of Europe did.

The Soviet strategy was to use Soviet military power to exploit fear of
nuclear war and to exploit the internal divisions of the West European
democracies, most of all in West Germany. In addition to its geostrategic
centrality, the Federal Republic was without a nuclear arsenal of its own
and was dependent on American nuclear deterrence. Hence, antinuclear
sentiment easily overlapped with feelings of national dependence and then
of national resentment. In Clausewitzian terms, the "center of gravity" or
most vulnerable point at which this strategy was directed was West German politics, from the level of elites to that of public opinion. Given this
strategic viewpoint, my primary interest in the West German political culture of the time was how it helped or hindered Soviet and Western
strategy.

To be sure, the West Germans were objects of international politics. But
they were also subjects, whose beliefs and convictions became an important
causal factor in the outcome of the euromissile dispute. This book is a
study of ideas and interpretations held by leading political figures and the
impact of these convictions on political decisions.[1] I want to call attention
to the role of subjectivity and intentions in the practical world of power
politics. The individuals who had the greatest impact were three West
German chancellors, Willy Brandt, Helmut Schmidt, and Helmut Kohl,
and the West German Foreign Minister, Hans-Dietrich Genscher. In the
parliamentary debates in the Bundestag (the West German parliament), key
figures were Egon Bahr, the leading foreign policy advisor to Willy Brandt;
Alois Mertes and Manfred Wörner, the leading Christian Democratic
speakers on foreign and defense policy during the euromissile dispute; leading West German political intellectuals, especially journalists on major
news magazines and newspapers; and strategists and critics of strategy
within and outside the West German government. All of these actors mattered. They were neither bit players in a structuralist's drama nor were

they faced with chaos and total indeterminacy. Rather they all had to make judgments in the context of real possibilities and consequences.

West Germany in the Context of German History

In the context of German history, the euromissile dispute raised the issue of whether West Germany would remain anchored in the Western alliance or wander back to a position between East and West. The existence of a German state, the Federal Republic of Germany or West Germany, anchored into a Western alliance was a novelty in the context of modern German history since the Reformation.[2] It replaced the concept of a German *Sonderweg*, or special path between East and West.[3] From the time of the French Revolution and the Napoleonic Wars, with the brief interlude of the Weimar Republic, Germany's national identity and central political institutions had been predominantly forged in opposition to Western—specifically, French and British—liberal political values and institutions. After 1945, as a result of changes within the West German political culture and the presence of the Western victors, the center of moral order of German society and politics became Western-oriented for the first time in modern German history.[4] The Sonderweg, the vision of an illiberal, anti-Western Germany that had led Germany and Europe to catastrophe, became peripheral to the political culture in the new West Germany founded in 1949.

The change of center and periphery in the late 1940s was most evident in the two major political parties, the Christian Democrats, led by Konrad Adenauer, and the Social Democrats, led by Kurt Schumacher. The Social Democratic party (SPD) in postwar West Germany was rooted in the old German center. It was the most important, intact political tradition that had predated Nazism. It had always been a democratizing force in German history. Before 1945, German conservatism had defined itself by its opposition to the Western liberal tradition and its affinity to the values of a strong and unified Prussian state and army. Adenauer's version of Christian Democracy, in the form of the Catholic Center party, had existed during the Weimar Republic. But Adenauer, then mayor of Cologne, remained a peripheral figure on the national stage. After 1945, Adenauer's variant of conservatism became the first in German history to unequivocally identify itself with, rather than against, the liberal democratic traditions of Britain, France, and the United States. The transformation of conservatism and the emergence of a West German in place of a German conservatism was a revolution in political culture without which a distinctively West German history would not have been possible. This Western-oriented Christian Democracy was the central new political fact of the Bonn Republic. West Germany's anchor in the Western alliance came to be most fiercely defended by the nominal parties of tradition, Adenauer's Christian Democrats along with the Free Democrats, West Germany's party of economic and political liberalism. Social Democrats, claiming they did not need any additional Westernization, initially opposed economic, military, and political integration into a Western alliance.[5]

The Basic Law or constitution of the Federal Republic was written with the experiences of the Weimar Republic in mind. To prevent a repetition of the destruction of democracy by extremists of the right and left, it provided for withdrawal of political rights from those who would use them to destroy democratic institutions.[6] In addition to these legal barriers, the founders shaped a political culture of "militant democracy," that is, one in which democrats of the right and left would unite in an "antitotalitarian consensus" against the undemocratic extremes.[7] It was the West German version of what Americans called "the vital center." A key question of West German politics since the 1960s was whether an erosion of these public moral boundaries between democracy and dictatorship on the left, especially in the era of détente, would lead West Germany to slip out from its Western ties to return to an older, once-discredited Sonderweg.

From the 1960s to the early 1980s, first conservatives and then increasingly centrists and some to the left of center worried that such boundaries were eroding on the West German left in the face of the combined impact of Social Democratic détente policy, the revival of Marxism in various forms, and the new left.[8] In place of a clear distinction between democracy and dictatorship, the new left attacked anticommunism and an alleged universal "system of domination," composed of two equally dangerous superpowers. The West German critics of SPD leader Willy Brandt's détente and Ostpolitik argued that his policies went beyond a pragmatic reconciliation of West Germans with the governments and peoples of Eastern Europe and the Soviet Union to include a declaration, in the words of one supporter of West German détente policy, of "the end of the ideological era," that is, an end of public, militant criticisms of communism and Communist governments by the West German government in the interest of détente.[9] Ending the ideological era meant a change in West German political culture, one which preceded change in the political systems of Eastern Europe and the Soviet Union, as a result of which leaders of the West German left ceased to publicly accentuate the moral boundaries between freedom and dictatorship. For the sake of a "peace policy" in which Europe appeared as a third force between "both superpowers," they spoke less about freedom or its absence in Eastern Europe and the Soviet Union.[10] The moral order of militant democracy began to hemorrhage on its left boundary. One result of this evolution in political culture that had direct consequences for the battle over the euromissiles was a taboo on blunt speaking about Soviet armament, including but not limited to the SS-20s, for fear of undermining peace and détente.

The new left and an adversary culture of intellectuals hostile to capitalism were not exclusively West German phenomena.[11] But in West Germany, the new left drew sustenance from the fact that both Marxism and romantic antagonism to capitalism were deeply embedded in German intellectual history. Because leftist intellectuals associated capitalism and liberalism with the United States, their revival of the old traditions of Marxism and romanticism brought with it criticism of the new and recent traditions of liberalism and capitalism that had pushed these older traditions to the periphery of national identity. The revival of Marxism and romanticism brought with it a revival of the German *Sonderweg* or *Sonderbewusstsein* (special consciousness) in new forms.[12] With the addition of the division of Germany, the revival of leftism from the 1960s to the 1980s brought with it a link to nationalism and tradition much greater than was the case in the new lefts elsewhere in Western Europe, Japan, and the United States.[13] If there was going to be a new version of the *deutschen Sonderweg* in the early 1980s, it was going to come primarily from the left rather than, as had been the case before 1945, the right.

The word that captured this yearning for a West Germany less rooted in a Western and American-led alliance is "neutralism." Neutralism in West Germany was less a set of diplomatic proposals than a moral stance with clear strategic implications. As a theory of international politics, neutralism stood for the proposition that the similarities between the armaments and foreign policies of the United States and the Soviet Union were more important than the differences between their forms of government and society.[14] The distinctive feature of the neutralist mood in West Germany lay in its connection to German nationalism. In a divided country, as the moral boundaries between social democracy and communism took a back seat to the attack on the "ideology of the Cold War," old boundaries of the German nation again reemerged, now in the form of "both Germanies" seen as the victim of "both superpowers."[15] As one West German commentator noted at the time, the transformation of West Germany into the victim of both superpowers represented a "rebirth of the nation." This feeling of shared victimization by the superpowers was a basis for a rediscovered common national identity.[16] The victimization of the West Germans at the hands of the United States became a central theme of the Soviet political offensive during the battle of the euromissiles.

Given these developments in the political culture of the West German left, West German liberals and conservatives bore the primary burden for making the public case for West Germany's Western orientation during the battle over the euromissiles. Beginning in the early 1970s, in response to the new left, a countermobilization of intellectuals and politicians took place, called the *Tendenzwende* or "change of tendency."[17] The Tendenzwende was, compared to the new left, a turn to the right. But the right to which it turned was the liberal democratic and procapitalist traditions of post-1945 West German conservatism. Just as the erosion of militant democracy on the left opened up opportunities for Soviet policy in West Germany, so the Tendenzwende of the 1970s was one necessary condition of its defeat in the early 1980s. Both of these intellectual developments of the 1970s, the shift to the left and the Tendenzwende, had direct consequences for the euromissile dispute.

Asymmetric Strategic Interaction

The battle of the euromissiles was a diplomatic struggle, in Clausewitzian terms, a strategic interaction between democracies and dictatorships. The question of whether or not a republican democracy would be strong enough in the face of internal divisions to effectively confront a hostile world played an important role in the arguments for a strong president made by the authors of the American Constitution and *The Federalist Papers*.[18] But recent American theorizing in international relations has devoted little attention to the peculiar features of such interaction. One purpose of this book is to call attention to a strand of the realist tradition that has emphasized the role of forms of governments in interactions between states. Realism is the dominant academic tradition of the study of international politics; within it, two schools of thought have contended. The first, the predominant view among American realists, has maintained that the pressures and the stakes of relations between states in a system of anarchy are so powerful that a common rationality is forced on them despite differences in forms of government or ideological perspectives. E. H. Carr and Hans Morgenthau, both of whom had a great impact on postwar American thinking about international politics, were confident that democracies could successfully compete with dictatorships.[19] Kenneth Waltz, another prominent representative of American realism, voiced similar optimism about the capacity of democracies to generate power in a 1967 study of American and British foreign policy since World War II.[20] In his theoretical works on international politics, sometimes referred to as structural realism, Waltz stressed the relative insignificance of the effect of forms of government on the behavior of states in world politics.[21] In a 1979 essay, Waltz abstracted "from every attribute of states except their abilities" to offer "a positional picture, a general description of the ordered overall arrangements of a society written in terms of the placement of units rather than in terms of their qualities."[22] While he acknowledged that the characteristics of states influenced how they responded to changes in the international system, such influence was a secondary feature of his realism.

A second school of realists argue that to show that democracies do not always perish and that dictatorships can make terrible blunders does not mean that the nature of regimes or their ideologies are insignificant for a theory of international relations.[23] Aaron Friedberg has recently focused attention on the difficulties British leaders had in coming to a proper assessment of the changing balance of power before World War I.[24] The West German historian of nazism, Karl Dietrich Bracher, has noted that Churchill's willingness to take Hitler's beliefs as the true basis of his actions made him a truer realist than Hitler's domestic and foreign adversaries who underestimated him by not taking those beliefs seriously enough.[25] Such approaches draw attention to the role of meaning and intentions, in plain language, to the role of ideas in politics and social action. They rest on Max Weber's insight that explanations in history and social science are causally adequate only if they are also adequate on the level of meaning.[26]

One purpose of the following study is to demonstrate the continuing validity of this interpretive approach in the study of power politics between states. Raymond Aron, as a sociologist, theorist of international relations and strategy, and contemporary historian combined the realist impulse in the study of power politics, with a Tocquevillian and Weberian sociological appreciation of the role of subjective factors and political institutions in social and political action. Aron put the character of societies, regimes, and ideologies at the center of his analysis of the ability of states to compete in international politics.[27] For Aron, the interaction of states could not be understood "except by reference to the established power in each of them, to the conception of legitimacy, to the external ambitions, and to the strategy and tactics of the ruling classes."[28] The nature of the "internal regime" affects the "degree of mobilization" of states and thus affects the "configuration of forces." "Calculation of forces and dialectic of regimes," considered jointly, not in isolation from one another, were indispensable for understanding diplomacy and strategy.[29] Writing of the Greek international system dominated by Athens and Sparta, Aron wrote that the system "depends on what the two poles, concretely, are, not only on the fact that they are two."[30] A change of regime—the French Revolution, the Nazi and Communist dictatorships—by affecting its capacity to mobilize potential into actual power could bring about a change in the international system.[31]

But such a change was no less dependent on the nature and will of other regimes. The experience of the 1930s left Aron with skepticism about the capacity of democracies to survive the challenge of dictatorships.

> The totalitarian nations were in peacetime, with equal forces, more powerful than the democratic nations. They presented a facade of unity, whereas the latter paraded their disputes. . . . Regimes in which one man commands, in which the deliberations occur in secret, are more capable of suggesting irresistible force and flawless resolution than those regimes whose press is free and whose parliament debates. In the diplomatic poker game the totalitarian state often bluffs and almost always wins—until the day when another nation calls the bluff.[32]

What Aron called "the theory of the insignificance of regimes," which he believed had become dominant in American realism of the postwar period, did not capture the nature of interaction between democracies and dictatorships in the twentieth century. In such interactions, democratic virtues could become strategic disadvantages, while dictatorial vices could emerge as strategic assets.[33] Aron, who had seen French democracy fall in 1940, did not share the confidence of Morgenthau and Waltz that democracies would not be crippled by their virtues.

Winston Churchill was a practitioner of realist politics who also appreciated the role of subjective factors in power politics. His *Gathering Storm* remains the classic analysis of what we could call *asymmetric strategic interaction* between dictatorship and democracy in the 1930s. Churchill wanted to show how World War II could have been prevented,

> how the malice of the wicked was reinforced by the weakness of the virtuous; how the structure and habits of democratic states, unless they are welded into larger organisms, lack those elements of persistence and conviction which alone can give security to humble masses.[34]

For Churchill, "British fatuity and fecklessness which, though devoid of guile, was not devoid of guilt" had played a "definite part in the unleashing upon the world of horrors and miseries which, even so far as they have unfolded, are already beyond comparison in human experience."[35] At the same time, Churchill continued, "two or three men" made policy in Germany with no political restraint and "no public opinion except what is manufactured by those new and terrible engines—broadcasting and the controlled press."[36]

Churchill's history of the democracies suggested that the political virtues of democracies that make them "open societies"—public debate, free elections, meaningful public opinion—can become strategic vices when confronted with regimes that are willing and able to exploit these virtues. Dictatorships can take advantage of the "closed" nature of their own regimes to prevent democratic governments from symmetrically influencing them. Their political vices—the absence of public debate, political pluralism, effective public opinion, or pressure groups—can become strategic virtues, immunizing them from foreign and domestic pressures. Given this structural asymmetry, he feared that the will of democratic states would be more difficult to sustain than that of dictatorships. As Churchill himself demonstrated, doing so required extraordinary leadership at crucial moments.[37]

The Soviet Union of Brezhnev and Andropov of the 1970s and 1980s was not the same as Hitler's Germany, nor was Western Europe identical to the politically divided and economically troubled British and French democracies, both of which were still traumatized by the horrors of World War I. But the 1980s, no less than the 1930s, offered a case of asymmetric strategic interaction between democratic and dictatorial regimes, in which the outcome of diplomatic crises depended largely on decisions taken as the outcome of debate in the open, democratic societies. In Western Europe in the 1970s and early 1980s, there was a growing sense among historians, strategists, and government officials that domestic politics in Western Europe would be central for Soviet–West European relations. In 1979, the British military and diplomatic historian Michael Howard called for renewed attention to "the forgotten dimensions of strategy," of political consensus and social cohesion.[38] Dissensus within Western Europe was of particular concern for those observers who believed Soviet policy aimed at the expulsion of American influence.

One of the most important and trenchant of these analysts was Lothar Rühl, a West German journalist and strategist writing on foreign and defense policy and a *Staatsekretär* (equivalent to an assistant secretary) responsible for international security affairs in the West German defense ministry during the euromissile dispute. In 1976, Rühl wrote that an American exit from Western Europe would leave the West Europeans with "no alternative to voluntary adaptation to this distribution of power" in which the

Soviet Union would be predominant.[39] Rühl worried that "the Soviet cause is slowly but surely finding wider acceptance in West European societies—not on the merits of the Soviet economic system or political style but on the strength of the awe-inspiring power of the Soviet military presence."[40] The more movements and parties in Western Europe directed their criticisms at the United States and/or adopted Soviet positions in arms controls negotiations, the more Rühl felt confirmed in his belief that military power was especially useful when directed against Western democracies.[41]

Soviet policy could succeed, in Rühl's view, only if it "finds supporters in the countries against whom the power politics are applied. Therefore the impact of Soviet diplomacy and political propaganda must necessarily be concentrated on the body politic of those countries."[42] It was in this sense that Soviet strategy bore comparison to Hitler's diplomacy of the 1930s. The Soviet Union used its totalitarian rule to prevent domestic dissent and took advantage of the pluralism and freedom of Western societies to advance its policy. As a result, the Soviet Union "has so far enjoyed a certain advantage over Western Europe in the field of international power politics. . . . This indirect drive for political influence on the home base of foreign governments is one of the main goals of Soviet policy in Western Europe and one of the major concerns of the Western countries exposed to it."[43] At the Ebenhausen Foundation for Science and Politics near Munich, a group of strategists led by its research director Uwe Nerlich argued that international arms control negotiations offered the Soviet Union the avenue of most direct influence on Western security policy and defense policy. As K. Peter Stratmann, one of the Ebenhausen analysts, put it, the primary danger for NATO in Europe lay not in the possible direct use of Soviet military power but in its indirect psychopolitical impact. "It is not 'aggression' or 'intimidation' that is [NATO's] greatest problem but rather the largely self-induced domestic blockage of its capacity for decision and action in defense policy."[44]

The vulnerability of democracies to dictatorships able to immunize themselves from diplomatic counteroffensives was the central theme of Jean-Francois Revel's 1983 book, *How Democracies Perish*.[45] "Only democratic governments are easily influenced" by the media and public opinion. Yet democrats could not plead their case in totalitarian countries, organize supporters or mass movements, or expect parliaments to "refuse or shave the appropriations requested by the Soviet Minister of Defense."[46] Michel Tatu, *Le Monde*'s diplomatic correspondent and expert on Soviet foreign policy, wrote that dictatorships saw the goal of negotiations as weakening the "other government's determination by applying extra pressure on it through its own public opinion. Here again, this instrument works in only one direction, since totalitarian states can 'protect' their own publics from foreign information and propaganda."[47] As a result, politically consequential fear of war and of nuclear war was unequally distributed, because of the contrasts of democracy and dictatorship. Only in the liberal democracies could such fear change government policy as a result of public pressure.[48] Tatu and Rühl worried that the fear of nuclear war itself had become a powerful tool of Soviet policy in Europe. Given their view of Soviet policy, strategists such as Rühl and Tatu examined developments within Western Europe and West Germany from the standpoint of how these affected Soviet policy as they interpreted it.[49] Nerlich stressed the strategic significance of the erosion of Social Democratic anticommunism and the ascendancy of Brandt's conception of détente within the SPD. This change, Nerlich argued, had transformed the Social Democratic party from a bulwark into a lever to be pulled by the Soviet Union in pursuing its strategy towards Western Europe.[50]

Rühl did recognize some disadvantages that the Soviet regime created for its policy in Europe. Outside the dwindling Stalinist remnants of the French, Italian, Portuguese, and Spanish Communist parties or parts of the Greek left, the Soviet political and economic system had no political appeal to Western Europeans. Repression in Eastern Europe was a constant reminder of this unappealing form of rule. An overly aggressive policy could rekindle Western unity and military countermobilization. But other disadvantages of the dictators and potential strengths of democracies received less attention from these strategists. For example, without political debate and criticism at home, the Soviet leaders were more prone to continue to pursue mistaken policies and to dismiss all criticism as imperialist propaganda. Such absence of criticism reduced the possibilities for strategic reassessment. In fact, Soviet policy under Brezhnev and Andropov suffered greatly from these drawbacks. Conversely, if the political battle were to take place in Western Europe, democratic governments had the advantage of familiarity with the political terrain and with the give-and-take of public debate. Further, as we will see, the peaceful alternation of government and opposition in West Germany rewarded political learning and renewal, which greatly contributed to democratic resilience in the early 1980s.

The Intellectuals and Power

The euromissile dispute was conducted by politicans and intellectuals, especially journalists. The ability of intellectuals to lend meaning to events is key to their power in politics.[51] In debates about foreign affairs, they are one of those "articulate minorities" who, in contrast to the "mass public," shape public debate and create "spirals of speech" about international politics.[52] From Tocqueville through Max Weber, another current of the sociological tradition has been a skeptical view of the inclination of intellectuals towards utopianism in politics.[53] The West German historian and political scientist Hans-Peter Schwarz has recently argued that the West Germans, including the intellectuals, moved from an "obsession with power" in the Kaiser Reich and Nazi Germany to a "forgetting of power" in the Federal Republic.[54] "Internationalism," he writes, "represents our great, fundamental ideology in international relations."[55] Schwarz worried that a complete rejection of power politics based on a simplified understanding on the Nazi regime could lead to a new antimilitarist vision of the old German *Sonderweg* between East and West. The result, he feared, could be a power vacuum in central Europe that could tempt the Soviets to strive again for hegemony in Europe.

While intellectuals may reject the doctrine of realism in international politics, this does not mean they do not seek power or understand it. The sociologist Helmut Schelsky saw West Germany's left-wing intellectuals as power seekers whose interpretations were a major source of power on the "long march through the institutions."[56] In 1983, a West German political analyst, Martin Kriele, argued that Western leftist intellectuals responded to winners and losers in global politics as much as anyone else.[57] Perhaps, he wrote, West European pacifists and antinuclear activists were not so much naive as quite realistic in adapting to the "normative power of military and power political developmental tendencies since Vietnam" in favor of the Soviet Union.[58] Whatever the reason, West German intellectuals of the left in the early 1980s did not focus their criticism on the Soviet Union and its armament directed at Western Europe, but instead directed their fire at both superpowers, a technology-driven arms race, and the United States.

In 1983, Christian Democrats led by Helmut Kohl joined hands with Hans-Dietrich Genscher's liberal Free Democrats to implement a decision initiated by Helmut Schmidt, a Social Democratic chancellor. In West Germany, just as in the United States and Great Britain, parties of the right implemented a decision whose origins lay in the decisions of the center left. The following study of recent German history and political culture may also shed light on developments elsewhere at this pivotal moment in recent history. It was in West Germany in these years that the conduct of power politics by means of diplomatic offensives directed at public opinion and counteroffensives aimed at taking a difficult case to democratic electorates, that is, a war by other means, found its clearest and most instructive expression.

2

THE ORIGINAL BOUNDARIES OF MILITANT DEMOCRACY

Adenauer and Schumacher

THE FEDERAL REPUBLIC OF GERMANY came into being in 1949. The essentials of its political culture were first articulated in the three preceding years, 1945 to 1948.[1] This political culture entailed the establishment of moral and political boundaries between a new "militant democracy" on the one hand and the Nazi totalitarian regime of the past and continuing Communist dictatorship in East Germany on the other. Konrad Adenauer and Kurt Schumacher, the leaders respectively of Christian Democracy and Social Democracy, through words and deeds were the leaders of this founding process. Schumacher led the Social Democratic opposition to the Communists in the late 1940s. Adenauer's emergence from the periphery to the center of right-of-center politics in postwar West Germany signified a historical turning point in modern German history. It marked the first time that the predominant current of political conservatism in Germany embraced liberal democracy, a market economy, and a foreign policy based on a pro-, not an anti-Western stance. Together, Adenauer and Schumacher formed the right and left poles of a liberal democratic "antitotalitarian" consensus.

Though Schumacher was a man of the left, it was Adenauer who represented a far greater change in political culture. Since the French Revolution, German conservatism had defined itself in opposition to the West, to American, British, and French liberalism and to their notions of parliamentary democracy, civil liberties, and religious and ethnic toleration.[2] This illiberal, anti-Western pre-1945 conservatism was discredited after 1945, a casualty of its contributions to the destruction of the rise of the Weimar Republic and to the rise of Nazism. Adenauer was convinced that democracy within Germany required moral, political, economic, and military integration into a Western alliance, a break with the German conservative tradition, and creation of a new West German conservatism.[3] Recasting the moral order went hand in hand with a new Western geopolitical orientation in international politics. The striking feature of the transformation of German conservatism into West German Christian Democracy was that it was led by a man whose ideas did not change at all. Adenauer, whose Catholic, Francophile conservatism had been pushed to the periphery by anti-Western, antidemocratic conservatism and by National Socialism in the last years of the Weimar Republic, now occupied center stage in the wake of the destruction and self-destruction of the predominant tradition of German conservatism. Not the ideas, but their predominance within the right of center spectrum defined the historical novelty of *West* German conservatism.

Part of the old German national identity associated with Nazism and with anti-Western and antidemocratic conservatism lay in ruins. But another part of the old national identity, German Social Democracy, survived the war and the Nazi era with its moral and political credentials intact. The party of progress became the most tradition-laden force in the Western zone, while the nominal party of tradition, Adenauer's Christian Democracy, was the truly novel feature in the postwar political culture. Traditional-laden Social Democrats envisaged a neutralist, united, democratic, and socialist Germany. The push for an Atlanticist, Westernizing anchor originally came from Adenauer and a new West German conservative tradition.

"Militant democracy," whose primary standard-bearers were Adenauer and Schumacher, was the key term referring to the moral and political boundaries that differentiated the new Bonn Republic from the Weimar Republic. Weimar, so the postwar Germans argued, had not been militant enough in protecting itself against primarily the antidemocratic right, but also the antidemocratic left. It also distinguished the new republic from the German dictatorships of the Nazi past and Communist present. Antitotalitarianism was the conceptual and moral core of both anti-Nazism and anti-communism and the common ground of the revived center right and center left. The responsibility of the democratic right was to guard against any revival of Nazism, as it had failed to do in the Weimar years, and to bring the tradition of anti-Western German conservatism to an end. The democratic left was to serve as a bulwark against Soviet appeals for a "popular front." Because postwar Social Democracy combined, at the outset, opposition to Atlanticism with opposition to Soviet expansion in Europe, it was the liveliest exponent of neutralist views in West Germany in the postwar decade.

Adenauer's partiality towards the United States rested on both balance-of-power considerations and moral convictions. He believed an American presence was essential to preserve a balance of power in Europe. He did not want to see a return to a Germany wavering between East and West and was convinced that the era of a strictly European balance of power was over. He wanted the Western half of Germany to be integrated into an American-led alliance. Democracy and political freedom in at least half of Germany was preferable to a unified Germany under Soviet influence. A neutral Germany would create a tempting power vacuum into which the Soviet Union could extend its influence. Neutralism, for Adenauer, evoked the spectre of a revival of the *Deutschen Sonderweg*. German hostility to the West and its values had led to war and catastrophe in 1914 and 1939. Now postwar democracy was to be unambiguously tied to the West, economically, militarily, and morally. West integration meant free markets, welfare capitalism, and parliamentary democracy at home. Political liberalism, economic liberalism, and the Western anchor were all of a piece in Adenauer's view. The prominence of this Western-oriented conservative and the discrediting of anti-Western sentiment among conservatives were key political presuppositions of the Bonn Republic.[4]

The second presupposition was the Social Democratic rejection of a popular front with the Communists. Antagonism between Communists and Socialists in twentieth-century Germany began with the outbreak of World War I, the civil war and failed revolution of the postwar years, and bitter disputes in the last years of the Weimar Republic. Because Social Democracy emerged from the ruins of nazism as the only intact and unbroken political tradition in German society, it became the standard-bearer of a democratic and socialist nationalism after World War II.[5] Its blend of nationalism, democracy, and socialism was closer to the traditional German center in Berlin than was the Rhineland-based, westernizing, Francophile, Atlanticist, pro-American West German Adenauer conservatism. The survival of this older German tradition within the context of the new West German center remained at the heart of the debate over neutralism and West integration in West Germany.

Konrad Adenauer and the Creation of a West German Conservatism

In 1945, Konrad Adenauer initiated a radical change in the character of German conservatism. Adenauer was the mayor of Cologne from 1917 to

1933. As mayor, Adenauer developed a reputation as a modernizer seeking to establish his native city as an economic and transportation hub linking Western Germany to France, Belgium, and Holland. A leader of the Catholic Center party, he was forced out of office by the Nazis in 1933. He survived the Third Reich largely in seclusion as an inactive non-Nazi. Though he knew members of the July 20, 1944, conspiracy to overthrow Hitler, he was not an active conspirator. Nevertheless, he was arrested by the Gestapo and placed in prison for two months.[6] In 1945, the combined effect of the repression of the conspirators of July 20, 1944, the moral disgrace to which Prussian conservatism had fallen, and Adenauer's own opposition to the Nazis facilitated his emergence as the leader of Christian Democracy in postwar Germany. West German conservatism after 1945 was not built on imported elements alone. Rather, the weight of the Western victors facilitated a shift in the center and periphery in the political culture within Germany. This was a shift from Berlin to Bonn and from Prussia to the Rhineland. Adenauer's emergence was not due to a change of views on his part but rather to a transformed political landscape in which the then-peripheral pragmatic, moderate conservatism of Cologne's mayor of the 1920s became the central tradition of postwar conservatism.

Adenauer's speeches of the postwar years document his commitment to a liberal, Western-oriented conservatism rooted in conceptions of Christian natural right and the dignity of the individual. His rupture with German conservatism entailed an analysis of the causes of nazism. He delivered his first major speech as chairman of the Christian Democratic Union in the British zone of occupation in March 1946. Adenauer told his listeners that National Socialism was not only the fault of big industry and the military; rather, the Nazis had had support in "broad layers of the population."[7] For decades, he said, the Germans had "made the state into a God, and raised it to an altar" and had failed to understand the role of the individual.[8]

This criticism of statism was a novelty in the history of conservatism in German history. But for Adenauer, materialism had also contributed to a celebration of state power at the expense of individual rights. He opposed socialism and communism, in part, because he believed they were forms of the centralizing traditions of German authoritarian statism.[9] In place of Prussian authoritarianism and National Socialist paganism, Adenauer sought to "rebuild the foundations of Christian natural right," which placed primacy on the "unique dignity, and the value of every individual human being."[10] His support for capitalism was combined with support for a mixed economy, welfare measures, and a balance of the common good with profit seeking.[11] The Christian Democratic Union, or CDU, was the political party that would embody these principles.

The moral boundary that Adenauer established between a new democracy and the old German dictatorship rested on identical principles of individual freedom, as did the boundary he articulated between a Western Germany and the Soviet Union. Anticommunism in postwar Germany had to rest on wholly different principles than the racist and totalitarian ideology of the Nazis. As the candidate of the Christian Democratic Union for the office of West German chancellor in the election of 1949, Adenauer declared the question of the division of Germany one of "life and death" and said that the Germans would "never" reconcile themselves to it.[12] Though granting that the Social Democrats had played a key role in the political struggle against the Communists in Berlin and in the Russian zone, he took the SPD to task for "breaking the unified resistance of the German parties in the Russian occupation zone against Communism and the Russians."

The Soviet Union, he said, was "a conscious enemy of Christianity, an enemy of God." It had "subjected all of the Eastern states, Hungary, Czechoslovakia, Bulgaria, Rumania, Poland, and nowhere has a socialist party in these countries been able to carry out resistance against Communism. Everywhere, resistance has come from representatives of the Christian churches." Saving Germany from the Soviets required a Christian rather than Socialist government: "We should be clear that socialism does not form a dam against Communism.[13]

From the outset, Adenauer stressed the stark moral and political differences between Soviet dictatorship and Western democracy. In October 1949, faced with the foundation of an East German Communist government, he contrasted the absence of free elections in the East to their presence in the West. As a result, he said, to applause from Christian Democrats and Social Democrats, the Federal Republic was "the *only* legitimate organization of the German people."[14] West Germany had to pay attention to the fate of the 17 million Germans in the Soviet zone. Forced to choose between reunification on Soviet terms and division with freedom in only the Western half of Germany, he opted for preserving a liberal democracy in the Western half. But an enduring aspect of the Adenauer tradition became the religiously grounded belief that genuine peace in Europe required freedom in its Eastern half and that, over the long run, freedom and the democracies would prevail over the dictatorships in Europe.[15]

Adenauer made a sharp moral distinction between the United States and the Soviet Union.

The two superpowers, the USA and Soviet Russia, are of totally different ideological structures. In Soviet Russia: massification and domination of the masses, ruthless exploitation by a small upper caste in the form of a totalitarian state, slavery, concentration camps, persecution of Christianity. In the United States: freedom, dignity and protection of the individual, protection as well of the person over against the power of the state. The contrast between the two superpowers is so great that in itself it is inclined to call forth tensions.[16]

Adenauer argued that the Soviet Union since 1945 had exacerbated tensions rooted in these fundamental differences by violently crushing hopes for democracy in Eastern Europe and by preserving large armed forces in the center of Europe. The Western allies had grasped the danger they faced, both from Russia and from its fifth columns. They had also, he said, learned the correct lessons from the experience of appeasement of Hitler in the 1930s. Had they demonstrated their willingness to use their power soon after Hitler seized power, Adenauer argued, World War II would never have broken out. Speaking to the Bundestag in November 1950, he said that

> after the experience that we Germans had with the totalitarian regime
> of the Nazi period . . . it should be a common conviction of all
> Germans that totalitarian states, especially the Soviet Union, do not
> know as democratic states know, that law and freedom are essential
> factors of the community of individuals and peoples. They know only
> one deciding factor: power. Therefore, one can conduct negotiations
> with any hope of success on international questions only if those
> conducting them with the Soviet Union are just as strong, if not
> stronger than the Soviet Union.[17]

Faced with pacifist protest from Protestant ministers Martin Niemoller and Karl Barth, Adenauer said that "what was true of resistance against Hitler, applies as well to resistance against Bolshevism."[18]

Adenauer's geopolitical revolution in creating a Western-oriented foreign policy presupposed continued American presence in the European balance of power.[19] Adenauer believed that a close relationship between West Germany and the United States was a precondition for democracy and stability in Western Europe. An American exit could lead to Soviet hegemony, and hence to the erosion of democracy and political freedom in Western Europe. "Without the help and protection of the United States, Europe would be powerless in the face of the pressure of Soviet Russia."[20] In his view, "the policy of the Soviet Union appears to me to be very simple: It wants to drive the United States out of Europe in order then to dominate Europe."[21]

Konrad Adenauer, the founder of a postwar West German conservatism, led two revolutions in the postwar era. For the first time in modern German history, a political right emerged as the dominant current of German conservatism that was morally and geostrategically oriented to the West, that is, to France, Britain, and the United States. The emergence of Adenauer as the leading figure of West German conservatism brought to an end the German *Sonderbewusstsein,* or special consciousness directed against Western liberal values, and the German *Sonderweg.* Adenauer's continuing effort as West German chancellor from 1949 to 1963 was to insure that this shift remained a constitutive element of West German politics.

Kurt Schumacher: Social Democracy as a German Tradition

In West German political culture, the term "restoration" has usually meant restoration of the social and economic forces that helped the Nazis come to power. In the realm of political culture, however, no German tradition was restored so completely as Social Democracy. Kurt Schumacher had been a Social Democratic member of parliament in the Weimar Republic. The Nazis imprisoned him in Buchenwald for all twelve years of the Third Reich. In 1945, he set about rebuilding the SPD. He was its party chairman from 1946 to 1952 and leader of the parliamentary opposition in the West German parliament from 1949 to 1952.

Schumacher represented the left side of postwar militant democracy. He spoke as a representative for "the other Germany," that is, for that minority of Germans who had actively opposed the Nazis. In his view, it was the duty and responsibility of Social Democracy, which had defended the Weimar Republic while the conservatives invited Hitler into power, to be the representative of the whole nation after 1945. Like Adenauer, he rejected "totalitarian" parties and movements of the right and left and sought a moral renewal. His speeches of the postwar era dealt extensively with the causes and consequences of nazism and with the Social Democratic response to communism. The postwar Germans had to understand, he said in 1945, that occupation and division, physical devastation, and moral collapse all were "the consequences of the Third Reich."[22] However, in the midst of the "spiritual and moral ruins the Nazis had left behind," he detected a "will for democracy" in large parts of the population and in the then 80-year-old tradition of the Social Democratic party (SPD), a party in which "democracy was not first the result of the victory of Anglo-Saxon weapons."[23]

Schumacher vehemently rejected the notion of a collective guilt of all

Germans and noted with irony the Communist party's willingness to accept it. He said it was understandable that the Communists should adopt the accusation of collective guilt because without the stance of the Communists—the Comintern attacked West German Social Democrats as "social fascists" from 1928 to 1933, thus preventing a united opposition to Hitler—the collapse of German parliamentarism (in 1933) and thus the possibility for the Nazis to come into government, "would not have been possible."[24] The Social Democratic party opposed nazism from the outset. The world had to be shown that "that not all Germans were Nazis, and that alongside Nazi Germany there was also another Germany."[25] Schumacher believed that *das andere Deutschland* had earned the right to be a determining voice in the formation of a new Germany. The SPD in the Weimar Republic was "the only party in Germany which held to the great line of democracy and of peace without concessions." All other parties were more or less guilty of helping the Nazis to power either by helping to create its intellectual and cultural foundations or by taking tactical measures that made possible its assumption of power in 1933. This unbroken democratic record, Schumacher said, was why the Social Democratic party had a unique claim to lead a "new construction" *(Neubau)* rather than a "reconstruction" *(Wiederaufbau)* of the forces that had made the Nazi seizure of power possible to begin with.[26] As the primary adversary of the Nazi dictatorship, the SPD was, he argued, the most legitimate democratic force in the postwar order.[27]

Schumacher's distinctive place in the history of German Social Democracy also lay in his opposition to the Communists in Germany in the immediate postwar years. Stalin's policy in Eastern Europe from 1945 to 1948 called for defeating and subordinating all noncommunist political groups. Schumacher led the Social Democratic opposition to Communist efforts to force the SPD into a united front under Soviet control and to coalesce with a party he described in 1949 as "absolutely undemocratic."[28] Further, he viewed the German Communists as advocates of the Soviet Union. It was clear, he said, that Russia wanted all of Germany to be a buffer state, a development that would be possible "if Social Democracy in the West would go along with a one-sided pro-Russian policy."[29] This, Schumacher would not do. He rejected the use of the idea of world revolution "for the benefit of a chauvinistic and imperialistic national state."[30] German Social Democrats remained committed to the idea of international socialism without a "fatherland" of the workers. The nationalism of postwar German Social Democracy conflicted with Soviet strategy.

Though he opposed Soviet policy, he rejected a Western, anti-Russian bloc in favor of "democracy and socialism between East and West." Germany, Schumacher said, "was neither Eastern or Western, but European" because "the essence of the bourgeois revolution had become an immanent component of the conscious or unconscious thinking of the majority of Germans."[31] He believed that the Communists, in making a virtue of the absence of individual freedom, had become alien to European traditions. Because German Social Democracy was rooted in German classical philosophy and the bourgeois revolutions, no new center, no new more-Western political culture or moral order was necessary.[32] His views on political culture and geopolitics diverged radically from Adenauer's in this regard.

Schumacher believed that Social Democracy, as the most intact current of German national identity after nazism, was the most able to serve as a bulwark against communism. In 1949, he said that the "most dangerous fifth column of world communism" was composed of big property owners and their political representatives because their "unsocial, un-Christian, and inhuman" response to suffering "created more bitterness and more mistrust of the fundamentals of democracy and of socialism than did all communist talk and all the political perfidy of the party of the Russian state on German soil."[33]

It was the democratic left, he argued, that was best able to win the political battle with the Communists.

> It is not for nothing that we (the Social Democrats) are the world enemy No. 1 for Soviet Communism. . . . The Soviets would prefer an extreme capitalist and reactionary state leadership to democratic socialism in all countries. This is so because democratic socialism is the only factor which can take the trust of the working masses away from the Soviets.[34]

Though a Western-oriented Germany was going to be capitalist, and hence not truly democratic in socialist eyes, Schumacher believed a Communist-dominated Germany would be absolutely undemocratic. Schumacher's choice was for democracy under capitalism rather than for another totalitarian regime in Germany. In that choice lay the first major political defeat for Communist strategy in the Cold War.[35]

The Communist party of the Soviet Union had, in 1945–46, made a "decisive error" in trying to force the SPD into uniting with the Communist party. German unity would be impossible with dictatorship in the Eastern zones and emergent democracy in the Western zones.

> If we were to join the SED (Socialist Unity Party) as German, national representatives we would represent the enslavement of 17 million Germans. . . . *Today, in 1947, we are in the same situation as in*

1933. We are faced with the question of whether we will bend before a brutal claim to domination or will oppose it from the beginning.[36] (emphasis added)

For Kurt Schumacher opposition to the Communist effort to impose a new dictatorship on the Germans in the postwar years rested on the same democratic principles that led Social Democrats to oppose the Nazi dictatorship in 1933.

While the Social Democrats, he said in 1951, had "grasped the essence of dictatorship no matter what color it may be painted," many others in Germany had "a very young connection to democracy and have struggled too little with totalitarianism." Summer 1945 was a time of "grand illusions" about the communists.[37] "People had not yet understood the structural identity [Gleichheit] of the Communist system with the system of the "Third Reich.'"[38] "The liberation from the pernicious illusion" that one could enter into an alliance with the Communists was, in Schumacher's view, carried out by the Social Democratic party.[39] The great decision in favor of freedom and against dictatorship took place in March 1946, when the Social Democrats rejected Communist efforts at a united front. The aftermath left Schumacher asking "how the East Zone can be liberated."

Schumacher, speaking to the Bundestag, left no doubt as to who bore primary responsibility for the division of Germany. "Every analysis should begin with the fact that it has been Soviet Russia that isolated and separated its zone."[40] In the process, the "strength of the totalitarian position" rested "largely on the ignorance and lack of clarity concerning the essence of totalitarianism in Western democracies, beginning with large parts of the German people. (Very true! from the SPD and the center)."[41] He also proudly asserted that it was the refusal of Social Democrats to form a united front with the Communists that manifested "the victory of the will for freedom over the propaganda of totalitarians. (Vigorous applause from the SPD, center, and right)."[42]

After the creation of a Communist state in the Eastern zone, Schumacher was unrelenting in his criticism. In August 1951, Schumacher said that the dictatorship of the proletariat had become a dictatorship over the proletariat. Capitalist exploitation had been taken over by the state. A dictatorial police state giving the ruling clique absolute power had taken shape. Exploitation existed beyond that possible in a capitalist country, where political freedom allowed workers to organize independent unions. There was, he said, "capitalist democracy," but there was "no proletarian democracy. Above all, there is nowhere in the world such nonsense as the word 'people's democracy.'" There was "only one democracy, that which is

made of the moral self-consciousness of the individual human being and
the cleverness, energy and willingness to sacrifice of a class."[43]

Schumacher called Adenauer a "chancellor of the allies," who subordinated reunification to formation of a West German state. But however
strong his desires for a unified Germany, Schumacher did not want reunification at the price of Soviet hegemony. Reunification could take place only
on the basis of free elections in all of the occupation zones. Because the
Soviets refused to permit such elections, the sole responsibility for the continued division of the country and of dictatorship in its Eastern half lay
with the Soviet Union.[44]

In foreign policy, Schumacher disagreed with Adenauer's Atlanticism.
He believed that a strictly European balance of power with a strong and
reunited Germany was both possible and necessary for peace and stability
in Europe. His conceptions of power politics were as traditionally German
as Adenauer's were novel and West German. For Schumacher, Social
Democratic Germany's European roots required no new, enduring link to
the United States. While he posed a political and moral barrier to Soviet
influence, he refused to draw Atlanticist conclusions. For all his policy
disagreements with Adenauer, he agreed that there was a meaningful moral
and political distinction between totalitarian dictatorships and liberal democratic governments. This juxtaposition of democracy and dictatorship became the object of intense criticism, especially in the 1960s, when the
founding political culture was challenged by the New Left.

The SPD After Schumacher

In the decade following the defeat of the Communist strategy of a united
front against the West (1945–1948), the Social Democratic party continued to oppose Adenauer's practical steps towards integration into the
Western alliance: rearmament and creation of the Bundeswehr, and arming
the Bundeswehr with tactical nuclear weapons in the late 1950s. Aware
that the criticism of "neutralism" was making the party unelectable, the
party leadership moved closer to acceptance of West integration in the late
1950s, while criticizing the "chancellor of the allies" for sacrificing German
reunification on the altar of West integration.[45] In the mid-1950s, the Social Democrats toyed with proposals for "collective security," involving an
exit by both West and East Germany from their respective alliances.[46] In
1959 the party supported the *Deutschlandplan*, a disarmament plan that
would create a "zone of détente" in Central Europe—East and West Germany, Poland, Czechoslovakia, and Hungary—from which foreign troops

and nuclear weapons would be withdrawn.[47] The agreement would be guaranteed by a system of "collective security agreements" of all interested states, including the Soviet Union and the United States. With the development of a "European security system," the states in the zone of détente would leave NATO and the Warsaw Pact, after which the two Germanies would initiate discussions about the German question.[48] The Central Committee of the East German Communist party responded the following month that withdrawal of Western troops to behind the Rhine and of Soviet troops back to Russian territory was insufficient. The Americans would have to return home.[49] The SPD's receptivity to proposals for "collective security" and neutralization faciliated Adenauer's election victories with slogans such as "no experiments."

But despite Adenauer's longevity and success, surveys of public opinion about foreign policy showed that during the 1950s respondents advocating neutrality outnumbered those favoring close relations with the United States until 1961.[50] However, polls conducted by the United States Information Agency in the 1950s indicated that support for close ties to the United States was higher among the university educated and among conservative voters.[51]

By 1959, it was apparent to the leaders of the Social Democratic party that class struggle in domestic politics and neutralism in foreign policy were recipes for continued national electoral defeat. In 1959, at its historic party congress in Bad Godesberg, the SPD officially became a *Volkspartei*, a people's party seeking support from all social and economic groups, in contrast to a class party appealing primarily to a working-class constituency. It embraced the mixed economy and moved away from Marxist dogma about capitalism and class struggle. At the SPD annual party congress in Hannover in 1960, Herbert Wehner, the leading electoral strategist of the party, declared an end to the party's neutralism. "In the contest between East and West, the position of the Federal Republic of Germany and thus also the position of the Social Democratic Party of Germany is irrevocably on the side of the West."[52] Wehner's speech and the adoption of his position by the party leadership marked the end of the predominance of official neutralism-nationalism in the party leadership.

The construction of the Berlin Wall in 1961 smashed hopes for a reunified Germany. It deepened West German anger at the Communist regime. As Willy Brandt, mayor of Berlin at the time of the construction of the wall, declared to the Berlin city council on the day the wall was built, "Berlin is being divided not only by a sort of frontier, but by the barbed wire fence of a concentration camp. . . . We will never reconcile ourselves to the brutal division of this city, or with the unnatural division of our country . . . !"[53] But, in the political culture of the détente era, the Berlin Wall evolved in the consciousness of the West German left from being a symbol of the failure of East German communism into a symbol of the failure of Adenauer's policy of West integration to bring about German reunification.[54] Rather than remain the advocate of oppressed workers in East Germany suffering under Russian imperialism and colonialism, as Schumacher had described it, the Social Democrats, led by Willy Brandt and a journalist and foreign policy adviser named Egon Bahr, suggested that the West Germans begin to deal with the East German government. As important as their policy, and in some ways more important, was Brandt's and Bahr's challenge to the political culture of the left side of militant democracy represented by Schumacher's social-democratic anti-communism. The blurring of boundaries between Social Democracy and the Communists that reached full fruition in the 1980s had its beginning in the political language of Brandt's and Bahr's foreign policy in the early 1960s.

3

BOUNDARY EROSION
Willy Brandt, Egon Bahr, and the Political Culture of Détente

WEST GERMANY'S *Ostpolitik* OR "EASTERN POLICY" operated at several levels. Economic links to the Soviet Union and Eastern Europe expanded. Families divided between East and West Germany were able to visit. The West Germans made loans to the East bloc. But the aspect of Ostpolitik with which we are most concerned is the political culture and language that accompanied it. Ostpolitik was in part a meritorious series of acts of atonement and reconciliation between Germans and the peoples of Eastern Europe and the Soviet Union, but it was also a diplomatic policy directed towards the existing Communist governments of the Warsaw Pact. At the level of political culture and public diplomacy, Ostpolitik in these years entailed a shift away from the vehement Social Democratic anticommunism of Schumacher. The boundaries of militant democracy were eroded and blurred. While the Soviet Union did not emerge in a favorable light, neither did Brandt and Bahr dwell publicly at length on its dark side. Instead, they elaborated an idealist and internationalist style as opposed to a realist and balance-of-power style in West German foreign policy. Motivated, in part, by a desire to overcome the legacies of Nazi aggression in Eastern Europe and the Soviet Union, they came to speak more about peace than freedom, more about negotiations than about the power balances that made successful negotiations possible. The West German historian Hans-Peter Schwarz has aptly described the political culture of détente as one in which the Germans moved from an "obsession with power" to a "forgetting of power."[1] Two figures stand at the center of West German Ostpolitik: Willy Brandt, West German foreign minister from 1966 to 1969 and West German chancellor from 1969 to 1974, and his longtime adviser, Egon Bahr. Together they changed West German foreign policy. Their ability, institutional position, longevity, and contacts with West German intellectuals in the worlds of journalism, literature, publishing, and the universities allowed them to exert a profound impact on West German political culture from the 1960s to the 1980s.

Willy Brandt (b. 1913) emigrated to Oslo following the Nazi seizure of power, where he was active in socialist circles. From 1945 to 1947, he worked as a journalist in Norway and Sweden before returning to Berlin, where he became active in the SPD. He was mayor of Berlin from 1957 to 1966, where he entered the world stage during the Berlin crises. In 1964, he became national chairman of the SPD, a position he held until June 1987. In 1961 and 1965 he ran unsuccessfully for the office of chancellor. From 1965 to 1969, he was the first Social Democratic foreign minister of West Germany in the Grand Coalition with conservatives. In 1969 he became the first Social Democratic chancellor of the Federal Republic, serving until 1974. A member of the West German parliament since 1969, he was elected chairman of the Socialist International in 1976, a position from which he spoke often about "north-south" issues. From 1974 on, after resigning as chancellor when one of his aides was revealed to be an East German spy, Brandt focused his energies on the Social Democratic party. A prolific author and essayist, he received honorary doctorates from leading universities in the United States, Britain, Scotland, France, Israel, and Latin America.

Egon Bahr (b. 1922) was the conceptual architect of Ostpolitik. Bahr served in the Wehrmacht during the war and worked as a journalist in postwar Berlin. In 1960, Brandt asked him to take the position of director of the Press and Information Office of Berlin, a position he held until 1966. He went to Bonn in 1967 to assist Brandt as director of the planning staff in the Foreign Ministry until 1969. When Brandt became chancellor in 1969, he appointed Bahr to the position of *Staatssekretär* and Bundesminister for special tasks in the chancellor's office, a position from which he performed the bulk of the negotiations for treaties with the Soviet Union, Poland, and East Germany from 1970 to 1972. From 1974 to 1976, he was Bundesminister for economic cooperation in the government of Helmut Schmidt. From 1977 to 1981, he served as the General Secretary (*Bundesgeschaftsführer*) of the SPD and was editor of the party weekly, *Vorwärts*. After the fall of the Schmidt government in the autumn of 1982, Bahr's influence over foreign and security policy in the SPD steadily grew. During the 1980s, he became the party's leading spokesman on foreign and security policy. He became, in 1983, the chair of a party committee on "new strategies" and, in 1984, director of the Hamburg Institute for

Peace Research and Security Policy, one of the peace research institutes established in the Brandt reform era in the early 1970s. Bahr was a member of SPD since 1957 and a leading parliamentary spokesman on foreign and security policy in the 1970s and 1980s.

Willy Brandt was a political leader convinced of the importance of ideas in politics and of "enlightening minorities, elites in the good sense of the word," in a liberal democracy.[2] Throughout his political life, some of West Germany's most prominent intellectuals were drawn to him, and to the prospect of being a democratic, enlightened minority that would influence the direction of West German politics and society. From the time he first returned to Germany in 1946, the ideas to which Brandt remained most committed were those of democratic socialism.[3] He initially opposed formation of a Western alliance and hoped for allied cooperation to facilitate an overcoming by the Germans themselves of legacies of Nazism, militarism, and racism.[4] He shared Schumacher's vehement criticism of communist practice in the postwar years.[5]

But Brandt introduced a different emphasis when he said that "our first task" lay in forming a bridge between the West and the Soviet Union to prevent a permanent division of Germany. He opposed West German rearmament and integration into a European Defense Community on the grounds that it would harden the division of Germany. He rejected conservative assertions that the Social Democrats were neutralists or pacifists.[6] His major criticism of Adenauer's policy of West integration was that it took place at the expense of reunification.[7] In the 1960s, he offered a policy of opening to the East without sacrificing West Germany's Western ties.

Brandt in the 1950s and early 1960s relished the intellectual confrontation with communism. Berliners and Social Democrats who had the most experience with the Soviet Union and with Communists did not, he believed, suffer from illusions about either. Where the Communists tried to seize power by force, they had to be confronted with force. But it was not necessary, he said, to be so fearful.[8] Brandt stressed throughout his public career that the confrontation with communism for the West Germans was also one with Russia and Eastern Europe. West German anticommunism labored under the "additional burdens" created by Nazi crimes in Eastern Europe and Russia. His conviction that communism was a failing system, as well as the burden of the Nazi era, led Brandt to criticize and mute the anticommunist political culture of the Schumacher tradition.

In November 1960, Brandt addressed the annual meeting of the SPD as its candidate for chancellor. He called for a "self-conscious Ostpolitik," for more attention to the "zone," the term used by West German politicians

to refer to East Germany.[9] Brandt's commitment to political change in East
Germany and his rhetorical commitment to the ideas of militant democracy were still apparent, as shown in the following passage from that 1960
speech.

> Today we call for resistance to every form of rule by force. We
> assume that among the people of the zone there is a readiness to
> engage in spiritual and moral resistance against a dictatorial regime run
> by Germans. We consider it as a pledge of future unity and freedom
> of our fatherland that in the zone, German patriots engage in
> resistance and as a result land in prison or leave their home. But just
> as the battle against communist inhumanity is a patriotic duty, so the
> battle against the brown inhumanity [Nazism] must not be measured
> on another standard.[10]

Brandt recalled Abraham Lincoln's words that a divided people cannot
survive and urged reconciliation of the Germans with themselves. "We are
all one family. Thus our people must finally make peace with itself."[11] Like
Schumacher, Brandt spoke in the name of an unbroken sense of the nation,
in contrast to the West German state associated with Adenauer.

Brandt's commitment to intellectual debate with Communists went hand
in hand with a defense position that was sharply at odds with Adenauer's
major decisions of the 1950s.[12] Though he affirmed support for NATO,
he rejected tactical nuclear weapons for the Bundeswehr and stressed the
importance of disarmament, a "European zone of détente," and armed
forces appropriate only for defense.[13] The Social Democrats were not in
favor of "one-sided weakening of the West," but strategic equilibrium was
not a "permanent condition," as new armaments always threatened to
upset this balance. Brandt spoke with pride about Berliners who were determined to remain free. "The spiritual and moral values of the West have
been preserved in Berlin."[14] The Federal Republic was not a "wanderer
between worlds" but a reliable ally whose foreign policy rested on a foundation of "unbreakable friendship with the USA."[15] He articulated a stance
of a political and cultural offensive against communism in the fall of 1960
in a speech titled "Intellectual Armament" *[Geistige Aufrustung]*. "We" in
the West, he said, "are in a life and death battle with an un-culture."[16] He
criticized the West German conservatives for having neglected the cultural
dimension of the conflict. Expanded education would serve to "arm ourselves in a spiritual sense. Only in this way can we see an alternative to the
totalitarian system of non-culture."

Despite these assurances, Adenauer defeated Brandt in the election of
1960. In 1961, Brandt published *Plädoyer für die Zukunft* (Plea for the

Future), a collection of essays and speeches. Brandt sought to reassure West German voters and West Germany's allies that his foreign policy views were compatible with West Germany's Western ties and a credible defense against the Soviet Union.[17] He expressed confidence that "we will win the spiritual and economic competition with Communism."[18] Khrushchev's wish to catch up with and overtake the Western economies placed the East–West competition in those areas where the West was strongest and the East weakest. From this position of strength, the West could normalize relations with the Soviets, conclude treaties, and continue the battle with the "ideological adversary."[19] Brandt argued that the democratic left was more capable of conducting a political offensive against Soviet expansion in Europe than were Adenauer and the conservatives. Though he paid little attention to the role of military power in Soviet policy in Europe, the Willy Brandt of 1961 did not shrink from applying the principle of self-determination of former colonies in Asia and Africa to the Soviet position in East Germany.[20] By the 1970s, talking about human rights in Eastern Europe was no longer part of the political culture of Brandt's Ostpolitik.[21]

In the Bundestag in December 1961, Brandt declared that the construction of the Berlin Wall meant that Adenauer's policy aimed at reunification had failed. However odd this reasoning was, he made clear his determination to seek political change in East Germany. "Mere preservation of the status quo is not enough. We will preserve our freedom only if we act for the freedom of the 17 million [in East Germany]."[22] Attaining the right of self-determination would be possible through normalization of relations with the Soviet Union in the context of agreement with West Germany's Western allies. However, in 1961, improved West German–Soviet relations did not, in his view, preclude a West German political offensive in East Germany and Eastern Europe, intended to change the status quo and fulfill demands of the West German conscience towards those living in unfreedom. For Brandt, in 1961, peace in Europe and freedom in its Eastern half were linked together.

In 1962, in two speeches at Harvard University, Brandt again expressed confidence that the West would win the battle of ideas with communism.[23] From his experiences in the anti-Nazi resistance in wartime Norway and as mayor of Berlin, Brandt drew the lesson that moral forces were a potent force in world politics.[24] While both instances lend support to such a lesson, it is a partial one, for the anti-Nazi resistance in World War II, no less than the West Berlin resistance to Soviet pressure from 1958 to 1962, would have been defeated without the military power of the Allies in the first instance and of NATO in the second. It was not "moral strength" alone that transformed an "apparently hopeless situation," but strong convictions in conjunction with military power. Brandt's "lesson" from modern history, a lesson that came to exert a powerful impact on West German political culture, was to relegate power, especially military power, to a secondary role in determining the outcomes of the conflicts in which he had been a participant.

In 1963 Brandt stressed ever more clearly the link between foreign policy and coming to terms with the Nazi past. Adenauer, he acknowledged, had prevented a "collapse of our people."[25] This success, however, was not the result of a thorough discussion and thus "unfortunately did not mean a reconciliation of our people with itself and with its past."[26] In postwar Germany, there was "too much opportunism and too little courage to face uncomfortable truths" about the Nazi past. He linked coming to terms with this past with recognition of "common security interests" with the Soviet Union.[27] He still rejected popular fronts with the Communists and saw no contradiction between German reunification and the unity of the West. Indeed, "only through the growing unity of the West" could the "German right to self-determination" be realized.[28]

On July 15, 1963, Egon Bahr spoke to the Evangelical Academy in Tutzing on the subject of *Wandel durch Annäherung* or change through rapprochement. Bahr began with a realist's appreciation of the fact of Soviet power in Europe. German reunification could be created "only with the Soviet Union . . . not in East Berlin . . . , not against the Soviet Union, not without it." Those, to his left, who thought reunification could be accomplished by talking to the East German government should reflect on the "presence of 20 or 22 well armed Soviet divisions" in East Germany.[29] Hence, reunification and by implication all inner-German relations, was a matter of West German–Soviet relations. While a man of the left, Bahr was a traditionalist focused on state-to-state relations.

Bahr identified his policy with the "American strategy for peace" enunciated by President John F. Kennedy, according to which "communist domination should not be replaced but rather should be changed." The United States, Bahr continued, "serves to overcome the status quo by first taking the position that the status quo should not be changed. That sounds paradoxical but it opens perspectives, after (it has become evident that) the hitherto existing policy of pressure and counter-pressure has only led to a rigidification of the status quo."[30] He contrasted the American position to Adenauer's policy of "all or nothing," free elections or complete rejection. This policy was "hopelessly antiquated, . . . unrealistic . . . (and) also senseless as a strategy for peace." Reunification, he continued, was "not a unique act which can be accomplished by an historic decision on one historic day at a historic conference" but "a process with many steps and stations." If, he continued, President Kennedy was correct in saying that

> one must recognize and consider the interests of the other side, it is certainly impossible for the Soviet Union to allow the zone (East Germany) to be used for the purpose of a strengthening of Western potential. The zone must be transformed with the agreement of the Soviet Union. If we went that far, we would be taking a large step toward reunification.[31]

The East German government could neither be torn out of the Warsaw Pact nor overthrown from within. "Changes and transformations are attainable only on the basis of the hated ruling regime of the present."[32]

Bahr argued that a policy of economic and political pressure directed against the Communist regime would only strengthen that Stalinist regime and deepen the division of the nation. Hopes for a revolt from below nurtured by the social democratic left were no less unrealistic. "Beneath the level of legal recognition," Bahr sought forms of interaction that were short of actual formal relations. Trade with the East "without damaging our security" could be considerably expanded. West German policy must be aimed at helping improve the lives of Germans in the Eastern zone. He argued that material improvements there would have a "loosening impact" in the zone. Improving living standards in the East bloc through expanded East–West trade generally was in the interest of the West.

He warned that discontent in the East could lead to "uncontrolled developments and to inevitable regressions," but there was no practical prospect of an overthrow of these regimes. Aid to individuals in small doses that would not lead to revolution and then to Soviet intervention was called for. It was necessary to reduce the "thoroughly justified fears" on the part of the East German regime that the relaxation and loosening of the borders and the wall would not bring with it unbearable risks. "This is a policy which can be expressed in the formula: *Wandel durch Annäherung* (change through rapprochement)." Bahr believed it could be pursued without illusion and in line with a Western strategy for peace.[33] *Wandel durch Annäherung* became the centerpiece of the new détente policy, which rested on the belief that reduction of external pressure on Eastern European governments would eventually lead them to tolerate political change and reform.

West German conservatives attacked any hint of recognition of the East German Communist regime. Reformers in Eastern Europe worried that *Wandel durch Annäherung* was a rapprochement between Bonn and Moscow at the expense of reform movements in Eastern Europe. Would it legitimize the Soviet presence in Eastern and Central Europe?[34] Where was the line to be drawn between recognizing the fact of Soviet domination in Eastern Europe and making a virtue of such recognition in the form of a "strategy for peace" in Europe? What would happen if there was rapprochement without change in Eastern Europe? Could the momentum of this policy be reversed? Would Bonn's Western ties be sacrificed to a policy towards the East?

In 1966, Willy Brandt became the foreign minister of the Federal Republic in a Grand Coalition led by the Christian Democrat Kurt Kiesinger. Speaking to the SPD party convention of 1966, Brandt stressed the importance of West Germany's Western ties. Social Democrats knew well that one cannot make Communists into democrats by talking to them.[35] Given the SPD's unhappy experience with Communist-dominated people's fronts in the past, the Communists, he said, "should bury all illusions" that the SPD would advocate a people's front in the present and future.[36] But he saw "no contradiction" between rejecting people's fronts with the Communists and conducting discussions with them. In the spirit of *Wandel durch Annäherung*, Brandt presented his policy as a diplomatic offensive designed to bring about political change and the emergence of "free opinion" in Eastern Europe.

In December 1967, NATO issued a report on "The Future Tasks of the Alliance," commonly known as the Harmel Report. Brandt, then West German Foreign Minister, played an important role in shaping the report. Its primary purpose was to reconcile West German détente policy with the balance-of-power policy of the alliance.[37]

> Military security and a policy of détente are not contradictory but complementary. Collective defense is a stabilizing factor in world politics. It is the necessary condition for effective policy directed towards greater relaxation of tensions.[38]

The Harmel Report defined a long-lasting NATO consensus: diplomacy and negotiations were a complement, not an alternative, to a policy of military equilibrium. Relaxation of tensions was "not a final goal" but part of a long-term process aimed at a European settlement. The "ultimate purpose of the alliance is to achieve a just and lasting peace order in Europe accompanied by appropriate security guarantees."[39] The Harmel Report urged a balance-of-power politics and diplomacy in the interest of resolving the political roots of tension in Europe. The status quo could not be changed by force, but neither was it an adequate foundation for a lasting peace. NATO was a militarily defensive alliance that, however, sought a fundamental revision of the postwar order. The key element of the Harmel

Report was the idea that a balance-of-power policy and diplomacy were not alternatives but complements to one another. Much of the debates in West Germany in the 1970s were about whether Brandt's diplomacy was neglecting its complement in the balance of military power. When he described détente policy as the "best and above all the cheapest security policy," he aroused concerns among those committed to the Harmel synthesis of diplomacy and military equilibrium.[40]

Brandt's *Friedenspolitik in Europa* [*A Peace Policy for Europe*] also appeared in 1968.[41] It is an important document of Brandt's public rhetoric in which "peace" became the primary theme at the expense of a rhetorical stress on "freedom." "The will to peace and to reconciliation is the primary idea and the foundation stone of our foreign policy."[42] And, "Germany cannot have any interest in letting the conflict between East and West go on, to say nothing to heightening it."[43] Germany still had to "bear the heavy burden that was imposed on it by unrestrained obfuscation and unscrupulous arrogance" of the Hitler regime. Its foreign policy now would consist of "general staffwork for peace." In the nuclear era, "war is no longer an alternative to peace."[44] In the long run, peace could not rest on a balance of terror but on "common interests that are recognized and desired as such."[45] Renunciation of force was a "logical consequence of our policy of peace."[46] Brandt wrote of a "Germany without megalomania" that proved itself through its peaceful accomplishments, a lucid and firm foreign policy, and an ability to "come to terms with the results of history" in place of the "missed opportunities" and "largely restorational reconstruction" of postwar West Germany.[47]

Determined as he was to bring the Nazi past to the forefront of German policy and politics, Brandt presented Ostpolitik as a policy that would lead to change in East Germany and Eastern Europe and therefore to a "European peace order." He was not willing to abandon peaceful efforts to overcome "the unnatural condition of the division of Germany and of the split within Europe." To renounce such efforts "would mean a renunciation of common sense."[48] Détente could not rest on an initial West German abandonment of the goal of German reunification. "Anyone who believes that all present day realities can be frozen for all eternity is a reactionary fool petrified to the point of utter rigidity."[49] His policy towards the German Democratic Republic was still guided by concern for the fate of 17 million Germans living in East Germany and a resolve not to recognize a regime that did not represent the will of the people and that survived only with the support of Soviet troops.[50] But Adenauer's "politics of strength" were based on illusions or the "widespread hope" that the East German government would collapse.

In place of Adenauer's stark juxtaposition of free and unfree polities in
Europe or Kurt Schumacher's stinging denunciation of Soviet imperialism
in Central Europe, Brandt now spoke in more distanced tones about the
division of Europe and the integration of its two parts into armed blocs.
Where Schumacher had spoken of the responsibility of the Soviet Union
for the division of Germany, Brandt referred to the division that "runs
through the continent and splits Germany. Consequently, one part of Germany has been drawn into the Western camp, the other into the Eastern."[51] To speak of having "been drawn into" both blocs was quite different than the stark juxtaposition of freedom and totalitarianism common
among West Germany's founding generation. Nevertheless, Brandt had a
sober view of Soviet diplomatic strategy in Europe. The Soviets would like
to limit détente so that "the status quo is congealed, the United States is
forced out of European politics, and NATO is dissolved; in that way the
Soviet Union would achieve the position of the premier power in Europe."[52] Brandt understood that, so long as NATO existed, the Soviet
Union would be unlikely to use military means to carry out these aims.
But *A Peace Policy for Europe* did not contain a discussion of how the global
and regional balance of military power affected Brandt's diplomacy.

The central hypothesis of Brandt's and Bahr's policy, namely, that rapprochement would bring about change in Eastern Europe, received an early
blow when the Soviet Union and its Warsaw Pact allies suppressed the
"Prague Spring" in August 1968. Reform tendencies in Czechoslovakia
fueled Soviet fears that relaxation of tensions and more contact with the
West would bring "ideological subversion." Brandt argued that the suppression of the Prague Spring made *Ostpolitik* even more important. But
was this not rapprochement with the repression of change? What incentive
did his policy give to the Soviet leaders to tolerate liberalization in Eastern
Europe if military intervention carried no risk of a slowing down in détente? Just as the speeches of summer 1963 had followed the construction
of the Berlin Wall, so Brandt's and Bahr's most intensive *Ostpolitik* immediately followed another act of Soviet repression in Eastern Europe, the invasion of Czechoslovakia in summer 1968. In both cases, Western rapprochement followed barriers to change in Eastern Europe. A separation
of peace policy and freedom in Eastern Europe was apparent in summer
1968, at the outset of the *Neue Ostpolitik*.

In September 1969, as leader of a coalition government with the Free
Democrats and a majority in parliament of six seats, Willy Brandt became
the first Social Democratic West German chancellor. On October 28,
1969, Brandt delivered the traditional statement of his government's intentions, the *Regierungserklärung*. It combined a broad program of domestic

reforms captured in the phrase "we will dare more democracy" with a statement of his intentions in foreign policy.[53] He said that on the basis of firm links to the United States and the NATO alliance, the Federal Republic would seek the "dismantling of the military confrontation in Europe."[54] The West Germans' national interest permitted no wandering between East and West, but favored cooperation with the West and understanding with the East.

> We are ready for an honorable effort at understanding so that the consequences of the hell brought on Europe by a criminal clique [the Nazis] can be overcome. . . . But our conversation partners must also know that the right of self-determination, as established in the Charter of the United Nations, applies to the German people as well.[55]

While willing to speak of self-determination for the Germans, he did not mention this principle in regard to the remaining countries of Eastern Europe, only a year after the Soviet invasion of Czechoslovakia.

Brandt's good will was not reciprocated by the East German Communists. The East German Communist leader Willi Stroph, following a 1970 meeting in Erfurt, East Germany, called the construction of the Berlin Wall a humanitarian act that preserved peace in Europe. He attacked monopoly capitalism and the imperialist West, voiced confidence in the ultimate "victory of socialism," and was certain that German unification would take place on the basis of "democracy and socialism."[56] Stroph's comments did not exactly "build bridges." Brandt responded that both states were committed to the unity of the nation, to mutual respect for existing borders, territorial integrity, peaceful resolution of conflicts, rejection of attempts to change the social order of the other state by force, technical cooperation, respecting the rights of the four powers in Germany, and improving the situation in Berlin.[57] While Brandt stressed elements of cooperation, Stroph emphasized the enduring nature of conflict.[58]

In August of 1970, Brandt signed a treaty on the renunciation of force and for cooperation with the Soviet Union in Moscow. It was time, he said, to "ground anew our relations to the East—on the basis of the unlimited mutual renunciation of force."[59] Russia, he said, was "inseparably intertwined in Europe history, not only as enemy and danger, but also as partner—historically, politically, culturally, and economically." Again, he stressed that the Moscow treaty "in no way affects the firm anchoring of the Federal Republic and its free society in the Western alliance."[60] By 1970, it had become apparent that the Soviet Union was engaged in a large military buildup, in its European theater and worldwide, and that this military buildup was not compatible with the synthesis of diplomacy and equilibrium presented in the Harmel Report. But Brandt did not raise an issue then that would have struck such a discordant note concerning this new "partner."

In Warsaw in December 1970, Brandt signed a treaty normalizing relations between West Germany and Poland. In his remarks on Polish television, Brandt recalled the deeds of the "criminal regime" and the "hell on earth" of Nazi policy in Poland, as well as the sufferings of German refugees after the war. He placed a wreath at the memorial of the Warsaw Ghetto and bent down on one knee, a gesture of atonement that received global attention. Again, he stressed that West German understanding with the East presupposed a firm anchor in Western Europe and in the Atlantic Alliance. Yet he did not combine all of these moving and important gestures with a straightforward appeal for internal change in the form of democracy and freedom to accompany rapprochement.

Brandt was awarded the Nobel Prize in recognition of his Ostpolitik. In his acceptance speech of December 1971 in Oslo, he offered a full treatment of the principles underlying his foreign policy. War could no longer be an instrument of policy. It had to be abolished. All foreign policy should serve peace and the dismantling of tensions.[61] He called his policy the "true *Realpolitik* of our era. What for twelve years in Germany was, in extreme form, called *Realpolitik*, was in fact a hellish chimera."[62] Brandt's domestic critics argued that Hitler's ideological fanaticism was not an example of realpolitik and that speeches such as the Oslo speech led to a forgetting of the power necessary for successful diplomacy.[63]

Such concerns were deepened when Brandt said that the lesson of the crises in Cuba and Berlin was the need to move from confrontation to cooperation or to seek the cooperation of states beyond the borders of the blocs.[64] In Oslo, Brandt criticized the Cold War itself, more than the Soviet challenges in Berlin and Cuba. Rather than view Berlin and Cuba as confirming the wisdom of containment and a firm response to Soviet expansion, Brandt spoke of how states had learned to control conflicts. In the context of his speech, the moral distinction between democracy and dictatorship, freedom and tyranny, appeared to be "sterile" sources of tension.

Brandt's goal was a "transition from classical power politics to sober peace policy. . . . It should lead from the sanctified egoism of the nation to a European and global domestic policy in which all feel responsible for human existence."[65] The principles of such a new policy included equilibrium; an end to the use of and threats to use force; arms reductions; nonintervention in the internal affairs of other countries; economic, technical, and cultural cooperation; social justice; and European responsibility for world peace by assisting development efforts in Africa, Asia, and Latin

America. As with previous Anglo-American efforts to reject power politics, the primary problem with Brandt's speech was that the world of states continued to exist and that included among them were dictatorships that continued to play the traditional game of power politics. How could a conflict be "transformed" by expressions of a desire to do so by one side? Would the West Germans misconstrue Soviet power in the 1970s out of a desire to overcome the German deeds of the 1940s?

Brandt's "peace policy" put his domestic political opponents on the defensive. Was pointing to Soviet military power a threat to peace because it reeked of "classical power politics"? How could one discuss the balance of power without opposing a "peace policy" and thus becoming an advocate of war? If the Cold War was sterile and obsolete, was anticommunism, not the Soviet Union, now a threat to peace? If West German foreign policy was intended to reassure the East European governments enough so that they would reform internally, those who pointed at the absence of freedom in Eastern Europe could also be criticized as threatening détente and hence undermining peace.

Brandt's Ostpolitik and the treaties it led to with Poland, East Germany, and the Soviet Union, as well as his program of domestic reform, led to his reelection in November 1972. The Social Democrats received just over 45 percent of the vote and formed a coalition government with the liberal Free Democratic party (FDP). But in 1974, Brandt had to resign as chancellor after it was revealed that his private secretary was an East German spy. From 1974 to 1987, Brandt focused his energies on the Social Democratic party, while Bahr became its leading speaker on foreign and security policy.

Brandt and Bahr accumulated a host of critics who believed that the intentions and certainly the consequences of their policies would in fact lead to a revival of German nationalism, neutralism, and a loosening of West German's Atlantic ties.[66] In 1973, Bahr assessed the policy of change through rapprochement which he had advocated in 1963. He said that, as long as Germany remained divided, change through rapprochement remained the only conceptual basis for the preservation of the nation.[67] Whereas Bahr had earlier argued that *Wandel durch Annäherung* would lead to reunification with the support or toleration of the Soviet Union, in 1973 he said that things had taken another path and that the two German states would pursue "coexistence German style" *(koexistenze auf Deutsch)*. An "abnormal normalization" had developed between the two states, neither of which "wanted to be enemies any more" and who, despite deep-seated differences of opinion, also had interests in common to develop. The principle of renunciation of force had become the leading principle of West German–Soviet relations. Trust between the two countries had grown since the Moscow Treaty of 1970. Negotiations on troop reductions would soon begin. The Soviet Union had accepted the proposition that the United States could not be pushed out of Europe and that security and détente required an American presence in Europe. The "nuclear pact" between the superpowers had created for the first time the possibility of circumnavigating the conflicts between East and West without unleasing a general war.

Bahr spoke of gradually replacing the balance of terror by a "balance of interests and of trust." Security could only be attained with "mutual dependence and confidence building measures, . . . not only through armaments but also through disarmament."[68] He asserted that *Wandel durch Annäherung* had created stability. An era of "negotiated self-limitations" had begun. In this era, each side had to consider and adapt to the interests of the other. Applied to inner-German relations, improvements in living conditions in the German Democratic Republic (GDR) must take place in such small doses that no danger of a revolt emerges. "Things must remain stable and controllable, if the transformation from conflict to cooperation is to function."[69] There was a need for agreements that "transcended the blocs. . . . transcended the systems" and ushered in a new system of "security by agreements."

Given that the East German communist government was the most orthodox Stalinist regime in Eastern Europe, it was hard to see what *Wandel* (change) Bahr had in mind as a result of *Annäherung* (rapprochement) other than ease of access for West Germans to visit relatives in East Germany. No political change of significance had occurred in East Germany as a result of increased trade and credits from West Germany. If the Soviet Union had finally accepted the principle that the United States ought not be pushed out of Europe and had made renunciation of force the leading principle of its relations with West Germany, its military buildup was an odd way to manifest this policy. While Bahr spoke of disarmament and confidence-building measures in 1973, the Soviet leadership continued its military buildup.

What began as a policy called "change through rapprochement" was continuing with far more rapprochement from West Germany than change in East Germany or Eastern Europe. Détente now had a pronounced conservative thrust directed toward preserving existing Communist governments. In fact, movements or political groups that challenged the status quo in Eastern Europe would appear to be threats to peace and détente, as Bahr conceptualized it. The "common" interests and security to which Brandt and Bahr referred applied to the interests of the West German government and the governments of Eastern Europe. If abnormality had become normal, if people were still shot at the border by East German soldiers or if the East German government prevented the flow of ideas into East Germany, then was this not a failure to deliver on change through rapprochement? Despite Bahr's assurances about West Germany's Western ties, rhetoric about "security by agreements" suggested that the military balance offered by the Atlantic tie was less than crucial. In the face of these questions, Bahr presented himself as a realist in contrast to the ideologues and crusaders of the "now obsolete ideology" of the Cold War.

Yet, despite his reluctance to mention the moral distinctions characteristic of the political culture of militant democracy, Egon Bahr insisted that he was not a neutralist. West Germany, he said, was "economically too strong, militarily too weak and geographically too unfavorably and unalterably located to allow neutrality between East and West. In addition, no one has suggested it. The discussion about neutralism is playing with mirrors *(reine Spiegelfechterei).*"[70] Neutralization of Germany or Central Europe, he said, was "nonsense." However, eventually "a security system for all of Europe will replace" NATO and the Warsaw Pact.[71] Despite his assurances about the importance of equilibrium, Bahr's statements only fueled fears that dissolution of the NATO alliance was precisely what he wanted to bring about. Why, his critics asked, would one even talk about the issue in a period of Soviet military growth? Policy differences aside, at the level of political culture, Bahr blurred the moral differences between the Soviet Union, the communist governments of Eastern Europe, and the Western democracies.

In January 1973, Günter Grass, the West German novelist, essayist, and early supporter of Willy Brandt, praised Bahr's efforts on the occasion of the latter's receipt of a peace prize for his diplomatic efforts. Grass called Bahr's diplomacy a demonstration that "negotiations for securing peace can only be successful when an irreconcilable concept of the enemy is abandoned."[72] He praised Bahr's thought and action for transforming the image of the Soviet Union and the Soviet threat in West German Social Democracy. The onetime totalitarian enemy was now West Germany's "security partner." In Grass's comments were evident a reversal of the meaning of ideology. Cold War anticommunism was itself a product of a rejection of ideologies of communism and nazism in the postwar decade. Détente and the peace policy of the 1970s was now the sober, nonideological approach to foreign policy in contrast to the crusading ideologies of the Cold War.

One result of the transformed political culture of the West German left was a rejection of the Carter administration's human rights policy. In July

1977, *Vorwärts* published a statement by members of the SPD parliamentary faction on the link between human rights and détente entitled "No human rights without peace."[73] Human rights, the parliamentarians wrote, must not become "an instrument of ideological battle" nor should it be considered "only from the perspective of the struggle with communism." A Western human rights campaign aimed at the East bloc would, they continued, erode progress made in economic relations, confidence-building measures, and humanitarian relief. By encouraging destabilization in the East, it would strengthen groups within Communist states that prefer an ideological confrontation with the West and repression at home. It would harm arms control negotiations, inner-German relations and humanitarian relief offered by the East German government and diminish moves toward independence by Western European Communists. Moreover, the authors criticized the American concept of human rights because it did not include freedom from hunger, illiteracy, and poverty. Above all, they said, there could be no progress in human rights without peace. If President Carter's human rights campaign became a threat to détente, it would become a threat to peace.[74] *Wandel durch Annäherung* had given way to security partnership with the governments of the East bloc. By contrast, West German conservatives were enthusiastic supporters of President Carter's human rights campaign.[75]

In 1980 Willy Brandt assessed the impact of détente on West German political culture in the following manner: "The great positive result of our détente policy was that we subordinated ideological differences to the necessity of peaceful coexistence between states. . . . We have determined that the undissolved ideological fronts have sunk into a long slumber without damage to one side or the other."[76] In practice, détente meant the end of the culture of militant democracy and the end of the Schumacher tradition within the Social Democratic party. The differences between Brandt and Bahr and their critics were only partly about policy. No one in the West German establishment opposed a diplomatic engagement and negotiations of some kind with the Soviet Union. But what for Brandt were "slumbering ideological fronts" remained for others very real differences between free and unfree political regimes. To make the irreversibility of détente his first priority was to admit that he and Bahr gave greater weight to rapprochement with the East bloc than to change within it.

Brandt did not change his view that communism was a failed project.[77] He continued to stress contradictions between communism and Social Democracy. But he did not raise the issue of the Soviet military buildup of the 1970s. Rather than admit that détente had raised false hopes about the Soviet Union, Brandt and Bahr increasingly blamed the United States for a cooling of world politics in the late 1970s. They lent halfhearted support to Chancellor Helmut Schmidt's efforts to raise the issue of Soviet armament. Consequently, as Helmut Schmidt grappled with the problem of sustaining a balance of power in Europe in the late seventies, he found that much of his own party had moved away from the intellectual and political assumptions on which a policy or equilibrium rested.

Boundary Erosion and the *Abgrenzungsbeschluss*

The Social Democratic leaders, Brandt included, were aware that the public language and the policy of détente could clash with the Schumacher tradition of anticommunism and militant democracy. Given that the Social Democratic–Communist split overlapped with a division of the nation, the possibility for East German appeals to the West German left were considerable. In addition, the emergence of a new left in the late 1960s enhanced further the erosion of the moral and political boundary between Social Democracy and communism and groups on the radical left. In 1971, concerned that the diplomatic opening to the East might further the erosion of Social Democratic anticommunism, the party's executive committee issued a position paper on the relation between Social Democrats and communism. Known as the *Abgrenzungsbeschluss* [decision on establishing boundaries], it made clear that diplomatic détente did not extend to an end to the ideological and political conflict with communism.

> Peace policy, security and freedom are inseparable for German Social Democracy. Therefore, in its efforts to arrive at a foreign policy understanding with Communist ruled states, it will never allow a blurring of the fundamental contradictions which separate Social Democratic and Communist goals and methods of implementing those goals. . . . Our security rests on a balance of forces. Treaties with our Eastern neighbors will increase our security, but do not make preservation of equilibrium superfluous. . . . the decisive contradiction between Social Democratic and Communist politics lies in the contradiction between a state based on law and on arbitrary power, between a free democracy and party dictatorship, between self-determination and domination from abroad.[78]

In spite of the *Abgrenzungsbeschluss*, Brandt chose not to stress these boundaries between Social Democracy and communism in his major speeches of the 1970s. Instead, he spoke about common interests, about the Soviet Union as a partner, and about the dangers of an "arms race" whose roots seemed to lie in the West as much as the East. Rather than conduct the kind of political offensive he had celebrated at Harvard in 1962, Brandt and Bahr appeared to reassure the Communist regimes of Eastern Europe that relaxation of tensions would not turn into another version of the Prague Spring of 1968. As a consequence, the boundary which the SPD sought to preserve in 1971 became a porous one. The blurring of the distinction between liberal democracy and dictatorship and its replacement with a language of common interests and common security in West German foreign policy effectively dismantled anticommunism on the West German left, especially among the political generations coming of age during the détente era. The political culture of the détente era also placed a taboo on discussion of power balances and of the extent and details of the Soviet military buildup. It was Helmut Schmidt's special burden to reverse the momentum of the regional and global balance of power at the same time as the political culture of militant democracy was unraveling within his own party.

4

HELMUT SCHMIDT
The Bulwark, the Balance, and the Two-Track Decision

FROM 1977 TO SEPTEMBER 1982, West German Chancellor Helmut Schmidt was the major West European player in the euromissile dispute. He was the first leader of the Atlantic Alliance to publicly call attention to the political consequences of the appearance of the SS–20 missiles. He played a central role in shaping the "two-track" NATO decision of December 1979, and he defended the deployments of 1983 even as his own party rejected them. His speech at the International Institute for Strategic Studies in London, calling attention to the political implications of an imbalance in intermediate-range nuclear weapons in fall 1977, was a turning point in the history of postwar Europe and in the rhythms of global politics. Yet this renowned world statesman was unable to sustain support for his policies within his own political party. In part, Schmidt was overwhelmed by the sheer numbers of the young left that streamed into the SPD after the 1960s. But more important than the young left was the impact of Brandt and Bahr on the SPD's foreign policy. Schmidt, the grand strategist of East-West relations, was outmaneuvered by Brandt and Bahr for control of the party. In 1974 when he became the West German chancellor, Schmidt didn't replace Brandt as chairman of the Social Democratic party with a figure more compatible with his views on foreign and economic policy. As a result, Brandt and Egon Bahr remained in very powerful positions within the SPD and placed their allies in important party positions. While Schmidt governed, they continued to transform the political culture of the SPD.

Helmut Schmidt was the chancellor of the Federal Republic from 1974 to 1982. This was the highpoint of a national political career that began with his election to the Bundestag in 1953. Schmidt was born in Hamburg in 1918. His parents were neither Nazis nor members of the anti-Nazi resistance.[1] He served in the Wehrmacht from 1937 to 1945 as a lieutenant in an anti-aircraft battery on the Russian front. Schmidt was drawn to Social Democracy because of its unequivocal defense of democracy during the Weimar era. After the war, he studied economics and wrote a doctoral dissertation on the currency reform in postwar Japan and Germany. His interest in military strategy and in the positive role economic markets had to play in a social democratic vision put him at odds with the SPD left. Helmut Schmidt was a centrist to the core. Coming of age during the Nazi era left him with a distrust for utopias and a commitment to pragmatism.[2] As chancellor, he urged cabinet members to read Karl Popper.[3] He regarded new left utopianism with unconcealed contempt. Though he had little taste for ideological combat with Brandt, Bahr, and the party's leftist intellectuals, he fought a valiant but losing battle to sustain the legacy of Schumacher's social democratic anticommunism.

Helmut Schmidt's contributions to West German intellectual life in the fields of political-military strategy were important and enduring. They consisted of two books, *Defense or Retaliation* (1962) and *Strategie des Gleichgewichts* [Strategy of equilibrium] (1969), and the initiation of annual public reports on the state of West German defense policy known as the *White Books*. In *Defense or Retaliation*, Schmidt presented the British and American literature on deterrence—Henry Kissinger, Bernard Brodie, Thomas Schelling, and Albert Wohlstetter—to a West German audience and made a case for strong conventional forces in NATO's strategy.[4] He believed that a combination of excessive conservative deference to military officers and Social Democratic ignorance of and disinterest in defense policy had led to a deficiency of informed public debate over defense issues in West Germany. He sought to encourage more public debate about such matters.

Schmidt called for stronger conventional forces in Western Europe and opposed land-based nuclear missiles in Europe. He argued that though such missiles helped to deter Soviet aggression against Western Europe and increased American involvement in any European conflict, they had a very small military utility. They were vulnerable to Soviet medium-range bombers and missiles and thus were "suitable only for a surprise attack or a preemptive first strike, and in no way for a second strike." Actually getting political approval to use them in a crisis would be very difficult. Instead of land-based missiles, Schmidt favored missiles on submarines and surface ships, far away from densely populated Western Europe and out of reach of many Soviet weapons. "Anything that attracts enemy fire is unwelcome to states with a high population density or a small area."[5] In the battle over the euromissiles of the 1980s, Schmidt's critics cited these arguments against him. The central motif of Schmidt's views then was the need for a politically credible defense policy that was not "tantamount to the destruction of one's national existence."[6] This was why Schmidt wanted to replace NATO's nuclear focus with an expansion of conventional forces.

Though Schmidt's views in 1962 echoed some of the antinuclear sentiments of the SPD, he delivered a hard line on the Soviet Union. He viewed peaceful coexistence as "a psychological smoke screen for obscuring the intentions of the Soviet Union and world Communism to use all methods beneath the level of actual war for extending its power." Coexistence "has room neither for the idea of balance nor of respect for law." It did not exclude support for and exploitation of revolutions in Africa, Asia, and Latin America and "by no means disavows the efforts, which are continuously being made to undermine the old continent spiritually and politically by infiltration of Communist ideology and propaganda." Khrushchev's view of coexistence was a "one-way street. Changes are only allowed if they benefit the Soviet Union; revolutions in the West are permissible and historically inevitable, in the East they are a crime against the people."[7]

The West would be best off, he continued, if it were able to place competition with the Soviet Union on the level of economic and technical competition. It could do so only as long as the West maintained equilibrium on the military level. Western strength lay above all in its political values and institutions and economic accomplishments. A Western strategy must be aimed at placing the competition with the Soviet Union primarily on those two levels where the West was strongest. However, the West would damage itself if it were restricted to "the familiar type of trite anti-Communism so often encountered in the Federal Republic and the United States."[8] Like Kurt Schumacher, Schmidt argued that the democratic left had a crucial role to play in confronting communism in Europe.

Schmidt identified with the effort of President John F. Kennedy to combine the "aggressive battle with communism" with social reform. To leave anticommunism to the conservatives would open up an "ideological vacuum," which would be a "heaven sent opportunity for Communist aggression."[9] But if the United States did not close the "missile gap" to sustain equilibrium, "the main weight of the real confrontation with Communism might very quickly shift from the economic and technological front to that of naked threats backed by military power."[10] In order for the West to place competition with the Soviet Union on the terrain most favorable to it, that of political and economic institutions, it had to sustain a military equilibrium. Schmidt's emphasis on military equilibrium as an indispensable foundation on which to wage a political battle with the Communists was an enduring theme of his thinking, and one which set him apart in style and tone—and eventually in substance—from Willy Brandt.

Helmut Schmidt took a sober view of the military power of the Soviet Union in 1962. "The Soviet Union," he wrote, "is now a power of unprecedented and commanding military potential" and "shows every sign of being aware of this advantageous change in the situation."[11] If Soviet strategic nuclear superiority in intercontinental ballistic missiles (ICBMs) continued to expand, so that the Soviet leaders thought themselves safe from American nuclear retaliation in the event of limited war in Europe, the possibility of limited attacks on European territory by the Soviet Union grew.[12] If the credibility of the American nuclear guarantee to Western Europe were to erode because of the increasing capability of the Soviet Union to strike the United States, the political pressure the Soviets could exert on Western Europe because of their military power would also grow. This concern over Soviet pressure on Western Europe if the link to the United States was broken remained an enduring worry. Unilateral disarmament in Europe or an American exit from Western Europe would expose the West Germans and West Europeans to possible "Soviet aggression and nuclear blackmail."[13]

In 1969, Schmidt became the defense minister in the social-liberal coalition led by Brandt and published *Strategie des Gleichgewichts*, which examined the German question in light of nuclear parity between the United States and the Soviet Union. The dilemma of the détente era for Schmidt was how to preserve a balance of forces when relaxed relations with the Soviet Union reduced the perception of threat in Western Europe. By diminishing fear of war in Europe, détente might loosen up the alliances on which equilibrium rested. Further, the United States and the Soviet Union might attempt to improve superpower relations at the expense of the security interests of their European alliance partners. Schmidt also worried about weakened American leadership during the era of the war in Vietnam and domestic turbulence, de Gaulle's nationalism, British isolation, and the lack of progress towards a European common market. Western disunity and an absence of strong American leadership could offer opportunities for Soviet expansionism.

At the beginning of the détente era, Schmidt recalled the political stakes in Europe. The main enemies of the East German communists, he wrote, were not West German conservatives but "right wing Social Democrats" in the Schumacher tradition, who refused to allow the communists to monopolize the mantle of German nationalism and the socialist tradition. The East-West political battle over the German question was also a battle between democratic socialists and communists, a battle whose central issue was "the question of whether Europe was to be democratic or dictatorial."[14] Schmidt stressed the central role of Social Democracy as a bulwark against communism. A new *Ostpolitik*, far from blurring distinctions between democracy and dictatorship, was a great political threat to the existing communist regimes. This was so, Schmidt argued, because Western social democrats made it more difficult for East German and East European Communist leaders to label the West, especially West Germany, as the reactionary, fascist, and revanchist enemy that justified their own political rule. In contrast to Brandt, he expected no grand changes from détente. A modus vivendi with some small improvements was attainable. To expect more than that would be to foster illusions.

Détente, he wrote, could be had by those who "do not see or willfully ignore dangerous facts," but political leaders ought not give in to such perfectly understandable feelings. They had to face facts and present them to the public. West Germany had to be calculable, predictable, a good alliance partner, and a country that maintained "military equilibrium as the sine qua non for the political stability of our security."[15] Schmidt summed up his argument in five principles of West German foreign and security policy: military equilibrium, defensive orientation of defense, alliance loyalty, appropriateness of military means to strategic ends, and NATO membership as indispensable for West Germany's security interest, as well as for advocacy of West Germany's special interests within the alliance. Schmidt did not seek a security system in Europe without the United States. He did not juxtapose a "peace policy" to power politics. He believed that diplomacy should rest on continued military equilibrium and a continued Atlantic link.

Faced with the challenge from the new left, Schmidt wrote that West German politicians had perhaps neglected to make their ethical-political maxims clear, "perhaps because many of us believed that the Germans should be spared that, after a time of the absolute misuse of such idealism."[16] Schmidt believed that the postwar West Germans had to relearn the facts of international life. Neither anticommunist rhetoric nor gestures of good will to atone for Hitlerism could preserve equilibrium. He evoked Kant's sense of duty and Max Weber's concern for the intended and unintended consequences of political action as warnings against the revival of German idealism in modern guises. Many leftist intellectuals of the 1960s dismissed Schmidt as a "technocrat." The mutual hostility persisted and grew over the coming decade.

The phrase "daring more democracy" associated with Brandt's opening to the left in social and educational policy applied equally to the publication of annual White Books begun by the West German defense ministry when

Schmidt was the Defense Minister in 1970. For the first time, the West German government presented to the public a detailed picture of the government's information on the military balance in Europe and on the strategy of NATO and the Warsaw Pact, although in the 210 pages in the 1970 White Book, only three were devoted to the NATO–Warsaw Pact military balance.[17]

The 1970 report painted a grim picture of Warsaw Pact improvements in the air, at sea, and on land, a picture at odds with visions of leaving the world of power politics in the past.[18] It concluded that "there is no conventional equilibrium in Central Europe."[19] Nevertheless, a "political psychological equilibrium of deterrence" existed because NATO's conventional forces were adequate to prevent the "creation of facts" by surprise attack and because NATO's conventional defenses would give it sufficient warning "to bring the nuclear component of deterrence into play."[20] Hence war was not likely,[21] but possibilities for Soviet political pressure and intimidation, especially in southern Europe and the Middle East and around West Berlin, remained. "The curtailment of its political freedom of decision due to pressure or threats is the real danger which could threaten West Germany and her allies."[22] The 1973 White Book, the last one of the Brandt government, informed its readers that the Warsaw Pact military buildup was continuing on land, in the air, and at sea.[23]

The first White Book in the Schmidt government, the volume for 1975–1976, continued to present the news of a military balance shifting in favor of the Soviet Union.[24] The White Book stressed that "despite efforts at détente, the ideological conflict between East and West persists. . . . Even in their incompleteness" the countries of the Atlantic Alliance "had nothing in common with an order which monopolizes almost all forms of expression of public and private life."[25] Beginning in 1975, the central chapters of the White Book presented the strategy of both alliances and their military balance. The White Book stated that for the Warsaw Pact the fundamental strategic idea was that of the strategic offensive. It could launch a surprise attack on Western Europe "with practically no preparation time at all" and could use the "inner weaknesses of Western democracies for its own goals with subversive action." The military strategy of the Warsaw Pact in Europe called for parity with the United States, and conventional superiority over NATO in Europe. The Warsaw Pact could be expected to "exercise political pressure [on Western Europe] with its military superiority."[26] Therefore, preservation of strong conventional forces and a credible nuclear deterrent were essential for NATO.[27]

The White Book reported that trends in the military balance were not favorable for NATO. The Soviet Union had overcome and surpassed the

United States in numbers of missiles and had narrowed the technological gap as well. American missiles had been MIRVed (MIRV refers to multiple independently targeted re-entry vehicles), while a new generation of Soviet ICBMs heavier than American missiles and outfitted with multiple warheads were operational. In submarine-launched ballistic missiles (SLBM), the Soviet Union had also surpassed the United States. Delta Class submarines with missiles of 7,500-km range now allowed Soviet submarines to operate farther from American shores. The Soviet Union had introduced the Backfire bomber, which could reach the United States from Soviet territory, while the B-1 bomber would not be introduced into the American arsenal until the early 1980s.

The most interesting new development reported by the 1975–1976 White Book concerned medium-range missiles. The Soviet Union had 600 launchers. "An additional threat potential can emerge from a new MRBM (medium range ballistic missile), the SSX-20, currently being tested by the Soviet Union."[28] The nuclear potential of Great Britain and France was an "additional risk factor for an aggressor but did not constitute a counterweight to the medium range missiles of the Soviet Union."[29] So the soon-to-be-famous SS-20 made its first, one-sentence appearance in the White Book, as did the argument that the existing British and French nuclear weapons were not "counterweights" to the medium-range weapons of the Soviet Union.

Trends in the maritime balance were also disquieting. The greatest threat came from Warsaw Pact submarines. From 1968 to 1975, there had been a 15 percent increase in conventional submarines with cruise missiles (from 59 to 67) and a 92 percent increase in the number of nuclear-powered submarines with cruise missiles (from 38 to 73). Naval aircraft had increased considerably. The numbers of cruise missile cruisers had doubled (from 9 to 21). Cruise missile corvettes went from 2 to 31. Destroyers carrying cruise missiles increased in numbers from 27 to 48. The ships of the Warsaw Pact were on average newer than NATO's. The Soviet naval policy was "one of the most important changing developments of the last ten years." Fleet maneuvers in 1975 indicated that the Soviet navy was now able to conduct rapid, worldwide, centrally directed operations, operations that were facilitated by a capacity for resupply at sea and access to a number of airfields in the Third World.[30]

On NATO's north and south flanks there were considerable numerical superiorities of the Warsaw Pact over NATO. Neither flank was defensible at all without American naval and air power. As for the Central Front, there remained a now-familiar Warsaw Pact numerical superiority in divisions (58:27, with 30 more in the Western military districts of Russia), tanks (6100:1900), with 8000 in the Western military districts), planes (2,460:1700, with 1290 in the Western military districts). Since 1968, the numbers of Warsaw Pact tanks had increased by 40 percent, as had the numbers of rocket launchers, antitank weapons, and artillery in each Warsaw Pact division. In 1975, twenty Warsaw Pact divisions had the same fire power as twenty-five did in 1968.

In the balance of air forces in Europe the Warsaw Pact was also superior. Largely because of the large number of fighter planes suitable for air defense, the Warsaw Pact had about twice the number of planes that were at NATO's disposal, even when American reinforcements were taken into account. While the number of planes had been constant since 1968, their quality was improving. NATO was incomparably more dependent on oil imports than the Warsaw Pact. Forty-three percent of the energy used in the world in 1974 was oil based, 30 percent gas, 20 percent coal, 7 percent from hydroelectric and nuclear energy. The Western industrial societies used 70 percent of the world's oil but produced only 22 percent. Western Europe was dependent for 90 percent of its oil on imports. The strong dependence of Western Europe on oil from Third World sources had a double risk: the sale as well as the transport of oil could be withheld or interrupted. The Soviet Union, on the other hand, was totally independent in oil and could supply its allies with their needs as well. The same dependence on raw materials characterized the West European dilemma regarding imports of raw materials, while the Soviet Union could supply itself and its allies with about 80 percent of their mineral resources. In 1973, West Germany was importing 100 percent of its bauxite, chromium, copper, manganese, molybdenum, nickel, phosphates, titanium, vanadium, and tin, with 95 percent of its iron, 85 percent of its lead, and 70 percent of its zinc equally divided between the Third World and other Western countries. As copper and tin come primarily from developing countries, security of sea control was vital for the economy of Western Europe. The growth of the Soviet navy had direct implications for West European security.

In the period from 1970 to 1974, the highpoint of *neue Ostopolitik*, West German defense spending increased at least 10.3 percent a year, then increased by 2 percent to 3 percent a year in the wake of the OPEC oil shocks in 1975 and 1976. In 1975, when the United States was spending about $432 per capita on defense, West Germany led Western Europe with $264 per capita. The percentage of the West German GNP going to defense increased from 4.2 percent in 1970 to 5.0 percent in 1975 and declined to 4.6 percent in 1976.[31] While the percentage of the American budget going to defense spending was declining as a percentage of the GNP in the aftermath of the Vietnam war, the West German contribution was increasing.

A regular public accounting of the Western assessment of the military balance also came from annual and biannual statements made by NATO officials in Brussels. The deteriorating global and regional balance of forces and the nature of the Western response were the central theme of NATO's public statements during the era of détente. The NATO communiques during the era of détente provide a running commentary on the shifting military balance. In Brussels in December 1970, the NATO ministers said that "the evidence thus far suggests that the USSR, intent on extending and strengthening its political power, conducts its international relations on the basis of concepts some of which are not conducive to détente."[32] In the same year, the Nuclear Planning Group asserted that Soviet defense spending from 1965 to 1969 rose at a rate of 5 percent to 6 percent a year at a time of declining NATO defense expenditures. It warned that improvement of East–West relations would depend on Soviet acceptance of a military balance.[33]

In June 1974, NATO's Defense Planning Committee stated that the growth of Warsaw Pact forces was "far in excess of that required for self-defense . . . such actions are difficult to reconcile with declared objectives of detente. . . ."[34] These concerns were repeated in the Defense Planning Committee reports of December 1974[35] and May 1975.[36] Similar reports appeared in January and June 1976, along with statements about the "possible improvements in NATO flexibility and selectivity" of NATO's theater nuclear forces.[37] In December 1976, NATO's Defense Planning Committee expressed "serious concern" over the "relentless growth" in the strength of the Warsaw Pact forces, which displayed an "increasing emphasis" on offensive capabilities. It was in this communique that the defense ministers first mentioned the SS-20.

> In the nuclear field significant improvements are being made with the appearance of new nuclear delivery systems equipped with multiple warheads; this includes the expected deployment of the SS-20 mobile intermediate range ballistic missiles capable of striking targets in the whole of Europe and beyond.[38]

By June 1977, the Nuclear Planning Group statements reaffirmed NATO's determination to maintain "essential equivalence" between NATO and the Warsaw Pact. In that regard, they discussed the utility of cruise missiles and possible approaches for theater nuclear force modernization.[39]

Helmut Schmidt's London Speech of October 1977

In January 1977, Jimmy Carter became president of the United States. He was committed to radical reductions in nuclear weapons. Helmut Schmidt was worried about the SS-20 arsenal, worried about coupling to the United States, and worried that Carter would neglect the European nuclear balance in his eagerness to reach an arms control agreement with the Soviet Union. In the spring and summer of 1977, Schmidt expressed his concerns to President Carter and his national security adviser, Zbigniew Brzezinski, but was not satisfied with their apparent lack of empathy for his concerns. He decided to raise the issue of the medium-range nuclear missiles at a speech at the International Institute for Strategic Studies in London in October 1977.[40] That speech marked the beginning of a historic reversal of the momentum of the global balance of forces, as well as the opening shot of the political battle over the euromissiles. It was the first time that a Western political leader had publicly raised the issue of the nuclear balance in Europe. In an interview with the author in 1985, Schmidt explained the background to the speech as follows:

> *I was fed up with Brzezinski and Carter who had told me that the Russian SS-20s did not matter at all . . . they didn't understand that the SS-20 was a political threat, political blackmail against Germany most of all and later on against others in Europe. . . .* In the course of 1977, Carter talked a lot of nonsense about deep cuts. . . . I told him [such an approach] would fail. Moscow would not accept this. . . . They [the Soviets] had been set on a certain track in Vladivostok and given their immobility, they would keep to their track. I forecast the breakdown of this deep cut approach. . . . Instead, [I said to Carter that] you should add to the so-called incomplete Vladivostok framework two medium range new weapons in the Soviet Union—namely, the Backfire and SS-20 to the Vladivostok framework. I had been in agreement with Gerald Ford that they would be included once Gerry had been reelected before finalizing the Vladivostock thing.
>
> Carter and Brzezinski rejected that idea. This was not my business, was the wording of Mr. Brzezinski. . . . The London speech was a reaction against being rebuffed twice by the White House in the course of 1977, telling them publicly in front of an audience that understood what I was talking about that it was not a good approach to let these missiles and weapons that were targeted against Europe and not against America be left out [of negotiations] as being a negligible quantity or quality. This was the sense of the London speech. The London speech said that there ought to be equilibrium on all levels.[41] (emphasis added)

The Soviet Union, he continued, had attained strategic parity in intercontinental nuclear missiles, yet it continued to accumulate more weapons.

This accumulation applied to the intercontinental level but also included weapons that could reach Western Europe but not the United States. Schmidt believed that the purpose of such weapons was, as he put it, to deploy "a weapon of political intimidation directed against the nonnuclear Federal Republic of Germany."[42]

In London, Chancellor Schmidt said,

> Changed strategic conditions confront us with new problems. SALT codifies the nuclear strategic balance between the Soviet Union and the United States. To put it another way: SALT neutralizes their strategic nuclear capabilities. In Europe this magnifies the significance of the disparities between East and West in nuclear tactical and conventional systems.[43]

Since the late 1950s, the Soviet Union had deployed medium-range nuclear missiles, the SS-4s and SS-5s, directed at Western Europe. Before that, it had manned bombers capable of reaching Western Europe with nuclear bombs.[44] Thus it was not only the fact of an imbalance of forces in Europe that concerned Helmut Schmidt. What worried Schmidt was the combination of unfavorable trends in the global and regional nuclear balance or, in his words, the "neutralization" of the American strategic deterrent and the growth of the Soviet medium-range nuclear forces directed at Western Europe. Disparities in Europe that were previously tolerable before the Soviet Union had attained parity were no longer tolerable, or were less tolerable, when American superiority had been lost. If the United States could be deterred from coming to Western Europe's defense by the growth of Soviet intercontinental nuclear weapons, the pressure and threat emanating from Soviet medium-range weapons directed by Western Europe would increase dramatically. This was the meaning of "decoupling," the nightmare of NATO strategists.

Schmidt stressed the "vital interest" of all in negotiations between the two superpowers on limitation and reduction of nuclear weapons.

> But strategic arms limitations confined to the United States and the Soviet Union will inevitably impair the security of the West European members of the (Western) Alliance vis-a-vis Soviet military superiority in Europe if we do not succeed in removing the disparities of military power in Europe parallel to the SALT negotiations. So long as this is not the case we must maintain the balance of the full range of deterrence strategy.[45]

A balance could be established by a Western buildup or by Warsaw Pact reductions leading to a balance at a lower level. Schmidt said he preferred the latter option.[46] To his ally President Carter, Schmidt's message was: do not sacrifice the security interests of Western Europe for the sake of an arms control deal with the Soviet Union. Take a harder look at the political purposes of Soviet military forces. His message to Leonid Brezhnev was no less clear: stop the buildup of medium-range nuclear weapons that was upsetting the balance of forces in Europe. If the balance were not restored, the possibility of new Western weapons of some sort could not be excluded. Norms of parity should be applied to Soviet relations with Western Europe no less than to the United States. Nuclear parity between the super-powers should not lead to codification of second-class security for West Germany and Western Europe.

Lothar Rühl on Decoupling and "Limited War"

Lothar Rühl, one of West Germany's most respected military strategists, discussed the political meaning of changes in the military balance in essays written in the late 1970s.[47] In 1977, he wrote that if the Atlantic Alliance dissolved and if American power no longer was extended to Western Europe, the basis of the postwar strategic stability in Europe would also collapse.[48] Then "the hypothesis of the improbability of a war in Europe" would lose its strategic foundations. The door would be open to the "active, direct and offensive use of superior military power by a state or a group of states." Europe would return to its pre-1945 condition, in which a state or group of states used military power in limited wars with the hope of success.[49] Short of an outright dissolution of the Atlantic Alliance, Rühl worried that an end to the threat of escalation to nuclear weapons able to strike the Soviet Union in retaliation for a Soviet attack on Western Europe "would liberate the offensive capacities of the Soviet Union arrayed against Western Europe and make possible a calculation of success for a war of aggression with calculable means necessary to carry it out." An interruption of escalation in the event of war, he continued,

> would mean that a limited war would be conducted in Europe. In such a war, the risk for Europe would always be maximal, that for the Soviet Union however would be smaller.[50] This situation of a limited war with conventional offensive forces and nuclear weapons used for a rapid decision appears to stand in the center of Soviet images of war in the event of a European war.[51]

Rühl believed that the Soviet conventional and nuclear buildup had taken place with such possibilities in mind. He referred specifically to the SS-20 and the Backfire bomber in connection with this analysis of a limited war of aggression in Europe launched by the Soviet Union. He argued for a Western strategy that would deny the Soviet leaders the possibility of limiting a war to Western Europe or to Western and Central/Eastern Europe. Soviet leaders had to know that retaliation against Soviet territory itself was possible and likely in the event of an attack on Western Europe.

However, if the Soviet Union succeeded in limiting the use of nuclear weapons to Western Europe and in "neutralizing" the power of American nuclear weapons in relation to the Soviet Union, the security of Western Europe could be "decoupled" from that of North America. *"Then a nuclear war limited to Europe would no longer be burdened with an unacceptable risk.* It would then become politically and strategically a real option" [emphasis added].[52] In other words, a Western Europe decoupled from the American nuclear guarantee would be made safe for a Soviet war of aggression. The "fundamental and unavoidable consequence" of the change to superpower parity or Soviet superiority was a "change in the fundamental conditions for nuclear escalation in the course of a limited war."[53] Only, Rühl argued, as long as the Atlantic Alliance and a credible threat of escalation to the American nuclear arsenal remained in place was war in Europe a suicidal proposition for the Soviet Union.

The primary political purpose, in his view, of the Soviet buildup was to bring about such decoupling by intimidating West European leaders and publics. Such a strategy was a means to preserve the Soviet empire in Eastern Europe and to extend Soviet influence over the governments of Western Europe. Refusal by Western leaders to talk clearly about the Soviet military buildup, combined with attacks on American policy, were in his view evidence that Soviet military power had already begun to intimidate parts of the West European elites. Neutralization of the Federal Republic in the wake of the disintegration of NATO would be a political result of Soviet military power.

If, Rühl continued, the link to the United States were broken, the states of Western Europe would have to do one of two things. They could appease the Russians so that their security became dependent on the Soviet Union in a European security system that it dominated, or they could reestablish a balance in Europe with a European nuclear deterrent. The most likely result of a break in the trans-Atlantic link would be a peace under Soviet hegemony.[54] From Rühl's perspective of 1977, the appearance of "peace movements" in 1981 in Western Europe directed against NATO policy or verbally attacking "both superpowers," while mounting no effective opposition against Soviet armament, was a powerful piece of evidence confirming his concerns that Soviet military power would pay rich political dividends in the form of fear and appeasement in Western Europe.[55]

NATO estimated that by the end of 1977 ten SS-20 launchers with a total of 30 warheads had become operational. By the end of 1978, that number had grown to 78 launchers and 210 warheads.[56] The SS-20s replaced older single-warhead, immobile SS-4s and SS-5s, which had been deployed in the 1950s. The SS-20s were mobile, fitted with three warheads and very accurate, with a range of 5000 kilometers. They gave the Soviet leadership the capability of launching a nuclear attack on civilian or military targets—command headquarters, airfields, missile silos in Britain and France, and communication centers—while keeping the bulk of its nuclear arsenal intact to deter American intervention or retaliation.[57]

Helmut Schmidt and Equilibrium in the "Gray Zone"

In the public case that Chancellor Schmidt made in the euromissile dispute, the key word was equilibrium. The Soviet Union, he argued, must apply principles of parity and equality previously applied to relations with the United States to its relations with the medium-sized and, in West Germany's case, nonnuclear powers of Western Europe. In order to get the Soviet Union to apply such norms to Western Europe, Schmidt argued, the threat of Western counterdeployments was indispensable. To bring about a Kantian world in which nations accepted common norms, Schmidt recalled the Hobbesian realities of power politics. In this sense, he was a classical European balance-of-power statesman seeking to combine diplomacy and equilibrium in the Grotian tradition manifest in the Harmel Report of 1967.[58]

The 1979 White Book, written under the direction of Walter Stützle, director of the planning staff in the West German Defense Ministry and a close adviser to Schmidt, recalled that the West German government had "very early"—in 1976 privately and then publicly in 1977—drawn attention to the threat to the Atlantic Alliance posed by the medium-range systems of the Soviet Union because they menaced strategic objectives in Europe and were a challenge to the cohesion of the Atlantic Alliance. Therefore, it was necessary to eliminate the risks associated with the growing preponderance of the Soviet Union in the domain of medium-range systems with a mixture of arms control and defense decisions.[59]

The White Book of 1979 also elaborated on points Schmidt had raised in the London speech of 1977. First, parity between the superpowers increasingly limited the function of intercontinental weapons to mutual deterrence. "Therefore the disequilibrium between arms of a medium range of the East and West plays an ever more important role in the global equilibrium." Second, SALT II, by focusing only on parity at the strategic level between the two superpowers, put the European disequilibrium into greater focus. Third, the SS-20 and Backfire bomber amounted to a "radical unilateral change in favor of the East" in global nuclear potential and created a "strategic threat of a new dimension" to the European members of the alliance. Fourth, in view of the principle of strategic parity between East and West, the existence of medium-range Soviet missiles "can no longer be justified" by a need to maintain a deterrent against Central Europe to counterbalance the—no longer existent—strategic superiority of the United States at the level of strategic nuclear weapons. The fact that the Soviet Union was, nevertheless, proceeding with a buildup of medium-range missiles suggested that the Soviets were seeking "superiority at the level of the global equilibrium." Yet these weapons were included neither in the SALT nor in the MBFR (Mutual and Balanced Force Reductions) negotiations and fell into a "gray zone" of growing disequilibrium in Europe. Finding a solution to the gray zone problem was "one of the essential tasks of the Alliance needed to guarantee our security."[60] In Chancellor Schmidt's public statements, as well as in the assessments of the West German Defense Ministry in the late 1970s, there lies abundant evidence that the West German Social Democratic government was very worried about the Societ buildup. It was not the case, as opponents were later to claim, that the United States forced the dual-track decision of December 1979 on its reluctant West German ally.

Between fall 1977 and December 1979, the foreign and defense ministries of the Western alliance worked out the details of what came to be called the "two-track" decision of December 1979.[61] Strategists on both sides of the Atlantic argued for new missiles on land in Western Europe to prevent "decoupling" and allow "selective nuclear options" to make more credible the existing strategy of flexible response.[62] They did not favor treating these weapons as bargaining chips and feared that the Soviet Union would use negotiations to gain a veto over Western defense policy.[63] Political leaders, especially Helmut Schmidt, hoped negotiations would lead to a balance at lower levels and initiate a process of reductions of nuclear weapons via arms control.

The strictly operational advantages for NATO of the Pershing II and cruise missiles were considerable. They had the ability to strike fortified targets with minimal collateral damage, penetrate Warsaw Pact air defenses, and allow NATO air forces to be used for attacking less-fixed targets, such as troop concentrations. The missiles could strike deep into Warsaw Pact territory at strategic reserves of personnel and material, helping to isolate the first attacking echelons of troops. They were useful in implementing a less static concept of flexible response, one less focused on stopping aggression primarily with use of tactical nuclear weapons near the German-German border. The West could respond to attack by taking the battle quickly to the western regions of the Soviet Union.[64] As a result the Soviet leaders would be denied the option of limiting war to Western and Central Europe, thus reducing the likelihood that they would start a war at all. Weapons able to reach the Soviet Union from Western Europe meant that the state that made the decision to attack would suffer retaliation for that decision. As Michel Tatu put it, war would "automatically extend to the territory of the aggressor, also probably to that of its protector. Is there a better guarantee that this war would never take place?"[65]

The 108 Pershing II missiles were too small in number and too short in range to reach more than a third of the SS-20 sites or the command bunkers in Moscow, while the cruise missiles flying at the speed of sound were too slow to prevent Sovit missile firings, nor could they reach the bulk of Soviet intercontinental ballistic missiles. They could not suppress the Soviet nuclear threat to Europe, which would exist in any case as long as the Soviet Union had intercontinental missiles. Neither system could be used to launch a surprise first strike against the Soviet Union's critical political and military targets. They could come into play only after a Soviet attack on Western Europe.

The Neutron Bomb Affair

The neutron bomb affair, a microcosm and foreshadowing of the battle to come over the euromissiles, put the issue of nuclear weapons in the West German public eye for the first time since the 1950s. In July 1977, the American Senate debated the issue of deploying the "neutron bomb" in Europe after a defense correspondent for the *Washington Post* reported that it had been successfully tested.[66] This "enhanced radiation" weapon reduced blast and increased radiation effects, making it a powerful tool against concentrated tank formations. The Soviet Union then launched a propaganda offensive describing it as a "capitalist" weapon that killed people but spared property.[67] In the July 17, 1977, issue of *Vorwärts*, Egon Bahr fired one of the opening shots in the battle of the euromissiles. In "Is humanity going mad? The neutron bomb is a symbol of the perversion of thinking," he linked the enhanced radiation bomb to a critique of the production of "more and more commodities."[68]

Reduced to a simple formula this is a weapon which causes no, or only slight, material damage, but "cleanly" kills man. This is to be the final progress? Is mankind about to go crazy? . . . Here the scale of all values is being turned upside down. The goal has become the preservation of the material things: man is secondary in importance. . . . With his mind man makes himself even less than the slave of the machine: In case of hostilities, it is the machine rather than man that is worth saving. The neutron bomb is a symbol of the perversion of thought.[69]

Helmut Schmidt and his defense minister Georg Leber pointed out the tactical advantages for West Germans of a nuclear weapon that caused a smaller blast than previous battlefield nuclear weapons.[70] *Der Spiegel,* West Germany's most influential weekly newsmagazine, entitled its cover story for July 18, 1977, "America's wonder weapon for Europe."[71] In what was to become a familiar pastiche, *Der Spiegel* presented pictures of Hiroshima, descriptions of the results of nuclear explosions in West Germany, technical detail concerning the effects of the bomb, and the comments of American critics of the weapon. *Der Spiegel* contrasted "American hawks" who wanted the weapon to "sober observers" who rejected their "panic messages" concerning Soviet military advantages in Europe. Though the balance of terror between the superpowers was stable, Jimmy Carter threatened to upset it by introducing the neutron bomb and cruise missile, "at a time in which the climate between the two superpowers has been cooled by Carter's human rights crusade."[72] *Der Spiegel* juxtaposed "technocrats," "nuclear war planners," "NATO's artillery officers," and "American hawks" to Germans defending human values.[73]

In September 1977, the Christian Democrats defended the neutron bomb decision. Manfred Wörner (then a CDU's defense expert in parliament), while stressing the defensive, war-preventing purpose of NATO's strategy, added that "whoever attacks us cannot delude himself with the illusion that he could plot a war limited to our territory while sparing his own territory."[74] The neutron bomb, he said, was well-oriented for damage limitation needed to credibly implement NATO's strategy of flexible response. "Precisely because this weapon reduces collateral damage for the civilian population, its use is more credible, the risk for the Warsaw Pact is higher and thus deterrence and war prevention is more effective."[75] It was no surprise, Wörner continued, that the Soviet Union had launched a worldwide campaign against this "capitalist weapon." The aim of this campaign was a "psychological disarmament" of the Western public. In view of the Soviet buildup of SS-20 missiles aimed at Western Europe, "it would be much better to draw attention to Moscow and its arms policies than to denounce the supposed perversity of thinking in the West. . . ."[76] Wörner warned that "it would be utterly catastrophic if in the area of external security it was Mr. [Egon] Bahr and others, and no longer the Defense Minister, the Chancellor and the government who had the last word in West Germany."[77]

The West German Defense Minister, Georg Leber, a Social Democrat, also defended deployment of the neutron bomb. Leber defended détente but distinguished it from a policy that assumed all conflicts between East and West were over or from one directed at changing "the inner constitution of the East." If, he continued, the East wanted its readiness for détente to be taken seriously in the West, it had to avoid, "as a result of a growing number of tanks and airplanes, a climate of distrust which is grist for the mill of those in the world who do not want any detente. Sometimes it seems as though the leadership of the Soviet Union is erroneously assessing the political effects of its increase in arms. . . ."[78] The Soviet buildup, Leber implied, was diminishing support for détente in Western Europe, undermining support for the West German Social Democrats and the Brandt-era détente policy, and building support for the right-of-center parties in West Germany.[79] The neutron bomb affair in West Germany made nuclear weapons and strategy a topic of public debate and offered a foretaste of the difficulties military strategists faced when engaged in public discussion of nuclear strategies.[80]

In April 1978, President Carter surprised Chancellor Schmidt when he decided to cancel production and deployment of the neutron bomb. For Schmidt and for the West German conservatives, Carter's decision amounted to submission to a Soviet diplomatic-propaganda offensive against the neutron bomb.[81] The decision was a particular shock and embarrassment for Schmidt and for James Callahan in Great Britain, both of whom had supported the weapon in the face of great opposition in their own parties.[82] The neutron bomb affair suggested that domestic divisions in West Germany could serve as an effective lever to veto Western defense decisions. Egon Bahr, then General Secretary of the SPD, welcomed Carter's decision. He had won a relatively easy political victory.[83]

Brezhnev in Bonn: A Military Equilibrium Exists in Spring 1978

In May 1978, General Secretary Brezhnev visited Bonn. With approximately 50 SS-20 then deployed, he announced that a military equilibrium existed in Europe. He also signed a West German–Soviet declaration that committed both sides to the principles of parity and détente.[84] Schmidt expressed concern about the accumulation of conventional and nuclear potentials and was "not silent about our conviction concerning the necessity of equilibrium." He stressed the need for a political-military equilibrium in Europe, expressing hope that American-Soviet negotiations in the SALT talks would soon lead to arms reductions that would "do away with the currently existing disparities also in the conventional sphere and in the sector of nuclear medium range missile potentials."[85] Schmidt did not accept Brezhnev's assertions about the existence of equilibrium and told Brezhnev that the SS-20 buildup was unacceptable.[86] He hoped to convince Brezhnev that continuation of the military buildup, including the SS-20, was putting détente at risk. Schmidt wanted Leonid Brezhnev to know that if he continued the SS-20 buildup, he would be doing so in violation of the principles stated in the joint Soviet–West German declaration ending their meeting in Bonn in 1978. Willy Brandt praised the accomplishments of détente in building trust and cooperation between West Germany and the Soviet Union and urged that it now be extended to include the area of arms control and disarmament.[87] He did not mention the Soviet military buildup.

Schmidt's warnings about the balance of power found faint echo in his own party. On the contrary, the foreign-policy left began to stir. In November 1978, Dieter Lutz, a prolific peace researcher at the peace research institute associated with the University of Hamburg, published an essay in the SPD's weekly magazine *Vorwärts* entitled "Is the third world war coming in 1983?"[88] The danger of war, he wrote, did not come from the Soviet threat but from a destabilized arms race due to technological developments driven by the United States. Both superpowers were developing additional heavy strategic weapons suitable for a first strike against the hard targets of the other. If current trends continued, Lutz predicted a third world war by 1985 at the latest.[89] Lutz's political style was long on references to abstract, subjectless processes and short on reference to specific actors with proper names. He stressed weapons and technological "logic" rather than governments and their policies, though the brunt of his criticism fell on American policy.

The Year of Decision: 1979

In January 1979, the leaders of the Western alliance, President Jimmy Carter, French President Giscard d'Estaing, British Prime Minister James Callahan, and West German Chancellor Helmut Schmidt, met on the Caribbean island of Guadeloupe. There they agreed to proceed with the key elements of what became NATO's two-track decision: Carter agreed to deploy American medium-range nuclear weapons in Western Europe and to combine the deployment decision with a negotiation "track." The leaders agreed that the new weapons should be deployed no later than 1983, leaving a three-year period for negotiations. In April 1979, NATO's Nuclear Planning Group agreed to deploy between 200 and 600 theater nuclear weapons. NATO also created a "special group on arms limitation" to work on negotiations with Moscow. In September 1979, NATO's High Level Group recommended deployment of 464 cruise missiles in five West European countries and 108 Pershing II ballistic missiles in West Germany.

On December 12, 1979, the NATO council of foreign and defense ministers in Brussels announced the "two-track" decision to deploy 572 medium-range nuclear weapons (108 Pershing II ballistic missiles and 464 air-breathing cruise missiles) and simultaneously to offer to begin arms control negotiations with the Soviet Union "as soon as possible." All limitations on American systems would be accompanied by limitations on Soviet systems. Limitations in LRTNF (long-range theater nuclear forces) would be negotiated bilaterally in the context of SALT III. The objective of the negotiations would be the establishment of agreed limitations on the LRTNF of the United States and the Soviet Union at the lowest possible numbers. All limitations had to be in accord with the principle of equality between the parties, and the agreement had to be verifiable. NATO also announced withdrawal of 1000 nuclear warheads from Western Europe. At the time of the NATO decision, the number of SS-20s had grown to 140, with 420 warheads.

The two-track decision combined the hopes of détente with the concerns created by the Soviet buildup. Linking the two tracks and creating a four-year period of negotiations highlighted the asymmetry of democracy and dictatorship in Europe. In the four years between announcement and deployment, the Soviet Union and domestic opponents in Western Europe would have many opportunities to try to stop the deployment. The absence of public opinion and open, legal political opposition in the Warsaw Pact ruled out a symmetrical diplomatic counteroffensive on NATO's part. NATO would be bargaining over weapons it had not yet deployed, in contrast to the already deployed and continuously growing number of SS-20s. The voluntary character of the NATO alliance and the need to attain consensus among democratically elected governments offered Moscow the possibility of encouraging divisions between governments, especially between West Germany on the one hand and France and Britain on the other.[90] The four-year period expanded opportunities for opposition in the democracies, but it also expanded the time for governments to make their case as well.

From Bulwark to Lever: The SPD in West Berlin

The struggle between Schmidt and the SPD was evident in the resolution emerging from the party congress in West Berlin in December 1979. "Peace and Security Policy: Security Policy in the Context of Peace Policy" was one of the key documents of the battle of the euromissiles. It was written in the language made familiar by Brandt and Bahr during the decade of détente. The resolution did not mention the Soviet Union by name, but it did affirm that "détente and disarmament presuppose equilibrium," that "global equilibrium must not be endangered by one-sided armament at the regional or global level," and that "in the establishment of equilibrium, arms control and disarmament have a clear political priority."[91] But it suffered from a certain vagueness. It referred to "competing states and alliances" instead of to NATO and the Warsaw Pact, who "must assume" that the "other side" began with a readiness for peace, to listen to its ideas and "not to assume the opposite." Defense policy should not be "over-reactions which originate in mistrust and Angst. The subjective need for security of the other side must be taken into account."[92]

The resolution reaffirmed membership in NATO and asserted that deterrence remained stable. However, "a growing military strengthening of the military capabilities of the Warsaw Pact could endanger the stability" Europe had enjoyed for so long. The SPD would support measures aimed at preserving NATO's strategy.[93] That was the extent of the discussion of the Soviet buildup in the resolution. The resolution did not refer to the SS-20s by name. In regard to the NATO two-track decision, the resolution stated that "disparities in nuclear medium range potentials must be handled with a combination of defense and arms-steering policies." Arms control should be given priority in such negotiations. There would be no "automatism" about deployment. The West German government should agree to the stationing of medium-range missiles in Europe only if negotiations did not lead to satisfactory results. *"The goal of negotiations is to make the introduction of additional medium range weapons in Western Europe superfluous as a result of a reduction of Soviet and medium range weapons and an agreed limitation on medium range weapons in general for East and West Europe"*[94] (emphasis added). The resolution did not mention the goals of reinforcing coupling, restoring a balance, eliminating the Soviet sanctuary, reinforcing deterrence, or establishing a balance at the lowest possible number, as the

NATO decision had put it. Rather, the primary purpose of the proposed talks was to make the deployments "superfluous" altogether. Further, the resolution left open the possibility that Soviet reductions short of zero could make new NATO deployments "superfluous." The West Berlin resolution of December 1979 contained the idea of a one-sided zero option, that is, elimination of any new American deployments on West European territory. In the battle of the euromissiles, Brandt's and Bahr's critics said they had changed their position. In fact, the West Berlin resolution of 1979 contained the seeds of their subsequent rejection of the NATO deployments.

Moscow's diplomats could reasonably interpret the SPD's Berlin resolution of 1979 to mean that there was strong support in the Social Democratic party for accepting reductions in the number of Soviet missiles, but not for eliminating them, in return for rejection of any American deployments. This accurate political assessment would suggest a political strategy aimed at gaining the support of the Social Democratic party and, more broadly, the West German left, to prevent implementation of NATO's decision. While Helmut Schmidt sought to play the role of bulwark in the face of this Soviet strategy, others in his party, intentionally or not, created a lever that the Soviet Union could pull to exert pressure on the governments of the Western alliance.

5

THE POPULAR FRONT
OF THE 1970s
Some Quantitative Measures

IN THE FOLLOWING THREE CHAPTERS, we take a step back from the political narrative of the euromissile dispute to look at the state of West German political culture from the sixties to the eighties. This chapter presents quantitative measures of the distribution of attitudes in the political and intellectual elites. Chapters 6 and 7 present the views of the foreign-policy left and of the intellectual and political center right, respectively. Taken together, these chapters offer a view of the balance of forces among West German political and intellectual opinion- and policy-shaping elites on the eve of the battle of the euromissiles. Far from being a tabula rasa on which the superpowers casually played out a game of global power politics, West Germans came to the euromissile dispute with well-developed interpretive perspectives and political convictions, which were an important causal factor in the outcome of events.

Everywhere in the most affluent capitalist democracies, the sixties left had had an enduring political impact. West Germany was no exception, and in some ways the persisting impact was even more potent than in the United States. Neo-Marxism of the 1960s in West Germany was, in part, a revival of the German Marxism of the 1920s and the Marxism of the German refugees of the 1930s. Unlike the United States during this time, where Richard Nixon won the presidency in 1968 on a platform of law and order, in West Germany the new left found a critically sympathetic voice in Willy Brandt, elected as West German chancellor on a program of "daring more democracy" in 1969. The new left's attack on anticommunism in West Germany went very deep, as did its rejection of the application of the term "totalitarianism" to both the Nazi regime and the Soviet

Union. In contrast to the United States, West Germany experienced a leftward shift of the whole political spectrum which included the capture of national executive power. In addition to the contrast between Brandt and Nixon, in West Germany of the sixties and early seventies the left benefited from initially favorable demographics and professional labor markets. Instead of their being seen as strictly a movement of youthful sixties "post-materialists," the West German left in the 1970s steadily accumulated institutional positions that enhanced its influence in national politics. At the same time, a minority among the intellectual and academic elites emerged in the early seventies which was critical of the left and began to forge links to the eventually resurgent Christian Democratic party.

The West German new left appeared at an opportune moment. From 1950 to 1970, the numbers of students attending West German universities nearly doubled every ten years, from approximately 120,000 in 1950 to 280,000 in 1960 and 400,000 in 1970. But in the five years from 1970 to 1975, when the baby boom generation entered the university system—ten years later than in the United States—the numbers of students doubled again, from 400,000 to 800,000. By 1980, there were over a million university students in the Federal Republic, and by 1983 almost 1.3 million. The size of university faculty also grew dramatically. In 1950, barely recovering from the Nazi purges and the war, the West German professoriate amounted to 10,000 members; by 1960 the figure was 20,000. It doubled again by 1965. The numbers increased to 50,000 by 1970, 110,000 by 1975, and 120,000 by 1980. This period of rapid growth coincided with the radicalization of the student body and younger faculty.[1]

Good Timing: Demography, Labor Market, and Politics

Certain peculiarities of the demographic structure of postwar West Germany combined with the politicization and expansion of the universities made the university generation of the 1960s a particularly fortunate one. First, wartime destruction and immediate postwar privation delayed a postwar baby boom in West Germany until the late 1950s. The combined effects of soldiers killed in two world wars and material deprivation in the decade following World War I and in the Great Depression left behind large gaps in the size of the cohorts, especially men, who would be in the midst of their careers from the late 1950s to the mid-1970s. Finally, reduction of the birthrate during and immediately after World War II meant that the cohort coming of political age in the 1960s and early 1970s was relatively small.[2] The result of this stormy demographic history, when combined with the dramatic expansion of the universities from 1964 to 1975, was that the generation moving left from 1960 to about 1975 comprised a relatively small number of people pursuing a relatively large number of slots in universities and professions. That meant employment and tenure as a civil servant with relative ease at a relatively early age.[3]

The political shift to the left in Bonn under Brandt from 1969 to 1974 helped the new left considerably both by the change in national political culture and in the tangible institutional benefits it brought about. In place of Schumacher's anticommunism, Brandt stressed "peace policy" and détente. His call to "dare more democracy" at home lent legitimacy to the new left's attack on "authoritarian" institutions. University reform proposals eased the path to tenure for young professors. Whole new institutions, such as peace research institutes, offered employment and political ties to an intellectual left associated primarily with the Social Democratic party.

Up to 1974, in all fields, there were more jobs available than graduates seeking employment. After 1974, the situation was reversed. The labor markets in the humanities and education were particularly depressed. By 1982, 100,000 graduates in the humanities were seeking 20,000 openings. Labor markets in medicine and engineering also showed a steady deterioration from 1974 to the early 1980s. Labor shortages became surpluses as two and three times as many applicants as positions flooded the market.[4] By the late 1970s, unemployment among university graduates appeared to encourage a mood of youthful, "post-Marxist," leftist cultural pessimism, as well as a market-induced pragmatic conservatism. At that point, however, a good number of the sixties left had already secured positions in the educational system, government, and media from which they could influence West German political culture. A conjuncture of forces—Brandt's election, the new left, expansion of the universities, expansive labor markets, superpower détente, a small fortunate generation following generations devastated by war—all combined to deepen the push to the left. While the West German left was not a new or dominant "class," as some of its critics suggested, neither was it the powerless group of outsiders besieged by an authoritarian state that it sometimes presented itself to be.

Oligopoly in the Markets of Political Opinion

Der Spiegel is West Germany's leading weekly newsmagazine and has been so since it was founded by Rudolf Augstein in 1947. Its annual reports on the market share of West German newspapers and magazines offer a detailed statistical assessment of the balance of power in West Germany's opinion markets in the years preceding and coinciding with the battle over the euromissiles. In the 1970s and 1980s, six newspapers and magazines addressed the educated and politically interested West German readership: the Hamburg liberal intellectual weekly, *Die Zeit*; the glossy, trendy, and leftish weekly, *Stern*, also published in Hamburg; the flagship paper of the conservative Springer chain, *Die Welt*, and its Sunday edition, *Welt am Sonntag*, published in Cologne; the national weekly magazine of business, *Capital*; the leading daily newspaper of the West German conservative and center-right establishment, the *Frankfurter Allgemeine Zeitung* (*FAZ*, as it is called); and the Munich centrist daily, the *Süddeutsche Zeitung*. *Die Welt*, with a readership of 500,000, is the smallest of these periodicals. The *Frankfurter Rundschau*, a Frankfurt/Main daily close to the SPD, the trade unions, and the intellectual left, is not included in the annual reports, because its circulation was 300,000.

From 1973 to 1985 *Stern* led in number of readers (about 9 million), with almost twice that of *Der Spiegel*.[5] The dominance of *Stern* and *Spiegel* and the relative positions of all of the major competitors remained stable over the period. The readership of the national political press in 1981, at the beginning of the public controversy over the euromissiles, was divided as follows: *Stern*, with 8 million readers, was the industry leader by far, followed by *Der Spiegel*, with 4.6 million readers. *Die Zeit*, *Capital*, and each of the leading regional newspapers had readerships of about a million readers.[6]

Stern alone had about half of the weekly newsmagazine market, *Der Spiegel* had about a quarter, and all the others amounted to about 27 percent of the market. Both vociferously opposed the NATO decision. The totals of the firm supporters of the NATO two-track decision and missile deployments—*FAZ*, *Capital*, *Die Welt*—amounted to about 18 percent of the market.[7] *Der Spiegel* had feeble competition in the weekly newsmagazine market. Though local newspapers tended to be more conservative than the national press, *Der Spiegel's* market dominance meant that readers of the conservative press were much more likely to read *Der Spiegel* than readers of *Der Spiegel* were likely to read them. For example, while only 7 percent of readers of *Der Spiegel* read the *FAZ*, 33 percent of readers of the *FAZ* read *Der Spiegel*.[8]

Der Spiegel's 1980 market report estimated that over 4.5 million people, about 10 percent of the population 14 years of age and older in West Germany, read *Der Spiegel* each week.[9] *Stern* and *Der Spiegel* dominated the market for the 1.53 million West Germans in leading professions, high-level executives, and high-level civil servants.[10] But this most-elite readership read a variety of the leading national papers and magazines covering political issues, most of which were, in varying degrees, more conservative than *Der Spiegel*, such as *Capital, Welt am Sonntag, Die Welt, FAZ, Wirtschafts-woche, Die Zeit* and the *Süddeutsche Zeitung*, and was less enamored of *Stern*. No other national publication reached both the national elite and a more mass-educated readership as effectively and consistently as *Der Spiegel*. Its influence and tone captured the mixture of power and dissent that so characterized left-of-center intellectual life in West Germany's 1970s.

Locating the Intellectual Left

In 1980, *Der Spiegel* published *Akademiker in Deutschland* [University Graduates in Germany], a survey of a representative sample of 2,500 West German university graduates carried out in 1979.[11] It surveyed graduates of the humanistic and technical universities, as well as graduates of colleges of business, education, art, theology, and medicine and vocational schools.[12] It also included data on fields of study.[13] A secondary analysis of the data offers a more detailed snapshot of the distribution of political attitudes among the most articulate sectors of West German society.[14]

In 1979, when asked which of the above-mentioned magazines and newspapers they "regularly or frequently read," 43 percent of West German university graduates said *Der Spiegel*, 30 percent *Stern*, 23 percent *FAZ*, 22 percent *Die Zeit*, 18 percent *Süddeutsche Zeitung*, 14 percent *Die Welt*, and 10 percent *Capital*.[15] Respondents were further asked to indicate the "magazine/newspaper you primarily use" for political commentary. Although only 23 percent answered that they read *Stern* for political commentary, 60 percent read *Der Spiegel* for that reason compared to 41 percent for the *FAZ* and *Die Zeit*, 37 percent for the *Süddeutsche Zeitung*, and 27 percent for *Die Welt*.[16]

Akademiker in Deutschland presented considerable—and for those convinced that university graduates leaned left—rather surprising data about the political views of the university educated. In contrast to the employed population in general, employed university graduates in 1979 showed a strong interest in politics, with 21 percent of graduates claiming a "very strong interest" compared to 7 percent of the general employed population.[17] But the survey found them to be less supportive of the Social Democrats than the employed population (33 percent compared to 45 percent), more supportive of the Christian Democratic–Christian Social Union (COU–CSU) (46 percent compared to 37 percent), still more supportive of the liberal Free Democratic party (18 percent compared to 7 percent), and about as uninterested in third parties (4 percent) as the general popula-

tion (3 percent).[18] (The survey was done just as the Green party was being
formed at the national level.) In 1979, university graduates as a whole in
West Germany leaned more to the right and center than did the employed
population in general. If leftism was coming from "the intellectuals," the
survey suggested it was coming from a particular part of the university-
educated. The survey also suggested that leftism was concentrated among
the aging sixties generation (see Tables 1 and 2 of Appendix 1).

   Akademiker in Deutschland found an intelligentsia as divided along disciplinary lines as did Everett Ladd and Seymour Lipset in their study of American professors in the 1970s. Like Ladd and Lipset, it also revealed a left-
right spectrum extending from the social sciences and humanities to the
natural sciences, law, medicine, and engineering (Table 3).[19] Social science
graduates, not including economists, were the most left-leaning, with 67
percent on the two furthest left groups compared to 36 percent among all
graduates, 13 percent among agriculture graduates, and 22 percent among
graduates in medicine. The range in the left-right spectrum was very large
between the social sciences and agriculture, medicine, and economics. The
leftism of graduates with degrees in education was also apparent. The left-
of-center stance of graduates of engineering offers some contrast to the
American data. Among American professors in the 1970s, the left-leaning
social sciences faced a right-leaning group in business, engineering, and agriculture. In 1979 in West Germany the central cleavage of disciplines pitted
left-leaning graduates in the social sciences and humanities against graduates
of the law and medical schools. But in both the United States and West
Germany, leftism among the intellectuals was concentrated among those
who had studied the humanities and social sciences. If by the term "intellectuals" we mean those who address a public about moral and political questions on the basis of inherited and reinterpreted traditions, then a majority
of the intellectuals in West Germany in this sense did lean to the left.

   Those most interested in politics were graduates of law and social science
(Table 4). Table 5 indicates a direct correlation between leftism and interest
in politics. Leftist opinion was also concentrated in the disciplines—the
humanities, social sciences, and education—most engaged in social and political issues. Conservative opinion was stronger in disciplines less focused
on politics—medicine, agriculture, natural sciences—with the important exception of law. Table 6 indicates the distribution of political attitudes of
graduates by occupation in 1979. Professors of the humanities and social
sciences, social workers, journalists, natural scientists, primary and secondary school teachers, and economists were to the left of the general sample
of graduates, while engineers, doctors, and lawyers were to the right. The
relative conservatism of lawyers is also evident from the table. The table

indicates that in those professions most engaged in the interpretation of society and politics, the mood of the late seventies was left-leaning. Lawyers were the only occupational group with strong or very strong interest in politics among whom right-of-center and conservative political views predominated over those of the left.

So, though West German university graduates in 1979 as a whole stood slightly to the right of public opinion, an intellectual left with a high interest in politics was concentrated in professions most devoted to the interpretation of society and politics. By 1979, this left was well represented among middle-aged graduates of the humanities, social sciences, and education. If we restrict the meaning of the term political intellectuals to encompass those people most engaged in commentary and judgment on contemporary political issues based on moral and cultural traditions, then *Akademiker in Deutschland* offered considerable evidence that in 1979 West Germany's politically active and interested "intellectuals" in this sense leaned to the left.

The West German Establishment Moves to the Center-Right: 1968–1981

Another piece of quantitative data comes from surveys of West German elites performed in 1969, 1972, and 1981 by Rudolf Wildenmann and his associates at the University of Mannheim.[20] The respondents in the three samples were persons in leading positions in the following sectors of West German society: political parties, national and local government bureaucracy, mass media, education, industry, employers' organizations, the military leadership, and trade unions.[21] The 1981 survey further delineated a cultural elite in the arts, literature, publishing, and film. By matching these institutional positions to political perspectives, the surveys described trends within the West German establishment. Asked to rank sectors of the West German establishment in order of political significance, respondents to these three surveys gave very high rankings to the national government, parliament, the Social Democrats (then in power), the trade unions, the Christian Democratic party, television, and the press (Table 7).

The Mannheim surveys also offered evidence about support for the major political parties in different sectors of the establishment. From 1972 to 1981, the Mannheim surveys showed a dramatic loss of support for the SPD in all sectors of the West German establishment, except for the trade unions and the "cultural elite" (Table 8). The most striking losses took place among elites in the mass media and the universities. The Social Democrats reached a highpoint of support in 1972, followed by a dramatic loss of support over the following nine years. In 1972, 44 percent of the mass media elites and 48 percent of the educational elites supported the Social Democrats. By 1981 those figures dropped by more than half, to 21 percent and 22 percent respectively. The Social Democrats lost support from all sectors of the West German establishment surveyed by the Mannheim survey over this period.

The gains for the CDU/CSU and the FDP among mass media and educational elites were no less dramatic. The percentage of mass media elites ranking the conservatives first rose from 40 percent to 53 percent from 1972 to 1981. The increase of support for the conservatives among educational elites was even greater, from 31 percent in 1972 to 54 percent in 1981. The West German elite as a whole was becoming more conservative over this period. As Wildenmann put it in 1982, the preferred political coloration for a Bonn government among respondents was the conservative-liberal coalition, in place of the then existing social-democratic-liberal coalition.[22]

The Soviet military buildup was one cause of this shift. In the three surveys respondents expressed increasing concern about "aggressive world communism which can only be met with firmness," though the degree of concern was greater among conservatives and liberals than among social democrats (Table 9).[23] The Mannheim data show continuing support for détente in 1972 and 1981 in all sectors of the West German establishment, though the conservatives and the business elites were much less supportive than Social Democrats, Free Democrats, cultural elites, unions, civil servants, mass media, and educational leaders.

By 1981, the Social Democrats' strongest elite ally came from the cultural elite. While the positions taken by Brandt and Bahr were arousing fears in Paris, London, and Washington of "self-Finlandization" in West Germany, the West German establishment as a whole was taking a harder line towards the Soviet Union. As Georg Leber argued in the neutron bomb debate in September 1977, Brezhnev's military buildup led to growing support for a firmer stance toward the Soviet Union within the West German establishment.

The *JUSOS* and the Popular Front on Campus

The erosion of the boundary between Social Democracy and the hard left was apparent in student politics at West German universities in the decade of détente. It was a period of a popular front of the left against "the right" rather than of, as young Christian Democrats hoped, a "coalition of democrats" against the "antidemocratic" extremes. The young left moved away from Social Democratic anticommunism in rhetoric and tactics. In the hundreds and hundreds of elections of student governments at West German universities taking place in the 1970s, students on the moderate left, especially members of the Social Democrats' youth group, the *JUSOS* (short for *Jung Sozialisten*, Young Socialists), had to make a decision. Should they, usually as the dominant member, form a coalition government with the radical left, a left that often included Marxist-Leninist and communist student groups, or should they form a coalition with the youth group of the CDU, the Ring of Christian Democratic Students (*Ring Christlich-Demokratische Jugend*), or *RCDS*, as it was called.[24]

The activities of the *JUSOS* were of concern to the parent Social Democratic party because entering into coalitions with communist groups contradicted the spirit of the *Abgrenzungsbeschluss* of 1970. Foremost among the Marxist-Leninist and communist groups active on campus were the *Marxistischer Studenten-Bund* or *MSB Spartakus* (Marxist Student Organization–Spartacists), *Sozialistischer Hochschulverband* (SHB) (Socialist University Association), communist, Stalinist, and Maoist sects, and a variety of ad hoc local groups, many of which were prefigurations of Green politics. The first three, *MSB Spartakus*, *SHB*, and the *JUSOS*, were the major student organizations with national networks. Throughout the 1970s, the *JUSOS* entered coalitions with them rather than with the young conservatives.

Student politics at West German universities were more than a barometer of the hothouse of student politics. They also played a role in the struggle for power over university governance. In 1976, a federal *Hochschulrahmengesetz* [Law on the Framework of the Universities] laid down the principles of democratization in all tertiary institutions.[25] The reform was based on a principle that grew out of trade union efforts in the sixties to develop more worker participation (*Mitbestimmung*) in industrial managerial decisions. Supporters of university reform viewed it as a long-overdue attack on authoritarian structures that had persisted from Germany's illiberal modern history. To its critics, the university reforms became a pretext for extension of direct state interference in the internal affairs of previously independent institutions.

The first reform at the Free University of Berlin in 1967 called for participation of university members in all decision-making councils based on the principle of *Drittelparität* (tripartite) governance with equal weight given to faculty, students, and staff. The university was to be governed on the basis of the *Gruppenprinzip* [group principle], and the resulting university would be called the *Gruppenuniversität* or group university. The "group principle" entailed a program of radical democracy in which clerical staff as well as student government leaders could actively participate in academic decision-making, including faculty appointment decisions. As the elected representatives of the student body, the student government leaders were also to be included in such tripartite schemes. Academic appointments could then be subjected to pressure from student political groups.[26] The result, in the view of many faculty members, was the politicization of scholarship and a decline in its quality. At large universities with over 20,000 students, mandatory student fees could place considerable funds, between 500,000 and one million marks a year, at the disposal of student governments to use for whatever political purposes they saw fit. Control of the *AStA* (*Allgemeine Studenten Ausschuss*) [General Association of Students], the student government formed by political groups based on their vote totals and coalition decisions, meant an opportunity to shape the public political culture of a university campus with posters, lectures, films, speakers, demonstrations, and student government resolutions.[27]

From 1968 to 1983, student voter participation in elections declined from about 50 percent in the late sixties to less than 20 percent by the late seventies. But despite low turnout, the student elections have the virtue of being a piece of evidence that, unlike sample surveys, documents the actual, public, political culture of the universities. They indicate that *Abgrenzung* and Social Democratic anticommunism gave way to a popular front.

According to the reports of the *Westdeutschen Rektorenkonferenz*, over the course of the 1970s there were between forty and fifty political groups active in West German university student elections. Of these, ten called themselves communist (*Kommunistischer Bund, Kommunistischer Studenten-Verband*, etc.), two were Marxist or Marxist-Leninist (*Marxistischer Studenten-Bund Spartakus*), five described themselves as "trade unions" (*Gewerk-schaften*) of students or faculty, eight were self-described socialist organizations (*Sozialistischer Büro, Jung-Sozialisten-Hochschulgruppen*), three were "basis" groups, that is, "anti-authoritarian" or anarchist groupings, three were self-described liberals (*Liberale Hochschul-Gruppe*), and three were conservative (*Ring Christlich-Demokratischer Studenten, Junge Union Hochschul-gruppen*).[28]

The most important of these sects was one oriented to the German Communist party (*DKP*), the *Marxistischer Studenten-Bund Spartakus* founded in May 1971. It sought inroads among university students by gaining influence in student governments.[29] The central slogan of *MSB* was "Marx in the university!"[30] Among the groups willing to enter student government coalitions with the *MSB Spartakus* in the 1970s were the *Sozialistischer Hochschulbund (SHB)*, the *Sozialistische Fraktion, JUSO Hochschulgruppen*

[Young Socialist University Group], and even groupings of young liberals, *Liberal Studenten Deutschland (LSD)* [Liberal Students in Germany], and the *Liberal Hochschulverband (LHV)* [Liberal University Association]. But the most important of its coalition partners were the *JUSOs*, the young socialists who comprised the youth organization of the SPD.[31]

The *JUSOS* were the key group. They pursued a policy of "no enemies on the left," in preference to a "grand coalition" of young socialists with young conservatives. They kept the young conservatives out of power by forming coalitions of "all left-wing and liberal groups."[32] At times, liberal student groups also entered into coalitions with *MSB Spartakus*, and some refused to coalesce with young conservatives.[33] In 1979, one liberal student leader said, in a message to *MSB Spartakus*, "now as before: the common enemy stands on the right!"[34] As a consequence, although the young conservatives were able to gain 35 percent to 45 percent of the student vote, student governments remained dominated by a popular front of the left, and young Christian Democrats remained out of power.

Table 10 summarizes data drawn from the reports of the *Westdeutsche Rektorenkonferenz* from 424 elections held during the "winter semester" at West German universities from 1969 to 1984. It shows the political tendency of the student councils at twenty-eight of the largest and most prominent West German universities and technical universities in the period from 1969 to 1984.[35] The number of universities represented in any given year varies slightly because some schools did not report their results, because elections were not held or because administrations had abolished their student governments because of student turbulence. But the data do include at a minimum the following universities: Berlin, Bielefeld, Bonn, Bremen, Cologne, Technical University Darmstadt, Erlangen-Nürnberg, Frankfurt, Freiburg, Göttingen, Hamburg, Hannover, Heidelberg, Konstanz, Mainz, Mannheim, Marburg, Munich, Tübingen. These are the largest and most well-known universities in West Germany.[36]

The table describes student governments as "conservative," "center right," "liberal," "social democratic," "leftist coalition," and "far left." "Conservative" refers to student governments with a controlling majority of members of the youth organization of the Christian Democratic party, the RCDS. "Center right" *AStAs* had a controlling majority of young conservatives in coalition with members of the youth organization of the Free Democratic party or other groups calling themselves liberals. "Liberal" *AStAs* were those composed only of these latter groups. "Social Democratic" refers to *AStAs* in which the youth organizations of the Social Democratic party, the *JUSOS*, had a controlling majority without having to coalesce with other groups. "Leftist coalition" refers to *AStAs* that included the *JUSOS*, new left groups, Green and "basic" groups, left-wing socialists, and groups with ties to the *DKP, Sozialistischer Hochschulbund (SHB)*, and *MSB Spartakus* or other Communist and Marxist-Leninist sects. "Far left" refers to *AStA*s in which the controlling majority was composed exclusively of Communist and/or Marxist-Leninist groups.

The numerical predominance of the left is immediately apparent. There were about six times as many left-of-center coalitions as right-of-center coalitions. From 1969 to 1984, 60 percent (254) of the governments were leftist coalitions, 23 percent (99) were social democratic or center-left, 16 percent (41) were center-right, 3 percent (14) were dominated by the far left, 3 percent (13) were centrist, and less than 1 percent (3) were conservative. There was no right-wing radicalism at all in West German student politics in this period. On only two occasions, once in Bonn (1973) and once in Erlangen (1974), were there coalitions of "militant democrats," of *JUSOS* and young Christian Democrats (*RCDS*). In all of the remaining cases, the *JUSOS* entered coalitions with young liberals, governed on their own or with small parties to their left, including with Marxist-Leninist and Communist groups. From 1969 to 1984, in hundreds of elections, at universities in all regions of the Federal Republic, the *JUSOS* faced a choice of sharing power in a "coalition of democrats" with young conservatives or dominating a popular front government that included Marxist-Leninist and Communist sects. They consistently opted for the popular front.

Tables 11 through 13 show more detailed results from the universities of Bonn, Frankfurt, and Hamburg. In Bonn, the popular front of the early 1970s gave way to a conservative-liberal coalition beginning in 1975. In Frankfurt, where the Frankfurt School, "anti-authoritarian" leftism, and democratic socialism were strong influences, a popular front of socialists, new leftists, and precursors of the Greens dominated student politics for the whole period. At the University of Hamburg, there was a no less striking continuity of domination by a popular front comprised of socialists and Spartacists. Perhaps, accustomed to a communist left that appeared so often in a minority position in student coalitions, the young democratic left coming of age in the 1970s in West Germany may have found it hard to imagine that the Soviet Union posed a genuine threat to Western Europe.

During the same period, in France, socialists were forming a common program with the communists. This popular front, far from being confined to the universities, led to the election of Francois Mitterand and a socialist government in 1981.[37] But in France, the socialist embrace of the communists turned out to be a near fatal kiss of death, hastening the decline of the French Communist party. It was a tactical coalition undertaking in an atmosphere of increasingly vocal left-of-center criticism of communism and the Soviet Union. In West Germany, on the other hand, the popular front of the 1970s was accompanied by criticism of anticommunism. Similar coalition behavior had a different meaning in the two political cultures. In France, it was accompanied by growing criticism of the Soviet Union, while the West German left muted its critical tone toward the Soviet Union and East European Communist governments. During the battle over the euromissiles, these differences between the French and the West German left came to the surface and made apparent how different the evolution of the left in the two countries had been since the sixties.

The picture of political life at West German universities in the 1970s that emerges from this and other data is of a student body leaning to the left in which small, organized political groups exerted disproportionate influence in student government as a consequence of the relative disinterest of the student body as a whole. It was a political culture in which the political boundary between the moderate and the hard left had blurred.[38] A 1979 survey of student political attitudes found student support for the political parties in West Germany in 1979 to be as follows: SPD (Social Democratic Party) 37.1 percent; CDU (Christian Democratic Party) 14 percent; FDP (Free Democratic Party) 14.0 percent; GLU (Green List) 13.3 percent; GAZ (Green-Alternatives) 5.5 percent; DKP (German Communist Party) 2.4 percent; Bürgerpartei (Citizens' Party) 2.1 percent; CSU (Christian Social Union) 1.7 percent; KPD (Communist Party of Germany) 0.7 percent; and KBW (Communist Association of West Germany) 0.3 percent. Combined support for the Green parties (*GLU* and *GAZ*) forming in the late 1970s exceeded that for the CDU, while support for the more conservative Christian Social Union was less than support for the *DKP*, the German Communist party.

Two surveys, one commissioned by the Friedrich Ebert Foundation, the research institute of the Social Democratic party, and another done by the Allensbach Institute of public opinion research whose director, Elizabeth Nölle-Neumann, was an adviser to Helmut Kohl's Christian Democratic Union, explored the student political landscape of the late 1970s in some detail. The Allensbach study questioned 500 students at thirty-three West German universities in winter 1977–78 with a focus on the issue of the "democratic potential" among students.[39]

Table 14 summarizes some of the Allensbach data. The Allensbach conclusions were that students who were very interested in politics, participated in student elections, served actively in student government, and believed student government should deal with national and international political issues in addition to specific student concerns were considerably to the left of students who were less interested in politics, did not vote in student elections or serve in student government, and did not think student governments should deal with general political issues beyond the university. The student left was more vocal and more active than were student conservatives and liberals. Nölle-Neumann described the situation as one in which a vocal, well-organized, active, articulate, and sizable left-leaning minority shaped the climate of opinion in the face of a relatively silent, unorganized, politically passive majority.

While the far left comprised only 9 percent of the student body (Table 14), 25 percent of the far left respondents had been in student government. Of those in student government, 45 percent came from the moderate left, still more than the 39 percent who described themselves as such. Conversely, though 35 percent described themselves as centrists, only 16 percent of centrists had been in student government. As for the moderate right, the comparable figures were 13 percent and 9 percent. The survey indicated that 6 percent of young conservatives were active in student government, compared to 30 percent of the *MSB Spartakus*.[40] Such disparities were partly products of the popular front coalitions. Compared to their support in the student body generally, conservatives and liberals were underrepresented in student governments while the *JUSOS, SHB,* and the *MSB Spartakus* were overrepresented. For example, while *MSB Spartakus* gained 8 percent of the student body's votes, 17.3 percent of students active in student government agreed with its views. Conversely, though 28 percent of the students voted for the *RCDS* (the young conservatives), only 21.4 percent of student government members supported it.

Table 15 presents the Allensbach data on whether or not students approved of the *JUSOS* decisions to "cooperate with Communist students." Of students involved in student government, 49 percent approved of SPD or FDP alliances with Communist groups, compared to 30 percent of all students and 34 percent of student voters. Only 28 percent of student government activists rejected the practice. While only 11 percent of centrist and 5 percent of conservative students approved of such coalitions, 44 percent of moderate leftists did, and an overwhelming majority of far leftists (81 percent) did as well. Only 7.3 percent of the far left rejected a policy of a coalition with the moderate left.

Table 16 presents the Allensbach data on student attitudes about the refusal of the *JUSOS* to enter coalitions with the young conservatives "under any circumstances." Of students voters, 40 percent supported this refusal. Only 26 percent supported it among nonvoters. Among members of student governments, 60 percent approved this stance, while 57 percent of those very interested in politics, 48 percent of those calling themselves moderate leftists, and 76 percent of those on the far left approved. Only 13 percent of conservative and 17 percent of centrist students approved.

However, there was also considerable opposition to the *JUSOS* refusal to coalesce with the young conservatives: 47 percent of all student voters, 67 percent of conservatives, and 55 percent of centrists opposed it, while 34 percent of moderate leftists, but only 9.8 percent of the far left opposed such a policy.

Finally, the Allensbach survey asked students whether communism was "a fundamentally mistaken idea," a "good idea that has been perverted in practice," or "a good idea and existing communist states are certainly superior to capitalism" (Table 17). The left-right cleavage between the student political elite and students generally is apparent in the responses, though the answers generally displayed an erosion of anticommunism. The only subgroup in which a majority thought communism was fundamentally mistaken were conservatives (58 percent), while 39 percent of self-described centrists thought so. Only 27 percent of the total sample took this view; and among those active in student government, only 16 percent of those active in student government. Among the key group, the moderate left, 10 percent thought communism was a fundamentally mistaken idea.

In 1978, according to the Allensbach study, the most prevalent view among university students was that communism was a good idea that had been perverted. That view was taken by 61 percent of students in general, 67 percent of student government activists, 48 percent of the centrists, 83 percent of the moderate left, and 59 percent of the far left. Though only 6 percent of the students in general approved of communism as an idea and as an existing reality, 15 percent of student government activists did, as did 37 percent of those on the far left. The student mood was neither procommunist nor anticommunist. *Abgrenzung* had given way to boundary erosion.

This picture of student radicalism in the late 1970s was not drawn only by anxious conservatives. In 1979 a basically identical distribution of political attitudes was found by researchers sponsored by the Social Democratic party. *Zwischen Revolution und Resignation* [Between Revolution and Resignation] offered a detailed statistical portrait of the student political culture at the universities in Bonn, Hamburg, Berlin, Frankfurt, and Heidelberg.[41] Like *Akademiker in Deutschland*, the study offered evidence of a left concentrated in the social sciences and humanities. More than other surveys, it drew attention to the differing political culture and political traditions at the universities of Bonn, Heidelberg, Berlin, Frankfurt, and Hamburg (Table 18).[42] Like the *Akademiker in Deutschland* survey and like the Ladd and Lipset study of American professors, *Zwischen Revolution und Resignation* found a very strong concentration of leftism in the humanities and social sciences (Table 19). Over 70 percent of students studying in the humanities and over 55 percent of those studying social science in 1979 described themselves as new leftists, socialists, or communists, while only 2 percent of the social science majors and 10 percent of those studying the humanities called themselves conservatives.

Finally, the Ebert Foundation arrived at results similar to Allensbach's concerning popular front governments in student politics.[43] It found that the most-favored student government coalition of the moderate left was an *AStA* coalition of the moderate left composed of the *JUSOS* alllied to some combination of the *MSB* and *SHB* and "undogmatic" new left groups, a preference which, as we have seen, was reflected in the actual political coloration of the great majority of student governments in this period. Young moderate leftists at these major West German universities were less willing to coalesce with young conservatives than with orthodox, Marxist-Leninist sects. Nevertheless, 62 percent of young conservatives still wanted to coalesce with the young socialists.[44]

In a previous chapter, we explored the erosion of the political culture of militant democracy in the public rhetoric of Brandt and Bahr. In this chapter, we've presented evidence of a popular front mentality where it was easily measured in West German university student politics. The change in the meaning of the democratic left from militant democracy to a popular front, from the left of Schumacher to that of Brandt, was the decisive change in West German political culture of the left in the détente era. In this political culture, it proved extremely difficult for Helmut Schmidt to find adherents for his effort to reverse the momentum of the global and regional balance of power. Conversely, this change in the meaning of democratic leftism represented a window of opportunity for Soviet diplomacy in the battle over the euromissiles. The West German Social Democrats in ths period were not pro-Soviet, in the sense in which the Stalinist wings of West European communist parties were. But on campus and among the generations come of age since the sixties, they were unwilling to focus on public criticism of Soviet policy or to reject, in principle, coalitions with communist and Marxist-Leninist groups. In West Germany, in contrast to France, the tactical toleration by the moderate left of the far left was of a piece with the intellectual dismantling of the tradition of vocal, social democratic anticommunism. The French and the West Germans were responding to different political clocks, the former rediscovering liberal and left-of-center anticommunism, while the latter were leaving it behind in the era of détente.

Sympathetic national political leaders, the revival of old and powerful national cultural traditions, and fortuitous timing of demographic and labor market realities all added impetus to the leftist push of the 1970s. We now turn to a part of that push, peace research and peace research institutes.

6

DARING MORE DEMOCRACY MEETS THE LONG MARCH
West German Peace Research

IN 1969, CHANCELLOR WILLY BRANDT, along with the Bundespresident, Gustav Heinemann, initiated government support for *Friedensforschung*, or peace research. At the same time, new left theorists articulated a framework for a radical version of this endeavor, which they called "critical peace research." The conjuncture of Brandt's desire to "dare more democracy" and the new left's "long march through the institutions" led to the creation of new institutions, which facilitated the development of an intellectual left inside and outside West German universities. It was also part of the process of the erosion of the boundaries of the political culture of militant democracy and Social Democratic anticommunism in the era of détente. In place of sharp distinctions between liberal democracy and communist dictatorship, the political culture of the détente era in West Germany presented a blurring or muting of such distinctions. In some of the prominent works of peace research, this erosion of boundaries found more elaborate theoretical foundations.

The phrase "long march through the institutions" was popularized by Rudi Dutschke, the most compelling public personality of the West German new left.[1] It combined the elan of Mao Tse-tung's original long march through the Chinese countryside with the conviction that revolution in the West would be the consequence of long-term changes in consciousness, rather than of violence and terrorism by armed vanguards.[2] In Dutschke's words, the long march was "the subversive utilization of the contradictions

and possibilities inside and outside the whole state-society apparatus in order to destroy it during and as a result of this long process."[3] In practical
terms, this meant transforming existing institutions, beginning with schools
and the media, as well as creating new "critical" or "counter" institutions.[4]
For Dutschke the long march was a strategy in a power struggle that sought
influence in the social institutions that formed or transmitted social consciousness.[5] Suggestions for an "alternative" or "proletarian public sphere"
hinted at similar outcomes.[6] Whether changes in West German consciousness were due to the conscious strategy of radicalized intellectuals or due
merely to the aging of the generation of 1968, the shift to the left in the
political culture of West German intellectuals, in institutions as well as
ideas, was notable.

By 1981, there were over sixty "alternative" left-leaning newspapers and
magazines in West Germany, including a left-wing national daily, *die Tages-
zeitung* or *TAZ*, with a circulation of about 100,000.[7] Several major West
German publishers linked authors and a public. *Suhrkamp Verlag* made
available the leftist cultural criticism and social theory of the Weimar Republic, and of the emigres in the Nazi years, as well as social theory, philosophy, and literature from the intellectual left in the Federal Republic. *Rowohlt Verlag* published inexpensive paperbacks on topical issues from a
leftist perspective. Beyond these two large, established publishers, a number
of smaller leftist presses emerged, such as *Verlag Neue Kritik, Roter Stern
Verlag,* and *Syndikat Verlag* in Frankfurt am Main and *Rotbuch Verlag* in
West Berlin.[8] And then, every week, there were *Stern* and, more important, *Der Spiegel.* Peace research found a place in some or all of the publications, as well as in the monthly journal of the SPD, *Neue Gesellschaft.*

The close links of government reform and the institutional anchoring of
left-leaning intellectuals were apparent in the formation of publicly financed
"peace research institutes." In 1970, a national center for peace research,
the *Deutsche Gesellschaft für Friedens- und Konfliktforschung* (DGFK) [German
Society for Peace and Conflict Research] was established near Bonn.[9] In
1970, the *Hessiche Stiftung Friedens- und Konfliktforschung* (HSFK) [Founda-
tion for Peace and Conflict Research of the State of Hesse] in Frankfurt
was established. Its members found ready access to the *Frankfürter Rundschau,* whose security correspondent, Andreas Anton-Guha, looked favorably on the efforts of the peace researchers.[10]

The *Max Planck Institut zur Erforschung der Lebensbedingungen der wissen-
schaftlich-technischen Welt* [Max Planck Institute for Research on Life Conditions in a Scientific-Technical World] was also founded in 1970 in Starnberg, south of Munich. Its codirectors were Carl Friedrich von Weizsäcker,
a physicist and philosopher, and later Jürgen Habermas, the sociological

theorist and philosopher. Alfred Mechtersheimer, a former officer in the Bundeswehr, joined the Starnberg institute to direct its program in peace research. In 1971, the private *Berghof Stiftung für Konfliktforschung* [Berghof Foundation for Conflict Research] in Munich began, as did the *Institut für Friedensforschung und Sicherheitspolitik an der Universität Hamburg* (IFSH) [Institute for Peace Research and Security Policy at the University of Hamburg].[11]

From 1975 to 1983, Rowohlt published about thirty paperbacks on war and peace, in editions ranging from 20,000 to 90,000. Suhrkamp published sixteen essay collections organized by the peace research institute in Frankfurt. The topics of the volumes published from 1975 to 1980 included images of the enemy (*Feindbilder*); armament; underdevelopment; peace movements; aggression, violence, socialization, and aggression; wars in Africa, Latin America, and Southeast Asia; détente; and the new peace movements.[12] *Der Spiegel* also ran articles by and about *Friedensforschung*. Leading politicians of the Social Democratic party such as Karsten Voigt, Oskar Lafontaine, and Erhard Eppler helped to diffuse the arguments of peace researchers in books and speeches.[13] In 1981 Roland Vogt, a member of the Green party, praised peace research as signifying "the transition from utopian . . . to scientifically grounded pacifism in the Federal Republic of Germany."[14] In 1983, Franz Alt, one of the country's most well-known television newscasters, drew on arguments of *Friedensforschung* in a best-selling book, *Frieden ist Möglich* (Peace Is Possible).[15] The vocabulary of peace research, perhaps not always recognized as such, reached a broader public through the electronic and print mass media.

From 1971 to 1979, the DGFK dispensed twenty-two million marks in support of peach research. These funds made possible 135 research projects, forty-eight conferences, and thirty-seven publications. The DGFK published yearbooks on détente, the Helsinki agreements, dependency theory, and development. It disbursed funds to support thirty-one studies on American foreign and security policy, sixteen on the arms race between East and West, seven on weapons exports to the Third World, fourteen on North-South issues and Europe and the Third World, twenty-one on "development of alternative viewpoints," sixteen on theories of conflict and crises, ten on images of friend and enemy, and fourteen on social psychological and pedagogical investigations. In the détente era, the DGFK funded few studies of Soviet foreign and security policy.[16] Though the total amount of funding was modest, it was sufficient to provide an institutional foothold to analysts sharing the perspectives of peace research and to enhance their capacity to reach an interested public.

Social Democracy and the new left developed an at times uneasy coexistence within West German *Friedensforschung*. Both currents rejected the realist tradition in the study of international relations, which was not well known in West Germany. Hans Morgenthau's *Politics Among Nations*, the major work of American postwar realism, which went through twenty-one editions in the United States from 1949 to 1967, was first translated in West Germany in 1963. E.H. Carr's *The Twenty Years' Crisis* was never translated. Reinhold Niebuhr, Arnold Wolfers, and Kenneth W. Thompson remained known to small groups of specialists. Raymond Aron's *Peace and War* did only somewhat better. Internationalist and legalist traditions in international affairs had a greater presence among West German scholars, who associated realism with the discredited power politics of the German Reich from 1870 to 1945.[17] Realism survived in university departments of history and political science, as well as at research institutes more closely associated with official policies. Peace research involved a "short-circuiting" or end run around these institutions.[18]

Peace research in West Germany was nourished by a revulsion for militarism associated with the Nazi regime, and by a rationalistic optimism rooted in the socialist tradition and the reforming spirit of Anglo-American liberalism.[19] Pessimistic assumptions about the behavior of states in an anarchic international order and the dangers posed by human capacity for evil, both so important to the realist tradition, did not sink deep roots in the political culture of postwar leftism. Instead, "critical" peace researchers exuded optimism about the possibilities for peace through "conflict resolution" with the help of a "science" of peace.[20] One West German analyst of peace research compared its effort to overcome prescientific utopias to Marx's effort to place socialism on a scientific rather than utopian foundation.[21] Indeed, *Friedensforschung* in West Germany was of two minds about positivism. On the one hand, it criticized "technocratic" Western strategy. On the other hand, it turned away from the historically oriented study of relations between states in favor of ahistorical social science modeling or policy-oriented technical recommendations on arms control negotiations of the 1970s.[22]

Tension between professionalization and political commitment was a continuing theme in the history of West German peace research. Karl-Heinz Koppe, the director of the DGFK throughout this period, wrote that the task of the DGFK was to link theory and practice by developing ways in which "the interest of public opinion in the problem of peace could be awakened."[23] Both the DGFK in Bonn and the regional peace research institutes went to great efforts to make their work available to a broader public through lectures, newspaper articles, and publications by the institutes made available to schools and universities. The DGFK also fostered contacts with peace researchers in other countries and with the United Nations, especially UNESCO. Johan Galtung, a Norwegian peace researcher whose work was influential among West German peace researchers in the 1970s, wrote that peace research without political action was pointless. The point, he said, was to "make propaganda" among intellectuals, to influence foreign policy elites and public opinion, and to "break the monopoly of governments on the making of foreign policy."[24]

Public funding of an intellectual enterprise with such an explicit political agenda evoked a heated conservative counterattack. Conservative journalists criticized peace research as a political maneuver by Brandt to create a stratum of subsidized intellectuals whose primary task was to justify his policies.[25] The conservative minority in the Bundestag voted against funding for *Friedensforschung* at the national level. Its continuation over the decade of the 1970s was due to Social Democratic city and state governments, especially in Hessen and Hamburg. Conversely, in conservative Bavaria funding was cut off in 1979.[26] But enough public support continued so that the publicly funded long march through the institutions could continue up to and during the battle of the euromissiles.

Dieter Senghaas and the Theory of "Organized Peacelessness"

One of the characteristic features of the political culture of the post-sixties left in West Germany was the salience and prestige of theory within it. Though there were many peace researchers whose work was primarily policy-oriented recommendations lacking any distinctive theoretical bent, a distinctive feature of West German peace research, in contrast to American arms control literature, was an attempt to link a critical theory of society in general to a particular approach to international politics. In 1969, Dieter Senghaas wrote the major West German work of "critical peace research" of this kind.[27] *Abschreckung und Frieden: Studien zur organisierten Friedlosigkeit* [Deterrence and Peace: Studies of organized peacelessness] synthesized the Frankfurt School's critical theory with American social psychological and game theoretical approaches to the study of international politics. Senghaas integrated American social science with West German critical theory in his critique of American deterrence theory. Published in 1969 and reissued in second (1972) and third (1981) editions, *Abschreckung und Frieden* was the most extensive West German leftist critique of American deterrence theory published from the 1960s to the 1980s. In the following decade, Senghaas remained a prolific scholar and public intellectual shaping the peace research and the language of West German political culture.[28]

Senghaas argued that since World War I the clear distinction between periods of war and of peace had become obsolete. Cold War and technological advances had led to an "organized peacelessness" [*organisierte Friedlosigkeit*].[29] For Senghaas, deterrence was the clearest example of organized peacelessness. "In deterrence policy, the systematic preparation for war becomes a permanent condition."[30] Senghaas' method was that of immanent critique, that is, reading texts as manifestations of social and political institutions and their "contradictions." Because he did not assess the claims of theorists in light of the history of modern international relations, his text has an abstract quality. American deterrence theorists had failed to reflect on "its prior precondition."[31] Senghaas intended to fill this gap. He took Raymond Aron, Bernard Brodie, Henry Kissinger, and Albert Wohlstetter to task for trying to save conventional power politics with theories of graduated and limited use of nuclear weapons.[32] These theories, Senghaas claimed, were theories of "organized peacelessness."[33] Senghaas saw a continuity between Clausewitz and "fascist" theories of war presumably present in the writings of the German World War I general, Ludwig von Ludendorff.[34] In so doing, he drew more on Herbert Marcuse's arguments about the supposed link between liberalism and fascism than on a historical examination of the political content of German strategy.[35] If "fascism"—he did not refer to National Socialism or Hitler—was the outcome of the Clausewitzian tradition, then "antifascism" meant rejecting the tradition of power politics per se. If deterrence too rested on Clausewitzian assumptions, and Clausewitz via Ludendorff contributed to fascism, then wasn't deterrence also somehow fascist? Senghaas himself did not extend his own case this far, but such a conclusion was certainly one plausible implication of his argument.

Senghaas adopted a distanced and sardonic tone toward the idea that there actually was a real conflict between free and totalitarian states in Europe. The deterrence theorists, in his view, wrongly dramatized the existing conflict as one between "civilization (i.e., freedom) and barbarism (i.e., tyranny)." Kissinger et al. were guilty of "hypostacizing the enemy . . . militant cultural pessimism . . . fatalism . . . obscurantism grounded in panic," all of which served to justify sacrifice and which culminated in propagandistic heroism.[36] In fact, "regardless of the actual behavior of the adversary," all of this antagonism was really "justification of one's own aggressiveness."[37] A Western social psychology of projection, not the behavior or nature of the Soviet Union, was the cause of the problem. The "Soviet threat" was a necessary fiction, a *Feindbilder* or image of the enemy, produced by a "deterrence system." It was not an actual, empirical reality. Therefore, the primary danger lay at home, in the democracies' exaggerated fears of the enemy.

Senghaas argued that the United States did not have a deterrence policy. It was a "deterrence society."[38] Deterrence was "collectively organized fear, socially organized aggression, a system of mobilized and dammed up *Angst*."[39] It pointed towards a military and psychological disciplining of the masses, a mixture of fear and violence that made the costs of deterrence appear plausible. Grounds for fear had to be found, leading to "manipulative control." Psychic manipulation was a product of the "structure of domination. . . . Interests and not mistaken knowledge blocks the way."[40] Senghaas argued that deterrence theorists invented anticommunism, the Soviet threat, and deterrence as an ideology that functioned to dominate the mass consciousness. In the United States, deterrence theory was a powerful instrument "to guarantee the wealth, influence, status and power interests" of the military-industrial-scientific-education complex and to serve "particular interests bound to a strategy of organized peacelessness. . . . It is in this that the *objective* function of deterrence lies, whatever the subjective intentions of its bearers may be."[41] Without an external foe, the masses would gain true consciousness and turn on the enemy at home. Hence, deterrence was "autistic." "Peace pedagogy" and "peace science" had the task of "working out the emancipation of human consciousness from the force of centuries of old traditions of *Realpolitik*, diplomacy of violence, and strategies resting on threats."[42]

Abschreckung und Frieden was the major theoretical attempt from the West German new left attempting to link a theory of society to a theory of international relations.[43] It lent theoretical weight to the refusal to discuss the Soviet Union and reinterpreted anticommunism as a social psychological pathology of late capitalism. The Senghaas book grew out of and contributed to a political language of abstraction and ambiguity, one largely bereft of historical referents, proper nouns and active verbs, specific individuals and states, and particular events. Theory, not history, was the coin of this intellectual realm. But in the transformed political culture of the West German left, this poverty of contact with the actual events of international politics came to signify theoretical profundity and insight.

Johan Galtung: Redefining Peace, War, and Violence

Johan Galtung, a peace researcher from Norway and a professor at the University of Oslo, was another important influence in the shaping of the political culture of West German leftism since the 1960s in the realm of international politics. An adviser to UNESCO, Galtung began to publish essays in West Germany in the late 1960s. In 1975, *Strukturelle Gewalt* [Structural Violence], a collection of his essays, was published in a Rowohlt paperback, which had sold over 25,000 copies by 1982.[44] Galtung's essays appeared in West German editions throughout the 1970s, some in inexpensive paperback books designed for a broader public.[45] Like Senghaas, Galtung combined leftist commitment with a social science oriented to ahistorical typologies and models. He also avoided examination of the history of actual states from the study of international relations.[46]

Galtung wrote in the abstract style and with a tone of moral equivalence.[47] Galtung's central contribution lay in redefining the meaning of words, especially of peace, war, and violence. "Violence," he wrote in 1969, "exists when individuals are influenced in a way that causes their actual somatic and intellectual realization to be less than their potential realization." Galtung contrasted this concept of violence with a narrower one, according to which violence was "mere physical damage or an attack on life and limb (with death as the most extreme form)—a subjective act which intends these things as its consequences." This narrow concept of violence, however, meant that peace was compatible with the existence of "utterly unacceptable social orders." Hence an "expanded concept of violence" was essential.[48]

> We define violence as the cause of the difference between the potential and the actual, between what could be and what is. Violence is that which enlarges the gap between the potential and the actual or which makes more difficult the reduction of this gap. If, in the 18th century, an individual died of tuberculosis, this could only with difficulty be called violence because it could hardly be avoided. However, if, in spite of all the medical assistance in the world, a person died of tuberculosis today, then according to our definition, this would have to do with violence. . . . In other words, if the potential is greater than the actual and the actual is *avoidable*, violence exists.[49]

Galtung called such suffering the result of "indirect violence" in contrast to the "direct violence" of war.[50] He defined illiteracy, inadequate health care, and even the manipulative psychological assaults of Western advertising as "indirect violence." "The decisive point in all this is that the concept of violence can be expanded in this direction."[51]

Violence could be "personal or direct" if caused by an individual or "structural or indirect" and without an actor. In both cases, individuals can be hurt or killed, but in the case of indirect violence, "the violence is built into the system and expresses itself in unequal power relations and thus in unequal life-chances."[52] "If individuals are hungry in a period in which this can be objectively avoided, then violence is being done, regardless of whether or not a clear subject-object relationship exists."[53] Was "personal violence" necessary to overcome "structural violence"? For Galtung "absolute answers" to the question did not yet exist. But his own left-wing variant of a cost-benefit analysis of the Cuban Revolution found that the "losses due to personal violence" were "without a doubt lower" than the "losses caused by the structural violence under Batista."[54] Though accompanied with the customary academic qualifications, Galtung's work could be and was read or misread as a justification of "revolutionary violence." Galtung himself stressed the role of nonviolent action.[55] But though he stopped short of advocating terrorism or "revolutionary violence," his many qualifications, typologies of direct and indirect violence, and the redefinition of liberal democracies with capitalist economies as forms of structural violence offered a bundle of arguments for those inclined to use violence to achieve their political ends.

Galtung's argument found a receptive audience in the West German new left, which was developing on its own some ideas about "revolutionary conflict research" or "participation research." In 1971, a conference on critical peace research in West Berlin encouraged study of the hypothesis that under certain social conditions groups suffering discrimination had no alternative means of articulating and realizing their interests other than that of "violent self-expression" (*gewaltsamer Selbstäusserung*). The statement criticized existing peace research for its "ideological fixation on a law and order standpoint."[56]

Galtung's redefinition of violence led to an "expanded" concept of peace "defined as the absence of personal violence and structural violence." Such a peace was "positive peace" in contrast to the mere absence of war, which he called "negative peace."[57] "Negative peace" was merely the absence of war. "Positive peace" meant the absence of structural violence. Positive peace called for the presence of a "nonviolent form of egalitarian, non-exploitative and non-oppressive form of cooperation" among states, nations, and individuals, rather than the negative peace of a balance of terror. The "classical" conception of prevention of war occupied "only a small space" of the more comprehensive conception of peace in peace research.[58] Instead of criticizing Soviet occupation of Eastern Europe as an element of a negative peace, he castigated the "war system."[59] He advocated nonviolent defense for the Western democracies.[60] At the same time, he expressed admiration for the—armed—anticolonial guerilla wars fought since 1945, because of their intense ideological content, mass mobilization of the population, and apparent engagement of the whole personality of individuals.[61]

Galtung blurred the distinctions between war and peace, between violence and its absence. Just as Bahr and Brandt blurred or muted the distinctions between democracy and dictatorship, Galtung's discussion of structural violence and negative peace, like Senghaas' reference to "organized peacelessness," blurred the distinction between war and peace. These were no small achievements in West Germany, where the memories of two world wars in which millions died were still vivid. Dieter Senghaas and Johan Galtung criticized defense experts from the standpoint of the traditional intellectual as moralist and critic. We now turn to the self-described "counter-experts," who entered the fray on the terrain of arms control negotiations and details of weapons systems.

Counter-Experts

"Counter-experts" included former military officers, physicists, and peace researchers. They were more at home in debates over policy than in the realm of theory. One of the most prolific of the counter-experts to emerge from peace research was the already mentioned Dieter Lutz, at the peace research institute at the University of Hamburg. In the late 1970s, Lutz warned that the "arms race," or American strategic doctrines and developments, not the Soviet buildup, were increasing the danger of nuclear war.[62] During the battle of the euromissiles, he was a tireless opponent of the NATO decision, presenting dozens of radio addresses and essays on behalf of the antimissile cause.[63]

Lutz's *Weltkrieg wider Willen*, published in 1981 as a Rowohlt paperback, was one of the most successful examples of West German "counter-expertise." Lutz intended to break the "monopoly" of existing security experts over discussion of defense policy.[64] He drew on American, West German, and NATO figures, as well as data from the Stockholm International Peace Research Institute (SIPRI) and the London International Institute for Strategic Studies (IISS), to arrive at no fewer than eleven possible assessments of the balance of forces in Europe. He argued that NATO's claims of an unfavorable balance were wrong. He saw the danger of war less in a "supposed expansionist thrust" by the Soviet Union than in the "mutual distrust based on the foundation of the doctrine of deterrence . . . its worst-case imperatives, as well in the inherent dynamics of weapons technology producing an inhuman armaments policy in East and West."[65] The best way for Western Europe to protect itself from the Soviet threat was to separate itself from American policy, especially from the NATO decision of December 1979, a decision he interpreted as an American effort to create a first-strike capability against the Soviet Union and to limit war to Western Europe.

Among physicists, the most prominent figure in West German peace research was Carl Friedrich von Weizsäcker (b. 1912). His father, Ernst, had been head of the Foreign Office in Hitler's Germany. His brother, Richard, a leader of the moderate right in the CDU, was elected president of the Federal Republic in 1982 and reelected to a second five-year term in 1989. Carl Friedrich von Weizsäcker studied physics with Werner Heisenberg, continued to work as a physicist in Nazi Germany, and taught physics at the universities of Strasbourg and Göttingen and philosophy in Hamburg from 1957 to 1969.

Weizsäcker has written that "it was clear to me since 1939 that the atom bomb meant, and contained a push towards radical transformation of world politics."[66] His first of many political essays on the danger of nuclear weapons was published in 1945. In 1959, he agreed to join other physicists in establishing the *Vereinigung deutscher Wissenschaftler* (Association of German Scientists) to warn of the danger of nuclear weapons and to encourage arms control and disarmament.[67] In 1963, in response to the publication of Herman Kahn's *On Thermonuclear War*, he initiated and gained financial support for a study of the consequences of a nuclear war in Europe.[68] It was Weizsäcker who conceived the plan for the Max Planck Institute.[69] The institute opened in January 1970.[70] For Weizsäcker, the driving force behind the establishment of such an interdisciplinary research institute was the "danger to humanity posed by the atom bomb."[71]

Weizsäcker drew inspiration from what he called "the most socially critical text of world literature, the Sermon on the Mount."[72] He envisaged an interdisciplinary institute that would combine politics, philosophy, and natural science. It was a vision that was attractive to Jürgen Habermas, who agreed to serve with Weizsäcker as codirector of the institute. Weizsäcker's cooperation with a former West German army officer, Horst Ahfeldt, led to efforts on behalf of "alternative strategies" and to a study of war prevention and the consequences of war published in 1971.[73] It concluded that small and densely populated West Germany possessed no effective defense with nuclear weapons that would permit any significant survival of its industrial capacity or civilian infrastructure.[74] Only ten nuclear warheads with an explosive power of two megatons exploded over the ten most populated areas would kill eight million people. But at that time the Soviet Union had 700 medium-range missiles, not including hundreds more short-range missiles and artillery shells, each of which could carry a nuclear weapon. Were some portion of them fired at West Germany, "life would be extinguished in our country."[75] Ahfeldt and Weizsäcker noted that other countries lived with the nuclear peril but that West Germany's geography and unsolved national problem made this situation more dangerous.

Von Weizsäcker's argument about deterrence and defense in West Germany focused on the theme that the use of nuclear weapons to defend the country would lead to its self-destruction. In 1976, von Weizsäcker published *Wege in der Gefahr* [Paths into Danger], a work that focused on the dangers of nuclear weapons.[76] In 1979, it was published in an inexpensive paperback by Deutscher Taschenbuch Verlag. By 1981, it was in its third edition, having sold over 25,000 copies. The core of his argument lay in a chapter entitled "Five theses on the third world war."[77] "The third world war is probable," he wrote, because the drive for hegemony in a system of sovereign great powers had led to wars in the past. There was no reason to assume such a system would not lead to war in the future. Neither change in political consciousness, changes in social systems, diplomacy, societal convergence, nor liberal and/or socialist hopes would prevent war. So long, he argued, as the system of power politics persisted, a third world war would take place if it could be won.[78] The belief that victory was possible rested on the development of counterforce weapons that threatened the security of second-strike forces. Weizsäcker estimated that there was only about a decade more of reliable and secure second-strike forces.[79]

Von Weizsäcker wrote that the greatest barriers to peace lay in what East and West had in common, namely the belief that it was the adversary, not oneself, who was responsible for world armament. Peace thus required a fundamental change in consciousness, specifically the adoption of the view that "war must and can definitively be overcome" and that our perceptions of ourselves and potential adversaries must change.[80] This change in consciousness "must encompass all social groups who exert a formative influence on political decisions, that is, wielders of power and opinion makers, and in a certain sense the whole people."[81]

Von Weizsäcker's pessimism about the stability of deterrence led him to examine what to do if it were to fail. Drawing primarily on the work of his Starnberg colleague Horst Ahfeldt, which was published as *Verteidigung und Frieden* [Defense and Peace] in 1977, von Weizsäcker sought a military as well as a political alternative to existing NATO strategy.[82] The core of "the Ahfeldt proposals" was the creation of highly mobile groups armed with antitank weapons or "technocommandos" who would fight hundreds of small battles and thus offer no large targets. Technocommandos could not completely stop a tank assault, but they could slow down a blitzkrieg without destroying what was to be defended. The proposals had the virtue of being strictly defensive and were thus not a cause for further arms races. They offered, so von Weizsäcker and Ahfeldt argued, a defense that was not tantamount to suicide and was, therefore, more credible and more capable of sustaining public support than was a policy of nuclear deterrence.[83] Defense analysts inside and outside the West German government scoffed at the idea, noting that a simple concentration of Warsaw Pact armor and air forces would obliterate small "technocommandos," but the Ahfeldt proposals contained a certain "low tech" elan that found its way into the SPD left and the Greens in the early 1980s.

In an essay published in *Die Zeit* in May 1979, "Moscow's Armament: Defensive and Threatening," von Weizsäcker agreed that a massive Soviet military buildup had taken place.[84] He compared the "strike for world power" of Wilhelminian Germany in 1914 to a Soviet Union encircled by the United States and China. The Soviet Union might conclude that a blitzkrieg attack on Western Europe followed by an offer of peace before the United States could respond would make sense. Therefore, a defense such as that offered by the Ahfeldt proposals, designed to prevent such a blitzkrieg from succeeding, would effectively deter the most likely source of war from a "defensive but threatening" Soviet Union. A change in West German strategy to prevent a quick victory would prevent a recurrence of the miscalculations of August 1917. If NATO was to have new nuclear missiles needed to encourage the Soviets to reduce their weapons, they should be placed at sea.[85]

Unlike Dieter Lutz, Carl von Weizsäcker did not dispute NATO's claims about the growth of Soviet military power. In an essay first published in 1981 but written in November 1979, Weizsäcker expressed the background to his fears of the danger of war in the 1980s. "The general ground for danger lies in the inner weakness of the Russian colossus."[86] Only military power gave it strength. Its economic crisis was deepening, and it faced a succession crisis. Aggressive foreign policy might become a response to deep-seated domestic problems. The Soviet Union, compared to the West, would reach the apogee of its military power in the 1980s, after which the American and then the European counterarmament would reverse the shifts in the balance of power toward the Soviet Union that had taken place in the 1960s and 1970s. That the Russians had not pursued an aggressive policy in Europe in the 1960s and 1970s did not mean they would not do so in the 1980s. "If they ever wanted to acquire political advantages from their superiority in arms, they would perhaps have to do so in the next ten years."[87] New deployments of American medium-range nuclear weapons in Western Europe would, in his view, only exacerbate Soviet fears and increase the danger of war. Such arguments were also made by Rudolf Augstein, but they were hard to sustain, coming as they did at the end of the decade of détente and Western restraint in Europe.

The intellectual left engaged in foreign policy was not part of a new "hegemonic" class, but neither was it primarily comprised of "anti-authoritarian" outsiders. Institutions and positions attained in the early 1970s proved instrumental in the political disputes of the early 1980s, allowed the intellectual left to reach a receptive, politically interested and active public, and served as a source of arms control and defense policy proposals for the Social Democratic party. Peace researchers displayed two stances toward the issue of the Soviet military buildup. Some disputed the factual basis of NATO's assessment of the balance of military power. Others accepted the facts as presented by Western governments and argued that Western restraint was necessary in order not to provoke an economically backward but militarily powerful Soviet government. Despite discussion of "negative peace," the peace research literature said little about the impact of dictatorship in Eastern Europe on peace in Europe as a whole. Instead, it focused on dismantling Western *Feindbilder* "enemy images" in the interest of peace. This ironic convergence with the relative neglect of the form of government in much of the realist tradition was little noted. As we will see, this political culture and its creators made an important contribution to the campaign against NATO's 1979 two-track decision.

The Return of Old Boundaries:
The West German Left and German Nationalism

Let us recall some strands of the preceding chapters. Beginning in the 1960s, Willy Brandt and his foreign-policy adviser Egon Bahr encouraged a change in the political culture of the West German left. This change entailed an erosion of the boundaries of "militant democracy" at the level of publicly expressed political ideas. Brandt and Bahr stopped talking or talked very infrequently about the sharp distinctions between democracy and dictatorship, between individual freedom and totalitarian dictatorship. The erosion of the political boundaries between democracy and dictatorship in the détente era left intellectuals with a vacuum of meaning and interpretation. By the late 1970s some figures on the intellectual and political left began to fill that vacuum by turning to commonalities of Germans in East and West Germany.

In a 1977 article called "The difficulty of being a German," Dutschke criticized the West German left for its lack of interest in the German question.[88] The DDR did not have "real socialism," while West Germany lacked "real democracy."[89] In both parts of Germany, "Americanization and Russification" had progressed but "not the reunification of the real historical consciousness of the Germans." The German left had identified with many foreign causes but had ignored the maxim that the international class struggle begins at home and is national in form. Like Ernst Schumacher, Rudi Dutschke spoke in the name of an intact German nationalism. Unlike Schumacher, he rejected any form of anticommunism and stressed instead the commonalities of Germans in the two Germanies.[90] Egon Bahr, then the general secretary of the SPD, Rudolf Augstein, the publisher of *Der Spiegel,* and Günter Gaus, the West German representative to East Berlin, also raised the issue of German identity from the perspective of the moderate left.

The primary thrust of West German political culture at the end of the 1970s was less a revived German nationalism than a blurring of distinctions that had once been clear. In the détente era, it became unfashionable in the West German intellectual left to make a sharp distinction between liberal democracy and totalitarian or authoritarian dictatorship or between political freedom in Western Europe and the absence of liberty in the East. At times, there was confusion about the differences and similarities between the military power of the Western democracies after 1945 and that of the Nazi regime. In Galtung's work, even the difference between war and peace, violence and nonviolence, became problematic. Helmut Schmidt was attempting to reverse the momentum of world politics with strategic and geopolitical arguments, but he was swimming against the emotional and moral currents of the détente era. Support for his policies was to come from political and intellectual currents to his right.

7

CONSERVATISM, *TENDENZWENDE*, AND MILITANT DEMOCRACY

IN THE EARLY 1970s, at the high point of the push to the left in politics and culture in West Germany, politicians and intellectuals of the center and right became more vocal in their criticisms of the spirit of the age. Intellectuals and scholars voiced criticisms of the new left and of aspects of Brandt's foreign policies. Conservative politicians, or rather some conservative politicians such as Helmut Kohl, argued that Christian Democrats must regain the capacity to articulate the moral foundations of their politics. This fusion of politicians seeking to reinvigorate their own traditions in changed circumstances with intellectuals discontented with the consequences of Brandt's policies contributed to the *Tendenzwende* or "change of tendency" in political culture that prefigured the change in national politics in 1982.

From 1949 to 1969, the Christian Democrats had been a governing party. From 1966 to 1969, they lost the support of the liberal Free Democratic party, largely because of disagreements over *Ostpolitik* and proposals for domestic reforms. In 1969, the Social Democratic–Free Democratic or "social-liberal" coalition led by Brandt and Walter Scheel won national elections, and Willy Brandt became the first Social Democratic West German chancellor. In 1972, Brandt won reelection when, for the first time, the Social Democrats alone received a larger percentage of votes than the Christian Democrats. From 1974 to 1982, Helmut Schmidt served as West German chancellor in a coalition with the Free Democrats, led by Hans-Dietrich Genscher.

In 1973, Helmut Kohl (b. 1930) became chairman of the Christian Democratic Union. Kohl understood that the path back to becoming a govern-

ing power clearly lay in the center, that is, in regaining the affections of
the West German liberals. Only in the election of 1972, when Willy
Brandt was at the height of his popularity in West Germany, did the Social
Democrats receive a higher percentage of voters than the Christian Democrats. In the 1976 election, the CDU/CSU outpolled the SPD 49 percent
to 42 percent but remained in opposition because the FDP coalesced with
the SPD. In 1980, even with the highly polarizing figure of Franz-Josef
Strauss as its chancellor candidate, the CDU received one percentage point
more than the SPD (44 percent to 43 percent) but suffered a decisive defeat
because the liberals, with a robust 11 percent of the national vote, remained
in the "social-liberal" coalition.[1]

The election of Willy Brandt in 1969 was also a victory for the West
German intellectual left. In the 1960s, the leftist intellectuals had criticized
the Adenauer era as one of delayed reforms, privatistic materialism, and
amnesia about the Nazi past.[2] Brandt's circle of closest advisers included
two journalists, Bahr and Günter Gaus.[3] One of his oldest and more ardent
supporters was the novelist Günter Grass.[4] Brandt and his intellectual supporters welcomed the unity of *Geist* and *Macht* in West Germany, and the
passing of anti-intellectual politicians and "unpolitical" intellectuals.[5] His
critics argued that this unity entailed the intellectual's loss of the critical
spirit.[6] Helmut Kohl argued that Christian Democracy, no less than Social
Democracy, had to develop good relations with West German intellectuals.

Helmut Kohl in 1973: Between Ideology and Pragmatism

Helmut Kohl had been a member of the Christian Democratic Union since
joining in 1947, at the age of seventeen, and had pursued a career in Christian Democratic politics ever since. A quintessential man of the party, Kohl,
who earned a doctorate in history from the University of Heidelberg, was
more attuned to intellectual currents than his many critics in the press
assumed was the case. From 1969 to 1976, he was the minister-president
of Rhineland-Pfalz. In 1973, he was election chairman of the CDU. From
1976 to 1982, he was the chairman of the CDU/CSU parliamentary fraction.

When he was elected party chairman in 1973, Kohl presented himself
as a man of the center critical of the "ideological absolutism" of the socialism of the Brandt years.[7] In both domestic and foreign policies, he called
for a renewed emphasis on the *Wertordnung* (value order) and *Wertprämis-
sen* (value premises) of West German democracy and the Atlantic alliance.

In his speech to the CDU party congress on the occasion of his election to the party chairmanship in 1973, Kohl turned to the condition of West Germany's political culture.

> But above all the inner coherence of the Atlantic community is threatened by the dwindling of the power of a previously shared value order (*Wertordnung*) which has been its foundation. The dismantling of the military danger by the policy of the Communist camp has brought the Cold War to an end. It has not, however, set this threat aside. This policy has only changed its character. Ideological aggression has emerged alongside military aggression. Today the conflict is conducted less with weapons than with words, concepts and ideologies. . . . The community of values and ideas must again emerge alongside the community of weapons. *It is decisive that the idea of a militant democracy remain the content of the Atlantic community and of the movement for European unity.* . . . [emphasis added][8]

Brandt's *Ostpolitk*, Kohl continued, had contributed to a separation of West German foreign policy from the "foundation of values and morals that defined the postwar position."[9] The SPD's foreign policy was threatening alliance stability, while its domestic reforms were leading to a disturbing expansion of state power.

Kohl elaborated these points in a 1973 book, *Zwischen Ideologie und Pragmatismus* [Between Ideology and Pragmatism].[10] He described himself as a politician who combined pragmatism with conviction and as an advocate of "critical rationality." Appreciation of human fallibility was a protection against the "positivistic belief in the total pliability of the world" or the secular religion of the possibility of the "perfect construction of society."[11] Pragmatism alone was insufficient: A party had to be able to articulate its fundamental beliefs. Intellectuals had a key role to play in this effort. They "structure the consciousness and the horizon of expectations of people." Politicians could "set accents, collect hopes, and awaken expectations only within, not against this framework and this political atmosphere. In this way, intellectuals naturally also attain political effect, and exert political influence in the society."[12] Unfortunately, he acknowledged, the CDU had poor links to the "majority of intellectuals," and he wondered what kind of "intellectual-cultural profile" the CDU could offer to "become an active and interesting conversation partner for the intellectuals?"[13]

Kohl's analysis of the alienation between Christian Democracy and West German intellectuals was as follows: In the immediate postwar years, Christian Democracy embodied the hopes of many intellectuals for moral and political renewal after Nazi totalitarianism. The alienation between the

CDU and the intellectuals came with the currency reform and the introduction of the social market economy in 1948. The more the CDU became identified with capitalism, the less appealing it was for an intelligentsia with a long and powerful anticapitalist tradition.[14] The relationship of the CDU to the intellectuals became even worse as it became a governing party.[15] Adenauer's decisions to join a Western alliance, to form an army, and to equip it with American tactical nuclear weapons were taken in the face of opposition from many West German intellectuals.

The party of governance in West Germany did not, he continued, sufficiently articulate the *geistige* or "intellectual-cultural" foundations of its politics. Hence "the real utopias of the CDU—social market economy, a free state of law, overcoming national states through European integration—are scarcely recognized as such."[16] The CDU, Kohl said, had lived on the cultural capital of its founding phase for twenty years. In the 1970s "this was no longer possible." A "theoretical new grounding" was necessary if the party were to regain the capacity to govern. Kohl saw the relationship of the CDU to intellectuals as "a question of the existence" of the party. It was time, he said, for the CDU to admit that it erred in the 1950s and 1960s when, while focused on reconstruction and economic recovery, "it treated the intellectuals as an undifferentiated whole."[17] Now the Christian Democrats had to make up for their previous underestimation of the "cultural-intellectual basis" of politics.[18] The result of Kohl's efforts was the beginning of a political dialogue between leaders of Christian Democracy and West German intellectuals critical of the policies of the Social Liberal government.[19] While the Christian Democratic leadership around Kohl decided to reach out to intellectuals, a "change of tendency" or *Tendenzwende* was taking place within West German intellectual life.

The Bund Freiheit der Wissenschaft
[The Association for the Freedom of Scholarship]

The reaction of West German university professors against the radical left was not only an intellectual or theoretical dispute about Marxism and liberalism. A history of the political turmoil in West German universities in the 1970s remains to be written. Though the 1970s in the United States were a period "after" the 1960s, the same period in West Germany was one of continuing bitter conflict, which at times led to violence and threats against students and teachers. In 1970, a group of West German professors who feared for the survival of academic freedom at their institutions, especially at the Free University of Berlin, formed the *Bund Freiheit der Wissenschaft*

[Association for the Freedom of Scholarship]. The organization presented itself as a defender of academic freedom and the autonomy of the university in the face of a pincers movement between the radical student left and the reform proposals of the Brandt government.[20] The political stance of the association ranged from center left to center right. In its periodicals, *Hochschulpolitische Information* [University information] and *Freiheit der Wissenschaft* [Freedom of scholarship], the *Bund* published reports on disruptions, violence, and student elections, as well as essays on the political and intellectual climate in the universities.

The picture of West German universities that emerges from these journals in the early and mid-1970s is grim. It includes Marxist-Leninist sects that inflicted physical violence and psychological intimidation, or "psycho-terror," on professors and students whose views they found unacceptable.[21] From 1970 to 1976, the reports included incidents such as the following: On three occasions in 1972 and 1973, communist students threatened to shoot a professor of English at the Free University of Berlin because he would not permit disruptions of his class.[22] In November 1973 at the University of Tübingen, following an open tribunal organized by one communist political group, a professor and two students were physically thrown out of a classroom and onto the floor. In December 1973, after an introductory economics course was disrupted for the fifth time, the president of the university closed the economics department for a week, and said the events recalled the beginnings of Nazi domination when Marxist and Jewish professors were attacked by right-wing extremists. In December 1973, a meeting of the young conservatives was disrupted by radical leftists who stormed the podium, beat up the panelists, and forced them out of the lecture hall. In February 1974 at the University of Heidelberg, radical leftists placed a stink bomb in the office of political scientist Klaus von Beyme and sprayed paint on the walls of his office after a lecturer's contract was not renewed.[23] In the fall of 1976 in Heidelberg the police were called so frequently to keep university buildings open that they were eventually required to remain permanently in the buildings. In December 1976, at the Free University in Berlin, communist students displayed the following opinions about faculty members on posters: "Hang Möller," "(Ernst) Nolte will be liquidated—Möller castrated—Miethke kidnapped—AND THEN studies can be done right."[24]

These reports, as well as reports on the emergence of "popular front" student governments of *JUSOS* and communist groups, filled the pages of the *Bund Freiheit der Wissenschaft* in the 1970s.[25] According to a survey of 3000 West German university professors conducted in 1977 by the Allensbach Institute, one in ten West German professors reported being personally attacked in leaflets and posters and one in five had had their teaching and/or research hindered or experienced some kinds of "interference or attacks" from the radical left in the 1970s.[26] Those who were outspoken in their criticisms of the radical left reported receiving anonymous late-night phone calls and threats of physical violence. Some were bitter at the reluctance of liberal colleagues to denounce the threat to academic freedom from the radical left.[27]

In the combination of intellectual radicalization and institutional change in the universities, leaders of the *Bund Freiheit der Wissenschaft* saw a threat to West German democracy.[28] As Thomas Nipperdey, a historian of modern Germany, put it in a 1974 essay, it was "not the [University of] Frankfurt excesses that capture the headlines but the silent conquest of the University of Marburg that is the actually dangerous development."[29] New universities in Oldenburg, Osnabruck, Kassel, and Bremen threatened to become "strongholds of radical ideological indoctrination [and] institutionalized counter-universities modeled on the University of Bremen."[30] Nipperdey said that those who criticize the threat from the radical left "will be attacked as an enemy of the mind, an enemy of freedom." But "enemies of our system," in a manner suggesting "something beyond liberality and tolerance," had used the university reforms of the 1970s to establish institutional roots.[31] Nipperdey had in mind plans for tripartite forms of university governance, which, he argued, enhanced the position of the extreme left and even of terrorist sympathizers. The universities had become more, not less, politicized.[32] Nipperdey argued that democratization of the universities combined with their expansion into mass universities had allowed political groups to seek and attain power in the face of the relative apathy of the mass of students. He expressed irritation with Social Democratic politicians who had failed to oppose the advances of the radical left and worried that the international standing and quality of teaching and research at all West German universities was suffering. The reforms were "a major cause of the misery."[33]

In Western Europe and the United States, the generation of 1968 had moved into university teaching posts. The university reforms in West Germany were not the only cause of the "strong anti-democratic current in the student body," but "that they have persisted and grown—in contrast to Anglo-Saxon countries" was, Nipperdey believed, due "to the fact that the university policies of particular states, and particular universities—perhaps not at all or only partly intentioned—have rewarded the enemies of democracy."[34] In 1981, Nipperdey wrote that "in contrast to other Western countries," the ideological revolt of the 1960s had been consolidated in the universities and from there was able to exert an impact on schools, churches, law, administration, the political parties, trade unions, and the media.[35]

The central conceptual point made by the leaders of the *Bund Freiheit der Wissenschaft* was Tocquevillian: reform from above combined with revolt from below enhanced the powers of government at the expense of previously autonomous institutions. Erwin Scheuch, a sociologist at the University of Cologne, spoke of "an alliance between those seeking to change the system and bureaucrats."[36] Rudolf Wildenmann wrote that the *Grüppenuniversität* [group university] was in fact a collection of fluid, changing, unstructured, largely individualized "masses," for whom symbolic, ideological politics held particular appeal. In these miniature mass societies, small minorities were able to exercise disproportionate influence because of the apathy of the mass of students.[37] The members of the *Bund Freiheit der Wissenschaft* believed they were living through a West German *Sonderweg* created by a conjucture of political traditions and contemporary government policies. A distinctively powerful persistence of radicalism in West Germany took place, in their view, because of the combined effects of government reforms and the revival of romantic, Marxist, and anticapitalist traditions.[38]

In response to criticism that the *Bund Freiheit der Wissenschaft* was resisting long overdue and necessary reforms of the German university, Nipperdey argued for rehabilitation of "the self-limitation of scholarship" in the face of "false claims to power" guided by politics or relevance.[39] The political theorist Wilhelm Hennis argued that plebiscitarian conceptions of democracy in the universities posed a threat to freedom of scholarship and facilitated a dangerous growth of state powers in the name of daring more democracy.[40] He wanted to restrain democratization in nonpolitical institutions. Universities rested on principles that established authority based on scholarly accomplishment. Hennis warned that to treat the universities simply as political bodies filled with competing interests ignored their distinctive features and opened the door for an expansion of state power.[41]

In West Germany's political culture, the *Bund Freiheit der Wissenschaft* and the advocates of an intellectual-political *Tendenzwende* were identified as "right wing" and "conservative." To the extent that they were to the right of the left, these labels had a certain meaning. They were also conservatives in their desire to conserve West Germany's liberal democratic polity and social market economy in contrast to socialist economics and "extraparliamentary" democracy. As is evident in the essays of Hermann Lübbe, one of the most outspoken figures of the *Tendenzwende* in the mid-1970s, the conservatism of the *Tendenzwende* also lay in a belief that enlightenment rationality alone was insufficient to offer a society binding values. More attention had to be paid to the value of traditions, which the parties of progress had too often neglected.[42] In a 1979 essay in defense of liberalism, Lübbe rejected utopias that promised the individual integration into a unified political collectivity.[43]

The sociologist Helmut Schelsky introduced another theme into the reaction to the new left: the theme of power. In essays and a much-discussed book, *Die Arbeit Tun die Anderen* [The Others Do the Work], Schelsky depicted a "new elite of reflection" whose power rested on its interpretive abilities. He saw, in Rudi Dutschke's plans for a long march through the institutions, a theory by which the radicalized intellectuals would become a significant power factor in West German society and politics. Unlike now-obsolete revolutionary strategies focused on armed assaults on the army and police, this new and more realistic strategy reflected the understanding that opinion rather than force was decisive in modern complex societies.[44] This explained the focus on schools from kindergarten to university, the press, radio, television, museums, theaters, artistic and literary associations, churches, and political parties.[45] The strategic goal of left-wing radicals as far as these institutions were concerned was "simply the 'seizure of power,' i.e., the occupation of the crucial positions of authority and determination of their policies by fellow believers, followers, and sympathizers."[46] In a 1974 essay, the sociologist Erwin Scheuch expressed similar views about the intellectuals as a power factor.[47] "Could it be," he asked, that "intellectuals had become part of the system of administration of power—at least some of them, if not the core group?"[48]

More important, however, than Schelsky's polemical arguments about the intellectuals as a new priesthood was a 1973 essay on the potential conflict between principles of democracy and freedom in West Germany.[49] Schelsky argued that the polarization of West German politics, popularly described in the traditional terms of left and right, was in fact defined by the conflict between two principles within free and democratic Western societies, "democratization" or "division of powers," Rousseau or Montesquieu. It was not a conflict between the establishment and radical leftist outsiders, though those seeking to "overcome" the political system benefited from it. Rather it was a conflict "immanent to the system," that is, one going on within the West German establishment, that would affect "our political fate" in the years to come.[50]

He argued that Brandt's determination to "dare more democracy" began the polarization. The Federal Republic of Germany, with the experience of totalitarian dictatorship in mind, had defined itself as a "free, democratic basic order." Brandt's decision to give primacy to "more democracy" reversed the order of these words. Schelsky, again in a Tocquevillian mode, suggested such a step could imply daring "less freedom." Schelsky criticized the demand for "more democracy" because it overlooked the "genuinely liberal form of the limitation of power," that is, the principle of the division of powers. West German liberalism had come to accept the need to keep political and economic power separate, to defend the autonomy of employers and unions and banks, in short, to defend a pluralist society resting on a principle of the division of powers. Only such pluralism could insure individual rights. Multiple institutions and "pluralization of power" offered the decisive guarantee for the freedom of the individual.[51]

However, he wrote, "in no institution(s) is the dismantling of the principle of the separation of powers and the consequences of its dismantling clearer than in the West German universities."[52] Schelsky attacked as a "fiction" the image of the *Ordinarienuniversität* in the Humboldt tradition as an authoritarian institution run by a small group. Instead, it rested on a division of powers among state authorities, faculty, administrators, and student governments that attended to concerns of students. It had been transformed by state reformers who, rather than sustain its institutional differentiation and complexity at a larger level, eliminated its division of powers in favor of a democratized university "in which everyone was able to participate in deciding about everything and in which no one any longer bore personal, concrete responsibility."[53] Transient majorities now were able to take power in the universities, thereby endangering freedom of research. Mediocrity rather than the personal initiative and creativity of individual scholars was the result, and politicized students were the beneficiaries.[54]

Schelsky warned of a "weakening of the liberal foundations of the Federal Republic." The Christian Democrats were too preoccupied with political maneuvering "to convincingly set against the growing democratization, the principles of a free order." The CDU had, in 1973, not yet understood that the "intellectual-political foundations" of the postwar years were no longer able to deal with the changed political and intellectual scenery of the 1970s.[55] Within the SPD, a conflict was taking place between an older generation more committed to liberal principles of the division of power and a younger generation uninterested in these "liberal" freedoms because they believed social and political change could be brought about by the centralized accumulation of power. Here as well the older generation had difficulty articulating its political and moral fundamentals. The nominally liberal party, the Free Democrats, was more noted for its tactical success in remaining in power than for its capacity to articulate fundamental liberal principles.[56] Therefore, said Schelsky, it fell to West Germany's intellectuals to restate the fundamentals of the West German liberal democratic order.

In the context of West German political culture of the 1970s, an option for Tocqueville and Montesquieu in place of Rousseau was a "right-wing" and "conservative" position on the then-existing spectrum, but it was not one with roots in German conservatism. Before 1945, especially in the Weimar and Nazi eras, conservative and Nazi intellectuals attacked the ideals of limited government and division of powers as threats to the totalitarian unity of the *Volk*.[57] Conservative in the context of the 1970s, Schelsky remained loyal to the liberal democratic traditions of militant democracy.

Alois Mertes: Militant Democracy and Foreign Policy

In foreign affairs as well, "conservative" intellectuals and politicians in West Germany based their criticism of Social Democratic foreign policy on liberal democratic principles. Hans-Peter Schwarz, a historian and scholar of international relations at the University of Bonn, wrote about about "Finlandization," a gradual process by which the West European countries gradually lost their freedom of action in foreign affairs and eventually in domestic politics as well. He criticized Brandt's and Bahr's reluctance to speak plainly about the persecution of dissidents in the Soviet Union, repression of liberalizing tendencies in Eastern Europe, Moscow's imperial adventures in Africa, and its arms buildup during the decade of détente. These, he wrote, were examples of Western self-censorship.[58]

Alois Mertes, the foreign-policy spokesman of the CDU parliamentary fraction from 1973 to 1982 and *Staatssekretär* in the Foreign Ministry until his death in summer 1985, took the Social Democrats to task for talking so much about weapons and so little about political intentions and the political purposes of Soviet military power.[59] In 1977, he argued that Soviet ideology still projected a "dynamic will to prevail" over the doomed capitalist West. He argued that the Russians used arms control negotiations to ratify military superiority designed to bring about an ultimate "victory of socialism" following a change in the correlation of forces favorable to them.[60] The Soviet détente strategy, in Mertes' view, was to have West Germany play a role in the Western alliance that "objectively" served the interest of Soviet foreign policy. The leadership of the Social Democratic party was key to this strategy. He argued that the Soviets hoped to separate West Germany from the Western alliance with the help of quasi-neutralist sentiment within West German politics. Soviet long-term goals were to diminish American influence in Western Europe; to erode Western defense either by a spectacular West German exit from NATO or, more likely, by a slow erosion of NATO's deterrent under the continuing pressure of a "German interest" in détente and reunification; to expand access to Western European capital, science, and technology; and to increase influence—and an effective veto power—on the foreign and defense policy positions of the governments of Western Europe by use of the lever of their own domestic politics.[61] In the neutron bomb affair, Mertes said that Bahr's statements, whatever their subjective motivations, "objectively served the interests of the Soviet Union."[62] Addressing Egon Bahr in the Bundestag in September 1978 during the neutron bomb controversy, Mertes said that Bahr's statements about the neutron bomb "encourage and favor a position which the Soviet Union justly sees as very useful and of service to its concept of détente."[63]

In addition to his warnings about the relationship between West German domestic politics and Soviet policy in Europe, Mertes was an enthusiastic supporter of President Carter's human rights policy. He believed it restored a balance between peace and freedom, which had been upset by Brandt's "peace policy." Human rights should apply with equal determination to all governments. As Mertes put it in a debate in the Bundestag in June 1978, the realization of human rights in all of Germany had nothing to do with an atavistic nationalism of the past. "Real détente, genuine peace will emerge for the first time when internationally applicable commitments to human rights will be strictly applied and adhered to in all of Germany."[64]

Mertes cited the argument of Polish philosopher Leszek Kolakowski to the effect that suppression of human rights and political freedom in its Eastern half, not reform movements seeking freedom, was the threat to peace in Europe. Lack of legitimacy by the regimes of Eastern Europe made them less able to respond to demands for human and political rights.[65] Peace in Europe called for freedom in Eastern Europe. The continuing violation of human rights in the Warsaw Pact states eroded the "much hailed process of détente." Détente could turn into an "empty formula, a smoke screen . . . one of the great lies of our time." East and West meant quite different things by détente. "For the West it means realization of human rights. For the Soviet Union, détente means: prevention of human rights."[66] It was, he said, "a perversion of international morality" that the majority of the United Nations talked about human rights and self-determination only in references to struggles against Western colonial domination, against South Africa's racism, and against the military regime in Chile, but not in respect to the "violation of human rights and of the right of self-determination of peoples by the Soviet Union and by the systems forced on those peoples by the Soviet Union. . . . The conscience of world public opinion must be sharpened so that the human rights of the individual and the self-determination of peoples are inseparable."[67]

West Germans in particular, he continued, must not close their eyes and ears to the question of human rights in East Germany. The German-German border was the "most inhuman in the world," but the will to freedom and human rights was certain to grow in Europe. "Must not," he asked, "Stalin's heritage be liquidated someday?" Under no circumstances should West Germans be intimidated by propaganda about "revanchism" into remaining silent before world public opinion concerning the self-determination and freedom of the Germans.

> After the experience with two totalitarian systems on German soil, both of which trampled on human rights—in the other part of Germany this is not history but the most acute present—there is a clear definition of our national interest: realization of the right of self-determination in all of Germany, human rights for all Germans—no more, but also no less.[68]

For Mertes, West German concern for human rights in Eastern Europe and in East Germany must not mean a return to an older German nationalism. Rather it should be the product of the political culture of West Germany's militant democracy. In the Adenauer tradition, he found a language for discussing the German question without abandoning the issue of democracy and dictatorship. Mertes warned that the national question and the question of political freedom and human rights should remain connected so that a reawakened German national feeling "never again falls into the hands of brown or red totalitarianism." It would, he said, serve neither West German nor Western interests generally if the German question were to be raised outside of or in antagonism to Western values of individual freedom and human rights. Yet, he said, this was just what Bahr was doing when he said that peace comes before the nation, "as if there could be a real, lasting peace without the realization of the German people's demands for human rights. As if suppression of human rights had something to do with peace!"[69]

By the late 1970s, the CDU made what it called "a search for a neutralist middle position for Europe between East and West in foreign affairs" by the Social Democratic party a key part of its political campaign.[70] The CDU resolution on security policy from its annual party convention of 1979 was entitled "security yes—neutralization no."[71] It expressed "deep concern" over the political goals of "European socialists" who tended to equate democracy and socialism and who had not proven able to maintain boundaries with "totalitarian ideologies."[72] It criticized the SPD for risking "an inner separation from our Western alliance partners and of a search for a neutralist middle position for Europe between East and West . . . ," understanding "the Atlantic Alliance as merely an alliance of interests" that would be superseded with a "dissolution of the military blocs."[73]

In 1980, an election year, the CDU/CSU's security resolution convention called for replacement of "socialist détente policy" with a "realistic peace policy." It described Soviet détente policy as "the policy of the Cold War with other means but the same goals: expansion of Soviet domination, dissolution of the Atlantic Alliance, and isolation of the Federal Republic of Germany."[74] As a result of "socialist détente policy," peace, especially following the invasion of Afghanistan, was less secure than at any time since World War II. West Germany needed a firm anchor in the Western alliance, something the SPD, with its excessive "understanding" for Moscow's "defensive" armament, was now not able to offer.[75] The platform promised to pursue an evenhanded human rights policy, that is, to criticize violations of human rights by communist as well as by right-wing dictatorships.

Helmut Kohl's speech to the annual party conference of the Christian Democratic Union in Berlin in May 1980 summarized the conservative critique of the Social Democratic party in the social-liberal era. "A strong faction within the SPD," he said, was "no longer ready to subscribe" to a policy that combined both peace and freedom. Though, he continued, only unambiguous alliance with United States guaranteed peace and freedom in West Germany, some of the Social Democratic leaders had "assiduously and sympathetically understood the security interests of the Soviet Union, but at the same time devalued and talked around solidarity with the United States in terms of 'if and but.'" There was, he continued, "no third way for the Federal Republic of Germany" between East and West. If there was a "special mission for us Germans, then it consists above all in our contribution to solidifying the Western alliance" and "not between the blocks."[76]

He criticized those who, "even after the Soviet aggression in Afghanistan, place the Soviet Union and the United States on the same moral plane," who sought to "decouple the Federal Republic of Germany ever more from America and from the Western Alliance, and who seek in domestic and in foreign policy a third way between East and West." He criticized the Social Democrats and the theory of change through rapprochement for having "created the illusions which feed doubts about our foreign policy position." He spoke of "a gloomy anti-Americanism" that had spread through the SPD, reminiscent of "the old SPD, the SPD before

Godesberg," and warned against underestimating "these signs of a harmful development."[77] The Social Democratic party of 1980 was no longer speaking the "language of Kurt Schumacher, Erich Ollenhauer, Fritz Erler, Ernst Reuter, Carlo Schmid, not the language of Herbert Weichmann," nor had the party responded effectively as its youth organizations in the universities formed popular fronts with communist groups.[78] Kohl warned that Helmut Schmidt would not be able to stop this trend in the SPD.

Franz-Josef Strauss, leader of the Conservative Social Union and the CDU/CSU candidate in the 1980 election against Helmut Schmidt, leveled a fierce indictment of the SPD in foreign affairs.[79] He spoke of "the growing understanding in the SPD for Moscow" which, Strauss feared, would lead to

> a neutralized, militarily defenseless Europe, one gradually shorn of American protection. That is the declared goal of the Soviet Union in the 1980s. . . . That is why following the overturning of the Brussels decision [of NATO] and a step by step neutralization of the Federal Republic of Germany with a loosening of ties to the USA there would follow a comprehensive and gradual reorientation of Western Europe to the Soviet Union.[80]

Strauss argued that neutralization and a pax Sovietica in Europe were real dangers if the illusory politics of the past decade were to continue. But Strauss was most unappealing to centrist opinion in West Germany, including that of the Free Democratic party. For the CDU/CSU leadership at the end of the decade of détente, West Germany's Western ties and the continuation of political freedom in Western Europe hung in the balance. For the Social Democrats, peace in Europe was at stake. The polarization of peace and freedom with left and right in West German political culture was firmly established before the battle of the euromissiles began.

In the Weimar Republic, right-wing intellectuals attacked parliamentary democracy and the principles of differentiation and individual freedom as threats to the unity of the *Volk*. Rather than defend the freedom of individual scholars from political interference, they took the universities to task for being repositories of "lifeless" learning. In foreign affairs, Weimar conservatism continued the legacy of hatred of France, Britain, and the United States as superficial, commercial societies. In the Rapallo Treaty, diplomats and military leaders secretly cooperated with the Bolsheviks during the 1920s. Conservative elites entertained visions of another effort at continental hegemony led by a Germany between East and West.

The leading representatives of "conservatism" in West Germany in 1980 remained loyal to Adenauer's legacy of a Western-oriented West Germany.

In the universities, they defended the separation and division of powers, the autonomy and freedom of scholarship, and individual freedom. In foreign policy, they defended West Germany's Atlanticist, pro-Western ties to France, Britain, and the United States and warned of the dangers of a German *Sonderweg* in a new form.

The *Tendenzwende* of the 1970s was the child of the transformation of conservatism in the postwar years, above all, in its Westernization and liberalization. Its advocates defended the political culture that had been shaped in the late 1940s and early 1950s. They spoke in the language of Adenauer and Clausewitz, but also in an international discourse of Tocqueville and Karl Popper, Raymond Aron and Leszek Kolakowski, Montesquieu and President Jimmy Carter. On the eve of the euromissile dispute, the conservatism of the *Tendenzwende* lay in the conservation of important components of the Westernizing traditions of West Germany and of the original boundaries of militant democracy. Helmut Kohl's 1973 opening to West German intellectuals, and the *Tendenzwende*, were as important to a shift of direction in the balance of power within West German political culture as Helmut Schmidt's 1977 London speech was to a shift in the momentum of world politics.

8

THE WAR
OF WORDS BEGINS
Reinterpretation and Response,
December 1979
to November 1981

THE ANNOUNCEMENT OF NATO'S two-track decision on December 14, 1979, marked the beginning of four years of public controversy in Western Europe over nuclear weapons. The controversy brought the strategic advantages and disadvantages of democracy and dictatorship into sharp focus. All of the war of words over the euromissiles took place in the West European democracies. Intellectuals were central participants. While opponents of the missiles believed they faced a choice of peace or war, supporters were convinced that West Germany's Western orientation hung in the balance. We have examined the contours of West German political culture and the beliefs of actors at the beginning of the euromissile dispute. We have also examined the links between ideas and institutions such as political parties, newspapers, universities, and research institutes. In the following four chapters, we examine the interaction of ideas and politics during the battle over the euromissiles in West Germany.

Support for the NATO two-track decision spanned a spectrum from the Schmidt wing of the SPD through the Free Democrats led by Hans-Dietrich Genscher, the foreign minister, and the CDU/CSU coalition led by Kohl and Strauss. In the press, supporters included the conservative *Die Welt*, the center right, *Frankfurter Allgemeine Zeitung*, and the centrist *Süddeutsche Zeitung*. *Die Zeit*, the leading intellectual weekly, was pulled in both directions. Opposition eventually encompassed the entire West German left. It initially included the Greens, a new national party of the radical left formed in 1979;[1] several leading figures of the left wing of the Social Democratic party, including Erhard Eppler and Oskar Lafontaine; the editorial boards and national security correspondents of *Stern, Der Spiegel,* and the *Frankfurter Rundschau;* several of West Germany's most well-known figures of the literary left, such as Günter Grass and Heinrich Böll; the foreign-policy left in the peace research institutes; and eventually a majority of the Social Democratic party. By its end, the overlapping of left-right divisions in domestic politics with left-right splits in foreign policy was complete and added to the bitterness and ideological polarization of the conflict.

The architects of the NATO two-track decision favored new American medium-range missiles in Western Europe in order to strengthen the coupling of Western Europe to the United States and to disabuse the Soviet leadership of the belief that the Soviet Union would be successful in limiting a war, conventional or nuclear, to Western Europe and Central Europe. The primary accomplishment of the oppositional intellectuals and politicians was to reverse the meaning of the 1979 decision. This reinterpretation imputed to the United States the intention of "Europeanizing" and "limiting" a nuclear war to Europe and the Soviet Union. The primary victim or victims of this attempt to threaten and if necessary wage a limited nuclear war in Europe would be West and East Germany, along with Europe and Russia. This was also the interpretation of the NATO decision offered by the Soviet Union.

In the fall of 1979, the Soviet Union increased its diplomatic efforts to stop deployment of any NATO medium-range nuclear weapons. On October 6, 1979, Brezhnev, in a speech in East Berlin, announced a unilateral reduction of 20,000 soldiers and 1,000 tanks in East Germany. He said new NATO deployments would lead to unspecified Soviet "supplementary measures." On October 25, 1979, Marshal Ustinov, the Soviet defense minister, warned that "appropriate measures" would be taken by the Soviet Union in response to Western deployments. On November 23, Foreign Minister Gromyko, speaking in Bonn, said that the Western decision to deploy new medium-range nuclear weapons in Western Europe would destroy the basis for any negotiations.

As we noted, at its annual party congress in West Berlin, which took place from December 3 to 7, 1979 in West Berlin, the Social Democrats defined the goal of negotiations over medium-range nuclear forces to be a reduction of Soviet medium-range nuclear weapons such that an agreement "would make the introduction of additional medium range weapons in Western Europe superfluous."[2] On December 9, 1979, 50,000 to 70,000 people demonstrated in Brussels in the first of many demonstrations against the NATO decision.[3]

On December 12, 1979, all of the foreign and defense ministers of the NATO alliance met in Brussels to announce the "two-track decision," or "INF" decision.[4] NATO would deploy 572 medium-range nuclear weapons in Western Europe able to strike targets in the Western parts of the Soviet Union. Of these, 108 would be single-warhead Pershing II ballistic missiles to be deployed in West Germany, while 464 were to be land-based cruise missiles, also with one nuclear warhead. At the same time, NATO offered to enter negotiations with the Soviet Union as soon as possible concerning such weapons. The "immediate objective" of the proposed negotiations was to be "establishment of agreed limitations on US and Soviet land-based long-range theatre nuclear missile systems," consonant with principles of parity and equality.[5] The communique also announced a decision to withdraw 1,000 nuclear warheads on short-range missiles from Western Europe. The NATO communique, in contrast to the SPD statement in Berlin, said nothing about a possible elimination of new deployments as a result of negotiations.

On December 14, 1979, TASS announced that the NATO decision had destroyed the basis for further negotiations on medium-range weapons. On December 20, 1979, the United States Senate Committee on Armed Forces recommended that the SALT II treaty not be ratified without major changes. On December 27, 1979, the Soviet Union invaded Afghanistan. President Carter then gave up efforts to have SALT II ratified by the Senate. At the end of 1979, when Soviet spokesmen claimed that "approximate equality" existed in the balance of forces in Europe, NATO estimated that the Soviet Union had deployed approximately 140 SS-20 missiles with 420 warheads within range of Western Europe, as well as the two-thirds of the earth's population living in Asia and the Middle East.

The West German Debate After the Brussels Decision

The fate of the NATO decision of 1979 was to be decided in West Germany, as in Great Britain, Italy, Belgium, and the Netherlands, by a vote of parliament. The battle of 1979 to 1983 in West Germany focused on the outcome of debates in the Bundestag. On over thirty-five occasions over this four-year period, the Bundestag engaged in long, thorough, often heated and acrimonious, and generally instructive debate. Following the NATO minister's meeting on December 12, 1979, the Bundestag debated the issue on December 14, 1979.[6] Hans-Dietrich Genscher, the West German foreign minister beginning in 1974 and leader of the Free Democratic party, presented the government's case. He argued that the public discussion that had already taken place was "not a weakness. It is a strength of our democracy," that would create broader support for a difficult decision.[7] He said that the open and public nature of Western decisions contributed to international security, in contrast to the nonpublic decisions leading to the SS-20 and Backfire bomber deployments. Genscher asserted that the foreign-policy consensus of all the major political parties—including, of course, the governing SPD—contributed to confidence in West German security policy.

Genscher referred to the NATO decision as the *Nachrüstungsbeschluss*, which translated literally means "decision to arm after." The offer of negotiations was intended to avoid a new arms race caused by what Genscher called the Soviet *Vorrüstung* [armament that comes before] and the Western response. Genscher said that the link of deployments and negotiations was in the spirit of the Harmel Report of 1967. Only a firm anchor in the Atlantic Alliance made arms control and détente possible. Genscher said that it was now up to the Soviet Union to prevent an arms race in medium-range weapons by entering negotiations to reduce its medium-range arsenal.

Manfred Wörner, the defense-policy spokesman for the Christian Democrats, vigorously supported both parts of the NATO decision. NATO had now confronted the "growing political and military threat by Soviet armament."[8] He supported the Brussels decision because it would stabilize peace in Europe by restoring a balance of forces and improve prospects for arms control. "Our place," he said, "is on the side of the Americans. That was the fundamental insight of Adenauer's policy. It was and remains the fundamental insight of the policy of the CDU/CSU. It is our standard in foreign and security policy."[9] Solidarity with the United States, Wörner continued, did not mean only military and economic cooperation. It meant above all, "political and moral help."

Wörner warned that the Soviet Union would try to undo the Brussels decision. "Every wavering in the Western camp will encourage the Soviets. . . . The more determined and united NATO remains, the more successful will the negotiations with the Soviet Union be. . . . He who now runs away from this decision must know that by so doing he hinders disarmament."[10] The Soviet leaders had to understand that they could not divide the West Germans. Wörner argued that history, including recent German history, indicated that when military power remained unbalanced, it would be used. "Weakness and adaptation" did not prevent war but led to it, as the history of the years preceding World War II indicated.

Alfons Pawelczyk, speaking for the SPD, repeated the essentials of the just-passed SPD Berlin resolution. Arms control was primary. An arms race must be avoided. New missiles should be made superfluous. The deployments were not automatic. West German membership in NATO was firm. There should be no Soviet superiority in medium-range nuclear weapons.[11] Jürgen Möllemann, speaking for the Free Democrats, stressed the link between equilibrium and the continuation of the "peace policy."[12] Imbalances made cooperation among equals impossible, as they led to intimidation by the strong and appeasement by the weak. Equilibrium, which the Soviet Union had upset with the SS-20s, had to be restored. In view of the Soviet SS-20 buildup, NATO needed new medium-range nuclear missiles to restore the credibility of a deterrent linked to a strategy of graduated response.

In January 1980, Helmut Schmidt had compared the world after the Soviet invasion of Afghanistan to Europe in the summer of 1914. In a debate in the Bundestag on foreign policy on January 17, 1980, Helmut Kohl disagreed. The Soviet Union, he said, bore responsibility for current tensions. Kohl criticized Chancellor Schmidt and the SPD for a reluctance to point the finger at Soviet aggression in Afghanistan and pressure on Poland and for its willingness to focus criticism instead on "cold warriors" in the West who urged a firm response.[13] Rather than worry about an American "overreaction," it was time to worry about encouraging Soviet aggression by failing to condemn it. The SPD peace rhetoric came from unwillingness to challenge the Soviet Union or face the implications for European security of Soviet actions in Southwest Asia.

In the same debate, Franz-Josef Strauss, leader of the Christian Social Union (CSU), said he would be most happy if, "without a sacrifice of the intellect," the conservative leadership could revise its somber view of the Soviet Union. But contrary to Brandt's and then Schmidt's assumptions, the military factor in Soviet policy had increased in importance while great Russian imperialism and world revolutionary aspirations continued to drive Soviet policy.[14] Strauss stressed that he was not opposed to détente, assuming it also meant more freedom for individuals in East Germany and Eastern Europe and an end to the order to shoot people trying to escape East Germany at the German-German border. Yet, in the current political climate, those who sought to recouple the issue of détente with that of freedom in East Germany and Eastern Europe were being attacked as cold warriors, enemies of détente and opponents of peace.

Détente must never be allowed to contribute to a political-psychological neutralization or to a dismantling of the will for defense. It was indeed one of the great mistakes of the governments of the 1970s, to let the consciousness . . . of the true character and true intentions of our détente partner to be numbed, put to sleep and broken in the West German public. This consciousness of the problem [*Problembewusstsein*] must be reconstructed.[15]

For Strauss, the "illusions of détente" now amounted to a "mountain of rubble." The conservative political task was to reconstruct a view of the Soviet Union that had been dismantled in the era of "socialist détente policy."

The "Kaiser Wilhelm Effect" and the Reinterpretations of 1980

Rudolf Augstein, publisher of *Der Spiegel*, was in the lead of the opposition to the NATO decision in the West German press, presenting his views in signed articles and in the focus, direction, and style of the flagship of West German weekly newsmagazines.[16] In the January 20, 1980, issue of *Der Spiegel*, he wrote of a "war in sight."[17] "Overnight, what has up to now appeared to be only an abstract possibility, namely the third, the largest, the last world war, the final Armageddon, has taken on concrete features. . . . Fatalism is spreading as it did before 1914."[18] Just as Europe in 1914 "slithered" into the Great War, so the world in 1980 faced a similar slide into catastrophe. Commenting on the invasion of Afghanistan, Augstein referred to "the Kaiser Wilhelm effect: because they feel encircled, they create new facts that make their encirclement perfect. . . . We must see the possibility that the Soviets may misunderstand NATO's objectively representable (*objektive vertretbaren*) missile decision in the context of 'encirclement' by Western Europe and China, and its mistaken policies toward Japan and in Europe."[19] A Western hard line and arms buildup would only accentuate the weakness of the Soviet economy, push the Soviets into a corner, and—because of the Kaiser Wilhelm effect—make war more likely.[20]

Following the Soviet invasion of Afghanistan, Wolf Perdelwitz, a senior editor at *Stern*, published a book entitled "Do the Russians Want War?"[21] His answer was "no." The Soviet Union, he explained, faced a "new holy-unholy alliance" between Islamic rebels and the CIA, an alliance which "must frighten" them.[22] He also noted the reasons why the Soviet Union had reason to be frightened by the NATO two-track decision of 1979. He argued that geography favored the United States over the Soviet Union because American territory could be reached from the Soviet Union only by strategic weapons, while the Soviet Union could be reached by the medium-range weapons of the United States in Western Europe. The medium-range missiles of the Soviet Union directed at Western Europe could not reach the United States. Because of this geographical asymmetry, the Soviet Union "must regard" NATO's offer of negotiations as an "artful attempt to push it into measures of unilateral disarmament."

Why, he asked, should the Soviet Union accept American missiles in Western Europe when the United States wouldn't accept Soviet missiles in Cuba?[23] The deployment of ever more accurate weapons suitable for a counterforce first strike threatened to shatter the balance of terror completely in the 1980s. A "mathematical formula" used in the SALT negotiations predicted that the

> capacity of the United States to launch a nuclear decapitation strike against the USSR will climb in the coming years and will reach its high point in 1985, when it will be twenty times as high as in 1980. This capacity will also increase for the Soviet Union, however with a five year delay behind the United States. During these years there will be a growing danger of war, unless détente is really once again taken up. . . . [24]

> In view of all these facts, NATO'S *Nachrüstung* decision *which came into being due to American pressure actually has only one plausible reason: The United States wants to remain outside a possible nuclear war between the Warsaw Pact and NATO. . . .* With the *Nachrüstung* decision NATO introduces an intermediate step in the ladder of escalation. Before the Americans fire their intercontinental missiles, they will start their "euro-strategic" weapons. For Europe, the result is the same. The Warsaw Pact and the European part of NATO are subsequently reduced to rubble. But the USA would have some chance to stay out of this inferno—then from a great distance emerge as the only superpower on earth.[25] (emphasis added)

This was the fundamental reinterpretation of NATO's 1979 decision. Rather than being the result of West German concerns, it was the product of American pressure. Rather than couple the United States to Western Europe more firmly, it was intended to serve American interests in staying out of a nuclear war in Europe and to enhance American capability to wage a nuclear war limited to Europe and the Soviet Union.

The reinterpretation of the NATO decision began to appear in signed statements of intellectuals that appeared soon after it was taken. On January

17, 1980, Gert Bastian, a general in the Bundeswehr, was relieved of his command by Defense Minister Hans Apel for his public criticisms of the NATO decision.[26] In February 1980, the "Berlin Initiative for Peace, International Settlement, and Security" announced its formation to support the continuation of peace policies in view of the "dangerous developments of recent weeks and months."[27] The signers included peace researcher Ulrich Albrecht, from the Free University of Berlin, as well as leading figures of the Protestant intellectual left in Berlin—Heinrich Albertz, Helmut Gollwitzer, Ingeborg Drewitz, and Kurt Scharf. They appealed to the West German government to do everything it could "to hinder stationing of atomic medium range missiles on German soil" and to enter negotiations with the Soviet Union to reduce existing nuclear weapons in Europe. The deployments would, they wrote, cause a new arms race and endanger the population of Central Europe. They did not mention the Soviet SS-20s as a source of new tensions.[28]

Writers such as Günter Grass were active in the antimissile campaign. On April 17, 1980, he signed an open letter to Chancellor Schmidt with three other West German writers—Thomas Brasch, Sarah Kirsch, and Peter Schneider.[29] In a situation "in which war could no longer be excluded," they appealed to Schmidt to take note of the special German responsibility for peace, given that Germany had twice laid waste to the European continent in war. "Do not let yourself be drawn into a policy of the American government—that at the latest since Vietnam, has lost every right to moral appeals—which could have as its consequence the destruction of all life on this planet." No one, the letter continued, threatened "us." Loyalty to the alliance had its limit in the face of willful threats to peace. Instead of boycotts and sanctions against the Soviet Union after the invasion of Afghanistan, the signers urged Germans to "really learn from their history, and for the first time save the peace, instead of, for the third and probably last time, allow it to be bombed."[30] What lessons West Germans should learn from German history was a most contentious question posed during the euromissile dispute.

Soviet public diplomacy directed at Western Europe and West Germany stressed that deployment in West Germany of nuclear weapons able to strike the Soviet Union would make the Federal Republic a major target of a Soviet nuclear counterattack.[31] But on July 7, 1980 at the end of a three-day visit to Moscow by Chancellor Schmidt, Leonid Brezhnev announced his willingness to enter negotiations if such talks included discussion of "forward-based systems," that is, American nuclear-capable aircraft in Western Europe, without a prior renunciation of the 1979 decision.[32] NATO rejected this precondition. In August 1980, the Carter administration published Presidential Directive 59. "PD 59" repeated long-standing concerns about NATO's ability to introduce selectivity and limitations into its nuclear strategy. It was not a shift to a doctrine of "first strike" or of "winning" a nuclear war, but the state of global tension lent weight to reinterpretations that linked the NATO double decision to a new American nuclear strategy in Europe that had shifted "from deterrence to war-fighting."

In October 1980, after a bitter campaign in which Helmut Schmidt ran as the peace candidate, the Schmidt-Genscher coalition handily defeated Franz-Josef Strauss, the standard-bearer of the CDU/CSU. The election was a sign of Schmidt's popularity and obscured the extent to which the West German political establishment was moving away from the policies of Brandt and Bahr. In the American elections of November 1980, Ronald Reagan was elected president, committed among other things to implement the Brussels decision initiated during the Carter administration. From mid-October to mid-November, preliminary discussions between the United States and the Soviet Union took place in Geneva. The disagreement was total. The Soviets insisted on including British and French nuclear forces in the discussions, while the United States insisted on limiting talks to American and Soviet weapons.

On November 15–16, 1980, a thousand people gathered in Kreffeld, West Germany, to support the "Kreffeld Appeal."[33] Signers included Gert Bastian, Petra Kelly, a leader of the new Green party, and the Protestant theologian Martin Niemöller. They proclaimed that "atomic death threatens us all" and that the NATO decision had been a "fateful mistake."[34] The statement criticized the United States for not ratifying SALT II and the delay in initiation of arms control talks about weapons in Europe. It spoke of a "suicidal arms race" and of the "apparent limitability of a nuclear war" that would expose Europeans to "intolerable risks." It called on the West German government to reverse its decision to deploy Pershing II and cruise missiles. West Germany should not be suspected of leading a nuclear arms race that would endanger Europe. The signers called for public discussion of "alternative security policy." "Women and men" through "untiring and growing pressure of public opinion" should bring about a security policy that "did not allow Central Europe to become a nuclear weapons platform for the USA."[35] The statement did not mention the SS-20s.

On December 10, 1980, the *JUSOS* issued a "Bielefeld Statement." The double decision was a "fateful mistake." The negotiations Schmidt had promised had not taken place. Without negotiations, a new arms race would occur, and West Germans would have their future "handed over to an American decision, that includes the notion that a nuclear war limited to Europe" could be fought.[36] Instead, the *JUSOS* urged a return to détente and renunciation of the NATO two-track decision.

> We do not want to abandon Social Democratic détente policy only because the USA wants to return to global confrontation, and knows no way other than building the Federal Republic up into a forward based missile base against the USSR. . . . We did not lead the fight and win against [Franz Josef] Strauss so the Social Democratic West German government could fall into the wake of the policies of a Ronald Reagan.[37]

The Bielefeld Statement did not refer to the SS-20s either. At the end of 1980, NATO estimated that the Soviet Union had deployed about 200 SS-20s with about 600 warheads.

In 1981, Peter Bender, an associate of Brandt and Bahr and an early advocate of détente, published *Das Ende der Ideologischen Zeitalters* [The end of the ideological era].[38] Bender reversed the meaning of "the end of ideology" from what it had meant when Daniel Bell used it to refer to the push toward a democratic center in the 1950s.[39] For Bender in 1981, the end of ideology meant an end to the "ideology of the cold war." Détente, he wrote, brought a mutual relaxation of tensions and decline of ideology (*Entideologisierung*). The conflicts between the alliances in Europe were becoming normal. Communists no longer spoke of their world revolutionary mission, while anticommunism in the West was no longer necessary, other than for domestic purposes.[40] What had made the division of Europe so difficult was not the contrast between dictatorship and democracy or the political division of two zones of influence of the great powers. It was the ideological division that had made Europeans enemies to one another. "With emancipation from the communities of faith, the old world opened a new chapter." Consciousness of "a European civilization" could re-emerge. The "East-West era" had come to an end. Europe's states and peoples had to redefine their interests and relations to one another.[41]

Bender wrote that both the United States and the Soviet Union had a diminished attractiveness for Western Europe. After Vietnam and the economic difficulties of the 1970s, European skepticism about the American model had grown. The Soviet Union repelled Europeans because of its economic backwardness, while the United States functioned well but seemed a threat to the soul. The Europeans were seeking a third way as Europeans. But the Soviets, in Bender's account, fit much more easily into the "Europeanization of Europe" than the United States. The United States had neglected Eastern Europe while the Soviets did not. "There cannot be an American interest in the fate of Europe as a whole. Such a Russian interest must exist."[42] Implicitly then, an American or West European interest in the political distinctions between democracy and dictatorship would be, in Bender's view, a return to an old ideological era. Bender wrote that "Europe's" threat perception had changed. The real threat to European and West German security was not the policy of the Soviet Union but "great power rivalry."[43] When the United States engaged in its anticommunist fixation, Europeans would have to take some distance from it in the interests of their own security. He rejected the NATO decision of 1979 because it would turn Western Europe into a base for American missiles able to strike the other great power.[44] Europeans had to leave the arms race or become satellites in a conflict that was not longer their own.

Eastern Europe, he argued, could not be emancipated unless Western Europe first emancipated itself from the United States. When Western Europe was no longer a base for American weapons and radio senders, and when human rights were no longer used as a weapon, then the Soviets could permit democracy to expand to their own borders.[45] Decoupling America from Western Europe would loosen the Soviet control over Eastern Europe. West European security would be enhanced by more distance from American policy.

Another important contribution to the emergent reinterpretation of the NATO decision came from Wilhelm Bittorf, the security correspondent for *Der Spiegel*. In February 1981, he published "Euroshima, my future . . . on the strategy of madness."[46] He argued that because NATO had sufficient nuclear weaponry to deliver an effective second strike against the Soviet Union, the Pershing II and cruise missiles "have nonsensical sense (*widersinnigen Sinn*) only as first strike weapons." He referred Mechtersheimer's warnings of "europeanization of nuclear war . . . (which would) . . . allow Ronald Reagan to operate with an offensive understanding of nuclear deterrence because American territory itself would no longer be immediately and automatically endangered by a nuclear exchange in Europe." Implementation of such a strategy meant that the West Germans, just like the residents of Hiroshima in August 1945, would suffer. Hence, he concluded, the new strategy should be called "euroshima."[47] Bittorf did not ask why, if the United States wanted to limit a nuclear war to Europe, it would introduce weapons that could strike the Soviet Union, which had publicly stated that it would retaliate against the United States if attacked by American weapons in Western Europe.

At the 26th party congress of the Communist party of the Soviet Union on February 23, 1981, Brezhnev proposed a moratorium on any new deployments of medium-range nuclear weapons in Europe as long as arms control negotiations were taking place. The following day, Egon Bahr suggested reconsideration of the NATO two-track decision in light of the failure of the American Senate to ratify SALT II. On February 25, Genscher rejected Brezhnev's moratorium proposal. In talks with American officials, Genscher stressed that West Germany was a firm, not a "yes-but" ally in regard to both shared beliefs and strategic conceptions.[48] Both Genscher and Chancellor Schmidt stressed that deployments or the credible threat of deployments were essential preconditions for the success of negotiations.[49] Schmidt continued to face opposition in his own party's executive committee, which in late March 1981 passed a resolution rejecting a nuclear freeze but favoring Brezhnev's proposal for a moratorium.[50] In April 1981, in an essay in the weekly *Vorwärts*, Bahr supported the Soviet proposal to include British and French missiles in the Geneva INF talks.[51] In so doing, at an early stage in the dispute, Bahr adopted a key element of the Soviet negotiating position.

In the same month, Erhard Eppler, then a member of the SPD executive committee with strong ties to the Protestant Church and ecological left, published *Wege aus der Gefahr* [Paths Out of Danger].[52] *Wege aus der Gefahr* was a response to Carl von Weizsäcker's *Wege in der Gefahr* [Paths Into Danger]. In contrast to von Weizsäcker's patrician skepticism about redemptive solutions, Eppler saw the moment of greatest danger as one which pointed to political salvation. Eppler criticized the 1979 NATO decision as a product of the *Ideologie der Sachzwang,* or "ideology of the force of things." Eppler expressed a suspicion of technology, "instrumental reason" or "technocratic rule," that had become a part of the political language of West German leftism since the sixties.

For Eppler, arms and the arms race were also examples of *Sachzwang* dominated by an *Expertokratie* or "caste of experts." In no other field did the *Expertokratie* have such an unbroken hold as in armament and arms control. It spoke a "secret language" that "followed the logic of computers." On the one hand, there was a "jungle" of terms—first and second strike, missile accuracies and warning times—while on the other, "on the margins of society,"—among peace researchers—a "qualified and . . . controversial" discussion of war and peace was taking place.[53] In Eppler's view, government officials were trying to avoid or restrict public discussion of defense questions. His task was to challenge this technocratic elite and to broaden public discussion.[54] In so doing, he turned to peace research literature. His targets were "the logic of thinking about parity and worst case thinking," the "mutual arms dynamic process" that "proceeded ad infinitum" and was driven by *Feindbilder.*[55] His analysis was devoid of proper nouns and historical actors. In place of the United States and the Soviet

Union there was "one side," "the other side," and "the two superpowers." This neglect of the subjectivity of identifiable nation-states or political leaders was particularly striking given the vehemence with which Eppler attacked *Sachzwang* and technocratic thinking.

Eppler described the two-track decision as an example of *Sachzwang* thinking. He repeated the case against it made by Bastian, Lutz, Mechtersheimer, and von Weizsäcker. Eppler argued that NATO had more than sufficient nuclear retaliatory capacity without new land-based missiles, that the expansion of already huge nuclear arsenals made no sense, and that more weapons of greater accuracy brought less security and raised the risk of war. New developments in technology and the evolution of American nuclear strategy—not Soviet policy—were raising the danger of a "Europeanization of nuclear war." Just as more growth did not promise a better life, so more armament did not promise more security. Only when people understood that "the risk of world armament was greater than the risk of disarmament" and when no one believed that more arms would lead to disarmament, when politicians were no longer able to stifle peace initiatives with recourse to arguments about equilibrium, then and only then would "peace policy" have a chance to overcome the *Ideologie der Sachzwang*.[56]

In a manner similar to Augstein's, Eppler saw a beleaguered Soviet Union. In 1981, Moscow worried about how the domination of the Communist party in Poland could be "stabilized." Its African adventures brought uncertain returns. China had begun to modernize its armed forces, as had Japan. The Communist parties of Western Europe had largely turned away from Soviet policy. The United States had embarked on a huge armament program. At home there was economic stagnation. The only consolation for Moscow was its military power. Therefore, he urged the West to take Moscow's *Angst* into account in order not to foster a Soviet "military overreaction."[57] One way to reduce Moscow's fears would be to adopt the Ahfeldt proposals for a defensive defense. "Those who do not threaten anyone are able, with an indisputable moral and political weight, to urge disarmament on others, and can more easily win and mobilize world public opinion."[58]

On May 17, 1981, faced with a growing revolt in his own party against the NATO decision, Chancellor Schmidt threatened to resign if the SPD turned against the 1979 decision.[59] Speaking to SPD delegates, Schmidt said:

He who neglects the balance of forces is an illusionist who endangers the peace. . . . With all of my force, I will work against a policy of inferiority and against a policy of Western superiority. . . . You must

finally stop acting as if the Americans were our enemies and the
Russians our friends. . . . There is no reason to believe that we would
be better off under the "protection" of a communist dictatorship than
we are at present. . . . Do you believe that the Sermon on the Mount
in the Bible is designed to correct the policy of the Soviet Union?[60]

Schmidt, perhaps distinguishing himself from the tone of the early Reagan
administration, cautioned against Western superiority, but in the main he
focused attention on the military imbalance caused by Soviet armament.
Willy Brandt focused his efforts on dialogue with Moscow and to saving
détente, while in interviews and public statements, Egon Bahr expressed
doubts that the United States wanted to negotiate seriously over the missiles. In early May, the Social Democrats of Baden-Württemberg, led by
Eppler, rejected policies aiming at "superior military strength" including
the use of "German territory for new eurostrategic weapons."[61] At the
end of May, Genscher, faced with a loss of support for the NATO decision
in the FDP, also threatened to resign as foreign minister and leader of the
party if the party voted in favor of a plan for sea-basing rather than land-
basing of missiles.[62] Increasingly, Schmidt's energy's were devoted to the
challenge of the left wing of the party.[63] Sustaining domestic support would
preoccupy an increasing amount of Schmidt's and, to a lesser extent,
Genscher's time and energy.

On May 26, 1981, Schmidt and Genscher gained support for a Bundestag resolution supporting "both parts"—negotiations and deployments—of
the NATO decision by a vote of 254 to 234.[64] Six SPD members voted
no, six withheld their votes, and 228 members of the conservative opposition voted no.[65] But the conservative "no" was a vote for an even stronger
stance. For Genscher, the resolution represented a commitment to proceed
with both parts of the NATO decision. For Brandt and Bahr, it meant
reserving judgment until the final moment.[66] Helmut Kohl was not convinced that passage of the resolution meant that Schmidt had sufficient
support in his own party to implement the decision.[67]

Jürgen Möllemann, in taking issue with Brandt's suggestion that armament was a "self-steering process," focused on the political differences between the alliances. Western societies were open. Policies could be changed
by criticism, elections, demonstrations, arguments, and parliamentary debate. In the alliance, policy was a result of discussion. But, Möllemann
continued, on the other side was a system with a closed party apparatus,
determination of goals from above, without demonstrations, meetings, or
"any possibility of an individual citizen . . . to protest against Afghanistan
or the SS-20." In the Warsaw Pact, the Soviet Union made decisions

largely on its own.[68] The debate of May 26, 1981, made clear that the
strongest opposition to the missile decision was coming from within the
SPD.

West German intellectual and political figures on the left continued to
mobilize against the NATO decision in more signed statements in late
spring 1981. On June 12, 1981, some of the leading figures of the left
wing in the SPD, Erhard Eppler, Oskar Lafontaine, the mayor of Saarbrücken and a rising star in the national party, and Willi Piecyk, the chairman of the *JUSOS*, met in Bonn with leading peace researchers and professors of political science including Dieter Lutz and Dieter Senghaas. On June
13, the group issued a "Statement of the Gustav-Heinemann Initiative."[69]
The statement asserted that since the beginning of the 1980s, as a result
of technological advances in weapons that had led strategists and political
leaders to conclude nuclear wars could be limited, fought, and won, the
danger of war had grown. These trends underscored the "fragility of the
deterrence system" and the "danger of the destruction of the Federal Republic" in crisis situations. The signers rejected the concept of equilibrium
for "a principle of stability through minimal deterrence." "No region of the
world" was "more threatened by a limited nuclear war than Europe." The
danger of such a war would be increased by the NATO decision of December 12, 1979, as would the prospect of a preventive strike against West
Germany by the Soviet Union. Such considerations made "clear the
security-political contradictions between the USA and Europe. Land based
medium range missiles on German soil are militarily, politically and morally
indefensible. We call on the West German government to use its influence
to overcome and retract the so-called *Nachrüstung* decision of December
12, 1979."[70]

The signers called on the Soviet Union "not to modernize its medium
range missiles beyond the numerical level of the already existing warheads
on the SS-4 and SS-5 [medium-range missiles,]." They wanted American
Trident submarines, sea- and air-based cruise missiles, nuclear battlefield
weapons, and British and French nuclear modernizations to be included in
any negotiations. They called on the West German government to foster
a public discussion with the "peace movement" over alternative security
policies, including defensive defense and nuclear-free zones.

The statement of the Gustav-Heinemann Initiative legitimated deployments of SS-20s not greater in number than the existing number of SS-4
and SS-5 warheads, which in June 1981 was between 250 and 350. The
signers thereby declared themselves willing to accept, as a suitable outcome,
a balance of between 250 and 350 SS-20s and no new Western deployments. They asserted that the NATO decision was linked to a "limited

nuclear war in Europe" and that West Germany was the primary victim of this decision. Here again, the intellectual opposition reinterpreted what officials and elected political leaders intended to be a decision to "couple" Western Europe more closely to the United States as just the reverse, that is, as an American effort to limit nuclear war to Europe.

On May 24, 1981, Rudolf Augstein escalated his criticism of the NATO decision in a signed essay in *Der Spiegel.*[71] He rejected the idea that the two-track decision came from superior wisdom or expertise. It was a "monstrosity" typical of the "abstruse nonsense" that often passed for military strategy.[72] There were no experts regarding nuclear weapons. "It concerns us all and we are all equally ignorant. No one should tell us, at any rate, that Reagan, Haig, Thatcher and Weinberger know more than any one of us."[73] Then, he turned around and said that, yes, there were experts among whom there "was unanimity . . . that *Nachrüstung* is superfluous from a military-technical viewpoint. Not a single expert would deny face to face that the Americans could still respond to the Russian threat of SS-20s directed at Western Europe in a crisis even without *Nachrüstung.*"[74]

If the decision made no military-technical sense and if Helmut Schmidt himself knew this, what meaning and purpose could it really have? "It serves," Augstein wrote, "to exert political-psychological pressure on the Federal Republic. Thus *Nachrüstung* aims not so much at the Soviets as against us [West Germans]."[75] The Americans were suspicious that the West Germans would decouple from the United States in response to Soviet pressure, "a suspicion that for the longest time we know has . . . no grounds at all." The Europeans, on the other hand, fear—"and the USA has given them very good grounds for this fear"—that in the event of war the United States "would like to fight a proxy war (*Stellvertreter-Krieg*) on European soil that would spare their own territory." Just as American troops stationed in Europe were hostages whose presence insured American involvement in any European war,

> so we must recognize that the *Nachrüstung* decision does not in the first place serve to fill a regional gap. Rather, it has a hostage function. It is supposed to keep the core of the European alliance, the Federal Republic, tied to the stake. To do that requires nuclear potential on West German soil that literally will stick the Soviets in the eye so that in the event of a crisis they will know very well where they should direct a first strike. . . . The *Nachrüstung* on the territory of the Federal Republic is a political-psychological preventive measure.[76]

The result, Augstein continued, was a "Europeanization" of nuclear war. Augstein referred to Helmut Schmidt as the source of "panic" by exaggerating fears of Soviet influence over Western Europe. Augstein accused Schmidt of acting like a "demagogue," an "absolute autocrat," and (worst of all?) a "functionalist." With his 1977 London speech, Schmidt had given the Americans the pretext they wanted to develop an option that both recoupled West Germany to the West and enhanced their own ability to stay out of a European war. Throughout the dispute, Augstein developed the theme of a West Germany victimized by its alleged protector with the aid and support of its own leadership.

Alois Mertes, as foreign policy spokesman for the CDU in the Bundestag, led the criticism of Soviet diplomacy in Western Europe and of West German domestic opposition to the NATO decision. Throughout, he analyzed domestic opposition in light of how it affected Soviet diplomacy and did so with civility and, at times, humor. In late June 1981, Mertes referred to Leonid Brezhnev's "chutzpah" in making "peace appeals" and moratorium proposals to the West in view of the Soviet Union's "massive overarmament," threats against Poland, war in Afghanistan, and stubbornness in the Geneva talks. The Soviet peace offensive was a diversion, "a large scale campaign of disinformation and intimidation which is intended to create fear in foreign policy, and pressure in domestic politics in the West by building Soviet influence on the formation of opinion in parliaments and the public."[77] Its purpose was to divert attention from their SS-20 buildup, and to use Western public opinion to undermine the NATO decision. The West German government, he urged, should confront the Soviet Union with its own campaign of information and refuse to give in to fears fanned by the Soviet peace campaign. Throughout the euromissile battle, Mertes returned to the theme of the strategic importance of Western public opinion in view of the confrontation of dictatorship and democracy in Europe.

An important document of the reinterpretation of the two-track decision was Wilhelm Bittorf's "Shooting Gallery of the Superpowers," a three-part series published in Der Spiegel July 1981.[78] Bittorf rejected the contention that NATO needed new missiles. Nuclear missiles on American submarines and the British and French nuclear forces were an adequate deterrent.[79] This deterrent had disappeared in Western assessments of the balance of forces "through crude manipulation which has remained just as hidden to the West German public as only some kind of statistical disappearance in the Soviet press is hidden to the population of the Soviet Union."[80] If one distinctive contribution to the political culture of the left from peace research was the abstract style, Augstein and Bittorf's distinctive addition was a cynical realism. Cynical realists blurred or abolished moral, political, and institutional differences between the United States, the Western democracies, and the Soviet Union. Hence Bittorf equated press manip-

ulation by NATO governments with the secrecy of the Soviet Union—
before *glasnost* and *perestroika*—despite the absence of a free press or even
reliable public figures on the Soviet defense budget. This was a period of
which the abolition of fine distinctions, and many not-so-fine distinctions,
was thought in some circles to be a mark of a sophisticated and disillusioned
piercing of ideologically grounded illusions.

For Bittorf, the real purpose was decoupling. Land-based rather than sea-
based missiles made it more likely that war would be limited to Europe
rather than escalating to involve the United States directly. "Only such
weapons were suitable for placing a barrier in the face of the dangers of
escalation for America, for blocking this danger and for shifting it to Europe."[81] He did not take seriously Soviet statements that attacks on the
Soviet Union coming from Western Europe would lead to retaliation
against the United States.[82] Therefore, Europe would be the "shooting
gallery of the superpowers," both of whom would remain sanctuaries.[83]

Another key word in Bittorf's reinterpretation was "horizontal escalation." American officials had spoken of it primarily in reference to use of
naval forces to deliver counterattacks in the event of a Soviet offensive in
a place where the United States was vulnerable, i.e., the Persian Gulf.
Bittorf linked horizontal escalation to the euromissiles. He argued that in
the event of a crisis in the Middle East where the United States was not
strong militarily, the United States would be able to threaten the Soviet
Union from Western Europe, where it would be strong. "It is in this
connection that the *Nachrüstung* must be seen." The new missiles would
offer a "flanking threat potential." The Pershing II would be stationed only
in West Germany, thus coupling the security of West Germany to the
"chaotic Middle East," among other crisis regions in the world. In the
event of superpower tensions, "the people of the Federal Republic will
impotently stand in the line of fire." To regard this as part of a West
German security policy was "mere self-deception."[84]

In 1970, West German writers on the left formed a national association,
the *Verbands deutscher Schriftsteller* (*VDS*). In August 1981, the chairman of
the *VDS*, Bernt Engelmann, organized an "appeal of European writers,"
signed, he said, by over 3,000 writers. The signers appealed "beyond the
borders" of all states and societies to governments to stop the arms race,
opposed "the criminal idea that a limited nuclear war can be fought," and
announced their determination to "act together so that Europe will not
become the atomic battlefield of a new and then final world war." "Nothing," they said, was "more important than the preservation of peace!"[85]
The idea that "nothing" was more important than the preservation of

peace was criticized by those in Western and Eastern Europe who believed that peace and freedom ought not be separated from one another.

Helmut Schmidt, for one, sought to hold in balance the values of peace and freedom. At a 1981 congress on "Kant in Our Time," he appealed to Kant's critique of judgment and to Max Weber's analysis of ethics of responsibility to underscore the need to examine the consequences of political actions.[86] He criticized what he called the unfortunate legacies of German idealism in which one value, such as peace, was made absolute and the consequences of pursuing that value for other, no less important values, such as freedom, were neglected. This was, he suggested, a recent variant of an old German idealism and lack of aptitude for politics.

But opposition within the SPD to Schmidt's policies was quite evident at a "peace forum" of leading figures of the party and prominent journalists and intellectuals held in Bonn in August 1981.[87] Egon Bahr presented ten "theses" on peace and disarmament, in which he developed the idea of "common security."[88] Security could "no longer" be attained militarily but "only politically, not against one another, but only with one another" for "we would all be united in catastrophe."

> Both alliance systems, NATO and the Warsaw Pact, without going into the differences in economic systems and political convictions which they represent, have in common the function of guaranteeing security in the face of one another. They are a peace-securing, stabilizing factor for Europe. Whoever wants to break a stone on this system endangers stability. Decoupling would endanger peace, whether it is the USA from Europe, the Federal Republic from NATO or Poland from the Soviet Union. Both alliances must develop into instruments that can together organize the common interest in security.[89]

Bahr did not say that there were no differences between the economic and political systems and convictions of the countries of the two alliances. But neither did he point out what those differences were. Instead, he focused on the "common . . . function" of the two alliances and equated West Germany's place in NATO—the result of a voluntary decision and electoral choices—to that of Poland in the Warsaw Pact—the outcome of military occupation. A Polish exit from the Warsaw Pact would endanger peace in Europe, but Solidarity was not talking then about leaving the Warsaw Pact but about freedom and democracy in Poland. Bahr's reference to the Warsaw Pact as a "peace securing factor" again manifested the separation of peace from freedom that upset those who recalled his claims that détente would bring about change in Eastern Europe. Bahr's notion of "common security" led his critics, aware of his formal support of NATO, to describe him as a neutralist in moral terms. From the perspective of East Europeans seeking political freedom and democracy, Bahr was in the Metternichian tradition of *Realpolitik,* in which peace was synonymous with the interest of the larger powers, in this case, West Germany and the Soviet Union, at the price of the freedom and self-determination of Eastern Europe.

Bahr argued that West German membership in NATO and Social Democratic support for the 1979 NATO decision were both levers that were to be used to insure that the United States negotiate seriously over the euromissiles. "If we would drop our support [for the NATO decision], the USA would be free to cease negotiating seriously," thus destroying the prospects for arms control.[90] Pressure could be exerted only as long as West Germany remained in NATO and supported the Brussels decision. This was a major difference between the SPD, the peace movement, and the emergent Greens. Bahr understood that because the Greens never supported the NATO decision, they were unable to threaten the United States with loss of such support, as the Social Democrats could. NATO membership was a precondition for influencing American policy.

Bahr did call the SS–20 buildup "unacceptable" and damaging to "détente and common security" and did support the Brussels decision. He understood the goal of negotiations as making new American deployments superfluous "and if that was not possible [to have deployments] at the lowest possible level."[91] A "zero option" would be the optimal outcome of negotiations, one including all missiles and planes affecting Europe not considered by SALT II. In reference to what was to become one of the central issues of the INF talks, Bahr said that "the medium range systems of France and Great Britain, which are not the subject of the negotiations, must be considered in determination of the [the meaning of] equilibrium."[92] He again supported including NATO aircraft and British and French missiles in the INF talks in Geneva. Before the American-Soviet negotiations began in the fall of 1981, Bahr had adopted elements of the Soviet negotiating proposals.[93]

In place of "ideological" distinctions between liberal democracies and communist dictatorships, Bahr stressed the distinction between "nonnuclear states" and "nuclear states." Nonnuclear states, such as West Germany, had a right of "codetermination" (*Mitbestimmung*) with nuclear states in making decisions about nuclear weapons. In one sense, because the NATO decision required support from democratically elected governments, including the West German government, Bahr's distinction was superfluous. No one could force weapons on the West Germans if their elected government did not want them. But the distinction highlighted West Germany's nonnuclear status and opened the door further to nationalistic themes.

The other main speaker at the forum was Anton-Andreas Guha, the defense correspondent for the *Frankfurter Rundschau*. Guha had described the NATO decision as a preparation for "Europe's Holocaust" in a book also published in 1981.[94] In Bonn, he summarized his indictment. Guha said that no military defense of West Germany was possible because its implementation would lead to the "annihilation of peoples who are supposed to be protected" and was therefore "irrational and unsupportable." West Germany security policy, however, contained "the risk of annihilation of the people (*Völkervernichtung*)."[95] His choice of the words *Holocaust* and *Vernichtung*, meaning "annihilation," evoked the death factories of the Third Reich. The link between Nazism and nuclear deterrence and German victimization appeared again.[96]

Guha presented an increasingly familiar indictment. While "tactical nuclear war limited to Europe" was a plausible and conceivable option "for both superpowers, the USA as well as the Soviet Union," it was inconceivable that an American president would risk an attack on the United States by ordering a first use of nuclear weapons against the Soviet Union.[97] NATO's threats of escalation against the Soviet Union to the level of "strategic Holocaust" were threats to commit suicide and thus not credible.[98] The United States, he said, was pursuing a doctrine that assumed that nuclear war with the Soviet Union was unavoidable, limitable to Europe, and thus winnable.

> Thus the vital security interests of the respective allies in NATO and the Warsaw Pact are not identical with the security interests of the respective leading powers. Rather, they are identical with the security interests of the non-nuclear powers in NATO and the Warsaw Pact.[99]

Included among "the respective allies" of both alliances were East and West Germany. West Germany, East Germany, and other "nonnuclear powers in NATO and the Warsaw Pact" had greater security interests in common than West Germany did with the United States.[100] The logical conclusion was that neutralism was the best security policy for the nonnuclear states of Central Europe.

The balance of the discussion arrayed two defenders of the NATO decision, Hans Apel, the West German defense minister, and Karl Kaiser, director of the German Society for Foreign Policy in Bonn, against critics Rudolf Bahro, Gert Bastian, Petra Kelly, Oskar Lafontaine, Josef Leinen,

Dieter Lutz, Alfred Mechtersheimer, and Willy Piecyk. Kaiser restated fundamentals of deterrence and its paradoxes. In order to deter war, one had to have the capability to fight it. He asked what alternative the critics had to offer. The two-track decision was an effort to establish that rules applied to all, including the Soviet Union. No one else had been able to offer any other way to get the Soviet Union to come to the negotiating table and to reduce its own weapons other than by threatening new deployments. How else, he asked, could one restore equilibrium in Europe?[101]

Hans Apel supported debate and criticism in free, democratic states, but he wished "to see all of us orient our criticism a bit more in Moscow's direction. Why has this unbelievable military machine been constructed? Why the tanks, missiles, naval forces, and aircraft? Why?"[102] Apel rejected the arguments of many participants that a "regionalization" of nuclear war was being proposed. He reminded them that "eurostrategic" components of NATO strategy had "always" existed and that, in this sense, the Pershing II and cruise missiles were "qualitatively not new." They were proposed to offer a "corresponding counter-threat to the SS-20."[103]

Assertions about nuclear war limited to Europe rested on imputation rather than on reference to government statements or documents, on a deep mistrust of the United States, a sense of West German victimization, and a belief that "real" motives were hidden and sinister. But there was nothing in the form of government documents or public statements to confirm that the United States supported deployments in order to facilitate the waging and winning of nuclear war limited to Europe. In interviews with the author, all of the members of Helmut Schmidt's cabinet and officials in the Foreign and Defense Ministries who had worked on the Brussels decision rejected as false the suggestion that the real purpose of the NATO deployments was to implement such a policy and strategy.[104]

The intellectual and political counteroffensive in favor of the NATO decision was only beginning in summer 1981. One of its leaders was Heiner Geissler, the general secretary of the Christian Democratic Union. He rejected the term "peace movement." He referred to the peace movement as "an *Angst* movement" that weakened the Western alliance and, intentionally or not, served the interests of the Soviet Union. Geissler criticized Bahr's view that "common security" was provided by both NATO and the Warsaw Pact as an "erroneous" and misleading assessment of the role of the two alliances in the postwar era.[105] Chancellor Schmidt, in an August 30, 1981, television interview, criticized the peace movement for its one-sided attacks against NATO and the policies of the West German government. The absence of any criticism of the Soviet Union from the peace movement would, he said, be pleasing to the Soviet leadership.[106] Alois Mertes said that the left failed to take the intentions of the Soviet Union seriously enough.[107] The SPD, he said, had closed its eyes to Soviet strategy in Western Europe.[108]

In the fall of 1981, the first high-level American official experienced firsthand the impact of the antimissile campaign. On September 13, 1981, Secretary of State Alexander Haig visited West Berlin. Some 30,000 to 40,000 demonstrators gathered to protest the NATO decision, and about 1,000 fought with police into the night. Hundreds were arrested, and hundreds more were injured, among them fifty policemen.[109] During Haig's visit to Bonn, Chancellor Schmidt and Foreign Minister Genscher urged the United States to adopt a "zero option" as the goal of the INF negotiations.[110] Schmidt emphasized that domestic political pressures from his own left wing made a publicly announced zero option necessary to retain the support of his party for the decision.

In September of 1981, Karsten Voigt, foreign-policy speaker of the SPD in the Bundestag, published *Wege zur Abrüstung* [Paths to Disarmament].[111] Voigt's central point was that technological development was creating weapons systems that destabilized the military balance faster than politicians and diplomats were able to control arms through negotiations.[112] "Armament cannot be seen only as the consequence of mistrust and conflicts, but also as a cause. Armament itself has become a driving force of armament."[113] He rejected assertions that the new NATO weapons were designed as first-strike weapons and argued that new nuclear capabilities were necessary to sustain "credible deterrence" in view of the SS-20 buildup. In the spirit of the SPD's 1979 Berlin resolution, he supported the decision as an effort to invigorate arms control.[114] He called for greater contact between the SPD and the peace movement, vigorously defended a traditional Social Democratic "active peace policy," which he called the "most important" Social Democratic and Social Liberal contribution to a peaceful and democratic Germany since World War II.[115] By fall 1981, Voigt was being outflanked on his left by those in the SPD who were abandoning the two-track decision. At the end of September 1981, the *JUSOS* announced their rejection of the NATO two-track decision.[116] On September 30, Oskar Lafontaine, chairman of the SPD in the Saarland, declared that the West was already militarily superior to the Soviet Union and that in the interests of peace and disarmament, "the most dangerous and most destabilizing weapons systems in the world—Pershing II and cruise missiles"—should not be deployed.[117]

In October 1981, in *Der Spiegel*, Rudolf Augstein said that a Western

policy of confrontation and rearmament would make it impossible for
the Soviet Union to dismantle "its most effective threat potential, the
SS-20."[118] "We" West Germans, Augstein continued,

> are not threatened because the Soviets would like to seize our .
> country. They lack both the desire and capability to do that. We are
> threatened because the USA is building into its defense budget . . .
> limited nuclear conflict. That is why we are threatened.
>   We are threatened because the new doctrine of the USA foresees in
> Central Europe, and indeed from Central European soil, threatening
> [the Soviet Union] with almost strategic nuclear weapons in the
> thoroughly conceivable case that the life interests of the USA and/or
> of NATO in Middle East or elsewhere—that is oil—appear to be at
> stake. . . . Who can assure us that the threat is not serious?
>   We are threatened not because the Soviet Union is militarily too
> strong but rather because it, as a communist country, is economically
> too weak. Who does it serve to push the Soviets to the wall until
> they collapse? Do we want to or must we participate in a showdown
> in which we will be the first affected?[119]

The West Germans, Augstein added, had to explain to the Americans that
they remained allies and that they would "rather be a US colony than a
Soviet colony." But if the choice came down to "Weinberger's transparent
war" or a "unified Germany under Hönnecker," that is, "if the question
were posed as it has not been posed before, 'rather red than dead,' in the
interest of my children, I know what I would do."[120]

On October 9, 1981, the day before a large antimissile rally in Bonn,
the Bundestag debated the missile issue. Schmidt warned that *Angst* could
paralyze reason.[121] He recalled his 1978 agreement with Brezhnev concerning the desirability of equality and parity as the precondition for cooperation between East and West. "Unfortunately," he continued, "the Soviet
Union as manifest in its continued medium range missile armament did
not hold to the common declaration of May 1978 . . . and that led to
. . . the double decision of the Western Alliance."[122] Schmidt stressed that
the "ideal result" of negotiations would be a "zero option for both sides"
resulting from a decision by the Soviet Union to dismantle its medium-
range missiles. He warned of those, including communist groups, who used
the desire for peace for their own political purposes. While communist
groups in West Germany had the right to demonstrate, young West Germans should remember that "my [Schmidt's] political friends are not permitted in the DDR or the Soviet Union to demonstrate."[123]

Willy Brandt rejected the criticism that the SPD was willing to work with communists. In view of the billions of dollars spent on armaments each year, "there was reason enough for those who want to demonstrate against further armament in East and West."[124] Helmut Kohl remarked on the difference between Schmidt's and Brandt's speeches. A majority of the SPD, he said, had "moved to another shore of German, and also international politics." Many of Schmidt's positions, said Kohl, were no longer held within the SPD.[125]

In October and early November of 1981, demonstrations of between 50,000 and 300,000 people against the NATO decision took place in Bonn, Madrid, Rome, London, Brussels, Paris, Milan, and Amsterdam. The demonstration in Bonn on October 10 of approximately 250,000 people was the largest political demonstration in West German history. Over fifty SPD members of parliament signed a statement supporting "nonviolent protest" against war. Brandt said that "we have seen worse things on German soil than young people committing themselves to peace and disarmament." Sixteen members of the FDP signed a statement saying that they "shared the concern of the demonstrators for the preservation of peace."[126] Erhard Eppler spoke at the rally. On the same day, Helmut Kohl warned that "the real problem in Bonn is that the contours between democrats and the enemies of democracy are blurring." The leaders of the SPD were "either too cowardly or too weak" to utter a clear "no" to cooperation with those who sought "another republic." The Bonn demonstration, Kohl argued, was the clearest demonstration of cooperation between Social Democrats and communists since World War II.[127]

A week after the Bonn demonstration, a journalist asked President Reagan if the use of nuclear weapons could be limited to Europe. Reagan responded that NATO's first use of tactical nuclear weapons might lead the Soviet Union to cease an offensive before escalating further. Asked if escalation were inevitable, Reagan answered that "he really didn't know," as candid and honest an answer as any strategist of flexible response could offer. The West German and Western European press, or parts of them, quickly reinterpreted Reagan's answer to mean that Reagan was advocating a "limited nuclear war in Europe."[128] Augstein, for example, wrote that Reagan had "uncovered NATO's life lie."[129] Neither the United States nor France was serious about committing national suicide for the sake of the defense of the Federal Republic. "We," wrote Augstein, "are Mitterand's *glacis* and that is all." As for the Americans, Augstein said that Caspar Weinberger, the Secretary of Defense, had "called for" conventional war, war that could be won and survived.[130] Weinberger had not "called for" a war but had discussed what the Western alliance would do if deterrence failed. The purpose of improved capabilities was to enhance deterrence. Nevertheless, Augstein bitterly wrote that "we would rather be and remain a protectorate of the US-Americans than the Russians."[131] For Augstein "the strength of the Soviet position and the weakness of American negotiating position" lay in the American effort to present a doctrine of limitations.[132]

Augstein's editorial nicely illustrated the strategic advantages of dictatorship and the burdens of democracy in the euromissile dispute. The Soviet Union, despite the fact that it had already deployed weapons capable of delivering limited attacks with nuclear weapons, could deny it had a policy of limitations. It had no press and or political opposition to ask why, if the Soviet Union did not have a policy of limitations, it had already deployed the SS-20s. NATO officials and West European and American political leaders on the other hand, had to explain the meaning of "coupling," "flexible response," and "extended deterrence" in a climate dominated by fears of imminent nuclear catastrophe.

On November 7, 1981, Günter Gaus, a prominent print and television journalist, former editor-in-chief of *Der Spiegel*, and at the time director of the West German representation to East Berlin, delivered a speech to Social Democrats in West Berlin on the topic of "the Social Democrats and German peace policy."[133] Gaus's interest in military strategy was recent. He had associated the military with World War II and the Nazis. "Ronald Reagan woke us up."[134] Gaus told his West Berlin audience that, "we are being lied to a great deal, every day."[135] There were, he said, differences between American and German priorities. It was not anti-Americanism to take note of these differences, unless the alliance was going to treat the Germans as "vassals." He attacked the "defamation and demonization" of the peace movement as being a tool of Moscow and as coming from the "ghostly landscape of political unculture" in West Germany.[136]

Gaus rejected joining a global "ideological crusade" led by the United States. Such a mentality would destroy NATO. Neither the Soviet invasion of Afghanistan nor the repression of Solidarity in Poland called for an end to détente. For Gaus, peace in Europe was bound to the "unconditional recognition of the status quo." Dreams of a rapid end to Soviet domination could become nightmares of war. Recognition of the status quo in Europe would bring change, but gradual change, not change due to a "primitive mentality of an anticommunist crusade," which would bring Europe again to a "prewar period." He attacked "verbal radicalism" aiming at a "defeat" of the other side. "Western Europe needs a stable Eastern Europe for survival—and vice versa."[137] Gaus did not advocate leaving NATO. On the contrary, "I am for NATO and the Warsaw Pact. I am against Communism and against the kind of anticommunism that sets the tone in West Germany."

Rather than rebuke the Soviet Union for its attack on peace and freedom in both Afghanistan and Poland, Gaus reserved his fire for the "streamlined adaptation" of West German conservatives to Washington's foreign policy. In November 1981, before any national elections had been conducted on the issue, Gaus asserted that it was attempts to implement the NATO decision that had been "rejected by a majority of the people," not the opposition of the West German left, that was damaging the alliance.[138] Without a "repoliticization" and "demilitarization" of the euromissile issues, "the end of this path can only be the Vietnamization of NATO: The apparatus of the NATO partners agrees within itself—high above and far removed from the people of the defense pact."[139]

The Americans, said Gaus, did not want war. But without Europe's direct experience of war, they displayed a certain "intellectual and emotional inclination toward war, which had nothing to do with enthusiasm for war."[140] NATO's problem was that Europeans had a different stance toward war, in thinking and feeling. No one wanted war but there existed a different attitude of many Europeans and Americans about "whether war is the continuation of politics with other means or the end of everything."[141] Gaus proposed that NATO should abandon flexible response and return to a policy of "immediate, total retaliation." This would end the problem of a nuclear war limited to Europe. He supported a nuclear-free zone in Central Europe, something that could be done more easily if NATO returned to a policy of massive retaliation. Finally, Gaus recalled a conversation with Rudi Dutschke in 1976 in which Dutschke said that the German left would get nowhere unless it took up the national question.[142] Thus, Gaus too linked opposition to the NATO deployments with a left willing to speak as the representative of the nation.[143]

I have argued that the gradual erosion of the moral and political boundaries of West German militant democracy from the 1960s to the 1980s left a vacuum of meaning and that one way of filling this vacuum was with older, national German boundaries. The reinterpretation of the Brussels decision of 1979 as a plan to wreak devastation on both Germanies was one manifestation, in the language of weapons and strategy, of this deeper cultural process. In 1979, the interest of the West German left in national identity was foreshadowed in an essay collection edited by Jürgen Habermas in which several contributors juxtaposed the "nation" to the technocratic, capitalist, parliamentary, and divided "republic."[144]

Wolfgang Pohrt, a freelance journalist who came of political age in the

1960s left, referred to the peace movement as a sign of "the rebirth of the nation."[145] Why, he asked, did the West German left not rally to the banner of Solidarity in Poland? Was "sacrificing the Polish freedom movement in the name of world peace" a new version of a German-Russian division of Europe?

> Must not the reawakening nationalism in the peace movement inevitably lead to a path of understanding with Soviet despotism? . . . Does peace . . . simply mean that the strong and the powerful, who are able to bring peace through force, will unite with one another at the cost of freedom loving obstructionists, rebels, separatists and other disturbers of the peace? Does peace mean that one may not stir oneself on behalf of any freedom movement because the USA and the Soviet Union would shoot intercontinental missiles at each other? Is peace only another name for a global rigidity?[146]

In fact, throughout the euromissile dispute, the repression of Solidarity remained a secondary issue for the West German peace movement.

Was it possible, asked Pohrt, that the American role in defeating Germany in two world wars was a factor in the unconscious life of left-wing nationalism and anti-Americanism in the 1980s?[147] Vivid images of imminent nuclear devastation at the hands of Russia and America could be "understood as memory of past defeats transformed into a vision of the future. . . . People say that America wants to turn Germany into a battlefield. Perhaps they mean that it has done it twice before."[148] Pohrt wondered if, in West Germany, protests against the United States war in Vietnam were "not the beginning of a revolutionary and anti-imperialist movement, but rather the beginning of a movement of national awakening."[149] He suggested that the peace movement of the early 1980s was the flowering of a nationalist movement found in embryo in the new left of the 1960s. The *Endstation*, last station, was a return home from Third World revolutions, a rediscovery of German rather than West German identity. A similar rediscovery, he suggested, lay in an image of victimization central to the reinterpretation of the NATO doubled-track decision in 1980 and 1981.

November 18, 1981: President Reagan's Zero Option

On November 18, 1981, President Reagan announced the "zero option." If the Soviet Union would agree to dismantle its SS-20s, SS-4s, and SS-5s, NATO would cancel deployment of the Pershing II and cruise missiles.

Chancellor Schmidt and Prime Minister Thatcher, who was in Bonn for consultations, immediately welcomed Reagan's initiative.[150] The Soviet Union immediately and vehemently rejected the zero option as "pure propaganda" resting on "absolutely fantastic facts" about the balance of forces in Europe. Soviet spokesmen referred to "irrefutable facts" that indicated that an "approximate balance" existed between NATO and the Soviet Union in Europe. Reagan's proposal was designed to place European opinion under "maximal pressure."[151] Reagan adopted part of the SPD's view that the best solution would be one that made any new missiles "superfluous." Unlike the SPD, Reagan insisted that such superfluity could come only with dismantling of the Soviet medium-range arsenal.[152]

From November 22 to 25, 1981, Prime Minister and Party Chairman Brezhnev visited Bonn. In contrast to Haig's riotous welcome in West Berlin, no antimissile demonstrators greeted Brezhnev. He reiterated his moratorium proposal of the spring, offered to reduce Soviet medium-range nuclear weapons by "hundreds" of units, asserted that "approximate equality" already existed, and called for turning Europe into a "nuclear weapons free zone." Brezhnev's claim of approximate equality in November 1981 was a slap in the face to both Chancellor Schmidt and Foreign Minister Genscher. It was the same Brezhnev who had announced that an approximate balance had existed in May 1978, who had committed himself to the principle of parity, and who then built up the SS-20 arsenal for the following three years.[153] At the time of their 1978 conversations, the Soviet side had 50 SS-20 missiles. In November 1981, there were 250 SS-20s with 750 warheads. With no new Western deployments in the interim, it strained credulity for Brezhnev to say that parity still existed. Schmidt rejected Brezhnev's offer of a moratorium, saying it would only ratify the Soviet advantage. Nor would Schmidt accept inclusion of American aircraft, submarines, and ships in the upcoming negotiations. If the Soviets wished to see no American missiles deployed on land in Western Europe, Schmidt continued, all they had to was dismantle their own medium-range nuclear weapons. The zero-zero option was the best solution.[154]

The INF Talks Begin: November 30, 1981

The focus of the battle over the euromissiles was the negotiations between the United States and the Soviet Union conducted in Geneva. The fall season of talks began on November 30, 1981. The United States presented the zero/zero proposal (frequently referred to as the "zero option"). The Soviets countered with a proposal calling for ceilings of 300 medium-range missiles and aircraft. The proposal precluded any new American medium-range nuclear missiles and included British and French nuclear forces in order to arrive at a balance between the Soviet Union and the West. The proposal also called for reductions in the numbers of American nuclear-capable aircraft in Europe. Each side rejected the other's proposal. The Soviet Union said it halted the buildup of SS-20 missiles on March 16, 1982, though NATO officials thought the Soviet buildup continued afterwards as well. On that date, when NATO estimated that the Soviet Union had deployed about 220 SS-20s with 760 nuclear warheads, Brezhnev announced a unilateral moratorium that would remain in effect until the United States decided to deploy Pershing II and cruise missiles.

The pattern of the asymmetrical pressures on the United States and the Soviet Union became clear as soon as the Geneva negotiations began. Schmidt, Genscher, and the conservative opposition supported the American zero option and rejected Brezhnev's moratorium proposals. Brandt, Bahr, and the bulk of the SPD looked more favorably on the moratorium idea.[155] The Greens and the peace movement attacked any American deployments. Supporters of the NATO decision, such as Manfred Wörner, argued that support for Brezhnev's moratorium or "freeze" proposal encouraged the Soviet Union in the belief that the West could be divided if it would remain unyielding in Geneva and wait for Western domestic politics to weaken the American position. Phillip Jenninger, speaking for the conservatives in the Bundestag, praised the "unequivocal statements" of Schmidt and Genscher, but expressed "great concern" that Brandt's and Wehner's proposals for a delay in deployment would eliminate pressure on Moscow to negotiate.[156] In the Bundestag, on December 3, 1981, Chancellor Schmidt said that he warned Brezhnev against "trying to replace politics between governments with an effort to influence the public opinion of other countries," to obtain a veto over Western defense policy.[157]

Helmut Kohl praised Schmidt and Genscher's commitment to the Brussels decision but criticized the Social Democratic party for eroding support for the decision and thereby relieving the Soviet Union of the need to dismantle its weapons.[158] Those, he continued, such as Bahr and Eppler, who wanted to prevent deployments, signaled to the Soviets that they need not negotiate seriously, aroused mistrust in the Western alliance, and concern among "our American friends" that the Soviet leadership would fill "the coming two years with cosmetic offers and thereby, with the help of certain forces in German politics, in the SPD, in the so-called peace movement, and elsewhere, prevent NATO's deployments."[159] Directing his attention to Chancellor Schmidt, Kohl suggested that in addition to continuing contact with the American and Soviet leaders, "above all, you should focus on contact with your own party."[160]

But by fall of 1981, it was probably too late. Schmidt, the most respected political figure in the country at large, had been outmaneuvered within the SPD. The extent of his defeat had been obscured in the purposefully vague language of the Berlin resolution of December 1979 and the Bundestag resolution of May 26, 1981. Beginning in London in October 1977, Helmut Schmidt began the process of a decisive shift in the momentum of the global balance of forces, but he was unable to shift the balance of power in his own party. With this gaze fixed on the world stage, the chancellor was unable to stem the tide of what he called a new wave of German idealism.

Political Culture and Politics in 1981

The major accomplishment of the intellectual and political left of 1981 was to reinterpret the meaning of NATO's two-track decision. While its originators intended it to be a policy that would couple Western Europe and the United States and thus decrease the likelihood that any war in Europe would remain limited to Central Europe, its critics argued that it would decouple them and increase the possibility that such a war would be limited to Europe and the Soviet Union alone. In West Germany, this suspicious conception of American strategy drew strength from a renewal of interest in German identity on the left, as well as from the deep tensions that accompanied a change of gears from détente to confrontation with the Soviet Union.

The reinterpretation of the two-track decision also rested on the transformation of West German political culture in both its new left and moderate left variants, which I have described. The mentality of the popular front ruled out specific and vigorous criticism of the Soviet Union. The language of abstraction focused attention on "the arms race" and its "dynamic" rather than on the specific history of the SS-20 buildup. Brandt's and Bahr's interpretation of détente separated the question of peace from that of freedom. In nuclear weapons and nuclear strategy, the revival of suspicion of science, technology, and technocratic rationality found the ultimate target. Over the course of the 1970s, parts of the Social Democratic party had evolved from a bulwark against Soviet policy into a lever that Soviet diplomats could pull. In the euromissile dispute, they did just that by means of arms control proposals. The erosion of the Schumacher tradition in

West German political culture was the "window of vulnerability" that would have an impact on the power balance between states.

By the end of 1981, the counteroffensive of the West German establishment gained momentum as well. It took the form of the reassertion of the moral boundaries of West German militant democracy and commentary on the day-to-day battle over the euromissiles. In 1982, as Helmut Schmidt was being overwhelmed by the forces in his own party, Hans-Dietrich Genscher and Helmut Kohl took over the role of bulwark against Soviet strategy.

9

SCHMIDT'S FALL, KOHL'S RISE
December 1981 to October 1982

PRESIDENT REAGAN'S ZERO OPTION of November 18, 1981, changed few minds on the antimissile left, judging from the minutes of a December 1981 peace congress in East Berlin, which brought together writers from Western Europe, Eastern Europe, and the Soviet Union.[1] Writers from the West were critical of the Western governments. Writers from East Germany or the Soviet Union criticized the West as well. They had few or no critical words to offer about their own government.[2] The participants debated whether both superpowers were equally responsible for the growing danger of a nuclear holocaust or whether the fault lay exclusively with the United States and NATO. No one suggested that the Soviet Union was the primary cause of the current crisis. Most of the East Germans in attendance defended their own government's official positions. Some made news when they dissented from that position. There was much talk of the international responsibilities of intellectuals, but participants from the East generally followed their government's position.

Günter Grass and the Great Equation

Herbert Marcuse called opposition to one-dimensional society the "Great Refusal." One could describe Günter Grass' political intervention of the early 1980s as the "Great Equation." Grass found parallels wherever he looked in the behavior of the Soviet Union and the United States. Like Gaus, Augstein, and Bahr, he too made a connection between the nuclear issue and German identity.[3] Grass saw many parallels between the United States and the Soviet Union, such as Vietnam and Afghanistan, Nicaragua and Poland. Both "bloc systems," with their threats and professions of peaceful intentions, were "infantile." Both systems sought an escape in foreign policy (*Flucht nach Vorn*) from political and economic crises at home. Both squandered resources on arms that should be used to relieve poverty. A peace movement in West and East would have to force politicians to come to their senses.

Grass believed that the two German states had a special responsibility for preserving peace.

> Two world wars began from German soil. Even today, the Germans bear the guilt and the consequences of the wars. Therefore, the political leaders of both German states are obligated to be critical, admonishing allies of the great powers to which they have been assigned. We owe this all-German responsibility for peace to ourselves and to Europe. We should be the pacemakers of disarmament in East and West.[4]

Grass noticed that writers from East Germany did not share his sense of "all-German" guilt and responsibility. Grass tried to sustain a symmetrical critique.

> If we now begin, to cite the insane publications of the United States, and find here one-sided origins and guilt, then we remain silent about what we know concerning similar plans and things on the Soviet side, that is, that during the period of détente, for example, a number of SS–20 missile bases have been constructed and that a threat has also emerged from the Soviet side. I believe that we won't get anywhere, if we here only direct our fire from one side and accuse the other, even though it is equally responsible in general.[5]

The Soviet and East German participants insisted that the issue must remain exclusively the Pershing II and cruise missiles, not the SS-20s. For Grass, the real problem remained both superpowers. "I know that there are ideological frameworks which seek to excuse or cover up this or that crime committed by both great powers and their bloc systems. The result is that poverty and suffering increase to a horrifying extent."[6] Grass did not criticize Soviet or Communist behavior without a parallel and equivalent criticism of Western, i.e., American policy. He linked a critical word about Poland with one about Nicaragua. "Little is left of our democracy" in the

West. "Capitalism is inherently sick." But Communism's economic system was immobile. Both tended to foreign adventures to escape from domestic difficulties, and so on.[7] Partisanship for one side or the other would, in Grass's view of 1982, suggest submersion in an "ideological framework."

Several writers who were living or who had lived in East Germany did comment on the asymmetric nature of the conflict in Europe. Jurek Becker, living in West Berlin since 1978, said that the "only reason" that there were no peace movements in the East bloc was that "they are forbidden." If peace movements were desirable in Western Europe, they were no less desirable in Eastern Europe.[8] Günter de Bruyn, also from East Germany, welcomed the peace movements of Western Europe but stressed that their use by the East German government was "questionable as long as the impression emerges that what is celebrated over there (in Western Europe) is unwanted here (in Eastern Europe)." If the East German government only supported officially sponsored peace movements while repressing the unofficial protests from the Protestant Church, it would "damage its own credibility," which is just what the Honnecker government did during the euromissile dispute.[9] In East Germany from 1981 to 1983, the small East German peace movement was not able to operate freely to protest the SS-20 buildup.[10]

Egon Bahr: What Will Happen to the Germans?

In late October and early November 1981, Egon Bahr offered his views on the German question in a long interview published in January 1982 under the title, "What Will Happen to the Germans?" [*Was wird aus den Deutschen?*].[11] The Germans, he said, were finally coming to terms with themselves. Substitutes for the nation, such as NATO or the European Community, were "without essence [*Wesenlos*]." Any German, he continued, who says that the nation no longer plays a role in German politics was either "stupid or ... lying and both are dangerous."[12] *Ostpolitik*, he said, had relegated "ideological questions" to a secondary status and affirmed that "the right of the Germans to pursue their national interests— subordinated to the duty for peace—is just as great as that of the English, the Americans and the Poles."[13] For Bahr, ideological questions were the issues of the Cold War, freedom and tyranny, democracy and dictatorship, while presumably the rights of the Germans were a nonideological matter.

Bahr insisted he was not a neutralist or pacifist because a "a state cannot escape" from world politics. Peace required the "alliance system" in Europe. "We attain security not against America and not without America.

We attain security not against the Soviet Union and not without the Soviet Union." "Common security," not neutrality, was necessary in Europe.[14] Common security meant that security was possible only "in common with the adversary, in common with the alliances, in common with the existing leading powers" for "we are all united in the catastrophe."[15] His discussion of common security placed West Germany's relations with its most important ally, the United States, on the same plane as relations with its most important potential enemy, the Soviet Union.

Among the sacrifices demanded by peace, Bahr included subordination of West German self-determination. This reality, he said, was as true for the Poles as for the Germans.[16] The implication was that both West Germany and Poland were equally lacking in sovereignty. Here, Bahr was equating the absence of an independent West German nuclear deterrent with Poland's absence of any national self-determination, involuntary occupation by the Red Army, and the absence of democratic institutions and political freedoms. He said that the great disappointment of German postwar history was the false hope raised by Adenauer that the politics of strength would force the Soviet Union to give up control of the East German zone. The Social Democrats had given up those "illusions" in recognizing the reality of the DDR (German Democratic Republic).[17] Bahr's critics thought the "great disappointment" of the postwar era was the construction of yet another German dictatorship in East Germany by the Soviet-supported Communists.

Bahr's view of the differences between the regimes of East and West was similar to Augstein's. There were "different forms of oligarchy in the world. . . . In their method, there is no principle difference between the 'kitchen cabinet' coalition talks and the politburo." The different systems were distinguished from one another primarily with regard to their forms of legitimacy.[18] Democracy was the indispensable and best form of control that human beings had to guard against the dangers posed by such oligarchies, but Bahr placed more weight on the distinction between states that did and did not possess nuclear weapons. In his view, the core of the Atlantic Alliance was that the American president had the final power of decision "over our existence." West Germany's "right of co-determination" was limited to "refusal" or "consultations," which amounted to a "very small degree of co-determination." Exercise of this right in West Germany "naturally means preventing that these missiles [cruise and Pershing II] will be stationed here."[19] Preventing deployments would enhance West German sovereignty by diminishing the American ability to decide West Germany's fate. Hence, opposition to deployments could mean defense of the not-fully sovereign nation.[20]

Bahr's central point was to link the missiles to the national question. The

United States, "not us," had the power of decision over nuclear weapons.
"It is at this point that German self-determination and responsibility
ends."[21]

> Our dilemma is the following: Others, not us, take the decisions that
> determine our existence. Our hope in this situation lies in the fact that
> we Germans are not alone. We share this fate with all the states in
> Europe which do not control their own nuclear weapons. All non-
> nuclear weapon states have the shared interest of not becoming
> hostages about whom decisions are made, as well as having a shared
> interest securing the stability of their alliances. They recognize that a
> common interest in peace with all states exists, that there are unequal
> rights of nuclear powers, and that from these inequalities grow
> different interests of non-nuclear powers.[22]

In the context of the euromissile dispute, this analysis was a recipe for
conflict between West Germany, on the one hand, and Britain, France,
and the United States, on the other. Its practical consequence was to support inclusion of British and French missiles in the medium-range balance
and reduction of the numbers of SS-20s down to the number of British
and French missiles already deployed, while preventing any new American
deployments.

The advocate of "common security" and "security partnership" mentioned three differences between the two Germanies. First, the West German economy was more effective. Second, Soviet troops in Eastern Europe
were not as dependent on deployment in East Germany as American
troops in Western Europe were on deployment in West Germany. Third,
the Soviet Union was "more dominant" in the Warsaw Pact than the
United States was in NATO. Egon Bahr wrote that "the sum of these three
factors comprises the difference between the political life of both German
states." In a crisis of war and peace, "there is no difference [between them]
at all." When, he continued, world tensions increase or war threatens, the
power of both German states approaches zero, as does the power of all
nonnuclear states in Europe.[23] He did not mention the difference between
parliamentary democracy and one-party Communist dictatorship, the presence and absence of free speech and freedom of the press, and markets
versus state control of the economy. Nor did he point out that the West
Germans could, if they wished, vote to leave the NATO alliance, while the
East Germans could not freely elect their own leaders, not to mention
democratically decide their alliance policy. What was clear was that assertion of West German sovereignty meant a "no" to the NATO deployments.

In winter and spring of 1982, the erosion of support for the Brussels decision and NATO doctrine continued. In January, Bahr called deterrence only a "transitional theory," which had to be replaced by a "doctrine of common security."[24] On January 24, the Hamburg SPD rebuffed Schmidt's pleas not to weaken his influence on the negotiators in Geneva and voted in favor of a nuclear-free zone in Europe and for a moratorium on Western deployments while negotiations took place in Geneva.[25] In late January, the party's executive committee prepared a resolution for the upcoming annual party congress that incorporated the Soviet position on consideration of dual-capable aircraft and British and French nuclear weapons in East-West negotiations. The resolution called for dismantling Soviet missiles so that new American deployments would be superfluous but appeared to leave open the possibility that not all the Soviet missiles would have to be dismantled.[26]

The British and French governments rejected any consideration of their nuclear weapons in the INF talks. They were weapons of last resort, intended for the defense of Britain and France. They had been deployed long before the SS-20. To include them in negotiations touching only a small part of the Soviet nuclear arsenal opened the door for unilateral nuclear disarmament via arms control talks. The more the West German Social Democrats insisted on inclusion of these weapons, the more tensions developed between them and the British and French governments. The issue of British and French missiles gave the Soviet Union an opportunity to drive a wedge between France and Britain, on the one hand, and West Germany, on the other. Faced with the Social Democrats' move toward the Soviet position in Geneva, Genscher warned that those in the West who rejected the possible missile deployments or even called for a moratorium "aroused Soviet illusions and thus undermined the Geneva negotiations."[27]

In February 1982, some leading figures of the political and intellectual left publicly rejected the zero-zero option. "A proposal which suggests that one side should dismantle everything it has built for 20 years so that the other side will refrain from taking several arms measures in the future is not to be taken seriously as a compromise."[28] Instead the signers of the "peace manifesto 1982" called for a moratorium on Western missile deployments and for Soviet missile reductions to the level of May 1978. They erroneously stated that Helmut Schmidt had agreed with Leonid Brezhnev in their 1978 meeting in Bonn that a military balance existed in Europe. In fact, Schmidt had called for ending the "currently existing" imbalances.

Though the SPD was moving quickly away from support for the Brussels decision, it was not moving fast enough for the new Green party, which was outflanking it on the left on the antimissile issue. Rudolf Bahro, a former East German dissident active in the Green party, attacked the SPD as the "party of moderate exterminism." It had to choose, he wrote in January 1982, between being a party of deterrence and a party of peace.[29] Security for Europe had to be found in "independence from the opposing blocs. . . . The whole of Europe, with our country in the lead, must cease to be one of the bases from which the Americans enact their global trial of strength with the Soviet Union."[30] Reagan's zero option, in Bahro's view, was a pure deception.

At the same time, Helmut Schmidt's center-right critics took him to task for failing to present all of the "uncomfortable truths" about the Soviet buildup earlier to the West German public.[31] A continuing theme of the editorials of the *Frankfurther Allgemeine Zeitung* was that Schmidt was not making a sufficiently detailed and frank presentation to the public.[32] In an ironic twist, this voice of the West German establishment criticized Schmidt for not daring more democracy in foreign affairs.

March 16, 1982: Brezhnev's Well-Timed "Freeze"

On March 16, 1982, Leonid Brezhnev announced that the Soviet Union would deploy no more SS-20s in the European parts of the Soviet Union and would begin to reduce part of its medium-range arsenal. He said deployments of American missiles in Europe would upset the strategic balance and warned of countermeasures that would affect the territory of the United States if deployments did take place.[33] In Bonn, Kurt Becker, Helmut Schmidt's government spokesman, said the Brezhnev moratorium proposal was in "crass conflict" with the principle of equilibrium that Brezhnev had accepted in Bonn in 1978.[34] Since then, when Brezhnev said a balance existed in Europe, the Soviets had deployed 250 additional SS-20 missiles, 200 since December 1979. In all there were now 300 deployed missiles, two-thirds of which were in the European parts of the Soviet Union. On March 29, Chancellor Schmidt said that Brezhnev's moratorium proposal was an "interesting gesture," but that he would prefer that such proposals be presented at the negotiating table rather than as public proposals directed at Western public opinion. A moratorium such as Brezhnev had proposed would have meant much more, he continued, in 1978, 1979, or 1980, before there were 300 SS-20s with 750 warheads aimed at Western Europe, in particular, at West Germany.[35]

Alois Mertes said Moscow was seeking a one-sided rejection of Western deployments while preserving its existing superiority. Jürgen Möllemann, speaking for the FDP, welcomed the Brezhnev proposal, but stressed the need for a "zero option" for both sides. In Washington, President Reagan said that the moratorium proposal did not go far enough and that it would leave a large Soviet arsenal intact. Egon Bahr welcomed the end of further Soviet deployments, said "discussion of the moratorium within the SPD has been made easier by the one-sided decision of the Soviet Union" and urged a Western response before the date of planned deployments in 1983.[36] Having built up its medium-range arsenal without public controversy, the Soviet Union was now able to announce that it wanted to "freeze" nuclear weapons at the same time that NATO was going to bring new ones to Europe.

Foreign Minister Genscher stood firmly by the zero option and noticed that his own views were closer to that of the conservative opposition than to those now coming to dominate the SPD.[37] On March 18, 1982, Genscher told the Soviet ambassador in Bonn that he stood by the zero option for both sides. It was, said Genscher, the only way "the concern of people in West and East and the danger created by the Soviet superiority in medium range weapons" could be overcome. He warned the Soviets not to make the "serious error" of thinking that NATO would be politically incapable of implementing the NATO decision, that domestic opponents would erode the government's stance, or that the American–West European bond would split apart. He urged the Soviets to negotiate in Geneva towards a zero option for both sides. He also told the ambassador that the Soviets should leave Afghanistan, lift martial law in Poland, and renew talks with the Polish church and Solidarity.[38]

In the same month, Egon Bahr and Alois Mertes continued a debate about the meaning of the militarization of foreign policy. In a number of essays in *Vorwärts*, Egon Bahr argued that "militarization of thinking" was weakening the NATO alliance and warned that "war is being prepared" by both superpowers.[39] Mertes himself complained of a militarization of public discussion. He said it was "the political will" standing behind weapons, not the weapons themselves, that posed a threat. There had been too little analysis of Soviet policy and strategy towards Europe and too much discussion of weapons. "Our major concern is that the [public] discussion must once again be conducted on a far more political plane and ought not be allowed to remain on a level that is strictly military and technical."[40]

It was in such terms that Oskar Lafontaine, in a speech in mid-March on "peace and security" to the Institute for International Politics and Economics of the Center for Marxist-Leninist Research on Imperialism in East Berlin, attacked the militarization of the foreign policies of both the United States and the Soviet Union.[41] He called for a nuclear weapon–free Europe and attacked the concept of equilibrium as one that justified armament and counterarmament.[42] Ever-new "gaps" could be discovered to justify more armament. With more than 50,000 nuclear warheads already existing, concepts of superiority and inferiority could no longer be defined. "The formula of equilibrium is senseless."[43] The only way out of the circle of "*Vor- und Nachrüstung*" was unilateral disarmament. Because of the excessive armament of both superpowers, unilateral disarmament could be pursued without danger to security. The Soviet Union could accept the American "zero option," while NATO could renounce its "so-called" *Nachrüstung* decision independently of the number of SS-20s.

Bahr was quick to respond to the challenge from the party left. In an article in *Vorwärts*, he warned against diverting attention from the Geneva negotiations with talk of a unilateral rejection of the Brussels decision. He recalled that such a step would undermine NATO's negotiating position in Geneva because only the possibility of deployments made reductions possible. If the SPD were to reject the NATO decision, it would also lose its leverage over the American position in Geneva.[44]

April 19–23, 1982: The SPD Party Congress in Munich

The SPD held its annual meeting from April 19 to 23, 1982, in Munich. Eppler and Lafontaine prepared a resolution calling for rejection of the armament part of the NATO decision and supporting a moratorium on all further deployments. Karsten Voigt and Horst Ehmke, leader of the SPD parliamentary fraction, urged postponement of judgment on the Geneva negotiations until fall 1983.[45] By the time the congress convened, 175 resolutions had been introduced concerning the NATO decision, calling for a moratorium, total rejection, or nuclear-free zones.[46]

In Munich, Helmut Schmidt urged the party to draw a clear line between itself as a *Volkspartei* (people's party) and the Greens and the peace movement.[47] He warned that internal conflicts were undermining support for the SPD and could only help the "neoconservative radicalism" waiting to govern. He criticized moratorium proposals, saying that the Soviet Union would negotiate seriously only if it believed NATO actually would go ahead with missile deployment. Without the time pressure of a deadline, the Soviets would not negotiate in good faith. In the current situation, no rational alternative existed to preservation of peace on the basis of a balance of forces. A moratorium now would preserve Soviet superiority. He warned the delegates that Soviet weapons without a Western counterbalance could be used to exert "political pressure on us and others." "In view of the totally unbalanced situation, the Soviet side is seeking with its moratorium proposals to create an overwhelming advantage for itself under the appearance of equality." West Germany, the chancellor continued, could not be equidistant between Washington and Moscow. The West Germans were loyal allies on the side of "free, equal peoples."[48]

Though Schmidt succeeded in defeating the resolutions of the party's left wing opposing the two-track decision, the SPD resolution on peace and security policy reflected Brandt's and Bahr's political language of peace policy and common security more than the chancellor's concerns over Soviet armament. It called for dismantling "enemy images" and establishing a "partnership for security." It declared a "nuclear weapons free Europe" to be the SPD's goal.[49] Though the resolution did not include support for a moratorium on medium-range nuclear weapons, it did include a clause urging inclusion of British and French nuclear weapons in assessments of the East–West balance by calling for inclusion of British and French missiles in the INF talks and seeking a "nuclear weapons free Europe."[50] With these resolutions, the SPD in Munich in 1982 emerged ever more clearly as a source of pressure on the West German and then the American governments to modify their negotiating position to approximate that of the Soviet Union in Geneva.

In late May, Bahr took another step in drawing out the practical implications of his distinction between states that did and did not possess nuclear weapons.[51] He called for withdrawal of all nuclear weapons from states that did not control them, including the two German states, in order to create a nuclear-free zone in Central Europe. It was time, he said, for both sides to accept the principle of common security in place of the endless game of alliances and arms races.[52] Bahr repeated his view concerning the common interests of all nonnuclear weapons states.[53] "Common security" in Europe meant that all nuclear weapons should be withdrawn from the European states that do not control them, leaving behind a nuclear-free zone in Central Europe, including the two Germanies. He called for an approximate balance of conventional forces between NATO and the Warsaw Pact, with both alliances and their guarantees intact. In a system of common security in Europe, the only land-based nuclear missiles would be those possessed by Britain, France, and the Soviet Union, while sea-based missiles in the American navy would still be assigned to Europe. The slogan of "no nuclear weapons for non-nuclear states" would "at last restore Europe to its natural power."[54] "Security partnership" would replace "ideological crusades," which had become too dangerous in the nuclear era.[55] If there were to be no nuclear weapons in "non-nuclear states," then this unequivocally ruled out any deployments under the Brussels decision, no matter what the state of Soviet armament was. Bahr's argument precluded implementation of the NATO double-track decision. How could nuclear weapons be deployed in a nuclear-free zone?

On June 10, 1982, President Reagan delivered a speech to the Bundestag in which he reiterated the zero-zero option and stressed the distinction between democracy and dictatorship in Europe.[56] It did not slow the move of the left away from its antimissile course.[57] Within the SPD, Lafontaine and Gaus increased their attacks on Schmidt's policies. Genscher's concerns about the direction of the SPD appeared in the press, and there was increasing talk of a possible end of the Social-Liberal coalition.

In May and June 1982, the *Verband deutscher Schriftsteller* [Union of German Writers] organized a writer's congress for peace in Haagen and Cologne.[58] At both meetings, participants from Western Europe, mostly from West Germany and the Netherlands, refrained from criticism of the Soviet Union. Sergei Michalkov, a Soviet participant, was not so reticent about criticizing the United States.

> The USA has announced the possibility of a nuclear war in Europe. Until today, it has not wished to abandon the so-called NATO doctrine which assumes the possibility of a nuclear first strike.
>
> Naturally, the farther away from Europe one is, the easier it is, apparently, to develop such a theory of war, the more acceptable are its prospects, the more it appears to many as possible and—to my horror—even attractive.
>
> Ideologists of nuclear war are not very concerned about the fate of European civilization on the territory of the Old World.[59]

Conference participants did not distinguish between a first use of nuclear weapons in response to a Warsaw Pact conventional attack and a first strike with nuclear weapons that would initiate a war.

Instead, Peter Hartling, a West German writer, rose to denounce technology, bureaucracy, and the language of military strategy. Dieter Lattmann, also from West Germany, praised the growth of the peace movement in Western Europe. Günter de Bruyn, from East Germany, said that because the missiles to be deployed in Western Europe were designed for "*our* annihilation" it was time that East Germans also protested against these Western deployments. Günter Gaus argued for combining realism with the peace movement by exerting pressure on existing governments rather than calling for immediate realization of a bloc-free utopia.[60] In spite of Gaus' realist caveat, the assembled writers agreed that "both power blocs should simultaneously and without preconditions be dissolved."[61] No one mentioned the continuing SS-20 buildup or the zero-zero option.

The INF Talks: November 1981 to Summer 1982

From the beginning of the Geneva talks in November 1981 until summer 1982, while debate raged about moratoriums, freezes, no first use, and nuclear-free zones, the Soviet Union did not change its basic position in Geneva. In August 1982, Defense Marshall Ustinov repeated that the Soviet Union would be willing to reduce its medium-range missiles to 300, a number equal to NATO's nuclear-capable aircraft and the combined British and French nuclear forces. A balance would thus exist without any new American deployments. He said that Reagan's zero option was "clearly intended to torpedo the goal of reaching an agreement."[62] From the beginning of the negotiations over the euromissiles, the Soviet Union consistently followed its own dual-track strategy. With no demonstrations or political oppositioin at home, it stood by its initial position and waited for the pressures created by the political opposition parties and movements in the streets to modify the Western position. It was a strategy appropriate to the asymmetry of democracy and dictatorship. By summer 1982, it had been successful in taking advantage of the split that had emerged between Helmut Schmidt and his own party, between the left in West Germany and the British and French governments, and between those in Western Europe who thought the United States was trying to facilitate a nuclear war limited to Europe and those who did not.

The summer of 1982 did, however, take on symbolic importance in the history of the euromissile dispute because it was in June that Ambassador Paul Nitze and the Soviet negotiator Juri Kvitsinsky had their "walk in the woods" talks. Nitze outlined four principles that would have to be reflected in any agreement acceptable to the United States: no compensation for British and French forces; no aircraft limits that would radically reduce U.S. contributions to the defense of Western Europe; no shifting of SS-20s to the Far East; and any agreement to be equal in overall effect.[63] Kvitsinsky insisted that the zero-zero option was unacceptable. Moscow viewed it as a demand for unilateral disarmament by the Soviet Union.

Nitze and Kvitsinsky developed the following package to present for consideration to their governments: the United States and the USSR would each have 225 long-range intermediate nuclear force (LRINF) missile launchers and aircraft in Europe; each would be limited to a ceiling of 75 LRINF missile launchers in Europe. The USSR would deploy only ballistic missiles. The United States would deploy only cruise missiles. The USSR would be limited to 90 LRINF missile launchers in the eastern USSR, and each ballistic missile launcher would have no more than one missile with no more than three warheads. Each ground-launched cruise missile launcher would have no more than four missiles, each with no more than one warhead. All LRINF missiles in excess of the limits would be destroyed. Limitations on aircraft included the American and Soviet planes capable of conventional and nuclear missions.

After consulting with his superiors in Moscow, Kvitsinsky backed off from this proposal. Moscow insisted on full compensation for third-country forces, i.e., the British and French missiles. There should be no U.S. deployments, no constraints on Soviet deployments in the Eastern USSR, radical reductions in dual-capability aircraft, and full adherence to the principle of equality and parity. Kvitsinsky told Nitze that the "walk in the woods" agreement had been rejected in Moscow, particularly because of the lack of compensation for British and French forces and that he, Kvitsinsky, had been told not to pursue any more informal discussions with Nitze. He told Nitze that the Soviet Union was not prepared to destroy a single SS-20. With the Soviet rejection of the substance of the package and the informal channel itself, the issue was closed.[64] From NATO's perspective, the walk-in-the-woods discussion did not live up to the principle of parity on several levels. It equated ballistic missiles able to reach Western Europe from the Soviet Union in six minutes to cruise missiles that took two-and-a-half hours to cover the same distance. Because the SS-20s had three warheads and the cruise missiles only one, there would be 225 Soviet warheads compared to 75 for NATO, a violation of the principle of parity. The reaction of the Kremlin made such considerations academic, for Moscow rejected any American deployments.

It was to be expected that the West European antimissile forces would blame the United States for the breakdown of the walk-in-the-woods agreement. But, in view of the fact that the agreement would not have made American deployments "superfluous"—the SPD's desired outcome—it was odd that the collapse of the agreement should have caused such consternation. The walk-in-the-woods agreement was exactly like the "arms control" agreements that had done so much to cast doubt on the value of arms control. It ratified by treaty an expansion of nuclear arsenals—75 cruise missiles in Western Europe and 75 SS-20s with 225 warheads pointed at Western Europe in the Soviet Union. From the perspective of those most interested in reducing the numbers of nuclear weapons, it was far inferior to NATO's zero option of November 1981, which called for elimination of all medium-range nuclear missiles in and for Europe. The only thing wrong with that proposal was that the Soviet Union rejected it. Neverthe-less, the legend of a great opportunity squandered by Pentagon hawks be-came part of the popular folklore of the battle of the euromissiles and confirmation for the West German left that the United States was not "negotiating seriously" in Geneva.[65]

By early September 1982, antinuclear sentiment in the West German political establishment was not restricted to the SPD. An antimissile faction among the Free Democrats had also emerged.[66] On September 12, 1982, Jürgen Möllemann, the security-policy spokesman of the FDP in the Bun-destag, who still supported Reagan's zero option, announced his support for transforming Europe into a nuclear-free zone.[67] Möllemann's condi-tions for such a zone were acceptance by the Soviet Union of Reagan's zero option, abandonment by France and Britain of their own nuclear arsenals, and a conventional balance of forces. Nuclear deterrence in Eu-rope would, in the future, be a strictly American task. The existence of France and Britain as nuclear and conventional powers was, Möllemann said, a "senseless splitting of limited forces," a view not likely to be shared in the government ministries in Paris and London.[68]

A Turning Point: Hans-Dietrich Genscher as the Bulwark

Hans-Dietrich Genscher became the pivotal figure in the West German euromissile dispute in late summer of 1982. By then he had concluded that Helmut Schmidt no longer commanded majority support for the double-track decision in the Social Democratic party. Genscher was concerned about the rise of neutralist sentiment in the party.[69] On August 21, 1981, Genscher addressed the Free Democrats of the state of Hessen. Genscher struck the chords of arms control, cooperation in the European commu-nity, and the special German responsibility for peace in Europe. Then, with developments in the Social Democratic party in mind, he said:

> We will not forget, who our friend and ally is, and who is not our friend and ally. We do not stand equally distant from the USA and the Soviet Union. Like the USA, we are a part of the West.
> One must say to those whose talk arouses another impression: American troops are in West Germany in order that free trade unions exist and Soviet troops are in Poland to see to it that free trade unions there do not exist. That is the difference.[70]

Genscher restated the moral dichotomies between dictatorship and democ-racy and the value of West Germany's West orientation and dispelled any hints of a new German flirtation with a third path between East and West. Foreign Minister Genscher did not accept the argument that opposition to the two-track decision was compatible with loyal membership in the NATO alliance, especially given the West German Social Democratic and Social-Liberal—not conservative or neoconservative—origins of the NATO decision. For him, support for the NATO decision was the litmus test of whether the West Germans were or were not good allies or were equidistant from the United States and the Soviet Union.

Genscher concluded that it was necessary, for the sake of continuity in foreign policy, to break up the (left-center) Social-Liberal coalition and to form a new (right-center) Conservative-Liberal coalition with Helmut Kohl's Christian Democrats. Without this shift to right of center in domestic politics, he believed the West German government would not have the basis to implement the foreign and defense policy he had shaped with Helmut Schmidt and the Social Democrats. Long-standing differences between the market-oriented liberals and the statist Social Democrats also played a key role in Genscher's decision to seek a change in government.[71] In the midst of an economic crisis with over two million unemployed, the SPD in Hessen was toying with the idea of an alliance with the Greens. Genscher warned of the "possible ungovernability" of West Germany due to a "red-green-alternative constellation." Genscher said "those who would actually abandon this highly industrialized country on the boundary between East and West to cooperation with spokesmen of neutralism and opposition to [economic] growth, obviously cannot also cooperate with us."[72]

On September 17, 1982, Genscher resigned as foreign minister, took his party out of the governing coalition, and brought the Social-Liberal era begun in 1969 to an end. Schmidt said he was willling to govern in a minority government until new elections were held. Kohl rejected that proposal. Genscher indicated an interest in entering discussions with Kohl about forming a new center-right coalition government. Though Schmidt spoke bitterly of betrayal by his coalition partner, Genscher's assessment of the balance of power in the SPD was correct: Schmidt no longer had the support of a majority of his party.[73]

Genscher saw that the Social Democratic party no longer served as a bulwark against Soviet pressure, so he formed a new barricade. Genscher's decision of September 1982 ranks with Schmidt's London speech as a decisive turning point in the momentum of East–West relations. It represented a most important defeat for the Soviet dual-track diplomatic offensive in Western Europe. In October 1982, Hans-Dietrich Genscher, along with Helmut Kohl, took over the role of "bulwark." Genscher's decision of September 1982 should be seen in the context of the elections of François Mitterand in France, Margaret Thatcher in England, Usiru Nakasone in Japan, and Ronald Reagan in the United States. The Soviet buildup and hard line under Brezhnev had contributed to the coming to power of leaders in the democracies committed to reversing the momentum of the military balance. When one adds China and the Islamic world, Soviet diplomacy had contributed to the formation of a global, counterhegemonic coalition by spreading fear among all of the Soviet Union's potential adversaries *at the same time.* Genscher's decision, filled as it was with considerations of West German domestic politics, was part of a countermovement of the global balance of power.

The Euromissiles and the Conservative-Liberal Coalition

The euromissiles figured prominently in the stormy parliamentary debates of September 9, 1982, leading to the "constructive no-confidence" vote on October 1, which brought the Christian Democratic/Christian Social-Free Democratic (CDU/CSU-FDP) coalition to power. Schmidt reiterated well-known convictions concerning the importance of a balance of forces attained through negotiations, but the irony of the debates was that the strongest supporters of his foreign-policy views were trying to push him or, more accurately, his party out of power.[74] Brandt dismissed charges of anti-Americanism as nonsense.[75] Horst Ehmke called for movement from both the United States and the Soviet Union in the INF talks.[76] Mertes asked Ehmke whether he thought Social Democratic doubts about American negotiating posture defined "being a good ally?"[77] Ehmke responded that he thought being a loyal ally meant that "the Europeans firmly represent their security interests."[78]

Helmut Kohl regretted what he saw as the sorry state of American–West German relations. Beyond the policy differences of the moment, West Germany's anchor in the moral values of the West had come unstuck. Whoever, Kohl said, argued that American and West German security interests were incompatible "destroyed not only the Western alliance, but the peace and freedom for our country."[79] Would the SPD, asked Kohl, stick to its support of the NATO decision, even if the Geneva talks did not reach a successful outcome? If not, would it at least refrain from engaging in a campaign that divided the West Germans into friends of peace and warmongers? He was concerned that the Soviet leadership would doubt NATO's will and pin its hopes on erosion of that will because of the domestic opposition in Western Europe.[80] The tone of the debates was bitter. Conservatives attacked the left for disloyalty to the alliance. Social Democrats attacked the conservatives for subordinating "German interests" to loyalty to the alliance.

On September 16, Karsten Voigt, speaking for the SPD, said neither the United States nor the Soviet Union had taken the security interests of the other side into account in the Geneva talks.[81] Volker Rühe, his counterpart in the CDU, criticized the SPD for failing to stress the shared values that held the Atlantic Alliance together.[82] For the CDU, he continued, the Atlantic community was in the first place "a community of values (*Wertgemeinschaft*)" rather than an "accidental geographical community of interests."[83] Manfred Wörner again drew attention to the interaction of Soviet policy and West German democratic politics in the following terms.

The Soviets sit [at the negotiations]. They have a clear position. They have a maximal position that they put on the table. They stick to this maximal position. They can count on the fact that five or six months later, Messrs. [Karsten] Voigt, [Egon] Bahr, [Willy] Brandt, [Horst] Ehmke . . . will demand movement, and movement not on the other side, but rather on our side. That means, that immediately the Western alliance will again be attacked from the rear.

Don't think that the Soviets don't notice all this! Why should the Soviets make concessions when they know that they can get all they want without giving up anything in return. This is the mechanism [of Soviet policy and strategy]![84]

Wörner said that the "yearning by democracies for peace should not be permitted to become a weapon of intimidation in the hands of the most ruthless" states.[85]

On October 1, 1982, Helmut Kohl became the West German chancellor after winning a "constructive vote of no-confidence" 256 to 249 with 7 abstentions in the Bundestag.[86] On Octobert 13, Kohl delivered his first government statement to the Bundestag. He placed great weight on continuity in foreign and security policy and emphasized that his foreign policy rested on the "fundament" of the North Atlantic alliance and friendship with the United States. This heir of Konrad Adenauer said that "the alliance is the core of German (*Staatsräson*) reason of state." It brought together values, the social order, and security.[87]

He intended to "free German–American relations from the twilight" of the recent past and to stabilize and strengthen this friendship. In tune with his emphasis on continuity, he evoked the Harmel formulas of equilibrium and defense, disarmament and arms control, dialogue and cooperation. In the spirit of "making peace with ever fewer weapons," Kohl stressed support for both parts of the NATO decision of 1979, which, he recalled, had its roots in a Social Democratic government and chancellor. Only, said Kohl, when the Soviet Union was sure that it would have to reckon with deployments of American missiles at the end of 1983 would it be ready to contribute to serious negotiations. He appealed to the Soviet leadership to accept the zero-zero option.[88] He stressed close relations with France and the European Community, promised continuity in relations with the Soviet Union, and expressed "great concern" over developments in Poland, calling for lifting martial law and legalization of Solidarity.

He was determined to end any doubts concerning West Germany's Western orientation. Less than two months after taking office, Kohl had met with Francois Mitterand in Paris, Margaret Thatcher in London, and Ronald Reagan in Washington to initiate the process of improving the atmosphere of West Germany's ties to her Western allies.[89]

Hans-Dietrich Genscher represented continuity in the West German government. In his address to the Bundestag on October 13, 1982, Genscher also focused on the need for reliability and calculability of West German foreign policy and on the need to strengthen the alliance with the United States.

> The path of German foreign policy began in 1949 with the fundamental decision for integration into the West. Then, it was not yet a decision for an alliance. It was—more fundamentally—the decision for a liberal, Western democracy. It was with heart and mind the firm and irrevocable fundamental decision for the value system of free democracy. This value decision is irrevocably rooted in the constitution. It is deeply rooted in our people. It gives our democracy its stability. It earns the trust which other democracies place in us. . . . There is much talk about equidistance, about equal distance to the USA and the Soviet Union.
>
> (Zander [SPD]: Not from us!)
>
> In fact, there are two superpowers, but we are allied with the United States, not because the USA is stronger, but because the United States is a democracy, as we are.[90]

Genscher took issue with SPD General Secretary Peter Glotz, who said West Germany would lose influence if it succumbed to "traditional anti-communism" led by the Americans and would gain influence by taking greater distance from the United States. On the contrary, said Genscher, it was the weight of West Germany in the Western alliance, in the European community, and in alliance with the United States that "determines our

importance in the face of the Soviet Union." Détente could continue only
on the basis of West integration.[91]

On November 11, 1982, a cultural critic and political analyst for the
Frankfürter Allgemeine Zeitung, Ernst-Otto Maetzke, analyzed the euromissile dispute in an editorial entitled "word-missiles."[92] Which alliance system, he asked, was better able to penetrate the public consciousness of the
other? "Who can aim word-missiles (*Wort-Raketen*) that explode in the
mind with greater aim, lasting effect, and successful effect?" In the euromissile dispute, the open societies of the West were far easier to penetrate than
the closed societies of the East. Soviet diplomats and scholars were invited
to "peace weeks" and conferences. They were greeted by West Germans
skeptical of their own government's claims and were able to give interviews
in leading magazines. But

> nothing comparable can be done on behalf of the Western side in
> regard to the East. On the contrary. Through the capabilities of
> totalitarian *Gleichschaltung* (coordination), communist states can keep
> possible discussants, who they see as unreliable customers, out of the
> game.[93]

As a result "only one side will be influenced" by the public controversy.[94]
The asymmetry of dictatorship and democracy appeared to give the advantage to the Soviet Union, which could fight the battle completely on the
terrain of its adversaries, taking full advantage of the virtues of their democratic political institutions. Over the course of the coming year, the West
German government displayed a capacity for democratic resilience that had
been quite unexpected by many of democracy's more pessimistic friends
in Western Europe and the United States.

10

HISTORY, LANGUAGE, AND STRATEGY
November 1982
to August 1983

HELMUT SCHMIDT'S DEPARTURE FROM BONN eliminated the major obstacle in Social Democratic politics to preeminence of the party's foreign-policy left. The major parties were now clearly polarized over the missile issue as they prepared for a special election scheduled for March 6, 1983, which would place the new government in parliament before the electorate. Without Schmidt's restraining influence, the SPD was free to run a campaign whose themes reflected the political culture of "security partnership" and "common security," as well as a definition of "German interests" espoused by a "patriotism of the left."

Egon Bahr: The Meaning of Security Partnership

In November 1982, Egon Bahr published an essay on American and West German neoconservative security policy and the meaning of "security partnership" *(Sicherheitspartnershaft)* in the SPD's monthly journal, *Neue Gesellschaft.*[1] He criticized neoconservatism as "first of all ideological thinking," whose "black-white" picture and visions of "victory over evil, victory over communism" were a "macabre luxury" of the prenuclear era.[2] Neoconservatism, in his view, meant a predominance of military over political thinking and more "domination" of Europe by the United States. Bahr criticized West German neoconservatives, such as Mertes, for speaking about the openness of the European and German question. In so doing, they challenged the legitimacy of the Eastern European governments, reduced the possibility of satisfying German interests there, and "degraded" West Germany to an outpost for American interests.[3] Neoconservatives, he wrote, simply could not see that the existence of nuclear weapons required agreements with the potential enemy. He continued that politics based on the principle of "security partnership," on the other hand, started from the idea that security in the nuclear era could be attained only with, not against the potential adversary. Thinking in terms of friend and enemy or of victory was antiquated and dangerous. Peace had the highest priority. Therefore, a policy focused on human rights in Eastern Europe and the Soviet Union would be "the opposite of coexistence and détente."[4] It would seem that a policy resting on "security partnership" with the Soviet Union would preclude a Western foreign policy that unsettled the Warsaw Pact governments, a policy, for example, seeking "change through rapprochement."

The Missile Election

In the year from November 1982 to November 1983 the Soviet Union pulled all available levers of West German politics. In November 1982, Juri Andropov became the new Soviet prime minister, following Leonid Brezhnev's death. On November 18, Hans-Joachim Vogel, former mayor of Munich and West German minister of justice, became the party's candidate for chancellor in elections to be held on March 6, 1983.[5] Egon Bahr and Carl Friedrich von Weizsäcker became advisers on foreign and security policy. On December 9, 1982, in discussions with American Secretary of State George Shultz, Vogel said that the SPD supported inclusion of Soviet SS-4 and SS-5 missiles as well as British and French missiles in the Geneva talks.[6] On December 20, while affirming the SPD's adherence to the Western alliance, Vogel said the party would not allow "others to take military decisions over our heads" and that the "rightist coalition" in West Germany served neither German nor American interests when it gave the impression that the United States could stick to its zero-zero option, its starting position of November 1981.[7]

On December 21, Andropov said that the Soviet Union would reduce the number of SS-20s in the European part of the Soviet Union to 162, the number of British and French nuclear missiles, if NATO abandoned its plans to deploy American missiles in Western Europe.[8] On December 23, Vogel called the Andropov proposals concerning British and French missiles a "realistic stance," while other SPD leaders criticized an overly quick

American rejection.[9] Manfred Wörner, the new defense minister of the West German government, responded to the Andropov proposals by noting that West Germany's nonnuclear status meant a continuing dependence on American nuclear deterrence.[10] He argued that the Soviet demand to include British and French missiles sought to take advantage of this West German vulnerability by preventing any American deployment while allowing 162 Soviet SS-20s to remain in place. The defense of West Germany would thus be decoupled from the United States, and the Soviet Union would preserve its monopoly of medium-range land-based missiles with the aid of an internationally recognized treaty. On December 29, Horst Ehmke said Andropov's proposals brought "movement" into the talks, while the West German government was failing to exert "pressure" on Washington to reciprocate. He urged inclusion of the British and French missiles and called the zero option a starting point that should lead to a compromise. Phillip Jenninger, minister in the chancellor's office, said the SPD was leaving the common Western position and increasingly approaching "the Soviet negotiating line."[11]

At the end of 1982, NATO estimated that the Soviet Union had deployed over 330 SS-20s, for a total of more than 990 warheads.

On January 7, 1983, the Bundestag was formally dissolved, and what became known as the *Raketenwahlkampf* or "missile campaign" began. Vogel said that if elected the SPD would proceed with deployment only in extreme circumstances.[12] Inclusion of British and French missiles had become the party's campaign position.[13] In a series of articles in *Vorwärts*, Bahr urged that NATO take up Andropov's proposals, especially the key issue of inclusion of British and French missiles. It was, he wrote, unrealistic to assume that the Soviets would reduce the number of their medium-range missiles to zero as long as the British and French deterrents were growing.[14]

The Soviet Union made its sentiments in the election apparent. A visit to Moscow by Vogel and Bahr in early January received extensive coverage in the Soviet press.[15] On January 12, Andropov threatened that "consequences, extremely dangerous to peace in Europe" would follow implementation of NATO's plans to deploy American weapons in West Germany. Vogel responded that "all forces committed to peace" had no task more important than curbing the arms race and removing the threat of nuclear war.[16] Vogel added that "the Soviet side has moved seriously in the direction of an understanding in Geneva."[17]

The Soviets juxtaposed the "misleading" Reagan zero option, "which is tantamount to an invitation to [Soviet] unilateral disarmament," to the Soviet plan of leaving the Soviets with just as many missiles as the British and French. In support of their proposal, they cited Western politicians who supported their proposals. On January 12, Izvestiya quoted Herman Scheer, an SPD deputy in the Bundestag, as having said that "we cannot expect the Soviet Union to reduce its medium range missiles to zero and still remain face to face in Europe with the French and British missiles. . . . A refusal to consider the French and British missiles at the talks would be tantamount to a covert bid for superiority." Izvestiya added, "Yes, a Western bid for superiority. And not so covert."[18] On the same day, TASS described Bahr as a one of the "realistically thinking politicians on the Rhine."[19] It criticized Foreign Minister Genscher for defending "the Reagan 'zero-option,' the absurdity and unacceptability of which is now obvious to any realistically thinking politician."[20]

The missile issue dominated the campaign. The SPD's central campaign slogan was "in German interests." It meant that the West German government should pursue "German" rather than American interests and ensure that new deployments were made "superfluous." Opposition to the deployments was, the SPD claimed, a manifestation of "leftist patriotism."[21] Vogel expressed support for important elements of the Soviet proposals in Geneva, and urged movement away from the zero-zero option.[22] The Social Democrats ran as the peace party but also as the true party of the nation, in contrast to the conservatives who were reducing West Germany to the status of a hostage of the Americans. Kohl and Genscher affirmed their support for the NATO two-track decision. They left no doubt that they would deploy new missiles if an acceptable agreement were not found. They warned of the unpredictability and unrealibility of the SPD in foreign policy and spoke of a "Moscow faction" and of neutralism in the SPD. On January 11, for example, Phillip Jenninger called Andropov's offer "small progress" compared to previous Soviet proposals, but it was in no way adequate. Jenninger said that Soviet goals remained unchanged: preserve "superiority in the realm of land-based nuclear medium range missiles— and with it the potential for political intimidation and blackmail against Western Europe—due to its own previous armament."[23]

Following Andropov's repetition on January 13, of the offer to reduce the number of SS-20s to 162 in exchange for no American deployments, Genscher and Wörner held a press conference to reaffirm their support for the zero-zero option. They said that the West German government was firm in its commitment to deploy missiles if the talks did not lead to a negotiated zero-zero option. They criticized the SPD for giving the impression that if the Soviet Union would reduce some of its SS-20s, NATO would abandon deployments. That would leave the Soviet Union with a monopoly in that category of weapons. The SPD, they continued, endangered prospects for a negotiated solution.[24] Genscher stressed that "the date of the beginning of deployment remains, as planned, the [coming] fall." Wörner criticized Soviet efforts to influence Western public opinion while formally agreeing to keeping negotiations confidential in Geneva. The Soviet Union, he said, would only modify its position in the face of Western unity and determination. He added that the public and the current SPD leadership had forgotten "astonishingly quickly" that it was Helmut Schmidt and the SPD who had originated the zero option. Genscher criticized those who spoke of "Reagan's" or "the Americans'" zero option. The zero option, Genscher continued, was an alliance decision that emerged from West German urging. A zero option only for the West would leave the Soviet Union with a monopoly of medium-range weapons and lead to a "practical decoupling of Western Europe from America." Wörner added that such an outcome would lead to an American exit from Europe. France and Britain could not replace the American nuclear guarantee for West Germany. Genscher and Wörner said a government statement at this time was necessitated by the lack of clarity about the Western position created by the SPD position. "There is no more critical moment than the coming weeks," Wörner added. At this key moment, he added, the SPD's path was all the more dangerous for West Germany and the Western alliance.[25]

Gert Krell, the director of the research group on "arms dynamics and arms control" at the Hessen Foundation for Peace and Conflict Research in Frankfurt, said a solution that set aside the NATO deployments in exchange for Soviet reductions—not necessarily down to zero—was "conceivable." An "interim solution" that entailed a small number of Western deployments was also possible.[26] But Egbert Jahn, director of the research group on socialist countries at the Hessen Foundation and a professor of sociology at the University of Frankfurt, described the Andropov initiatives as a "clever psychological measure in the direction of Western public opinion." No sooner had large parts of the peace movement justified the SS-20 buildup as only a modernization of obsolete SS-4s and SS-5s, than the Soviet proposals undermined these arguments by accepting the notion that the West also felt threatened by the SS-20. The peace movement, he continued, would have to be "more autonomous" in regard to the Soviet Union. "Just as the peace movement adjusts its position to that of the Soviet Union, the Soviets change their position, and then everything falls to pieces."[27] As the Soviets shifted away from earlier positions, those in the West who believed them to be accurate statements about the balance of forces in Europe were placed in the embarrassing position of being more pro-Soviet than the Soviets. Their claims to being opposed to "both superpowers" collapsed in tatters.[28]

On January 14, Vogel, back from Washington and then Moscow, said that "the last word" on the negotiations had not yet been spoken. He said "we do not want any missiles from the East directed at us. Just as little do we want missiles on our soil that present a threat to the East."[29] But Vogel did not explain how he expected to convince the Soviets to eliminate their medium-range arsenal without "presenting a threat to the East." It was now clear that the Social Democrtatic party was willing to accept a medium-range imbalance as an acceptable outcome.

On January 16, Andrei Gromyko, on a three-day visit to Bonn—again the West German peace movement did not organize a protest to greet him—rejected NATO's zero option as "amounting to a unilateral disarmament of the Soviet Union."[30] Western refusal to take British and French systems into account was an attempt to establish NATO superiority and was "completely unrealistic."[31] But Foreign Minister Genscher was not convinced. He responded that the "ever clearer readiness of the SPD" to reject Western deployments while putting up with Soviet medium range missiles endangered both the Geneva negotiations and "German and European security. We do not want to live with a permanent, one-sided Soviet missile threat ratified by a treaty."[32] In his talks with Gromyko, Genscher rejected Soviet proposals for a partial reduction of SS-20s if the NATO decision were rescinded and affirmed the desirability of a zero-zero option.[33] The following day, Kohl assured Gromyko that Bonn was not wavering from the Western alliance. As a result of his talks with Kohl and Genscher, Gromyko knew that this Bonn government could not be split from the American position.[34] The only hope for the Soviet position would be for the SPD to win the election.

The foreign-policy direction of the West German Social Democrats and the emergence of the Greens and the peace movement caused concern in Paris. The political culture of Paris was quite different from that of West Germany. Distinctions between liberal democracy and totalitarian dictatorship were rediscovered and reinforced rather than blurred. Aron's warnings about "decadent Europe" were taken seriously by leftist intellectuals, such as Cornelius Castoriadis and Andre Glucksmann, who wrote essays on Soviet armament and West European pacifism that presented a dark picture of the Soviet threat.[35] The French intellectuals abandoned the Communist party and enthusiasm for Third World revolutions, warmly received Solzhenitsyn, and revived Tocqueville's liberal democratic warnings of the dangers of democratic despotism.

These changes in French political culture led to a greater interest in France in talking about the distinctions between freedom and totalitarianism, distinctions that had become so unfashionable in the era of West German peace policy. It also led to concern about what some French observers saw as the neutralist-nationalist mood in the era of détente.[36] In December 1981, there was a sharp difference in tone in France and West Germany in the reactions to the repression of Solidarity in Poland. With the exception of the increasingly discredited French Communist party, the French political class sharply criticized the repression of human rights in Poland. In West Germany, similarly sharp reactions came more frequently from the centrists and conservatives. The Schmidt government focused on the need for stability. The antinuclear and peace themes of the West German left superseded a public effort to focus on repression of human rights in Eastern Europe.[37]

French observers worried that the Soviet Union would capitalize on neutralist and nationalist sentiment in West Germany to establish a veto over alliance military decisions, weaken NATO's nuclear deterrent, and eventually draw West Germany out of the Western alliance.[38] The emergence of the peace movement directed against the NATO decision rather than the SS-20s deepened fears that *Ostpolitik* had fostered a new German nationalism that would weaken the Western alliance.[39] Partly as a result of French fears of growing Soviet power and of neutralist sentiment on the West German left, the French government moved demonstrably closer to strong supporters of the Atlantic Alliance in West Germany. Giscard d'Estaing had a close relationship with Helmut Schmidt and supported Schmidt's efforts to move NATO toward the two-track decision in 1979. The Socialist Francois Mitterand defended the Gaullist legacy of an independent French nuclear deterrent with equal fervor and was more outspoken about the Soviet threat, freedom in Eastern Europe, and the need for a military balance and strong links to the United States than his center-right predecessor.

In the middle of the West German election campaign of 1983 Mitterand went further: He all but endorsed the conservative-liberal ticket in a speech to the Bundestag on January 20, 1983, on the occasion of the twentieth anniversary of the signing of the treaty of German-French cooperation.[40] Mitterand stressed the need for equilibrium and warned against decoupling Western Europe from the United States. He stressed that, in the INF talks, only comparable weapons could be compared. Soviet missiles were not equal to American aircraft. French missiles were, unlike the thousands in the American and Soviet arsenals, the French deterrent of last resort. They could not be dismantled without eliminating the French nuclear deterrent, which remained independent and sovereign. As a consequence, he rejected the Soviet proposal to incorporate French nuclear weapons in the INF talks.[41] Given the polarization over the missiles in the election, Mitterand's speech amounted to an endorsement of the conservative-liberal coalition in the forthcoming national elections. The following day in Paris, Helmut Kohl stressed the commonality of West German and French interests and assessments. He said "we [West Germans] are not wanderers between two worlds. Our place is in the Atlantic alliance and on the side of our American and French friends."[42] West German Social Democrats and Greens now found themselves in conflict not only with British and American conservatives but also with French Socialists and with Bettino Craxi's Italian Socialists, who also came out in support of the NATO deployments.

The Soviet Union made no secret of its hopes for an SPD victory. On January 19, *Literaturnaya Gazeta* stated that it was crucial to save "Europeans from a nuclear Auschwitz."[43] On January 22, TASS noted that the SPD election program stressed the importance of Andropov's initiatives and of including all nuclear weapons in Europe, British and French missiles among them.[44] With these same resolutions in mind, Helmut Kohl called the SPD a "security risk" for West Germany. He said that the SPD's positions and neutralists leanings could lead to an exit from NATO, which in turn could lead to Soviet hegemony in Europe.[45]

January 30 was the fiftieth anniversary of Hitler's seizure of power. Günter Grass spoke at an SPD meeting in the symbol of German political liberalism, the Paulskirche in Frankfurt/Main, "on the right to resistance."[46] Grass saw a connection between the question of nuclear weapons in 1983 and the Nazi era and spoke of a "right of resistance" to the government's security policies.[47] Grass said that the Geneva negotiations offered little hope for the West Germans. The CDU/CSU-FDP government was "too mindless and too powerless" to defend "Germany's special interests against the allied superpower and our neighbor France. In place of a firm policy, it offers only toadying." Now only resistance could prevent deployment of "instruments of genocide." Deployment of medium-range missiles was not comparable with Auschwitz.

> But there is no great difference between the cynical disregard of the basic ethical values by the ill-famed Wannsee Conference, which decreed the 'final solution,' and the cynicism that in our own day produces war games simulating nuclear combat with projections of here fifty, there eighty million dead. Every German should know that we would be first to feed our numbers into the fighting machine.[48]

Agreement to placing medium-range missiles on German soil would commit the Federal Republic to "nothing less than calculated genocide." The West Germans were "catching up with Orwell's vision of 1984, if not surpassing it." He urged the political leadership of the Federal Republic to "recognize the democratic right to resist, lest the lesson of January 30 be in vain."[49] The lesson was that resistance to the NATO deployments in 1983 should make up for the deficiency of resistance to Nazism in 1933.

The American government also took a keen interest in the West German elections. On February 1, Vice-President George Bush arrived in West Berlin. Five thousand West Berlin leftists demonstrated against his visit, resulting in injuries to ten policeman and damage to store windows and telephone booths in the city center.[50] Bush read an "open letter" from President Reagan that included an offer to meet Andropov anywhere or anytime to sign a zero-zero agreement to "banish from the earth all land-based medium range nuclear weapons, be they American or Soviet." Helmut Kohl urged Andropov to accept the offer. Andropov rejected it as "not serious." The Soviets called the zero option a propaganda maneuver designed to justify deployment of American missiles in Western Europe.[51]

In the first week in February, Hans-Dietrich Genscher, in a speech to the *Wirtschaftsclub Rhein-Main* in Cologne and an interview in *Die Zeit*, discussed neutralism and the SPD.[52] In Cologne, Genscher criticized the SPD's use of the term "German interests" in the context of opposition to American policy, as well as the phrase "both superpowers" to refer to the United States and the Soviet Union. This political language was, he said, an "inclination to equidistance," a step on the road to neutralism, and a "very dangerous development." A neutral Germany outside the Western alliance would be dependent on the Soviet Union. A West Germany wavering between East and West would succumb to Soviet influence and would be an incalculable factor in Europe.

Though the Greens and communist groups called for immediate exit from NATO, Genscher said that the real debate over neutralism had remained hidden. It was present in calls for a nuclear-free zone between the two Germanies or in acceptance of a Soviet monopoly of medium-range land-based missiles. Genscher argued that while these proposals were not neutralist "in themselves . . . their consequences however had to mean the European or German decoupling from the Western security organization."[53] The Social Democrats, he continued, were pursuing a "dangerous course" away from the foreign policy they had previously supported. Because of their approach to the Greens and alternatives, and the potential pressure these groups could exercise on the SPD, the Social Democrats could lead West Germany to neutralism.[54] The SPD's acceptance of a monopoly of medium-range missiles by the Soviet Union was a first step on this road. The prospects of an SPD-Green coalition were another.

Zeit: In Vogel's statements, what you present as the SPD or Vogel position does not appear in such clarity.

Genscher: Isn't what I just said clear enough? But any ambiguity in these questions is dangerous for our country! We cannot become wanderers between worlds. After the Second World War, our contribution to stability in Europe was that we had clear positions: Member of the Western alliance, and a country that sought détente and compromise. . . . If, among these preconditions, one or two become ambiguous or doubtful, then we [West Germans] are no longer a factor of stability in Europe. Rather we become a factor of destabilization.[55]

For the West German foreign minister, the debate over details of the arms control talks was also a debate about neutralism and West orientation in the Federal Republic of Germany.

On February 11, 1983, Alois Mertes spoke of the Vogel's "capitulation" to Egon Bahr and of "the danger of national-neutralism" in the SPD.[56] Bahr's positions in the euromissile controversy rested on his long-held "national-neutralism." To his honor, Mertes said, Bahr was a patriot seeking to overcome Germany's division. But the fact that Bahr was successfully pushing the SPD to a plan for overcoming the division by "gradual decoupling of the power that guarantees our freedom is justifiably causing alarm to all of those in positions of responsibility in the Western world."[57] Bahr's "strategic goal," he continued, was "overcoming Adenauer's *West* and *Deutschlandpolitik* by a thoroughgoing distancing from the USA and an equally thoroughgoing rapprochement with the Soviet Union." Mertes argued that Moscow's goal in Europe was not to wage war but to make

the non-nuclear Federal Republic of Germany including Berlin politically pliable in a process of growing intimidation through the use of pressure, threat and blackmail. The presupposition for the success of this strategy—with formal acceptance of German membership in the alliance—is [West] Germany's internal turn away from America as well as the military and psychological dismantling of the credibility of the American guarantee.[58]

Given this view of Soviet policy, Mertes viewed "national-neutralism" in the SPD to be of key strategic significance.

In mid-February, in *Vorwärts*, Bahr called NATO's strategy of flexible response "unacceptable" and urged Vogel to do "everything possible in order to make new missiles superfluous, not only in German but also in NATO's interest."[59] On February 24, Andrei Gromyko adopted a more threatening tone. He called on Western Europeans to "demonstrate their political maturity" by resisting American missiles. Europeans, he said, had no right to remain "non-participant observers" or "popularizers of American positions."[60]

West German voters faced a clear choice in the election of March 6, 1983. The SPD defined "German interests" as opposition to deployments and accused the conservative-liberal coalition of subordinating the interests of the German nation to those of Western nuclear powers, especially the United States. The Soviet Union favored an SPD victory. The CDU/CSU-FDP coalition presented itself as a *West* German coalition that supported deployments if necessary and accused the Social Democrats of reviving German nationalism and neutralism at the expense of West Germany's Western ties. The Reagan administration—as well as Britain's Thatcher and France's Mitterand—hoped for a conservative-liberal victory.

The CDU/CSU-FDP coalition won a clear victory. The results were: CDU/CSU, 45.8 percent, FDP, 6.9 percent, and SPD 38.2 percent, and the new antimissile Green party 5.6 percent.[61] The SPD lost 4 percent compared to 1980, to the Greens on its left and to the conservative-liberal coalition on its right. The FDP barely escaped extinction after Genscher's unpopular change of government in October 1982. The Greens rode the antimissile, peace, and ecology sentiment into representation in the Bundestag. West Germany became a four-party, rather than three-party system with a left-wing and a right-wing bloc in parliament.[62] The Reagan administration interpreted the conservative-liberal coalition victory as an affirmation of West Germany's Western ties and of plans to deploy the euromissiles if necessary in the coming fall.[63] In Moscow, commentators explained the conservative-liberal victory as a result of the deepening economic crisis, growing unemployment, and, as one put it, "the intensive psychological brainwashing in favor of the right-wing parties carried out against the voters by the Washington administration and NATO circles." This policy amounted to "overt and crude interference by external forces in the internal affairs of a sovereign state."[64] The Soviets also threatened to place nuclear missiles within a six-minute flying time of the United States in case of deployments in Europe.

The election of March 6 was a turning point in postwar history and a continuation of the reversal in the regional balance of forces in Europe that Helmut Schmidt had set in motion in October 1977. The outcome was a defeat for the Soviet Union's diplomatic offensive and for missile opponents in West Germany. The Social Democrats had run the campaign as a referendum on the euromissiles. No one could claim that the West German electorate had not had an opportunity to vote on the missile issue. In response to defeat, the foreign-policy left in the SPD became even more dominant in the party, and there was talk of an SPD-Green coalition.[65]

Both parties had placed the missiles before the voters. There could be no doubt as to which party was more supportive of the NATO decision. Kohl and Genscher sought a mandate from the voters to continue the foreign policy initiated by Helmut Schmidt. Over the next nine months, the opposition turned, without political success, to public opinion polls to reinterpret the meaning of what appeared to be a clear electoral mandate.[66] But Kohl and Genscher's decision to seek a mandate in foreign policy in March 1983 bore fruit in the strength of political support they were able to generate for implementation of a difficult decision. Alois Mertes, now a *Staatsekretär* in the Foreign Ministry, announced his intention to break with the political culture of equidistance in West German foreign policy by again stressing the moral distinctions between freedom and dictatorship, and by giving the public a fuller presentation of Soviet policy and strategy.[67]

On March 29, President Reagan proposed an "interim agreement" in which the United States would agree to deploy a reduced number of Pershing II and cruise missiles provided that the Soviet Union would reduce its weapons to an equal number, without considering British and French weapons. The final goal would remain the elimination of all medium-range missiles. On April 3, Andrei Gromyko rejected the interim solution. On May 3, the Soviets agreed that not only launchers but warheads would serve as the units to be counted in the balance, but the Soviet demand that the Western side reduce the number of its warheads to a number equal to the combined warheads in the British and French forces remained unchanged, as did Soviet opposition to any American deployments.[68] Again, NATO rejected the offer, saying it would codify a Soviet monopoly of medium-range missiles and help to decouple the United States from Western Europe.

In the spring, summer, and fall of 1983, the SPD continued on a foreign-policy course largely charted by Bahr and Brandt. A party commission led by Bahr on "alternative security" policy called for an alternative to nuclear deterrence, for no first use of nuclear weapons, no expansion of conventional forces, and a policy resting on security partnership with the Soviet Union.[69] Rudolf Augstein in *Der Spiegel* continued to assert that the real purpose of the NATO deployments was to limit nuclear war to Central Europe.[70] The superpowers were simply following their interests, and now, he said, the West Germans should pursue theirs.[71]

On April 22 and 23, about forty writers from West and East Germany, the Soviet Union, Denmark, England, Hungary, Austria and Switzerland met in West Berlin for the "Second Berlin Meeting for Declaring Peace."[72] Günter Grass was again a central figure.[73] Grass said that the Soviet Union had made "several disarmament proposals worth examining" while the

American government had rejected them without serious examination. Worse, he continued, the Reagan administration was striving for nuclear superiority for the West and had declared a goal of bankrupting the Soviet Union by an arms race. It was "clear" that the U.S. administration was ready, now as before, for a nuclear first strike and believed that nuclear war, be it limited to Europe or conducted worldwide, to be winnable. The policies of the United States were a "danger to the world community." He said that "nothing can absolve the West if it continues to place its trust in a leadership that threatens genocide." He again appealed for West Germans to engage in resistance. "It is first of all German history, including the resistance that failed to develop in 1933 against the [plans for] genocide announced [by the Nazis] that impels me to this decision."[74] He favored *Vorleistungen* or unilateral gestures or concessions for nuclear disarmament by the West. He hoped for comparable efforts from the East Germans based on

> the German responsibility for peace and the German duty for resistance against the nuclear genocide that is being prepared here [West Germany] and there [East Germany]. [This responsibility] is indivisible because it was and remains Germans who until today and into the future are responsible for Auschwitz.[75]

As we will soon see, the suggestion of such a link between the Nazi past and nuclear deterrence became the cause of one of the most bitter debates in the Bundestag during the whole euromissile dispute.

As they had at the first Berlin meetings, participants from the Soviet Union and East Germany offered a tepid response to Grass's appeal to resist the arms race in the East. A few of the East German writers criticized the repression of the peace protests in the East, though they did not announce plans to "resist" Soviet missile deployments.[76] The Soviet representatives completely rejected Grass's suggestion that writers oppose their government's policies. Sergei Baruzdin, editor of a Soviet journal entitled *Völkerfreundschaft* [Friendship between Peoples], was delighted that the West German writers had spoken out so clearly against the arms race and for peace. Soviet writers, he said, had been doing so for a long time. "We have," he said, "the good fortune . . . that our position accords with the position of the leaders of our state."[77] Baruzdin rejected Reagan's zero option—"You expect us to act as if the English and French missiles or American bombers don't exist."—and repeated the current Soviet proposal in Geneva to reduce the number of SS-20s in European Russia to 162. In fact, he proudly noted that in a special issue of his journal devoted to the theme of "the writer and the preservation of peace," Soviet Foreign Minister Gromyko had repeated recent Soviet negotiating proposals in Geneva. Forty Soviet writers and thirty-five writers from abroad were in this issue. "Why," Baruzdin asked, "can't other countries publish a magazine like this one?"[78]

Grass responded that "it frightens me, when I have to listen to you say that writers are completely and totally in agreement with their government's policy." We should recognize, he continued, that it was the Soviet Union that deployed large numbers of SS-20s during the 1970s and that now "we had to deal with these missiles as well." Baruzdin, Grass continued, served his country badly when he claimed that "love of peace comes exclusively from the East bloc" and that only the West was guilty. Such assumptions were part of "the language of the 1950s."[79] In refusing to criticize their own government's policies, the East bloc representatives fostered the "old hysteria of the new cold war." But Baruzdin was not deterred and met only mild criticism from the conference participants.[80] In response to the Western writers' assertions that political freedom and human rights were related to peace, Herman Kant, president of the East German writer's organization, said that "the first human right is the right to live. We've come together to defend that right." He called the "balance of terror . . . a huge violation of human dignity (applause)."[81]

The Hungarian novelist Georgy Konrad did say that "peace and freedom are parallel." Where individual rights were violated, a "false peace" existed. Yet, for Konrad, the primary evil was "the confrontation of the blocs." He thought that the "democratic movement and the peace movement in Eastern Europe are the same thing," that there was a "new internationalism, extending beyond the blocs," and that "the peace movement in both blocs is the representative of this new internationalism . . . is opposed to nationalism of the blocs and against ideological war."[82] However, whatever Konrad's intentions, the absence of democracy in the Soviet Union and Eastern Europe left made this "new internationalism" impotent to affect the policies of the dictatorships. This particular conference ended without criticizing Soviet armament. Despite the rhetoric of a "new internationalism," the meeting reflected the asymmetry of regimes: all pressure was directed at NATO and the United States. The "writers" at the Berlin peace conferences from the Soviet Union and Eastern Europe echoed the official line of the Soviet government while the dissidents such as Andrei Sakharov and Vladimir Bukofsky, among others, who directly criticized Soviet policy and strategy paid for their outspokenness with internal exile, emigration, or prison.[83]

In May 1983, Erhard Eppler published *Die tödliche Utopie der Sicherheit* [The deadly utopia of security], which presented a revisionist history of the NATO decision that juxtaposed American to German interests.[84] Following the reinterpretations of 1980 and 1981, he said that the new American missiles would serve an American strategy of horizontal escalation.[85] If the Geneva negotiations failed, the Europeans will not reach their goal—dismantling the SS-20s—but the Americans will attain an "optimal capacity for 'decapitation' of the other side."[86] While he did not blame the American government for trying to keep nuclear war from its territory, "no one should hold it against German politicians when they have the same thought about exactly the same thing."[87] The United States had used "German fears of Soviet intimidation to blackmail the Soviets with the permanent threat of 'decapitation' [with the Pershing II]." The result would be that "the Soviets would have little alternative" but to place the Pershing II in West Germany "at the highest spot on its list of target priorities."[88]

Eppler did not revise his position after the announcement of the American zero-zero option of November 1981. Rather, he supported Andropov's offer of December 1982. The Soviet Union "cannot offer much more in Geneva," while the United States could not "make corresponding concessions in Geneva without overthrowing its whole strategy." The Pershing II was central to the American strategy of fighting a nuclear war. "The issue in Geneva is ultimately if this strategy is or is not valid. Up to now, in spite of a clever policy of disinformation and much propaganda, there is no indication that Weinberger's plans [for being able to fight and win a nuclear war] are to be sacrificed in Geneva."[89] Again, Eppler did not ask why the United States proposed to abandon such weapons in a zero-zero option if it were intent on implementing such a strategy.

He argued that the Russians were more serious than the Americans in Geneva "because they have more to fear from Pershing II on German soil than the USA does from SS-20s which cannot reach American territory."

> A nuclear war limited to Europe . . . would totally radiate Germany, leave hundreds of wounds in the Soviet Union while the USA would remain intact. Thus it is in the German interest, to prevent such a conflict, a more urgent interest than for the Soviet Union and still more urgent than for the Americans. The American planners can engage in reflection over the nuclear holocaust in Europe with a cool head. The Soviets can do so less. We Germans cannot do it at all.[90]

If, for the sake of argument, one assumes that American leaders would view death and devastation in Europe "with a cool head," it is not apparent why they would regard the deaths of over 300,000 American soldiers and their dependents in Western Europe with similar detachment. Though Eppler and other members of the antinuclear campaign spoke of dismantling

"images of the enemy" *(Feindbilder),* the image he presented of a technocratic, heartless, American policy intent on threatening a nuclear war limited to Europe was sinister indeed.[91]

Another far more widely read expression of West German Protestant
pacifism was Franz Alt's *Frieden ist Möglich: Die Politik der Bergpredigt* [Peace
Is Possible: The Politics of the Sermon on the Mount]. It appeared in early
1983 and sold more than 200,000 copies before the year was over.[92] Alt
was one of the country's most well-known news personalities. The essay
juxtaposed the Sermon on the Mount to nuclear deterrence. Alt wrote
that the world had to be saved from destruction at the hands of politicians
and military experts. Now it was time to reject the split rationality of minds
contaminated by nuclear weapons. The conflict of systems had become
unimportant. The main enemy was nuclear weapons themselves. The
peace movement in East and West Germany was a German liberation
movement that brought East and West Germans together in a common
yearning for peace. This most successful book from the antinuclear campaign was further evidence of the intertwining of antinuclear and nationalist sentiment in West Germany.

In spring 1983 the Schmidt wing of the SPD was on the defensive. In
late May, ten professors of history and political science, members of the
SPD, publicly criticized the party's transformation towards a redefined
left.[93] They argued that the SPD was too defensive towards the Greens
and alternatives. With its electoral slogan "in German interests," it had
created fears within and outside West Germany about a new "equidistance" from East and West. The SPD, the signers wrote, had ceased to
speak "openly about the purpose of Soviet missile armament: in the short
run, exerting pressure on West Europeans, in the medium run, decoupling
of Europe and the United States, and in the long run a change of European
relations in favor of the soviet Union."[94] The impression was widespread
that a Social Democratic West German government would accept a regional monopoly of the Soviet Union in the sphere of medium-range missiles. In the name of exerting justifiable pressure on Washington and Moscow, "the Western negotiating position had been weakened." The
boundaries between the SPD and the peace movement during the election
were so "formulaic and abstract" that the SPD gave the image of a party
beginning to leave the West German security consensus.[95] Hans Joachim
Vogel said there were "no new elements and no new thoughts" in the
statement, which was true, but neglected the issue of its validity.[96] The
position of the last West German Social Democratic chancellor was now
voiced by a distinct minority in the SPD.

In the Bundestag, in May and June 1983, there was a great deal of repetition about the euromissiles. Kohl affirmed West Germany's Western ties. Vogel warned of the nuclear peril and urged inclusion of British and French missiles. Genscher criticized the illusions of West German neutralism.[97] The presence of the Greens, on top of the high stakes of the issue, produced a number of sharp and interesting exchanges.

Alfred Dregger, a parliamentary leader of the CDU/CSU from Frankfurt/Main, noted with regret the "deficit of information by our people," which, he said, was due to the reluctance of Western governments to present uncomfortable facts to the public. As a result, the Soviet Union had been able "to influence the consciousness and the opinion formation of a party of our citizens to greater extent than at any time in the postwar era."[98]

> In this effort to win the souls of Europeans, the Soviet Union can use the differences in the political systems of East and West. A public discussion of the missile issue exists only in the West, not in the East. The East intensively takes part in our discussions, and influences it through disinformation, propaganda, and focused efforts to foster fear. On the other hand, we do not take part in the Eastern discussion. In the East, this discussion is only conducted by the Politburo and the General Staff. Free media and free parties, who could participate in a free discussion, do not exist there.
>
> (Call from the SPD: Not even in the Politburo?)
>
> All of this had led to confusion in Western opinion formation, to turning the facts on their heads.[99]

The Soviet Union, Dregger continued, not the West, advocated offensive, war-fighting strategies. At the level of intercontinental missiles and short-range missiles, no less than for medium-range weapons, the Soviet Union strove for superiority, not a balance.

> The arrogance with which the Soviet Union has sought to influence the domestic political decisions of the West, and the readiness to surrender which it finds among a part of Western public opinion, raises the impression that such a military superiority of the Soviet Union already exists and has begun to have a psychological impact.[100]

In his assessment of the asymmetry of open and closed societies, he wondered if NATO had overburdened the Western public. Dregger argued that after years in which Soviet "overarmament" was inadequately reported, it would have made more sense for NATO immediately to deploy its new missiles and then to offer negotiations. "Probably, with an equality of starting points, an agreement on missile limitations would have been concluded long ago."[101] By March 1983, the Soviets had deployed 351 SS-20s, with 1053 warheads, and no new American missiles had arrived. In such circumstances, when, as Mitterand was reported to have said, the Soviets were deploying missiles while the West was deploying pacifists, it was not surprising to see concern about the capacity of democracies to resist dictatorial diplomatic offensives.[102] Even in his pessimism, Dregger regretted the absence of public discussion in the East and the inadequacy of the job done by Western governments seeking to make their case. He was not seeking to reduce public discussion in the West.

The Soviet military buildup helped to solidify a global counterhegemonic coalition. On May 29, 1983, in Williamsburg, Virginia, the leaders of the United States, Canada, France, Great Britain, Italy, Japan, and West Germany gathered at the world economic summit took the unprecedented step of issuing a declaration concerning security policy. American officials interpreted the willingness of all the participants to agree to a statement as evidence that the Soviet effort to separate the United States from its overseas allies had backfired. Instead of splitting the United States from its European and Asian allies, it had fostered a deeper sense of unity among the democracies.[103] The U.S. State Department said that the SS-20 buildup represented a "demand for military superiority and thus world domination."[104] The joint statement rejected inclusion of French and British missiles in the INF talks and criticized the Soviet effort to include them as part of its effort to attain military superiority and eventually global domination. Nor would the participants "agree to a treaty which shifts the SS-20 threat to our friends and allies in Asia."[105] Not only had the Soviet effort failed to separate Western Europe from the United States, but it had also led to a strengthening of alliance bonds between the United States and its allies in Western Europe and Japan in questions concerning the military balance of power.

At Williamsburg, Helmut Kohl received much needed support, as did the British and French. After Williamsburg, Kohl could now make the argument in West Germany that the genuine "new internationalism" was that of the governments of the democratic states and capitalist economies. He, not his Social Democratic adversaries, was in step with the leaders of all the major democracies. In his report to the Bundestag of June 9, he said that Japan's decision to sign the Williamsburg statement indicated that the danger for peace in the world was not "divisible" and that "the Soviet overarmament is felt to be a global threat."[106] He warned the Soviet leadership not to make the mistake of taking its own propaganda seriously and doubting the determination of the West to fulfill the NATO decision. The

Soviets, he said, would be "ill-advised" to base their negotiating strategy on such a mistaken assessment of the political situation in Western Europe.[107]

On June 15, a very extensive debate on the euromissiles took place in the Bundestag. Genscher warned that "whoever moves away from the NATO two-track decision, whoever gives up one of its two parts endangers the disarmament negotiations in Geneva."[108] New Western deployments could be wholly or partially avoided if the Soviet Union would wholly or partly abandon its own preceding armament. The "key to success in the negotiations lay in Moscow." Positive results in Geneva, possibly the elimination of all intermediate-range nuclear weapons, would arrive only when the Soviet Union had no doubts about the West's determination.[109]

In the same debate, Egon Bahr took the unusual, for him, step of criticizing the Soviet Union. "No one in Moscow," he said, had been able to offer a "plausible explanation" why the Soviet Union had deployed "250 SS-20s with 750 warheads" (according to NATO sources, the actual number then was 351 launchers and 1053 warheads).[110] Bahr continued that if there had been a balance in 1978, it no longer existed. He said that the SS-20s could not be a response to British and French programs that had not yet been implemented. What "additional targets" had to be covered that had not been covered by the SS-4s and SS-5s? What political considerations stood behind the "rapid growth of the SS-20s" that outweighed the damage they had already done to detente? The Soviet armament in this matter was "not acceptable," and when it persisted, the West "must do something against it." Bahr asked why, if Andropov was willing to reduce to 162 missiles, he would not agree to even lower numbers?[111] Perhaps Bahr understood that Andropov's and Gromyko's hard line was making it difficult to convince the West German electorate that the United States was the main barrier to a negotiated solution.

Yet Bahr did not go so far as to support the NATO position. His primary goal remained attaining enough reductions in the SS-20s to make any new American deployments "superfluous. That was our zero from the beginning. It did not include zero on the Soviet side."[112] Bahr interpreted the NATO decision of 1979 to mean that only SS-20s deployed after December 1979 would be affected by the negotiations. The zero option was an "extreme starting position." The current Western position was "not only absurd but abandoned above all the foundation of the NATO double-decision." Bahr's was now willing to accept a state of affairs which, in 1977 and even more in 1979, led Helmut Schmidt to initiate and support the two-track decision.

The Greens were the novel element in the Bundestag debates of spring 1983. Gert Bastian, now a member of their parliamentary delegation, presented the Green's indictment.[113] It ran as follows: the American position in Geneva was a hoax. Its purpose was to create a failure of the negotiations that would legitimate deployments. The SS-20s posed no new threat to Western Europe that had not previously existed from the SS-4s and SS-5s. In view of the Western nuclear deterrent, the Soviet Union was not in a credible position to threaten or intimidate Western Europe. A balance did exist when the sea-based missiles of the United States, France, and Britain were taken into account. The zero option was "not serious" because it asked the Soviets to reduce already-existing missiles, in exchange for which the West would not deploy missiles in the future.

Bastian asserted that the Pershing IIs were "ten times" more accurate than the SS-20s. They served to "make possible a nuclear war that is not burdened with the danger of escalation." Their purpose was to facilitate a "decapitation strategy" against military and political leaders.[114] The 108 Pershing IIs would be adequate to paralyze the most important Soviet leadership centers. In a crisis, there would be great pressure to use these weapons before losing them. Thus, the Western negotiating position should change. Not only should the SS-20s be reduced but so should "already existing" weapons of the West.[115] The Green's opposition to the NATO decision was unequivocal, no matter how many SS-20s the Soviet Union had.

The interventions of Manfred Wörner, like those of Alois Mertes, did not fit the image of a depoliticizing, technocratic government facing a politicizing, democratic opposition. It was the political dimensions of military affairs that were most in evidence in the defense minister's remarks in the June 15 debate. Wörner said that it was not the arms race that created the East-West conflict "but the suppression of the freedom of European peoples" and the expansive policies of Soviet power-politics.[116] As the Berlin Wall and the killing apparatus on the German-German border indicated,

> the tensions between East and West are not founded in missiles, but in the conflict between freedom and dictatorship. Peace is not threatened because weapons exist but rather because powers exist which use these weapons for political purposes or for domination. . . . The real threat to peace exists where people are separated by violence, where human rights and human dignity is trampled, and where freedom is suppressed.

(Ms. Beck-Oberdorf [Greens]: Chile, for example!)

When you interrupt, I can only say: Nowhere is this clearer than in the treatment of the members of the peace movement in East and

West. . . . Here you can argue freely. You can protest. You can demonstrate. There you will be imprisoned or forcefully sent over to us. . . . That is the reason we cannot permit the peace discussion to be reduced to a discussion about weapons. Peace between peoples does not exist without freedom and human rights.[117]

Wörner recounted and assessed Soviet claims about the balance of power in Europe from 1977 to 1983:

When we took the double-decision in 1979, the USSR already had 140 SS-20s. We had none. In 1979, Brezhnev declared that an equilibrium existed. In February 1980, the Soviets already had 210 SS-20s. We still had none. And Brezhnev again declared that there was an approximate equilibrium. In March 1982, when the USSR had 300 SS-20s, and we still had none, the Soviets declared a unilateral moratorium. . . . Despite the moratorium, in August 1982, there were 320 SS-20s. And the Soviet Defense Minister declared that today there still exists an approximate balance of forces. Now the Soviet Union has 351 SS-20s. We still have not deployed any weapons.[118]

What more evidence, he asked, could one seek of a readiness to make concessions than the Western policy of 1977 to 1983? But one-sided restraint would not secure peace.[119] He criticized those who called nuclear deterrence ethically unacceptable. Such views lead to "capitulation of the peaceful before the practitioners of violence, of freedom in the face of unfreedom, of law before illegality" and would give "license for nuclear intimidation by aggressive dictatorships."[120] Didn't, he asked, World War II break out because "the Western democracies had unilaterally weakened themselves?"[121]

Wörner addressed Egon Bahr. It was the Social-Liberal coalition government that took the deployment decision.[122] The West Germans asked for land-based rather than sea-based missiles in order to deepen the coupling of the United States to Western Europe. Bahr, he said, "knows better" than to say that the United States was not negotiating in good faith. "It was you who pushed the Americans to the zero-option." How, he asked Bahr, could the Social Democrats criticize the Christian Democrats for adopting the zero option that the Social Democrats had first proposed? Rather than criticize American stubbornness, it was better to "cast your gaze towards Moscow, and not so much to Washington![123] . . . Consider very carefully the way you are arguing here and what signals you are sending the Soviet Union."[124]

The defense minister rejected the Soviet demand that British and French missiles be included in the Geneva talks. The Soviets knew that American weapons were intended to guarantee the security of "non-nuclear" states in Western Europe and that British and French weapons were weapons of last resort to be used in the event of attacks on those countries. The Soviets, Wörner argued, sought a triple-layered system of security in Europe. At the top would be the Soviet Union. In the second tier would be France and Britain. The nonnuclear states, especially West Germany, would be in the third tier, and the United States would have a much diminished presence and political status in Europe.[125]

Wörner rejected the case against the euromissiles built on the reinterpretations of 1980 and 1981. The Pershing II and cruise missiles could not be used for a "decapitation" strike. The Pershing II could not reach Moscow. Only a tenth of Soviet missiles and very few military and political command centers were within their range. The SS-20s had flight times as short as the Pershing II. Didn't West German citizens have a right to security equal to that of Soviet citizens? He attacked as a "fairy tale" the idea that the NATO euromissiles were designed to fight a nuclear war limited to Europe. He quoted Soviet Defense Minister Ustinov to the effect that the Soviet Union would retaliate against the United States if it were struck by Pershing II and cruise missiles from Western Europe.[126] Finally, he pointed out that since November 18, 1981, Moscow had had it within its power to prevent deployments of new American missiles in Western Europe. All it had to do was to dismantle its own preceding armament, armament which it "absolutely does not need for its own defense, or for preservation of its own legitimate security interests."[127]

Whether or not there may have existed a "depoliticized public sphere" in West Germany in the past, as had been asserted by some West German social scientists, it was nowhere in evidence in the Bundestag during the euromissile debates. There was no dimension of the political issue that did not receive a full hearing. To win a battle for majority sentiment in West German democracy, a plausible case was most important. The Soviet disadvantage in this instance was that its case did not stand the test of extended public scrutiny. At the end of debate on June 15, the Bundestag, on a party-line vote, passed a CDU/CSU–FDP resolution supporting the government's position.[128]

The Nazi Past and the Nuclear Present

As we have seen, the association of Auschwitz and the Holocaust with nuclear weapons had been a part of the antimissile opposition from its beginnings in 1980 and 1981. In addition to the comments by Anton

Andreas-Guha and Günter Grass, this theme figured in Soviet propaganda of a "nuclear Auschwitz" and in the Greens' organization of a "Nuremberg trial" of the superpowers. In June 1983, the shadow of Auschwitz fell on the debates in the Bundestag after two prominent members of the Green parliamentary faction, Joschka Fischer and Otto Schilly, gave an interview to *Der Spiegel.* In the course of the interview Fischer said the following:

> It is certainly true, that the uniqueness of the crimes which the National Socialists perpetrated on the Jews cannot be covered up with quick analogies. But I find it morally horrifying that apparently in the system-logic of the modern, even after Auschwitz, that it is not yet taboo to continue to prepare means of mass annihilation—this time not on the basis of racial ideology but on the basis of the East-West conflict. I am not making an analogy with Auschwitz, but I say that Auschwitz warns us to denounce this logic where it surfaces and to fight it politically.[129]

With due allowance for Fischer's nuance, his comments blurred the distinction between nuclear deterrence and "calculated genocide."

It was at this point that Heiner Geissler, the general secretary of the Christian Democratic Union, entered the fray. In late May, Geissler had called an "ethical grounding of defense policy" the most important task of the CDU in the coming months.[130] Geissler wanted to focus attention on questions such as whether West Germany was worth defending or if it faced a real threat. If the state was worthless, the threat nonexistent, no weapons were needed. Geissler believed that these questions had been neglected in what he regarded as the overly technical public focus on weapons and negotiations.

In the Bundestag debate of June 15, Geissler said that the "intellectual-spiritual foundations" (*geistigen Grundlagen*) of the "future of our free democracy and of the Western alliance" had been lost in the discussion of the details of arms and arms control talks. He was determined not to make the same mistake as the Schmidt government, which, he said, "remained in the military-technical details of defense policy, but lost the *geistige* (intellectual-moral) leadership in the debate over the proper defense policy."[131] He referred to "a wholly unbelievable reversal of concepts and values" evident in Joschka Fischer's comments linking "our defense policy of nuclear deterrence and a 'second Auschwitz.'"[132]

> Mr. Fischer, as my answer to what you said, I would point out the following. The pacifism of the 1930s, which in its foundations in an ethics of conviction (*gesinnungsethischen Begründung*) is distinguished

very little from the pacifism of today, this pacifism of the 1930s first made Auschwitz possible.

(Applause from the CDU/CSU—Schilly [Green]: That is an absolutely shameless statement!—Further objections from the Greens and the SPD)[133]

As a storm of protest exploded in the Bundestag, Geissler urged the members of the Bundestag to read the debates between Churchill and Chamberlain in the British House of Commons about "how the free, Western democracies should have behaved towards the totalitarian dictatorship of National Socialism . . . there is absolutely no question . . . but that National Socialism would not have been in a position to begin the war in 1939 if the Western powers had taken a clear position in their own defense."[134] In the face of a growing din of catcalls and objections, he said that

the whole horrible and murderous development in the National Socialist regime with death and murder of millions of people would not have been possible if the weakness of the free democracies had not made it easier for the National Socialist regime to begin the war. That is the truth. . . . I fear that in the ongoing world-wide, ideological civil war now going on, if those win who want us, the free democracies to pursue unilateral disarmament, and in particular at the level of nuclear weapons

(Fischer: [Frankfurt] [Greens]: Going from five times to four times needed for overkill!)

then a world-wide Gulag Archipelago would be the result. I'm convinced of that.[135]

Geissler's point, that pacifist sentiment in Britain in the 1930s weakened British resistance to the Nazis, was not a novel one.[136] On the contrary, it was a key theme in the realist tradition in the study of international politics in postwar Britain, France, and the United States.[137] Judging by the outraged response to Geissler's statement, it was not a common theme in West German political culture. His critics accused him of blaming German pacifists for Nazi aggression. Geissler responded that Neville Chamberlain himself was not a pacifist but that in French and British democracy pacifist currents could influence the government while in the Third Reich they had no such opportunity. "Today we find ourselves in the same situation. We must discuss the consequences of pacifism in free democracies."[138]

Horst Ehmke, the leader of the SPD parliamentary fraction, stressed that

Chamberlain was not a pacifist but a "British right-winger" who hoped to turn Hitler against the Bolsheviks.

> It was the German Right in Weimar that made Auschwitz possible by helping put Hitler in the saddle. . . . If there was anything interesting in the Geissler speech, it was that it once again underscored what a tie there still exists between this tradition [the German Right] and parts of both conservative parties today.[139]

In the American or British context, Geissler's remarks, while perhaps a bit startling coming from a West German politician, restated historical lessons about which many conservatives and liberals were in agreement. The SPD and the Greens were so infuriated by Geissler's statements that they tried to have him dismissed from his cabinet position as Minister of Youth, Family, and Health.

On June 23, for only the fifth time in West German history, the Bundestag debated a resolution to dismiss a sitting cabinet member.[140] Hans-Joachim Vogel attacked Geissler and Dregger, the latter for raising the specter of the "stab in the back legend" of the 1920s and the former for obscuring the roots of the Nazi crimes with his comments about pacifism.[141] Vogel asked if Chamberlain was a pacifist or if the Maginot Line had been built by pacifists? Was it not the nationalist right in France that looked favorably on Hitler's anticommunism? Was today's Soviet Union to be compared to Hitler, and NATO's weaknesses with those of Britain and France before 1938? Vogel accused Geissler of a "dangerous falsification of history," which diverted attention from the real sources of the Nazi seizure of power. He insisted that Kohl distance himself from Geissler's remarks, which only served to divide the country into two hostile camps, and he rejected suggestion that the SPD was less than patriotic.[142]

Kohl, speaking in defense of Geissler, referred to "the so-called peace movement" that had attacked Western defense policy "with concepts intended to destroy the moral substance and foundation of this defense policy."

> It began, and is constantly and at every opportunity morally equating the policy of the United States and that of the Soviet Union.
>
> (Fischer [Frankfurt] [Green]: In the consequences of annihilation, they are indeed the same!)
>
> The claim has been spread that the West . . . is preparing an atomic Auschwitz. . . . In this manner, this concept of an atomic Auschwitz became a political and moral slogan of battle with which the defense capability, the will for defense, and the ethical foundations of the

defense capability of Western democracies were placed on the same level with National Socialist crimes. . . . The goal of this action is perfectly clear. [It is] to place those who represent the position of Western defense policy on the moral defensive.[143]

Kohl stressed that Geissler did not intend to make German pacifists responsible for Auschwitz or to divert responsibility for it from its Nazi perpetrators. But it was a "historical truth" that neither French Prime Minister Edward Daladier or British Prime Minister Neville Chamberlain were ready to resist the German dictatorship. Kohl, describing Winston Churchill as "one of the great statesmen of this century," quoted from Churchill's *Gathering Storm* concerning the contribution made by British appeasers to the coming of World War II. Kohl said that Geissler's point about the peace movements of the 1980s was the same as Churchill's was about appeasement in the 1930s. One-sided disarmament by democracies faced with dictatorships, in the 1930s and in the 1980s, was not an effective guarantee of peace.[144]

Otto Schilly, the Greens' leading debater in the Bundestag, interpreted the Greens to be heirs of the "German anti-fascist resistance," which, he said, was "our [the Greens] historical reference point, to which we have oriented ourselves politically."[145] Schilly continued that, instead of creation of "another Germany" on the foundation of the antifascist resistance, the politics of the two German states became instrumentalized into "vassals" in the Cold War, as a result of which "old traditions and social structures were reinstituted. The restoration began."[146] Schilly blamed Adenauer's policy of West integration for foreclosing the option of a neutral, unified, and demilitarized Germany.

Jürgen Schmude, a Social Democratic member of the Bundestag, in his speech calling for Geissler's dismissal, accused him of obscuring the responsibility for the murder of the Jews and fostering "hatred and intolerance" against the peace movement and contemporary pacifists.

> Under any conceivable point of view, it is misleading and contemptible to bring the pacifism of the 1930s into any kind of causal connection with racial hatred and mass murder. . . . But that is precisely what Mr. Geissler did. . . . take your expressions back without conditions and evasions!"[147]

Schmude said Geissler had "damaged our democracy" to such an extent that dismissal was in order.

The debate ended with comments by its two original protagonists. Joschka Fischer said that "Auschwitz was the result of a perverse will for annihilation of the German government; the atomic holocaust will be the result of [*Sachzwängen*] objective technical necessities."[148] Fischer continued:

> You continued with the old German nationalist whining fairy tale: Foreigners are guilty for everything. For the German Right, it was always the others—other countries, Versailles, the November criminals, the Bolsheviks, the stab-in-the-back, and now pacifists. Only it was never the perpetrators themselves, these clean, orderly Germans in evening dress, uniforms, and of course with national commitment.
>
> (Applause from the Greens and members of the SPD)
>
> Before you, Mr. Minister, in a measureless lie, accuse the peace movements of the 1930s in England and France for the guilt for Auschwitz, you should think about this: Was it foreigners who helped Hitler to power in 1933? Was it not the German National Party, the Hugenbergs and Papens, the Krupps and Flicks?[149]

It was, Fischer continued, only the communists and social democrats who had resisted the creation of a "brown dictatorship."

> The German Right—including you, Mr. Geissler—will never be able to talk itself out of its responsibility for the genocide in Auschwitz. This legacy, which your party always purposefully neglects, has been saved and continued in the West German postwar republic. The Globkes, Oberländers, Vialons, Kiesingers, and Filbingers have existed without doubt
>
> (Applause from the Greens—Boos and vehement objections from the CDU/CSU)
>
> just as all of the civil servants, judges, doctors and economic leaders who first made possible or at least acquiesced in the brown mass murder. They too were main pillars of this republic and of the governing Christian parties![150]

The central indictment against the West German conservatives, made especially by the Greens and at times by the SPD, was that West German conservatism was not so Westernized and democratic after all, but had strong resemblances to German conservatism of the 1920s and 1930s, and even to Nazism. Geissler's comparison of the pacifism of the 1930s and 1980s was said to be evidence of this continuity. In this climate, it was not surprising that the idea of an "atomic Auschwitz," would emerge as a potent weapon of rhetorical combat.

In his response, Geissler said that the German and British pacifists of the 1920s and 1930s were not responsible for Auschwitz. The responsibility, he continued, lay with the Nazis, right-wing extremism and hatred of the Jews. He acknowledged that he should have made this point more clearly in his remarks of the previous week. Rather than refer to Auschwitz, "I should have said: The war would not have been possible." But Auschwitz would not have been possible without "Hitler's totalitarian military attack." He had used the word "Auschwitz" in response to the term "atomic Auschwitz," which had been introduced as a "battle slogan" directed against our defense policy.[151]

Geissler continued that the pacifists he had in mind were not German pacifists but those in England and France who encouraged a policy of appeasement and weakened the defense of the democracies against Hitler. British appeasers and pacifists had "played the same role in England as does today's so-called peace movement" because "in all of the crises unleashed by the National Socialists, they spoke out for non-intervention by England," supported Germany in the Czech crisis, and celebrated the Munich agreement as "an act of justice."[152] Geissler suggested that the members of the Bundestag read Churchill's memoirs on these matters. After apologizing to those whose feelings he had unintentionally hurt, he said he stood by his original statement.

> Those, faced with the dictator, for whom peace at any price was a higher good and for these reasons did not take up arms with the dictators although they could have done so made Hitler's crimes possible. They did not want them, intend them but they made them possible through error, through neglect, as described by Churchill, as the Chancellor quoted this morning
>
> (Vigorous applause from the CDU/CSU and FDP—Objection from Dr. Ehmke [Bonn] [SPD])
>
> for—I am convinced of this—if Hitler had not been able to conquer Europe with this insane war, Auschwitz would not have been possible.[153]

In 1983, Geissler continued, the West Germans were faced with the dilemma of whether a freely elected West German government could implement the NATO double-track decision "against the domestic political pressure of the so-called peace movement." Discussion about the relationship between the 1930s and the 1980s was therefore necessary. Members of the peace movement as well had to "radically think through the consequences to their end," which would emerge "if their political ideas of radical, unilateral disarmament were to attain a political majority in the Western democracies. . . . Auschwitz cannot be undone. But those of us living today can preserve our freedom, if we learn from history."[154] In a straight party-line vote, the conservative-liberal coalition defeated the motion supported by the SPD and the Greens to dismiss Geissler 279 to 210 with one abstention.[155]

Geissler's speech, far from suggesting an unrepentant and unlearning "German Right," was evidence of its Westernization after 1945. German conservatism did not attack British appeasement policy in the 1930s. The conservatives of the Weimar era, rather than worrying about how to defend democracies against dictatorships, thought a great deal about how best to destroy the Weimar Republic. Geissler and Kohl were correct. The political intent in the use of terms like "nuclear Auschwitz" in West German politics was to make a connection between the NATO decision and Nazi criminality.

Perhaps the greatest threat that Heiner Geissler posed to the West German left was that he was breaking a claim to monopolize the moral high ground in the interpretation of the Nazi past. There were a plurality of lessons for West Germans to learn from German history in 1983. Though Hitler's Germany was not Brezhnev's Russia, the neutralist currents of the West German 1980s shared some of the illusions of the appeasing and pacifist left in Britain of the 1930s. Geissler's speech and Kohl's defense drew out lessons about democracy and dictatorship in modern European history and power politics that were quite different from those drawn by a left that assumed that mention of the Nazi past in West Germany would lead almost automatically to rejection of balance-of-power politics.

In the political culture of the West German left, it seemed that "coming to terms with the Nazi past" did not extend to analysis of appeasement, Munich, and the origins of World War II, and that any effort to compare the Nazi and the Soviet dictatorships in regard to their conduct of foreign policy was taboo. None of Geissler's critics entertained the possibility that power politics and moral purpose in mid-1930s Britain might have stopped Hitler. Geissler had put the West German left on notice that he was determined to make a vigorous argument about the multiplicity of lessons that the Nazis held for West Germans. As subsequent events were to show, the West German conservatives were not always successful in combining resolution in the present with openness to the dark memories of the Nazi years.

Summer 1983

Antimissile sentiment in the SPD was now unstoppable. On June 26, 1983, the executive committee of the SPD of Baden-Wurtenburg, following the SPD organizations in Bremen and Central Rhine, rejected the proposed deployments.[156] On June 29, the report on "alternative strategies" by an

SPD group led by Bahr and Apel was presented to the party.[157] In addition to repeating familiar themes of security partnership, common security, and transforming the East-West confrontation into a European peace order, the report called for "replacing the strategy of nuclear deterrence."[158] Short- and medium-range nuclear weapons should be eliminated by negotiations. West Germany should remain in NATO but adopt a program of a "con-ventionalization" of its military strategy.[159] There should be agreements to withdraw nuclear weapons from all states that did not themselves possess them. Then all nuclear weapons should be withdrawn from Eastern and Western Europe, leaving behind a "nuclear-free Europe."[160]

The "new strategies" report of summer 1983 was an argument for de-nuclearization of NATO strategy. A nuclear-free West Germany would mean the end of NATO's previous flexible response strategy. It would fit into long-held Soviet hopes for a denuclearization of Western Europe, which would enhance the power of the Warsaw Pact's superiorities in conventional forces. The new strategies report was clearly incompatible with deployments of any Pershing II or cruise missiles. It also rested on the—erroneous—assumption that the United States would be willing to continue to protect West Germany without any nuclear component in Western Europe.

As pleased as the Soviet Union may have been with these views in the SPD, it made no effort to conceal displeasure with Helmut Kohl and Hans-Dietrich Genscher. In Moscow on July 4 and 5, for meetings with Andro-pov, Chancellor Kohl was told that deployments of American missiles would lead to a "brutal aggravation" of the European situation, to Soviet countermeasures, and to a deterioration in Soviet and East German rela-tions with West Germany. Kohl told Andropov that acceptance of the zero-zero option remained the optimal outcome for all concerned.[161]

In West Germany, the Social Democratic abandonment of the two-track decision continued unabated. On July 6, the Bremen regional SPD an-nounced that "parliamentary majorities do not legitimate the NATO gov-ernments to raise the danger of a nuclear war in Europe which would make their own peoples victims" and therefore there was a "right of resis-tance" against the deployments.[162] On July 20, the SPD organization in Munich rejected the deployments.[163] In late July, Oskar Lafontaine called for the denuclearization of West Germany.[164]

On August 28, in preparation for the last round of negotiations before deployments, Yuri Andropov again proposed that the Soviet Union would reduce the number of its SS-20s to a number equal to that of the British and French missiles.[165] The proposal was identical in essentials to previous Soviet proposals that would have prevented any American deployments and preserved a Soviet monopoly. The NATO governments rejected it.[166]

Andropov followed his proposal with letters to the Western governments threatening a cooling of relations should the West deploy missiles.[167]

In August, Oskar Lafontaine published *Angst vor den Freunden: Die Atomwaffen-Strategie der Supermächte zerstört die Bündnisse* [Fear of One's Friends: The Nuclear Weapon Strategy of the Superpowers Destroys the Alliances]. By the end of September, it had sold 40,000 copies.[168] Lafontaine wrote that technology and the rivalry of "both superpowers and their global imperial policy" were the causes of the worldwide arms race. He called for a Gaullism of the left, a West German exit from the integrated military command of NATO in order to escape from the nuclear rivalry of the superpowers.[169]

Lafontaine equated the role of the United States and the Soviet Union in world politics. The imperial components of both were directed against freedom of other countries. The Soviet Union oppressed Eastern Europe and justified the invasion of Afghanistan with anticapitalism. The United States supported the most brutal dictatorships in Central and South America and a dictatorship in Turkey in the service of anticommunism. The military blocs led by the superpowers guaranteed that hunger, suffering, and environmental destruction would increase. Lafontaine wrote that the continued confrontation of the blocs made the survival of humanity impossible.[170] Europe had to be "Europeanized," and the blocs dissolved. The United Nations should establish an international security system as "an alternative to the bloc system."[171] The SPD should realize that "democratic socialism is a bloc-free ideology," return to its security policies of the 1950s, and support creation of a "collective security system in Europe in which a reunited Germany would be effectively embedded."[172] The current system of alliances and deterrence was a "declaration of war" on life in the third world and was incompatible with détente. West Germany should opt out of the arms race. The confrontation of the blocs itself was a barrier to solving the world's problems.[173] In view of the specter of a limited nuclear war in Europe, there were more than enough reasons "why the Europeans—especially the two German states—must separate themselves from the deadly grasp of both world powers."[174] Lafontaine's argument led in the direction of neutralism, as well as to contacts with members of the Green party willing to accept a parliamentary road to ecological, bloc-free socialism.

In a number of articles and interviews in 1983, Alois Mertes drew some lessons from the euromissile dispute. The SPD's move to the left, the emergence of the Greens, and a peace movement directed against NATO policy were proof of "how justified were the Western fears of the political consequences of a military superiority of the Soviet Union in Europe."[175] Moscow's strategy of making West Germany politically pliable by use of military threats and intimidation "through the use of pressure, threat and blackmail" required "West Germany's internal turn away from America as well as the military and psychological dismantling of the credibility of the American guarantee."[176] It was, he thought, a strategy that had met with some success. He criticized Bahr's application of terms such as "security partnership" and "common security" to the East-West relationship because it was political language that was a "short formula for neutralism" in suggesting that West Germany had similar relations with its American allies as with its Soviet adversary.[177] He criticized what he saw as a depoliticization of public discussion over peace and security in Europe from the left. "Without a repoliticization, the debate over peace and security will degenerate into the expert jargon of the military and disarmament diplomacy."[178]

Mertes believed that, from 1979 to summer 1983, a "gap of political insight" had characterized too much of the public debate in West Germany. He called for replacing the "grotesque militarization of the peace debate since the West German elections of 1980" with a discussion conducted on "political lines, not military-technical lines."

> The people that brought forth Carl von Clausewitz, should remember his message: Politics, that is, the human being, is primary, not military matters—whether it be the development of power or the diplomacy of disarmament. . . . Whoever wants to diminish tension and armament, must above all stress their political roots.[179]

For Mertes, the mistake of the peace movement was to assume that the source of the problem was "both blocs" and their weapons. Rather, in Aron's terms, it was the "dialectic of regimes," the interaction of their forms of government, their values, and their intentions that was decisive and that had been neglected.

In the summer of 1983, the interaction of West German domestic politics and international politics, between political culture and political power, was now apparent to the leading actors involved. There were no more innocents in the euromissile dispute by spring 1983, or at least none who had not heard arguments about how intentionality and consequence were related to one another and how domestic politics in West Germany affected the Geneva negotiations. With a minority in Parliament, and no more elections scheduled on the euromissiles, the only hope for antimissile forces lay in overturning the results of the March 6, 1983, election through extraparliamentary means, in the streets. The West German government braced for a "hot autumn" of 1983. In Geneva, the Soviet Union's hard line continued unabated.

11

DEMOCRATIC RESILIENCE
Fall 1983

WITHOUT ANY MAJOR CHANGE in the negotiating positions in Geneva, the euromissile dispute in West Germany continued in now well-worn paths. Moscow's hopes of gaining more support in Western Europe were dealt a blow when on September 1, 1983, a Soviet air-force plane shot down a Korean Air Lines flight over the Sakhalin Islands, killing all 269 people on board. In September and October, in preparation for a special SPD party congress to be held in Cologne in mid-November, SPD organizations in Baden-Württemberg, Schleswig-Holstein, Hamburg, Bremen, Niedersachsen, Berlin, Nordrhein-Westfalen, Hessen, Bavaria, Rheinland-Pfalz, and the Saar passed resolutions opposing deployments.[1]

On September 16, the Bundestag held its thirtieth debate on the euromissile issue since 1979. Hans-Dietrich Genscher called the Soviet proposal for inclusion of British and French missiles the major barrier to a negotiated solution, and he urged the Soviets to drop this demand.[2] Horst Ehmke criticized the United States for its refusal to include British and French missiles; Gert Bastian repeated that new American missiles were designed for a nuclear offensive from European territory.[3] Manfred Wörner criticized the Greens and the SPD left for neglecting the connection between peace and human rights.[4] In mid-September, Heiner Geissler again raised the temperature of the controversy when he said that the Social Democrats had to understand that "a party which criticizes only the West and simultaneously takes up the arguments of the Soviet Union . . . a party which introduces these arguments into domestic political discussion, such a party—whether it wants to or not—will in the intellectual and moral debate in the Federal Republic become a fifth column of the other side."[5] Willy Brandt called Geissler the "primary defamer" of the CDU. Vogel said he was spreading an atmosphere of "hate." A leader of the *JUSOS* said Geissler employed "Nazi methods." He called him "a fascist" and suggested he would have been a good "propaganda minister" if the Nazis were in power.[6] Yet, while the intentions of the Social Democratic leaders were not to aid Soviet policy, the consequences of support for inclusion of British and French missiles, for nuclear-free zones, and denuclearization of Central Europe were to strengthen the Soviet side and weakened the Western position in the Geneva talks. In Geissler's view, ritual formulations of support for NATO could not obscure abandonment of a decision that a Social Democratic Chancellor had set in motion.[7] By the beginning of October, twelve regional organizations of the Social Democratic party rejected deployments, and it was now clear that the national party would reject deployments at its special meeting scheduled for November 18 and 19 in Cologne.[8]

The Schumacher Tradition and the Euromissiles

By the fall of 1983, the Schmidt faction of the SPD was defeated within the party. Its intellectual traditions were preserved by the Seeheimer Circle, a group of intellectuals long bound to the SPD who regarded its neutralist drift with dismay. Several members of the Circle spoke out against the development of the SPD. On September 3, Karl Kaiser, of the German Society for Foreign Policy in Bonn, spoke to the Seeheimer Circle about "Priorities of Social Democratic Foreign and Security Policy." At the beginning of October, his speech was reprinted in the *Frankfurter Allgemeine Zeitung*, *Vorwärts*, and the *Frankfurter Rundschau*.[9]

Kaiser criticized what he called neutralist inclinations in the SPD. "A new German neutralism would lead to isolation, followed by dependency."[10] In the 1970s, he said, contact between social democrats and communists at the diplomatic level had had the unintended consequence of pushing into the background the traditional function of social democracy as the bulwark against communism. Hence, the generations coming of age in the era of détente lacked an understanding of repression of freedom and human rights in communist regimes. While the Soviet Union was "breaking out of the rules of parity," the SPD party leadership created a taboo on criticism of Moscow.[11] As a result, Schmidt's challenge to the Soviet Union beginning in 1977 lacked support in his own party.

During the détente era, Kaiser continued, the SPD had neglected the ideological conflict with communism. It had ignored repression of human rights in Eastern Europe. In so doing, it undermined its historic role in

West German politics, defined by Schumacher, of resistance to totalitarianism on the left.[12] Kaiser singled out Egon Bahr for having subordinated freedom and human rights to peace. No amount of talk about the arms race, Kaiser continued, could obscure the continuing fact of the conflict between repressive communism and free democracies, between the expansive hegemonial policy of the Soviet Union and the status quo orientation of the Western democracies.

> Equidistance to both world powers is the beginning of the end of German and West European security. When Egon Bahr defines the struggle for peace as a struggle against the hegemonial powers [as he was reported to have done in a speech in Beijing in fall 1982], then he misconstrues and obscures the real basis of West European security. West Berlin, with all that it means for we Germans and the West, can only remain free, because the Americans are risking their lives for it in Germany and at home.
>
> In the 1960s, Soviet armament or the contradiction between Communism and Western democracy as the origin of increased East-West tensions disappeared from the analyses and explanations of the young socialists; in the 1970s and 1980s this tendency entered the statements of the party and prominent Social Democrats, including the party chairman. Instead, one finds as the origin of tension an anonymous "arms race," American rhetoric about nuclear war, horizontal escalation and the like. When the Soviet Union as the origin of the threat is excluded, the USA is stressed as the problem. People repeat confessions (of loyalty) to the [Western] alliance. But it is no longer clear against whom this alliance secures the peace.
>
> Why can't we, like other European socialists, clearly state that the policy of the Soviet Union is the origin of the East-West conflict and the reason for our alliance?[13]

Kaiser urged the SPD to return to its bulwark role against Soviet policy, to grasp the political purpose of Soviet armament, and to stand in the way of efforts to push the United States from Western Europe.

Egon Bahr responded to Kaiser in the October 13 issue of *Vorwärts*.[14] Kaiser was a "Don Quixote" tilting at windmills when he pointed to neutralist currents in the SPD. The SPD in the détente era did make ideological confrontation with communists secondary to the presevation of peace. But that was because West German Social Democrats regarded communist governments as "indispensable partners" as well as competitors. In domestic politics they remained an adversary. One of the great successes of social-liberal foreign policy, in Bahr's view, was making peace its first priority.

"Without the preservation of peace, freedom is not possible."[15] Bahr wrote that the CDU, the American government, and Karl Kaiser sought to place ideology at the same level as the preservation of peace, but doing so had been the "principle of the Cold War." It would require a disciplining of the masses, restrictions on freedom, and a push to the right "that no Social Democrat should support."[16]

The impact of Brandt's and Bahr's foreign policy on the political culture of the Social Democratic party was also a central concern for Gasine Schwan, another member of the Seeheimer Circle, a professor of political science at the Free University in Berlin and a member of the SPD's "commission on basic values." In an essay on "The SPD and Western Freedom" published in the October 1983 isue of *Neue Gesellschaft*, Schwan argued that the controversy over missile deployment in the SPD was not primarily about changing nuclear strategies or technical imperatives of weapon systems.[17] It was a symptom of a deeper and widespread "disorientation" concerning the question, "How important is the preservation of Western freedom?"[18] The East-West conflict, she wrote, was not only one between the United States and the Soviet Union but also a confrontation between Western democracies and communist one-party dictatorships. However, she continued, opponents of the *Nachrüstung* decision, who had become ascendent in the SPD, did not agree. She wrote that opponents of the two-track decision felt "ideologically neutral" regarding competition between the superpowers "because they no longer believe the Soviet Union threatens Western freedom" and instead saw the major danger to peace coming from the United States, "as well from an anonymous arms race whose political motivations are obscured."[19]

Schwan wrote that the revival of Marxism and neo-Marxisms in the 1960s played an important role in fostering this ideological neutralism. Young Social Democrats attacked anticommunism, worked with communist groups in the universities, minimized the values of Western freedom, and placed a taboo on criticism of the Soviet Union and its oppression of human and civil rights. However, "behind the superficial *(Verharmlosung)* minimization of the danger posed by Soviet policy lies a deep fear and resignation in the face of its miliary strength and its political lack of transparence."[20] Schwan also expressed regret that the West German Social Democrats had allowed the desire for peace to mute their concern about freedom in Eastern Europe and to lead them to underestimate the importance of preserving Western freedom.[21]

Schwan focused her attention on the role of Willy Brandt. In the 1970s, Brandt did not mention or mentioned only in passing the distinction between democracy and dictatorship. When he proudly claimed that the "great and positive result of détente policy" was that ideological differences had been subordinated to the necessity of peaceful coexistence, he meant that no intellectual-political conflict should stand in the way of arms control agreements. "Under Brandt's leadership," Schwan wrote, the party became prisoner to a "mystified détente policy." It refused to recognize that securing peace through decreasing East-West contradictions had been only partially successful. The Soviet Union had not "moved away from its goal of expansive hegemonial policy."[22] Yet, she continued, as the Soviet military buildup continued, Willy Brandt never revised his view that détente had made peace more secure, placed blame for the danger of war on the West generally and the United States in particular, and undermined Helmut Schmidt with "countless utterances of mistrust" towards American policy and trust towards Soviet policy.[23]

She concluded that, as a result of the transformation of the West German Social Democrats, by 1983 Social Democratic foreign policy was being determined by Egon Bahr, Oskar Lafontaine, and Erhard Eppler. The common denominator of these three figures was "critical distance toward the West, mistrust to hostility to the policy of the USA and the encouragement of nationalist resentments against the superpowers, especially against America."[24] With a taboo on criticism of the Soviet Union, the SPD became "de facto one of the most effective instruments of Soviet hegemonial policy." It aroused nationalistic sentiments, which in the future could be the source of a new chauvinism of the right.[25]

In October, Manes Sperber, another leading figure of the West German democratic left, delivered a speech on the occasion of receiving the Peace prize of the German Book Fair in Frankfurt. He was critical of the peace movement and the drift of the SPD.[26] His experience of the Third Reich taught him that a "totalitarian regime" believes itself endangered if it cannot extend its power over neighboring states and then over the planet.[27] In the 1930s, he and others who argued against giving in to Hitler's threats were called warmongers. Europe now shared the continent with another totalitarian power supported with "terrifying nuclear threats," whose rulers viewed their own regime as endangered as long as it did not extend to the Atlantic and "if possible over the whole earth." The impact of Soviet intimidation "is unintentionally proven by those who today march through the capital cities of the democratic European countries in order to protest against deployment in Europe of means of defense against this blackmail, against the threat of nuclear weapons."[28] Sperber said Europe needed the "courage of self-assertion. . . . We old Europeans, who hate war, must unfortunately become dangerous, in order to preserve peace."[29] Those who claimed that Europe was threatened as much by the United States as by the Soviet Union were "blinded by aggressive ingratitude."[30] Sperber's comparison of the totalitarianism of the 1930s in Germany to totalitarianism in the Soviet Union in the 1980s, indeed the use of the word at all, had long gone out of fashion in the West German left.[31] Kaiser, Schwan, and Sperber were in the minority among political and intellectual figures of the West German left.

In political culture and practical politics, Egon Bahr was a more representative figure. In mid-October, he accepted Andropov's offer to cut the SS-20 arsenal to the number of British and French weapons if NATO would abandon deployments. In his words, "if Brezhnev had offered what Andropov is now offering, there would have been no double-decision."[32] The following day, October 19, 1983, Mertes said that Bahr had to understand that the result of his position was to favor Soviet policy. Mertes argued that Bahr's adoption of the Soviet position and the evolution of the SPD in the euromissile dispute were evidence that Helmut Schmidt's fears concerning the political impact of the SS-20 arsenal had been well founded.[33]

The White Book of 1983

Hans Ruhle, formerly director of the Christian Democratic Union's research arm, the Konrad Adenauer Foundation, became director of the planning staff in the West German defense ministry in fall 1982. One of his responsibilities was writing the White Book. Ruhle was determined to make a more vigorous presentation of the government's case in the euromissile dispute.[34] The planning staff devoted twenty-five pages of the report to the INF controversy and offered a much-expanded analysis of the nature of the Soviet threat to Western Europe.[35]

The White Book critically and at some length studied proposals for unilateral disarmament, nuclear-free zones, no first use of nuclear weapons, technocommandoes, social defense, and defensive defense.[36] It made an extensive case for the two-track decision: The SS–20s were an attempt to separate Western Europe militarily and politically from the United States. Should that effort succeed, the possibilities for Soviet intimidation of Western Europe would be greatly enhanced. The existence of the Soviet medium-range nuclear missiles was tolerable in the era of American nuclear global superiority but not in an era of strategic nuclear parity between the United States and the Soviet Union. Because of their limited numbers and range, cruise and Pershing II missiles would not be able to "decapitate" Soviet command centers or deny a second-strike capacity to the Soviets. Rather than constituting a destabilizing first-strike potential, they deterred the Soviet Union from limited use of its already deployed medium-range system. The "only function" of the missiles was preserve the coupling of Western Europe's deterrent capability to the United States and thus to "preserve the capacity of free Europe to protect its self-determination."[37] This deterrent function was evident in the fact that the United States had agreed to suspend deployments if the Soviets agreed to dismantle their medium-range arsenal.

One of the major themes of the White Book for 1983 concerned the relationship between the global and regional balance of forces, a theme that had not figured prominently in West German public debate. The global growth of Soviet air, sea, and land forces made the conventional imbalance in Europe less tolerable than ever. Warsaw Pact conventional superiority had increased NATO's dependence on the early supply of reinforcements from across the Atlantic and had increased the importance of nuclear deterrence. At the same time, the credibility of Western nuclear deterrence was declining, both because of the deteriorating imbalance in medium- and short-range nuclear weapons in Europe and

> the sinking acceptance of nuclear weapons in Western societies. A continuation of these two unfavorable developmental tendencies would seriously place into question the credibility of our measures for deterrence and defense and dangerously worsen our security situation.[38]

The Soviet monopoly of medium-range nuclear weapons had to be ended. Western conventional capabilities needed to be strengthened to reduce the need for early first use of nuclear weapons, and the public acceptance of nuclear deterrence in the democracies had to be restored. If NATO was unable to do these things, the Soviet strategy of applying political-psychological pressure on Western Europe through the buildup of military power would have a much better chance of succeeding. That, in turn, would reduce the independence of the countries of Western Europe. These, in the minds of West German government strategists, were the stakes in the euromissile dispute.

Cologne and the Prelude to Bonn: November 1983

Over the weekend of October 22 and 23, peace demonstrations took place all over West Germany. Over half a million people attended a peace demonstration in Bonn. There Willy Brandt, with the support of the SPD's executive committee, delivered a clear and unambiguous "no" to deployments, while affirming West German membership in the Western alliance.[39] The largest mass demonstration in the history of postwar Hamburg took place, as 200,000 people formed a human chain between Stuttgart and Neu-Ulm. Meanwhile, in Munich, Franz-Josef Strauss spoke in favor of the NATO decision to a mere 15,000 people. Whatever the popular sentiment may have been concerning the deployments, there was no question but that the antimissile forces were more able and willing to take their politics to the streets.[40]

On November 18, the West German Social Democrats began a special party congress in Cologne to consider whether or not to support the deployments.[41] Helmut Schmidt defended his foreign policy and again criticized what he called the "absolutization" or exclusive focus on any one value, whether freedom, justice, or peace. He appealed for appreciation of the "conflicts within political reason."[42] Schmidt criticized the Soviets as mistaken in deploying the SS-20s, and the United States for rejecting the walk in the woods formula. But by 1983, the SS-20 buildup posed a threat to fifty countries, giving the Soviet Union additional ability to exert pressure on nonnuclear West Germany. He spoke of the traditional Russian drive to expansion and of the Soviet perception during the Carter administration of disunity between Western Europe and the United States.[43] The West Germans were a main target of Soviet psychological propaganda, which took advantage of conflicts within the Atlantic Alliance. Schmidt again asserted that the Soviets had deployed the SS-20s to take advantage of a "psycho-political vulnerability" of the Western Europeans in order to attempt to divide them from the United States.[44] Though it was "hard to bear," the West Germans remained dependent on the United States for nuclear protection. Schmidt took issue with the revisionist account of the history of the NATO two-track decision. At first, "Carter and Brzezinski rejected our proposals" to make an issue of the eurostrategic balance.[45] He said that the idea that the United States forced the missile decision on an unwilling West Germany was not true.

In spite of superpower mistakes Schmidt urged the delegates to support the deployments for the following reasons. First, the West German government had to keep its word and could not allow the Soviet Union to have a veto over its defense decisions. Second, the political equilibrium in Europe must not be upset by the Soviet Union's unilateral buildup. Third, Moscow had to know that West Germany would fulfill its alliance commitments, that it wanted the United States to remain in Western Europe, and that any effort to threaten Western Europe would inevitably involve the United States. Fourth, the two-track decision was also important because it reaffirmed the link between military equilibrium and diplomacy.

Schmidt then challenged the antimissile arguments. Those who pointed to the Sermon on the Mount could not restrict their objections to nuclear weapons, but no people had survived without armed defense. Fears that nuclear arms could destroy humanity were reasonable, but they overlooked the fact that mutual vulnerability due to nuclear weapons had prevented war in Europe for forty years. Yes, the Pershing II's flight time was short, but so was that of the SS-20s. The Pershing IIs were too few in number and of too short a range to reach the Soviet strategic weapons. They were not useful for a first strike, while the SS-20s "can destroy all of Germany."[46] The West German Social Democrats, Schmidt continued, should not neglect the interests of Britain and France or become isolated from the Italian and Spanish socialists. Demanding the inclusion of British and French nuclear weapons in the INF talks and rejecting the NATO deployments was having just that effect.

Schmidt concluded wth a critique of idealism in its American and German variants.[47] The Germans were not immune from a "false consciousness which presumes to possess a higher morality."[48] Schmidt reminded the delegates that the SPD itself had a tradition of linking peace and freedom and that its own party executive had declared in the 1971 *Abgrenzungsbeschluss* that "no peace policy can overlook the contradiction between the system of free democracies and Communist dictatorship."[49] The Germans must not be "once again held to be unpredictable *(unberechenbar)* and unreliable."[50] "We need friends and partners. Friends in the West and partners in the East must always be able to rely on our steadiness."[51] Though he received long and enthusiastic applause, he did not change minds. Only 14 of the 400 delegates voted with Schmidt to support deployments. The other 386 voted with Brandt to oppose them.[52]

In Cologne, Willy Brandt, evoking the European and democratic lineages of German Social Democracy, led the opposition to the deployments.

> Both superpowers are strong, stronger than they have to be, stronger than is good for the world. Both feel weak for different—sometimes the same–grounds. Both experience crises of leadership. In both the "military industrial" or "military-bureaucratic complex" have become dangerously more powerful.[53]

In this situation, it was important for Europeans to increase their political weight in the respective alliance in security policy. This did not mean the end of alliances but a power shift within them. Europe had to take up its own responsibility in security policy. In fall 1983, such "self-assertion" meant rejection of the NATO decision.

The key concept in such European self-assertion for Brandt was "security partnership." Security partnership meant that "the task of politics must be to dismantle the East-West confrontation and transform the relationship between the alliances into a European peace order" which both world powers should participate in and guarantee. Détente and effective defense should be continued, and an "effective . . . war preventing defensive strategy" should bring about change in security policy.[54] An examination of ideas for nuclear and chemical weapon-free zones was in order. Brandt asked "if it was so difficult to understand" that the Germans, who already had so many nuclear weapons in their country, did not want any more. Who could blame the Germans "if they were not happy about handing over decisions about their children's future to computers or politburos, or to distant, often strange power structures?"[55]

The Cologne congress resolution was entitled "Yes to a European peace order! NO to ever more nuclear weapons!" According to the resolution, in the four years since the Brussels decision, not all possibilities for a negotiated solution had been used. For example, Soviet medium-range missiles could be reduced to their 1978 level, and British and French missiles could have been included in the INF and/or START talks.[56] Such efforts were not undertaken, the resolution continued, because the Kohl government stopped exerting pressure on the United States. However, it continued, critical assessment of the Western position in the INF talks did not mean a position of "equidistance." The communist social system was unacceptable for the SPD. The United States and West Germany were bound together by common traditions and values of human rights, law, and pluralist democracy, but in their foreign and security policies, world powers followed their interests often without regard to principles of humanity or human rights.[57] Presumably the United States was now doing just that. Therefore, the West German Social Democrats rejected deployments of American missiles in West Germany and called for further negotiations. If missiles were deployed, the SPD would do its best to get them dismantled.[58] The bulwark was now a lever.

The Last Bundestag Debate: November 21–22, 1983

On November 21 and 22, 1983, the Bundestag held the decisive debate and vote over the euromissiles.[59] It was the thirty-seventh debate held on the issue in the Bundestag since December 14, 1979.[60]

Helmut Kohl, as he had since the early 1970s, made the preservation of both peace and freedom the centerpiece of his remarks.[61] He said that the NATO two-track decision was not primarily a technical question of armaments. Other questions were central. Could there be a balance of military forces in Europe at lower levels? Could arms control lead to such a balance? Would West Germany remain a reliable member of the Western alliance? Were West Germany and its allies willing and able to stand up against a "claim for hegemony" by the Soviet Union? The Chancellor believed that West Germany's foreign-policy orientation "hung in the balance." The Soviet Union must not be permitted to intimidate Western Europe, to narrow its scope of action, and to separate it from the United States. Only, he stressed, when Western Europe succeeded in preventing the Soviet Union from implementing such a policy would there be a possibility for a genuine "peace order" in Europe. It was the "political will" of the Soviet Union, not weapons in themselves, that constituted the threat to Western Europe. That will had to change if there were to be a stable peace in Europe. The only way to influence that will was Western deterrence policy. "Peace in the nuclear era is only as secure as the danger of catastrophe for those who break it." A one-sided rejection of deterrence would be an "incalculable risk." Therefore, one had to live with nuclear weapons and with the tension between their destructive force and their ability to secure peace.[62]

Kohl cast the NATO decision in the context of changes in the nuclear balance between the United States and the Soviet Union since 1960. He told a story of American nuclear superiority giving way to parity in intercontinental weapons. "For us Europeans and for us Germans, the loss of nuclear strategic superiority of the USA is one of the most important developments of the last two decades." Europe was threatened by the Warsaw Pact's conventional superiority, by the Soviet Union's medium-range as well as by its intercontinental nuclear weapons. NATO's two-track decision, he continued, was designed to correct this imbalance. Either the Soviet Union could accept facing the same double threat from intercontinental and medium-range missiles as Western Europe had, or it could eliminate or reduce the medium-range threat by eliminating or reducing its own medium-range arsenal. In refusing to take these steps, he said, the Soviet Union was destroying a historic opportunity for disarmament.[63] Was it compatible with West European security and independence that the Soviet Union turn Western Europe into a zone of diminished security? Should the Soviet Union retain "an instrument with which it could decisively influence the history of Europe?"[64] He answered "no" to both questions.

He defended the two-track decision as a manifestation of the philosophy of the Harmel Report, that is, as a combination of military security and détente. He stressed that he had consulted closely with the Reagan administration in determining Western negotiating positions. The zero option of

November 1981 and the interim solution of March 1983 were indications of Western compromise. He contrasted Western flexibility to the rigidity of the Soviet position, one which absolutely ruled out any new American deployments.[65]

Kohl rejected the Soviet demand to include British and French missiles. It was, he said, a demand that aimed at driving the United States out of Europe in the long run. In the near future, it would deprive nonnuclear West Germany of protection from the United States. The grounds for an agreement were at hand if the Soviet Union would agree to abandon its insistence on a monopoly of land-based medium-range missiles. Kohl stressed the agreement among the positions of the West German government, the United States, Canada, and the other Western European allies concerning the negotiating proposals for the INF talks. Now, he said, deployment of new American medium-range weapons had to begin. Deployments need not mean the end of negotiations.

Kohl then turned to the Social Democrats. Why, he asked, hadn't they focused on Soviet armament? Why did they "again and again take up the Soviet arguments," even though in so doing they became isolated from the socialist parties of France, Italy, and Spain? Why had they not recognized the efforts of the American and West German governments to reach a negotiated solution?[66]

He returned to what he saw as the fundamental principles of West German security policy: Western orientation, preservation of the Atlantic Alliance, and continuation of relations based on equality with the Soviet Union.[67] *"We [West Germans] are not wanderers between East and West. . . . There is no middle way between democracy and dictatorship. We stand on the side of freedom"* (emphasis added).[68] Kohl concluded by turning to the "lessons of history." No democratic political leader, he said, should forget the "bitter knowledge" of Neville Chamberlain following the Munich agreements: military weakness led to diplomatic weakness.

Those who are weak encourage hegemonial claims and call forth threats. They expose themselves to blackmail and place at risk their freedom and thus also peace.

(Objections from the Greens)

Only the determination of free peoples can show totalitarian states their limits.

(Applause from the CDU/CSU and FDP)

We can never allow peace and freedom to be played off against one another.[69]

Kohl recalled the experience of two world wars and the Nazi dictatorship. "Weapons and military strength have no power of fascination for us. We are not eager for missiles." However, in a world where peace was threatened, the Germans could not step aside into a "niche of history" and hope that others would do what was necessary to secure peace and freedom. In 1983, the West Germans had a responsibility to defend democracy and freedom against dictatorship as the Germans had failed to do in 1933.

In his remarks, Alfred Dregger warned that if the Soviets succeeded in preventing NATO from implementing the two-track decision, there would be no limits to Soviet superiority in Europe, while an abyss of mutual incomprehension would emerge between Americans and Europeans, especially West Germans.[70] While the West talked and negotiated, the Soviet Union created facts, that is, ever more SS-20s. The Soviets had "used all the possiblities of their totalitarian system" to spread propaganda and disinformation in Western public opinion, while remaining "completely immune" from Western media.[71] He believed that the Soviet leadership conducted the Geneva negotiations with the purpose of preventing any American deployments. This, he added, had been the purpose of its proposal to include British and French missiles in the determination of a balance of medium-range nuclear weapons. The Social Democrats, Dregger continued, had made this Soviet standpoint their own. He "could not understand" why "the friends of peace on the left side of the house" did not support the zero-zero option. Why didn't they believe Soviet leaders when they spoke of retaliation against the United States, thus ruling out a nuclear war limited to Europe, yet accepted their promises about peace in an era of nuclear-free zones? He said that the Social Democrats had not only weakened the Western negotiating position but bore a "large degree of responsibility for the previous failure of the Geneva negotiations."[72] The Federal Republic could not do without an SPD with Helmut Schmidt's "conviction, clarity, and realism," and he spoke of the need to rebuild the national consensus on security policy.[73]

The following day, Manfred Wörner again took the Social Democrats to task for their "wrong headed policy of one-sided pressure on the Western position," which "only aided the Soviet tactic of delay and playing for time. . . . For the Soviet Union does not stand under the pressure of [public] opinion. It has no opposition to contend with. It determines its interests only according to the possibilities offered it by negotiations and the political card game."[74] Those who rejected the Western deployments

> give the Soviet policy of Vorrüstung (initial armament) a great triumph. They confirm the judgement of all those politicians and

military leaders in the Soviet Union who resort to power and arms, and they create an invitation for one side to continue arming without any risk.[75]

How, he asked, could arms control agreements with the Soviet Union be achieved if the West entered talks with "empty hands"?[76] As he had throughout, Wörner was in the forefront of those examining asymmetric strategic interaction between democracy and dictatorship.

Again, Foreign Minister Genscher, speaking on November 21, raised the issue of West orientation and neutralism.[77] In view, he said, of the past four years of Western restraint and continued Soviet buildup, the Bundestag in 1983 faced the decision of whether or not it would stand by the decision made in 1979. It was not a matter of pleasing or not pleasing the Americans. The history of the two-track decision, he recalled, began with European and West German concern over the danger of Soviet armament. The decision over whether or not to remain faithful to commitments already made was also a decision over the fundamental orientation of West German foreign and security policy. Would West Germany remain firmly in the West, or would it become "a country drifting out of the community of Western democracies"? In the past other countries, he said, had expressed fear of German militarism. In 1983, their concern was over "an incalculable German neutralism," a concern that had to be laid to rest.

> It is the concern that we Germans, like sleepwalkers caught up in a dream, could walk out of the Western community in the hope that we could best solve our national problem by opting for neutralism. . . . Today we have bound our national question to the fate of Europe. If we break out of this responsibility, if we seek the path of going it alone, then much of the stability in Europe to which we have all contributed since the Second World War, would be lost. . . . *A drift of our country out of the Western alliance—at first verbally rather than by actions—would mean a dangerous destabilization. This time, it would not be Germany's strength that would create problems in Europe. This time it would be the weakness of the Federal Republic of Germany that would create dangers for Europe.* . . . A weak Federal Republic of Germany outside the structure of the Western alliance would create a power vacuum around it which would become the object of rivalries. This must not be permitted to happen.[78] (emphasis added).

Genscher insisted that a yes or no to the NATO decision was also a decision about the Western alliance or neutralism. The Social Democratic party, he continued, had become a factor of uncertainty. It was "too large, too

important, and too strong to permit such doubts" to emerge. The SPD
was needed for a strong NATO. Genscher warned that failure to proceed
with deployments in November 1983 would be the "beginning of a path
towards the political strangulation of Western Europe. We must not go
down this path."[79]

The Social Democratic resolution in the Bundestag was identical to the
resolution passed several days previously at the Cologne party conference.
In his remarks, Hans-Joachim Vogel spoke bitterly of the "defamation" of
the peace movement and the SPD by the conservatives and of Heiner
Geissler's "slander" that the Social Democrats were a fifth column of Moscow.[80] The peace movement was one of the "broadest and most engaged"
of recent movements. The consciousness of the West German people
about the nuclear arms race had changed in recent years. Vogel insisted
that theologians, doctors, philosophers, and natural scientists who were
alarmed about the nuclear arms race could not be dismissed as subversive
or disloyal.[81] It was, Vogel continued, Helmut Kohl who was weakening
West German democracy and destroying its political consensus by his insistence on proceeding with the NATO deployments. Conversely, he called
Brandt's speech to the peace demonstration in Bonn a contribution to restoring consensus. Kohl had failed to offer the promised "intellectual-moral
renewal." Now, Vogel claimed, the majority of the West Germans were
opposed to the deployments.

Vogel affirmed his commitment to the Atlantic Alliance. He stressed that
no détente or European peace order would be possible outside the alliance,
but support for the alliance in the population would decrease, not grow, if
deployments took place against the will of the majority. Kohl had confused
"friendship with a desire to please, and cooperative membership in an alliance with the loyalty of a feudal vassal."[82] It was "false" to say that Kohl
had done all he could to bring about an agreement in Geneva. Turning to
Kohl, he said that "in the central question, namely the consideration of
third country systems [i.e., Britain and France] you have not done what is
necessary. On the contrary. You have neglected to do it."[83] Vogel criticized
Chancellor Kohl for not exerting more pressure on Washington to modify
its negotiation position to include the 162 British and French missiles in
the balance. Their presence meant that talk of a Soviet "monopoly" of
such systems was mistaken. In any case, he said, nuclear deterrence could
only be a transitional theory. He called for restoring a primacy of politics
over military strategies and weapons technicians.[84]

Vogel described the proposals of the Soviet Union to reduce the number
of its missiles directed at Western Europe to 140 in exchange for abandonment of American deployments as "worthy of negotiation." If the alliance

went ahead with deployments, Vogel said, the Soviets would only add to their existing arsenal. East-West relations would deteriorate, and acceptance of the alliance would decline in the West. If the West Germans rejected deployments, a "drastic reduction" of Soviet missiles would take place. The confrontation "between the superpowers" would diminish. Détente and arms control would be encouraged. German-German relations would continue to improve, and acceptance of the Atlantic Alliance would remain firm. "This is our [the SPD's] option."[85]

In his contribution to the last debate, Egon Bahr rejected the idea that the deployment decision was also a decision over the Atlantic Alliance. A yes to rearmament would "permit" Moscow to produce and deploy more SS-20s and shorter-range SS-22s. Bahr said that because the Kohl government had given up the possibility of a West German "no" to deployments, West German leverage in the Western alliance was reduced. "The obsequiousness with which the government of the Federal Republic has followed every change in American policy is horrifying."[86] If, he continued, the United States were to support inclusion of British and French systems, so would the Federal Republic. While Brandt and Schmidt were in office, West Germany had its own voice. With Kohl, "Bonn [became an] echo of Washington." In contrast to Genscher's interpretation, Bahr said that fundamental disagreement about the double-track decision had existed from the beginning. Bahr viewed it as a means of starting negotiations to make new missiles superfluous, while the conservatives saw the decision as a means of introducing the missiles. He repeated that the "Reagan zero option" was "divorced from reality" and "not serious."[87]

Bahr again said that the Soviets had offered reductions that were so significant that, had they been offered in 1979, the two-track decision would not have been taken. Meanwhile, "the Americans are moving away from the Harmel Report" by neglecting diplomacy. "I criticize the Soviet Union for not beginning with one-sided reductions . . . but I raise greater criticisms of our own side because the absence of our own cleverness pains me more."[88] Bahr's argument, in effect, was that the United States and the West German government had abandoned the negotiating track of the two-track decision of 1979, and therefore the West Germans were not under an obligation to proceed with deployments.

Willy Brandt doubted that more security would result from "continuing to stuff both German states with ever more launchers and atomic weapons. . . ." The current American administration had arrived at the fixed idea "that deployment of Pershing II was more important than dismantling of SS-20s."[89] No West Germans, he said, asked for new missiles. He rejected claims that the protest movement was neutralist or nationalist.

It was for defense but simply "against new missiles." He was for defense and for friendship with the United States, but not for "an artificial alliance which was limited to friendships between ministers and heads of states."[90] He justified his rejection of deployments by pointing to the refusal of the American Senate to ratify SALT II, the statements of Defense Secretary Weinberger about limited nuclear war, and what he said was neglect by the United States of the arms control aspects of the double two-track decision, which had accomplished its intended effect of getting the Soviet Union to agree to reduce its SS-20 arsenal.

As he had in Cologne, Brandt called for a "Europeanization of Europe." Europe would serve as a "moderating and stabilizing force" in world politics. The task of German politics must be "to dismantle the East-West confrontation" and to transform the relation between the alliances into one of a "European peace order. In order to do that we need security partnership instead of a policy of confrontation."[91] Both world powers should participate in and guarantee such a peace order. They should continue détente and adopt defensive strategies. The West Germans, he continued, were not "idiots" because they were critical of a policy that would bring about their annihilation if it were ever implemented. Brandt sought a defense policy that again could be supported by the "great majority" of the population.[92]

Helmut Schmidt's Bundestag speech was similar to his Cologne address. He spoke up for pragmatism and against yearning for "absolutely ideal solutions" to political problems.[93] As for the Geneva talks, the West, just like a trade union, could not enter such talks with empty hands. He recalled that in summer 1980 he had promised the Moscow leadership that, if the negotiations did not lead to agreement, he would support deployments of American missiles. "I have not changed my mind."[94] Schmidt supported the deployments on the following grounds: The Federal Republic should keep to its word. If deployments were rejected, the political balance of forces in Europe would be destroyed and a severe crisis in the alliance would develop. The two-track decision was still an expression of the Harmel Report, but he felt that neither side had made "great efforts" to reach an agreement. He criticized Kohl for reducing the weight of West German policy in the alliance.[95]

In fact, however, it was hard to see what Schmidt could have done differently than Kohl, given the rigidity of the Soviet position in the INF talks. The juxtaposition of ballistic missiles with slower-flying cruise missiles in the "walk in the woods" agreement was not an example of the parity and equal security Schmidt had always supported. Furthermore, Ronald Reagan had adopted the zero option partly in response to Schmidt's pleas in the spring, summer, and fall of 1981. If implemented, the zero option of November 1981 would have made American deployments "superfluous." Given Schmidt's clear understanding of British and French defense policies, it is hard to imagine that he would have supported inclusion of their missiles in the INF talks. In fact, Kohl and Genscher had implemented his own policy at a time when his own party had turned against it.

The Greens' resolution called for unequivocal rejection of the American deployments, withdrawal of chemical weapons from West Germany, and a reduction of the number of SS-20s to the number of British and French missiles. The goal of INF negotiations should be abolition of all remaining medium-range nuclear weapons as a step toward a Europe free of weapons of mass destruction.[96]

Otto Schilly, speaking for the Greens, described the decision of the West German government to begin deployments as "an act of subjugation under the increasingly aggressive military strategy of the United States government, a capitulation of reason, a fiasco for peace in Europe."[97] He argued that the purpose of the American missiles was to facilitate new nuclear war-fighting options such as a "decapitation strike" against the Soviet Union, and "horizontal escalation."[98] Schilly also drew lessons from German history. The Europeans could not leave their fate in the hands of the American president. "We Europeans must take another path. . . . We Germans" had to learn from the dark past in which the striving for military power had led to catastrophe. Now the Germans should dissolve the blocs, neutralize Central Europe, and replace military thinking with political thinking. "True Christian love of one's neighbor" would do more for security than weapons could. Faced with the choice of the risk of the arms race and nuclear war or the rejection of nuclear weapons, Schilly said that only the second path held out hope for a reasonable future.[99]

Petra Kelly, also speaking for the Greens, said the "atomic situation" itself was the greatest enemy of all humanity.[100] "We, in the peace movement are not ready to become mass murderers in order to make the concept of deterrence credible."[101] The Greens were not irrational to abandon the "bloc logic . . . deterrence thinking . . . and bilateral negotiations." Rather, continued armament had become "completely senseless" in a world of nuclear overkill. The appropriate response was nonviolent civil disobedience.[102] Marieluise Beck-Oberdorf, another Green representative, presented the NATO decision as a breakdown of West German democracy. A "dangerous minority" had caused panic and fear in the population. It had thus lost the right to command loyalty to the government. What were people supposed to do "when all democratic paths were blocked" if not engage in resistance? "How great is the guilt of those who did not oppose the Holocaust? How great would our guilt be if we did not oppose a nuclear Holocaust with all our power?"[103] Alois Mertes rose briefly to respond to Beck-Oberdorf and to put the issue of democracy in a different light. He referred to an "imbalance of consensus formation" between NATO and the Warsaw Pact, which had indicated that "the forms of Soviet influence on West Germany are often more subtle than primitive blackmail."[104]

At the end of the debate on November 22, 1983, the resolution supported by the governing CDU/CSU and FDP coalition supporting deployments and urging continued negotiations passed the Bundestag.[105] All 286 members of the CDU/CSU-FDP coalition voted in favor of the resolution, while 226 Social Democrats and Green members voted against it.[106] On the weekend of November 26 and 27 the first Pershing IIs arrived in West Germany. In the view of all of the NATO governments, the alliance had implemented both parts of the 1979 double-track decision.

The Soviet Reaction: Revival of the German Threat

The following day, Soviet negotiators walked out of the INF talks in Geneva.[107] The Soviet Union announced expanded deployments of short-range nuclear weapons in East Germany and Czechoslovakia and in the oceans near the United States. It also announced an end to its moratorium on further SS-20 deployments. NATO officials believed the Soviets had already broken the moratorium. The decision to place short-range missiles had been taken long before. As for submarines, the new Delta III and Typhoon class carried missiles with a range of 8000 kilometers, allowing them to stay away from the more dangerous waters near American territory. Soviet nuclear missile submarines had been located off the American coast for years.[108]

The tone of Soviet pronouncements directed at the Kohl-Genscher government was very hostile.[109] Pravda denounced Kohl's arguments as fabrications, disinformation, and lies. Kohl had "scraped the bottom of the barrel" by comparing "those people in the West who seek to meet the USSR's constructive proposals halfway with those who capitulated to Hitler in Munich." To draw a parallel between the USSR and Hitler's Germany was "blasphemy for a politician heading a 'Christian' party and an outrage against the memory of the millions of Soviet people who died in the struggle to rid Europe of fascism."[110] On November 23, TASS said that "obedient to Washington's will and disregardful of the will of peoples, including their own," the West German parliament had adopted a "decision giving the green light to the transformation of West German territory into a launch pad for American first-strike nuclear weapons targeted on the USSR and the other socialist countries."[111]

> The Bonn politicians from the CDU-CSU camp together with their FDP coalition partners have fulfilled the irksome assignment of their overseas patron contrary to the will of their own nation. . . .
> Although three quarters of the population, including a large part of supporters of the ruling parties, as numerous public opinion polls show, reject the deployment of American missiles, the Bundestag endorsed by the formal majority the decision that *turns the country into a testing ground for overseas nuclear maniacs.*[112] (emphasis added).

On November 29, Karl Feldmeyer, who wrote on defense and security affairs for the *Frankfurter Allgemeine Zeitung,* analyzed the outcome of the euromissile dispute.[113] The NATO deployments, he wrote, undermined the political and military purpose of the SS-20s, which had been the decoupling of Western Europe from the United States by the creation of differential spheres of threat. Implementation of NATO's rearmament or *Nachrüstung* decision undermined the credibility of a Soviet threat limited to Europe alone. The Soviet Union's strategic dilemma, he wrote, was reflected in its reaction to the euromissile defeat. The Soviet Union was a world power, Feldmeyer argued, only because of its military power. If military power could not break up the alliances of its adversaries, its whole foreign policy was undermined. The Soviet leaders understood that they were not competitive with the West in political, economic, and social aspects. Therefore they had played to their strength and relied exclusively on military power to remain a world power.

> The neutralization of the political effect of the SS-20 program by the *Nachrüstung* means at the least the temporary collapse of the effort to extend the Soviet sphere of hegemony over all of Europe, and thereby to decisively improve the basis for competition with the United States. For the challenge that Moscow faces is rivalry with America. The political collapse of the SS-20 program is of such far-reaching significance, precisely because it is obvious to political leaders and strategists that in the nuclear era Moscow can attain success against the other world power and its allies only through the political use of military power (its use in war would bring about everyone's destruction).[114]

Feldmeyer expected further Soviet efforts to use its military superiority to decouple Europe from the United States. But, he thought that if NATO's determination persisted and such efforts failed again, the Soviet leadership would be forced to rethink its strategy. Such a rethinking, he speculated, could lead to a "new political order in Europe" including conceding "the right of self-determination to the Germans." Such possible changes of policy in Moscow required that NATO remain firm and implement its decisions.

From the Soviet perspective, the virtue of the hard line pursued by Brezhnev, Gromyko, and Andropov was that it played to the strengths of the Soviet Union, its military power, and to real divisions, sentiments, and fears within Western Europe, especially in West Germany. But the democracies proved able to compete on the terrain of power politics. Once defeated, a policy of military threat and bluff only reinforced the global counterhegemonic coalition that had emerged most clearly at the Williamsburg summit of summer 1983. Karl Feldmeyer's analysis proved to be quite sound. The course of events from 1983 to 1989 confirmed his view that successful implementation of the NATO two-track decision of December 1979 in the fall of 1983 was one of the major turning points of postwar European and international history.

12

AFTERMATH AND THE INF TREATY, 1983–1987

THOUGH NUCLEAR WAR DID NOT BREAK OUT after the deployments, Soviet relations with the West and with West Germany were frigid. Kohl and Genscher rejected pressures to rescind the deployments. The Soviet Union described them in harsh terms as German revanchists. The Social Democratic party continued to pursue the foreign-policy course it had adopted after Helmut Schmidt left office. At an SPD party congress in June 1984, the party's resolution on peace policy stated that

> due to its geopolitical situation, the security interests of Western Europe cannot be identical (*deckungsgleich*) with those of its Atlantic partner . . . the security philosophy of nuclear powers is different than that of non-nuclear powers.
>
> The Federal Republic must not be permitted to become a *glacis* for the interests of great powers. It is incompatible with its interests to become a theater for a proxy war (*Stellvertreterkrieg*).[1]

The party's goal was "to create a European peace order on the foundation of the existing military blocs which overcomes these blocs."[2] A new security concept should "move away from nuclear deterrence and gradually create a defensive conventional structure," leading eventually to a "structural inability for attack" (*strukturelle Nichtangriffsfähigkeit*)."[3] Other practical steps included a gradual elimination of tactical nuclear weapons and creation of a nuclear-free zone extending 150 kilometers East and West from the German-German border, as suggested by the Palme Commission. Conventional arms should replace the role of short-range nuclear weapons, such as the Lance and Pershing I. The resolution called for dismantling the Pershing II and cruise missiles, which began to arrive in West Germany in December 1983. The Soviet Union should eliminate its new SS-21s, SS-

22s, and SS-23s deployed in East Germany and Czechoslovakia and carry out a "drastic reduction of the SS-20s to the level before 1979." The goal of all these proposals was a Europe free of nuclear weapons and all other weapons of mass destruction, including the European parts of the Soviet Union. American government officials, Richard Perle in particular, warned that the Atlantic Alliance could not survive divergences of views as profound as those expressed in the Essen resolution.[4] But while the SPD's critics accused them of pliability in the face of Soviet power, Horst Ehmke spoke of "the self-assertion of Europe," and a "community of responsibility" (*Verantwortungsgemeinschaft*) between the Federal Republic and the German Democratic Republic.[5]

Chancellor Helmut Kohl had difficulties building on the victory of November 1983. The Soviet Union unleashed a furious propaganda blitz against "West German revanchism." The West German left attacked him for being a vassal of the United States. Kohl blundered badly in the Bitburg episode, when in spring 1985 he insisted that President Reagan visit a cemetery that contained graves of members of the Nazi SS troops.[6] In going to Bitburg in the hopes of fostering American-German reconciliation, Kohl forgot that Adenauer's accomplishment lay in forging an alliance between West Germans and Americans, not in reconciling Americans with the SS.[7] With his attention focused on the neutralist currents in West Germany, Soviet pressure, and what appeared to be the fragility of the Atlantic tie, Kohl's insistence on going to Bitburg made it appear as if West Germany's West integration would be preserved at the expense of facing the Nazi past directly.

In the mid-1980s, West German conservatives continued to worry about decoupling and Soviet pressure. Michael Stürmer, a historian and adviser to Chancellor Kohl, was still very worried about the interaction of Soviet pressure and West German "anti-capitalist yearnings, pacifist remoteness from the world, and the search for anticipatory capitulation."[8] In the mid-1980s, he worried that the "the utopia of a world without nuclear weapons" would help the Soviet Union to erode the Atlantic tie. It was a goal the Soviets could achive only if the Germans "lost their nerve. This is the historical irony of German pacifism, its contradiction and its destabilizing impact."[9] If, Stürmer warned, as a result of American withdrawal, Soviet superiority, or "German blindness," the Atlanticist arrangement were to fall apart, "then the days of German democracy would probably be numbered, and with it the existence of a free Europe."[10]

In 1985, Mikhail Gorbachev was elected general secretary of the Communist Party of the Soviet Union and initiated a diplomatic policy superbly designed to take advantages of the fissures and vulnerabilities of West German political culture. The legacy of the Brezhnev and Andropov era in foreign policy was a global counter-Soviet coalition symbolized most dramatically in the statement made at the Williamsburg summit in summer 1983. As we have seen, Moscow's foreign and military policies in the Brezhnev era had pushed all of its potential adversaries closer to one another and had solidified, rather than fractured, America's alliances to its European and Asian allies. Brezhnev and Andropov did bequeath to their successor a massive military machine and a potent diplomatic peace campaign that had been successful in bringing some of the Western left closer to Soviet positions in arms control negotiations. Building on these assets, Gorbachev introduced a new era of relaxation of tensions that would possibly reopen splits between the United States and its overseas allies and perhaps help the Western left return to power.

In spring of 1987, Gorbachev accepted President Reagan's zero-zero option of November 1981 as the basis for an agreement eliminating all Soviet and American medium-range nuclear missiles. This was the same zero-zero option that his predecessors had rejected as a propaganda ruse and that Western and West German missile opponents had described as "not serious" and "absurd." On December 8, just over six years after Ronald Reagan had proposed the zero-zero option, Reagan and Gorbachev signed the INF Treaty eliminating all of the SS-4s, SS-5s, and SS-20s as well as the cruise and Pershing II missiles. With Gorbachev's decision to agree to eliminate the Soviet SS-20s, all of the Soviet arguments of 1979 to 1983 were retrospectively discredited. There was no more talk of an "approximate balance" with several hundred SS-20s deployed or of "compensation" for British and French missiles. It was a far superior agreement from the standpoint of "German interests" than the last Soviet offer of fall 1983, one which would have left 162 SS-20s or 162 nuclear warheads on SS-20s in place, with no Western deployments.

Gorbachev may have concluded that continuation of the hard line only promised to deepen Western resistance and strengthen America's alliances to Europe and Asia. Gorbachev's report to the 27th Party Congress of February 25, 1986, offered "new thinking" that contained many elements of traditional Leninism.[11] He called capitalism "the ugliest and the most dangerous monster of the 20th century," one which converted scientific and technical ideas into weapons of mass destruction.[12] He took a traditional view of relations between the Soviet Union and the United States. "The decisive factors here will be the correlation of forces on the world scene, the growth and activity of the peace potential, and its capability of effectively repulsing the threat of nuclear war."[13] That is, as part of his assessment of the balance of forces between states, Gorbachev included the balance of forces within their societies as well.[14] He referred to the social democratic and liberal parties in Western Europe who "have begun to discuss openly whether present U.S. policy coincides with Western Europe's notions about its own security and whether the United States is going too far in its claims to 'leadership.'"[15] It was important, he said, "to find ways for closer and more productive cooperation with governments, parties, and mass organizations and movements that are genuinely concerned about the destinies of peace on earth."[16] Across their ideological differences, he thought communists and Social Democrats could agree on issues such as renunciation of war, nuclear and conventional, prevention of an arms race in outer space, lower levels of military spending, and disbanding alliances. In a sense, Gorbachev's "new thinking" of the 1980s was an appeal to revive the popular front mentality of the détente era, this time with a more appropriate diplomacy than that of his immediate predecessors.

In foreign policy, Gorbachev's speech echoed many themes evident in Soviet peace offensives in the "era of stagnation" under Brezhnev. Brezhnev, after all, had had a long and enduring relationship with Brandt and carefully cultivated West German Social Democrats. The juxtaposition of a peace-loving humanity with an aggressive, imperialist United States was hardly an example of "new thinking." Stopping SDI had been a concern of the Soviets since Reagan had proposed it, despite their own significant programs on missile defense.[17] Delegitimating nuclear deterrence had been a long-term goal of Soviet diplomacy. It was, in short, the speech of an intelligent Leninist who understood that his aging predecessors had undermined a political offensive in Europe with an overly heavy-handed military buildup.[18]

In 1987, in *Perestroika: New Thinking for Our Country and the World*, Gorbachev spoke of "our common European home."[19] Again, though he spoke of "new thinking," his explanation of the division of the continent was quite familiar. He rejected "old political thinking," which, he said, led to the divison of Europe into two opposed military blocs, though he placed the blame for Europe's division on the West.[20] Gorbachev's Europe extended from the Urals to the Atlantic. It shared memories of war and a rich common heritage. It did not extend across the Atlantic to include the United States. It was in his discussion of disarmament in Europe that Gorbachev's "new thinking" most resembled that of Brezhnev, Andropov, and Gromyko. His proposals for denuclearization, for zones free of nuclear and chemical weapons were identical to those offered by Brezhnev and Andropov.[21] If implemented, they would indeed lead to a denulcearized Western Europe. This had been a Soviet goal for years.

Gorbachev's message was very warmly received in Western Europe and in the West German Social Democratic party. In August 1987 the West German Social Democrats issued a joint statement of West German Social Democrats and East German Communists entitled *Die Streit der Ideologien und die gemeinsame Sicherheit. Das gemeinsame Papier der Grundwertkommission der SPD und der Akademie für Gesellschaftswissenschaften beim ZK der SED* [The Battle of Ideologies and Common Security: The common paper of the commission on basic values of the Social Democratic Party and of the Academy for Social Science of the Central Committee of the Socialist Unity Party].[22] Leading the discussion were Erhard Eppler, from the SPD, and Otto Reinhold, the rector of the academy for social science of the central committee of the East German Communist party (called the Socialist Unity Party, SED). The SPD and the SED agreed that the threat of nuclear war called for "historically unprecedented" political thinking. Social Democrats and Communists "must reconcile themselves for a long time to existing alongside and with one another. . . . Criticism, even in sharp form, may not turn into interference in the internal affairs of the other side."[23] In agreeing not to interfere in one another's internal affairs, the signers suggested that concern for human rights set forth in the Helsinki process should not apply to East Germany. The peace theme completely displaced the question of human rights and freedom in the East German communist dictatorship. It was further evidence that the boundary between West German Social Democracy and East German communism was more porous than at any time in the postwar era. It was a long way from the letter and spirit of the SPD's *Abgrenzungsbeschluss* of 1971.

In 1988, Egon Bahr published *Zum europäischen Frieden: Eine Antwort auf Gorbatschow* [On European Peace: An Answer to Gorbachev].[24] In Gorbachev, Bahr believed he had found a convert to the doctrine of "common security." Change through rapprochement was now a realistic possibility. For the first time in postwar history there was an offer from Moscow to set aside the threat that had been the root of the deepening of the division as well as the impotence of Europe. Gorbachev understood that in the nuclear era security was possible only with, not against the adversary.[25] Bahr was delighted to see that concepts emerging from West German Social Democracy in the early 1980s—common security, security partnership, structural inability to attack, alternative strategies—"suddenly became internationally interesting and became part of an international discussion."[26] Gorbachev's policies meant "the end of the Soviet threat period. . . . The vital interests of Europe permit no other answer to Gorbachev than a yes to new thinking and a yes to common security. For he is not describing his goal, but rather our goal."[27]

In a section entitled "from confrontation to security," Bahr said nothing about the zero-zero option of 1981 and the INF treaty of 1987. Instead, he wondered what Europe would look like without British and French nuclear missiles. He said that nonnuclear states like West Germany should be allowed to sit at negotiations over nuclear weapons that would affect them, and he advocated the Palme Commission proposals for a nuclear-free zone in Central Europe. He said nuclear weapons in states that did not control them were in conflict with national self-determination. He foresaw an end to the era of military confrontation with a guaranteed peaceful political competition of systems and economic cooperation."[28] A "qualitatively new era" would break out in which violence would be excluded as the ultimate recourse, and American and Soviet forces would be withdrawn from both Germanies.[29] With armies unable to go on the offensive against one another because of their "structural inability to attack," Bahr envisaged peaceful competition, growing cooperation, and "change through rapprochement in a European house."[30] Rather than view Gorbachev's turn away from Brezhnev, Andropov, and Gromyko's hard line as a confirmation of Western resolve, Bahr argued that Gorbachev had seen the wisdom of the West German Social Democrats' own views on foreign and security policy.

In 1988, with the momentum of antinuclear sentiment moving in his direction, Gorbachev then proposed another zero option to eliminate short-range tactical nuclear weapons in Central Europe, the only land-based missiles left in NATO's arsenal once the cruise and Pershing II missiles were withdrawn. Such a proposal would denuclearize the defense of West Germany while the Red Army was still in Central Europe. American troops would not stay without a nuclear deterrent on the ground. This "third zero" would make Western Europe far more vulnerable to the Soviet Union's conventional forces.[31] The SPD supported Gorbachev's proposal and, in contrast to the dispute over medium-range missiles, so did Foreign Minister Genscher.

From 1985 to spring 1989, Helmut Kohl saw his political fortunes sag. SPD-Green governments replaced Christian Democratic governments in Frankfurt-Main and West Berlin. A new, radical right-wing party, the *Republikaner*, spouting anti-American and anti-immigrant resentments, picked up themes of old German right-wing nationalism. Until May 1989, when President George Bush shifted the focus of the debate in Europe away from tactical nuclear weapons and towards Soviet conventional superiorities, "Genscherism" was causing tensions within the conservative-liberal coalition and between the United States and Soviet Union. The peaceful East German revolution of 1989, the stunning center-right victory in the March 1990 elections in East Germany, and the prospect of German unification thwarted the advance of the *Republikaner* and placed Kohl in a very powerful position.

The collapse of communist dictatorships in Eastern Europe had many causes. It is beyond the scope of this study to explore them. However, certainly one necessary precondition was the emergence of new leadership in the Soviet Union. It is difficult to imagine what incentive the Soviet leaders would have had to change their foreign policy had they won the battle over the euromissiles. For had Brezhnev's and Andropov's policies of threat and intimidation worked, had the "old thinking" proven successful, would not the incentive to try "new thinking" have been far less? It will be the task of future historians with access to Soviet documents to study the strategic reassessment that went on in Moscow following the euromissile dispute. Yet from the perspective of 1989, public events lend plausibility to the claim that the resolve of the Western alliance from 1977, when Helmut Schmidt first raised the issue of the SS-20s, to 1987, when Ronald Reagan was able to attain the zero-zero option as the basis for the INF treaty, was one of the preconditions for the flowering of freedom in Eastern Europe.

13

WAR BY OTHER MEANS
Theoretical Implications
and Political Consequences

THE PRECEDING STUDY has incorporated the study of political culture and intellectual history to enrich the realist approach to international relations. More so than is the case in much of the realist tradition, we have focused on the role of actors' ideas and intentions and on the impact of forms of governments on, in Clausewitz's terms, "will" and "strategic interaction" between states. In Aron's terms, we have simultaneously examined the correlation of forces and the dialectic of regimes. We have done so in the belief that the study of political culture and power politics should be mutually illuminating rather than mutually exclusive endeavors. Before the direction of the balance of power between states from 1979 to 1983 took place at the level of policy, a change in political consciousness had occurred within West German and Western society and politics. This is why understanding West German political culture and intellectual history is important for understanding the battle between states over the euromissiles. The realist understanding of the changing balance of power and the strategies of states offers a plausible account for the timing and focus of the "antinuclear" agitation of the early 1980s. An interpretive grasp of West German political culture accounts for how West German politicians and intellectuals interpreted these changing international factors. Combining the two approaches frees realism of some of its deterministic elements and encourages the student of societies to examine how they are affected by relations between states.

We have also focused attention on the asymmetrical nature of strategic interaction that occurred between dictatorship and democracy. We have not asked whether dictatorships or democracies considered in isolation from one another are or are not aggressive or prone to war. Rather, we have drawn attention to the instability and pressures inherent in a situation in which political debate about international politics takes place on only one side of a political dispute. Looking at this example of asymmetric strategic interaction has offered insight into the sources of democratic resilience in 1983. Seen from the perspective of the battle of the euromissiles, the spread of democracy, and hence of transparent and open societies, in Eastern Europe is not only a moral advance from the viewpoint of supporters of liberal democracy. In eliminating dictatorships, it eliminates a major source of instability and tension built into the postwar order.

We have also examined the battle over the euromissiles in the longer perspective of German history. In that context, it represented an affirmation of West Germany's Western and Atlanticist ties in contrast to a return to a hard-to-define neutralist or eurocentric stance in political culture and foreign policy. The West German roots of the NATO decision lay in Helmut Schmidt's courage and insight into the need for a balance of power in Europe. The roots of the implementation of that decision in fall 1983, when Schmidt's party had turned against that decision, lay in the reinvigoration of the Adenauer tradition begun by Helmut Kohl in 1973. He helped to give voice to a quality of mind then out of fashion, a quality of making distinctions between freedom and tyranny, liberal democracy and dictatorship. The making of such distinctions was the meaning of his assertion that "we are not wanderers between two worlds. There is no middle ground between democracy and dictatorship. We stand on the side of freedom." In a period in which parts of the West German intellectual and political establishment equated "both superpowers" and "both blocs," the willingness to restate differences between the dictatorships of Eastern Europe and the Soviet Union and the democracies of Western Europe and the United States was an essential precondition for a reversal of trends in the East-West balance of power.

German conservatism of the 1920s elaborated an anti-Western and antidemocratic political culture that contributed to the destruction of the Weimar Republic. Westernizing democratic conservatives, liberals, and the remnants of the Schumacher tradition around Helmut Schmidt in the SPD defended West German democracy against a Soviet strategy of divide and conquer. They did so by daring more democracy, by taking their case to the electorate, and by making it again and again in parliament. These militant West German democrats of the 1980s demonstrated to themselves, their fellow citizens, their alliance partners, and their adversaries in the Soviet Union that democracy's virtues need not become strategic vices.

The pace at which history accelerated in 1989 is partly measured by recalling that, in the preceding decade, Western government officials and commentators devoted their efforts to preventing the Soviet Union from exploiting domestic division in Western Europe to expand Soviet influence over Western Europe. Instead of that "decoupling," the missile deployments of fall 1983 completed a reversal in the global balance of forces that began with Chancellor Helmut Schmidt's speech in London in October 1977. These deployments dealt Soviet foreign policy one of its most decisive defeats of the postwar era and were the indispensable precondition for the INF Treaty of December 1987. The Western victory of fall 1983 may have contributed to the emergence of "new thinking" in the Soviet Union and to the subsequent collapse of communist dictatorships in Eastern Europe. It is hard to imagine the political transformation of 1989 without the deployments of 1983. Instead of democracies perishing, it is the dictatorships of Eastern Europe that have perished, while the Soviet Union has entered a period of still uncertain steps towards reform. The argument for the euromissile deployments was a judgment based on historical experience, not a scientific proposition. In the past, military imbalances between politically antagonistic coalitions had led to a loss of autonomy or to war. Western leaders believed that if the Soviet Union had succeeded in preserving an imbalance of medium-range nuclear missiles and in defeating NATO's efforts to rectify that imbalance then, sooner or later, Soviet political influence in Western Europe would grow and American influence would decline. Further, the open, liberal democratic political institutions of Western Europe would be subject to the political pressure emanating from the Soviet Union, none more so than a nonnuclear West Germany.

In the preceding chapters, we have examined the ideas and leaders in West Germany who made such a reversal of the momentum of international politics possible. Helmut Schmidt, Helmut Kohl, and Hans-Dietrich Genscher insisted, at bottom, that there was no middle ground between democracy and dictatorship. Kohl, in particular, did so at a time when the political and moral boundaries of "militant democracy" had been replaced by older, national boundaries of Germans seeking "security partnership" with the Soviet Union. A reinvigoration of the Adenauer tradition and of the original political and moral boundaries of a West German republic filled a gap created by the weakening of the Schumacher tradition of Social Democratic anticommunism during the détente era. Over the course of four years for negotiations, the Social Democratic party moved away from support for deployments. It fell to Kohl and the Christian Democrats to implement the decision initiated by Schmidt. In the years of opposition, Kohl learned that West German conservatism had once again to articulate its basic political and moral values. This lesson enhanced his ability to take a case to the electorate during the battle over the euromissiles.

The preceding narrative draws our attention to the significance of timing. The West European "antinuclear" movement first emerged in Western Europe after NATO took its decision in December 1979, rather than when the Soviet Union began to deploy SS-20s in 1975 and 1976 or when Helmut Schmidt first raised the issue in October 1977. The "freeze" proposal was offered by Leonid Brezhnev at a time when its implementation would have undermined NATO's plans to deploy new missiles. Egon Bahr made his public distinction of the gap in interests between nuclear and nonnuclear powers in 1981 and 1982, when the Soviet Union was seeking to include British and French missiles in the INF talks. Though the reinterpretation of the NATO decision by Rudolf Augstein, Wilhelm Bittorf, Anton Andreas-Guha, and Wolf Perdelwitz in 1980 and 1981 drew on a decade-long resurgence of national feeling within the West German left, it also overlapped with themes of the propaganda offensive being waged by the Soviet Union. The SPD's election slogan of winter 1983, "in German interests," linked German nationalism to the antimissile cause.

Conversely, Helmut Kohl's assertion in fall 1983 that there was "no middle ground between democracy and dictatorship" must be understood in the context of a climate in which many West German opinion-makers were reticent about making such distinctions. Manfred Wörner's comments on the impact of Social Democratic positions on the INF talks or Alois Mertes's warnings about the impact of Soviet power on West German politics draw attention to the impact of particular statements in the context of ongoing negotiations. Hans-Dietrich Genscher's decision to leave the coalition with Schmidt and form one with Kohl in the summer and fall of 1982 is understandable only in light of the developments within the Social Democratic party during the preceding year.

Raymond Aron and the West European strategists who wrote about the centrality of West European domestic divisions for Soviet strategy remain the exception in the American study of power politics. The euromissile dispute reminds us how important the link is between the correlation of forces and the "dialectic of regimes." It is an ideal typical case of asymmetric strategic interaction between democracy and dictatorship, between open and closed societies and polities. There were good grounds for strategic pessimism about the prospects for Western democracy in the early 1980s. The West German Social Democratic party was not the bulwark against Soviet policy it had once been. Yet the concern over perishing democracies underestimated the capacity of liberal democracies to renew their own traditions with the punishments and rewards of peaceful electoral competition. The resilience of democracy in West Germany lay in the lessons learned by Christian Democrats while in opposition in the 1970s, lessons that taught their leaders the importance of integrating the best aspects of a policy of reconciliation with Eastern Europe and the Soviet Union with West Germany's Western ties. With their view focused on Western divisions, the strategic pessimists of the late 1970s spent too little time examining whether Soviet rigidity would be pushed so far that it would lead to a Western countermobilization. Soviet miscalculation also contributed to democratic resilience.

The euromissile dispute revolved around the question of whether or not the Soviet Union would be able to erode the will of the NATO alliance by taking advantage of internal divisions within individual societies and by exploiting potential conflicts of interests between member states of the Atlantic Alliance. The focus of the latter effort was on potential splits between the United States and Western Europe, and between Britain and France, on the one hand, and West Germany on the other.

In such efforts, the Soviet Union had the advantage that, because of the contrast of dictatorship and democracy in Europe, the political effect of the fear of war and fear of nuclear war could change the policy of only the democratic governments. Only one side had to concern itself with sustaining political support at home. The object of asymmetric pressures was NATO's negotiating position, which the Soviet Union tried to present as an exclusively American, as opposed to European, view. The lever for exerting this pressure in West Germany was the combination of the Social Demoratic and Green parties, the peace movement, and the dissenting press. There were no corresponding levers that NATO could pull, no public opinion and open political life in the Soviet Union or Eastern Europe that could change the Soviet position in Geneva.

Despite the asymmetrical nature of popular pressures, the political virtues of West German democracy did not become a fatal strategic vice. There were a number of reasons for democratic resilience. The United States, less subject to Soviet intimidation and pressure than the West Germans, had in Ronald Reagan a president determined to proceed with the NATO decision in the face of protests in Europe and in the United States. In contrast to West Germany, bipartisan support for the NATO deployments remained largely intact in the American political establishment. Reagan could rightly claim that he was implementing a decision taken by President Carter, his Democratic predecessor. France was determined to do all it could to ward off the specter of neutralism in West Germany, as Francois Mitterand's intervention in the midst of the 1983 election made apparent.

Moral and political support from all of the other NATO allies and, at Williamsburg in 1983, from Japan as well certainly helped Chancellor Kohl present his position as the truly internationalist one. Soviet armament brought the allies together and undermined Soviet efforts to divide them.

From 1980, when the Soviet negotiating position was defined, to December 1983, when the Soviets walked out of the Geneva talks after the first NATO deployments, the Soviet Union never offered to give up all of its SS-20 arsenal for the sake of an arms control agreement. All of the proposals offered by Brezhnev or Andropov between 1979 and 1983 sought to keep some of this arsenal intact while preventing any American deployments. Not until NATO deployed its missiles and had defeated the Soviet strategy of the early 1980s did the Soviet leadership change its position. The history and outcome of the euromissile dispute in West Germany and in Western Europe demonstrated again that effective diplomacy and the establishment of norms of equality between states in international politics required restoration of a balance of power. Without the NATO decision of 1979 and the deployments in 1983, the Soviet Union would have had no incentive to dismantle its SS-20 arsenal. Restoration of the military balance, not only the goodwill demonstrated in the willingness to enter negotiations, was decisive for the shift in the Kremlin's position. The "hard line" of the Reagan White House, of the West German government under Helmut Schmidt, Helmut Kohl, and Hans-Dietrich Genscher, and of the NATO alliance in general from 1979 to 1983 was an indispensable precondition for the diplomatic agreement of 1987.

There was considerable debate during the euromissile dispute about intentions and consequences. Beginning with Tocqueville, a considerable body of literature has examined intellectuals in politics with an eye towards their naivete, utopianism, and reluctance to grasp the relationship between intentions and consequence. But the facts of military power and political success have also exerted a normative power over Western intellectuals. Whatever the mixture of naivete or rational fear in each case may have been, the coincidence of growing Soviet military power pointed at Western Europe and at "nonnuclear" West Germany with political opposition directed primarily against the Western negotiating position, without equal pressure against the Soviet position, suggests that the hypothesis that Soviet power could intimidate West European elites has a certain plausibility. Soviet leaders could not be faulted if they concluded that their military arsenal was earning political dividends in Western Europe.

I have argued that this effect was also due to changes in West German political culture. The most important change in the political culture of militant democracy was a turn away from Kurt Schumacher's understanding of the Social Democratic tradition during the era of détente. Just as Social Democracy after 1945 had been a restoration of an intact political tradition, so the new left and the political culture of détente also restored older German political traditions: Marxism, critical theory, romanticism, and a German national identity seeking to balance Western and Eastern components. Ironically, the dismantling of the political culture of militant democracy took shape soon after the construction of the Berlin Wall. Willy Brandt and Egon Bahr were the key figures in the redefinition of the meaning of a Social Democratic left. They set aside what became known as "the ideology of the Cold War" and its vocabulary of contrasting polities—freedom vs. totalitarianism, democracy vs. dictatorship, individual liberty vs. collectivist conformity. In its place, they developed a new political vocabulary whose effect was to blur these distinctions and to stress "common" interests.

The key words and phrases of the new political culture included the following: *Wandel durch Annäherung* (change through rapprochement), European peace order, common security, both superpowers, security partnership, community of responsibility, patriotism of the left, German interests, and defensive defense. In place of old distinctions of freedom and tyranny, which were criticized as the ideology of the Cold War, came the distinction between nuclear and nonnuclear powers. What was "neutralist" about the political language of Brandt, Bahr, Rudolf Augstein, Günter Grass, and others was not primarily a policy option for transforming West Germany into a variant of Switzerland or Austria, nor did they propose a spectacular leap out of the Western alliance in exchange for reunification of the two Germanies.

Rather, their neutralism lay in a quality of mind and language distinguished first and foremost by a reluctance to make clear public distinctions between democracy and dictatorship, freedom and unfreedom, and open and closed societies and polities in Europe. Instead they spoke of security partnership, common security, both superpowers, or both blocs. Détente, however, did not bring change through rapprochement. Instead there was rapprochement without change, with the separation of the issue of peace in Europe from that of political freedom in Eastern Europe. This reluctance to make explicit these distinctions shaped a political culture that precluded discussion of Soviet armament in the 1970s and early 1980s and that led to the erosion of boundaries between young Social Democrats and Marxist-Leninist sectarians in the student politics of West German universities. The emergence of an "antinuclear" movement that focused primarily on the nuclear weapons of the democracies was one consequence of a political culture in which the making of such distinctions had gone out of fashion.

As we saw in the interaction of the Geneva talks and West German politics between 1981 and 1983, the stance of "a plague on both your houses" favored the negotiating positions of the Soviet Union in Geneva. The Social Democratic party's positions favored the Soviet negotiating position in several key instances. In West Berlin in 1979, its statement that making new American deployments "superfluous" should be the primary purpose of negotiations helped the Soviet Union, whose weapons were already in place. When it urged inclusion of British and French missiles in the talks and spoke favorably about a nuclear-free zone in Central Europe, it adopted important elements of the Soviet negotiating positions in the INF talks. By defining "in German interests" to mean opposition to the missile deployments, it echoed the Soviet effort to use German nationalist sentiments to separate Western Europe from the United States. In the Bundestag vote of November 1983, the Social Democratic rejection of deployments meant acceptance of Soviet conditions for a missile agreement. Whatever the intentions behind such stances were, it is evident that their consequences were to aid one side in an ongoing political battle.

The idea that intellectuals in democracies have little political significance, especially compared to their counterparts living in dictatorships, does not find confirmation in the euromissile dispute in West Germany. The reinterpretation of the meaning of the NATO two-track decision that took place in 1981 in the SPD, in *Der Spiegel* and *Stern,* and among the critical peace researchers and the mobilized intellectual left had political consequences. Without the labors of reinterpretation by intellectuals, the mobilizations in the streets during the subsequent two years would be hard to imagine. Not all the intellectuals who mattered leaned to the left, as the term was then defined. Participants in the *Tendenzwende,* in the *Bund Freiheit der Wissenschaft,* and the editorialists of the *Frankfürter Allgemeine Zeitung,* who were called "right-wing" and "conservative," relegitimated the institutions of liberal, pluralist democracy and the idea of West Germany's political and military West integration, both of which had come under attack from the intellectual left. This Tocquevillian defense of liberty in a period focused on more democratization is still poorly understood in the United States. Though there were some prominent figures of the intellectual left, notably Heinrich Böll, who made freedom and human rights in Eastern Europe a priority, those who spoke most vigorously and most often about the issue came, on the whole, from the center and right of the West German political spectrum.

As Günter Grass's comparison of the Wannsee Conference with Western nuclear strategy and Heiner Geissler's comparisons of British appeasement in the 1930s and the peace movements of the 1980s demonstrated, the battle over the euromissiles was also a battle over which lessons West Germans ought to learn from German history. In the simplifying pressures of public controversy, the antimissile advocates assumed that the recollection of Auschwitz would undermine the case for Western defense, while supporters of the government's case argued that the lessons of Munich were no less clear in leading to support for the deployments. A striking aspect of Geissler's counteroffensive in spring 1983 was that a leader of West German conservatism would recall the historical lessons taught by Winston Churchill about the dangers of appeasement in the 1930s, something which in itself was indicative of the Westernization of West German conservatism. Geissler's intervention was such an important moment in the euromissile dispute because with it he publicly introduced the idea that there were multiple lessons entailed in "coming to terms with the Nazi past." His lessons about how democracies face dictatorships was quite different from the rejection of balance of power politics that was so pervasive among antimissile advocates.

The debates in the Bundestag, in particular the interventions of Manfred Wörner and Alois Mertes, are interesting in light of an image, common in Western social theory since the 1960s, that governments seek to "depoliticize" public debate through a "technocratic" language. Yet Wörner and Mertes repeatedly took the opposition to task for talking a great deal about weapons but very little about the political intentions and purposes of the Soviet Union. The euromissile dispute revealed government officials more engaged in ferreting out the intentions of adversaries than the conventional social-science images of depoliticizing technocracy would suggest. Conversely, opponents were more fixated on weapons technology than the picture of a politicizing, antitechnocratic stratum would suggest. This is not to say that technical arguments were not to be found among supporters and that a political analysis of intentions was absent among opponents. It is to say that the assumption, rather widespread in Western social theory in the last decades, that technocratic and political approaches to politics overlap neatly with the division of right and left does not withstand scrutiny in this instance.

Before the collapse of dictatorships in 1989 in Eastern Europe, the erosion of the political culture of militant democracy on the West German left created a powerful lever for Soviet policy in West Germany. So long as Europe remained divided between democracies and one-party dictatorships, the antinuclear mood worked to the advantage of the Warsaw Pact. That is why democratization in Eastern Europe and possible reforms in the Soviet Union are so important for the stability of European peace. Freedom in Eastern Europe and peace in Europe generally are indeed intimately linked to one another. When the fear of war and the causes of peace are debated in all of Europe as extensively as they were in Bonn in the battle of the euromissiles, when all governments must face a legal political opposition and an inquiring press, the kind of secret military buildup and disregard of norms of equality in international affairs represented by the SS–20 arsenal will become far more difficult to implement. A repeat of the asymmetric strategic interactions of the INF negotiations of 1981 to 1983 in which all of the public pressures were on only one side would be out of the question. Democratization can mean stability in a more complex and more welcome fashion.

Before 1945, German conservatism defined itself in opposition to Western values of liberal democracy. The revolution in its political culture which took place in the postwar years ended that anti-Western tradition and made it a Westernizing force for the first time in modern German history. During the euromissile dispute, when the Western orientation of West Germany hung in the balance, it was the Westernized and Westernizing tradition, whose prominence was established by Konrad Adenauer and revived by Helmut Kohl, that made possible implementation of a policy initiated by Helmut Schmidt, an heir of Kurt Schumacher. In 1989, the peoples of Eastern Europe confirmed the wisdom of the belief of the founders of West Germany and the Western alliance in the late 1940s that freedom in the Western half of Germany should precede unification. Eventually, preservation of a balance of power by a link to the United States and of free political institutions in Western Europe would lead to the dissolution of dictatorship in Eastern Europe. By reaffirming such insights Helmut Schmidt, Hans-Dietrich Genscher, and Helmut Kohl made a distinctively West German contribution to the spread of democracy, freedom, and peace in Europe.

1

TABLES

Table 1. Political Attitudes on a Left-Right Spectrum of West German University Graduates, 1979

	Age (Years)						
Political Position	29 and Under (%)	30–34 (%)	35–39 (%)	40–44 (%)	45–49 (%)	50 and Over (%)	Total
Very Left (n = 61)	1	1	2	3	5	7	2
Left (n = 428)	10	12	16	23	22	25	17
Center Left (n = 328)	7	11	15	14	17	21	13
Center (n = 669)	31	26	27	25	25	21	27
Center Right (n = 353)	16	21	14	13	12	6	14
Right (n = 391)	22	18	16	12	11	7	16
Very Right (n = 278)	14	11	11	10	9	15	11
N = 2508	572	299	489	561	460	127	
% Left minus % Right:	−35	−26	−8	6	12	25	

Table 2. Party Preferences of West German University Graduates, 1979

	Age (Years)				
	29 and Under *(%)*	*30–39* *(%)*	*40–49* *(%)*	*50 and Over* *(%)*	*Total* *(%)*
SPD	20	27	37	51	33
CDU/CSU	60	52	37	24	46
FDP	17	18	18	16	18
Other	3	3	4	8	4
N	(505)	(707)	(860)	(180)	(2252)
	22%	31%	38%	8%	100%

Tables 1–6 are the result of secondary analysis of the data from E. Witte, *Akademiker in Deutschland* (Hamburg: Spiegel Verlag, 1980).

Table 3. Positions on Left-Right Scale of University Graduates by Discipline, 1979

Field of Study	Left %	Moderate Left (%)	Center (%)	Moderate Conservative (%)	Conservative (%)	% Left minus % Right
Political Science/Sociology	29	38	20	9	4	54
Humanities	16	32	29	18	5	25
Fine Arts	9	28	42	9	11	17
Education	16	25	30	21	8	12
Mathematics/Natural Sciences	11	28	26	25	9	5
Engineering	7	28	31	23	11	1
All Graduates	10	26	29	25	11	0
Law	8	24	26	30	13	−11
Economics	8	22	25	29	16	−15
Medicine	5	17	29	32	17	−27
Agriculture	2	11	41	28	19	−34

Table 4. Degrees of Interest in Politics by Discipline Among West German University Graduates, 1979

Field of Study	Very Strong %	Strong (%)	Moderate (%)	Little-None (%)	Strong + Very Strong (%)	Discipline as % of Sample
Political Science/Sociology (n = 51)	57	26	16	2	83	2
Law (n = 329)	38	41	20	1	79	14
Economics/Administration (n = 277)	25	47	24	5	72	11
Humanities (n = 280)	31	39	26	4	70	12
Agriculture (n = 57)	23	40	44	4	63	2
ALL GRADUATES	24	38	33	5	62	100
Math/Natural Sciences (n = 328)	21	47	24	6	61	13
Education (n = 172)	22	32	39	8	54	7
Engineering (n = 612)	16	36	44	4	52	25
Medicine (n = 253)	19	32	42	8	51	10
Fine Arts (n = 81)	17	25	49	9	42	3
General Employed Population	7	17	47	28	24	

Table 5. Degree of Interest in Politics by Political Position Among West German University Graduates, 1979

Political Position	Very Strong %	Strong (%)	Moderate (%)	Little/ None (%)	Strong + Very Strong (%)	Position as % of Sample
Very Left (n=61)	66	18	16	0	84	3
Left (n=425)	30	46	23	1	76	18
Center Left (n=328)	20	44	33	3	64	14
Center (n=668)	20	33	39	8	53	29
Center Right (n=352)	24	36	37	3	60	15
Right (n=391)	23	43	29	4	66	17
Very Right (n=90)	34	24	37	4	58	14

Table 6. Political Views of West German University Graduates by Occupation

Occupation	Left %	Moderate Left (%)	Center (%)	Moderate Right (%)	Right (%)	% Left minus % Right
Professors of Humanities/ Soc. Sci. (*n*=81)	40	14	20	9	19	16
Social Work (*n*=43)	30	14	33	7	16	21
Journalism (*n*=31)	26	19	29	3	23	19
Natural Science (*n*=103)	25	19	29	13	17	14
Teachers/Primary Secondary Schools (*n*=550)	24	16	28	13	19	8
Econ/Business (*n*=200)	25	14	23	16	23	4
Total Sample	20	13	27	14	26	-7
Engineering (*n*=491)	17	14	30	13	26	-8
Medicine (*n*=491)	17	14	30	13	26	-8
Arts (*n*=31)	16	23	32	3	26	-10
Law (*n*=345)	19	10	24	18	29	-18
Others (*n*=244)	12	9	27	18	34	-31

Table 7. Assessment of Political Influecence of Sectors of West German Establishment by the West German Establishment, on Six-Point Scale, 1972

Sector	Score (Points)						
	Average	SPD	CDU/CSU	FDP	BUR	MI	MM
1. National government	5.6	5.6	5.5	5.6	5.7	5.6	5.6
2. National parliament	5.3	5.2	5.3	5.2	5.5	5.5	5.2
3. SPD	5.1	4.9	5.1	5.0	5.2	5.3	5.2
4. Political parties	5.0	4.9	4.8	4.8	5.1	5.4	5.1
5. Television	4.6	4.4	4.7	4.5	4.6	4.7	4.2
6. Trade unions	4.6	4.0	4.6	4.3	4.5	4.7	4.4
7. CDU	4.6	4.3	4.4	4.4	4.5	4.7	4.8
8. Press	4.5	4.3	4.6	4.5	4.5	4.7	3.9
9. CSU	4.3	4.2	4.3	4.4	4.3	4.6	4.5
10. Civil service	4.3	4.4	4.7	4.7	4.1	4.0	4.4
11. State governments	4.1	4.1	4.2	4.1	4.1	4.6	4.2

12. *Bundesrat*	4.1	4.2	4.2	4.3	4.1	4.1	4.1
13. FDP	4.0	4.1	3.6	4.1	4.1	4.2	4.0
14. Employer organizations	3.9	4.0	3.7	4.2	3.9	3.9	4.1
15. *Bundesbank*	3.9	3.7	3.8	3.7	3.8	3.7	3.9
16. Supreme Court	3.8	3.7	3.9	3.8	3.7	4.2	4.1
17. Radio	3.7	3.6	3.9	3.7	3.7	3.6	3.3
18. Large employers	3.7	3.9	3.5	4.0	3.6	3.6	4.0
19. Electorate	3.6	3.6	4.0	3.7	3.3	3.8	3.6
20. Banks	3.6	3.7	3.5	3.9	3.5	3.5	3.8
21. Farmers' associations	3.6	3.6	3.3	3.7	3.5	3.4	3.5
22. Catholic Church	3.5	3.9	3.1	4.1	3.4	3.3	3.7
23. Protestant churches	3.0	3.2	2.8	3.1	2.9	2.9	3.1
24. Education/university	2.8	3.1	3.2	2.9	2.8	2.7	2.6
25. Students	2.8	2.7	2.8	2.7	2.7	3.4	2.7
26. Youth	2.7	2.7	2.9	2.6	2.7	2.7	2.7
27. Federal President	2.7	3.0	2.7	2.9	2.6	5.6	2.7
28. *Bundeswehr*	2.3	2.2	2.3	2.3	2.3	2.8	2.3

SOURCE: Rudolf Wildenmann and Werner Kaltefleiter, *Westdeutsche Führungsschicht 1972* (Mannheim: Universität Mannheim, 1973).

Table 8. Members of West German Establishment Except Leaders of Political Parties Ranking Political Parties First, 1969, 1972, 1981

	SPD			CDU/CSU			FDP			Greens
	1968	1972	1981	1968	1972	1981	1968	1972	1981	1981
Mass media	37.1	44.4	20.6	53.9	39.6	53.3	17.5	15.6	22.8	3.3
Education	28.9	47.9	21.5	52.6	31.3	53.8	23.7	22.9	23.7	1.1
Culture	—	—	39.2	—	—	21.5	—	—	25.3	13.9
Bureaucracy	37.4	37.4	35.3	57.2	48.2	43.1	9.9	15.6	21.2	0.4
Industry	22.6	12.9	10.0	68.6	78.2	75.1	19.4	10.1	14.1	0.8
Employer org.	12.0	7.6	2.6	69.6	73.9	79.1	25.0	19.3	17.6	0.7
Military	—	13.5	2.9	89.2	82.4	—	2.7	11.8	2.1	—
Trade unions	88.2	85.7	84.3	10.3	12.5	13.3	1.5	2.0	1.2	1.2

SOURCE: Rudolf Wildenmann, *Eliten in der Bundesrepublik 1968* (Mannheim: Universität Mannheim, 1969); Rudolf Wildenmann and Werner Kaltefleiter, *Westdeutsche Führungsschicht 1972* (Mannheim: Universität Mannheim, 1973); Rudolf Wildenmann et al., *Führungsschicht in der Bundesrepublik Deutschland 1981* (Mannheim: Universität Mannheim, 1982).

NOTE: Large gains and losses in support among particular groups, especially mass media and education, are italicized.

Table 9. Degree of Concern About World Communism by Sectors of West German Establishment, 1968, 1972, 1981*

"The greatest danger for the Western democracies is now, as before, aggressive world communism which can only be met with firmness."

1. – 3 Disagree
.
.
6. + 3 Agree

						Sector†						
	Average	PS	PC	PF	BUR	BUS	BU.O	UN	MM	ED	MI	CU	MISC
1968	3.6	2.4	4.7	3.1	3.9	3.8	4.4	2.8	3.2	2.7	—	—	3.8
1972	3.7	2.7	5.0	2.6	4.0	4.5	4.6	2.8	3.3	3.0	4.9	—	4.0
1981	4.0	2.8	5.2	3.4	3.9	4.5	4.9	3.5	3.8	3.9	4.6	(2.9)	3.8
Average	3.8	2.6	5.0	3.0	3.9	4.3	4.6	3.0	3.3	3.2	4.8	2.9	3.9

SOURCE: Rudolf Wildenmann, *Eliten in der Bundesrepublik 1968* (Mannheim: Universität Mannheim, 1969); Rudolf Wildenmann and Werner Kaltefleiter, *Westdeutsche Führungsschicht 1972* (Mannheim: Universität Mannheim, 1973); Rudolf Wildenmann et al., *Führungsschicht in der Bundesrepublik Deutschland 1981* (Mannheim: Universität Mannheim, 1982).

*Score determined by ratings given to question shown here, on 6-point scale as given.

†Sector names are abbreviated as follows: PS, Social Democratic Party; PC, Christian Democratic/Christian Social Party; PF, Free Democratic Party; BUR, National Civil Servants; BUS, Business and Industrial Leaders; BU. O, Business Organizations; UN, Unions; MM, Mass Media; Ed, Education; MI, Military; CU, Cultural; MISC, Miscellaneous.

Table 10. Political Character of Student Government (AStA) at the Twenty-Eight Largest West German Universities and Technical Universities, 1969–1984

	Winter Semester															
	69	70	71	72	73	74	75	76	77	78	79	80	81	82	83	84
Conservative	1	0	0	1	0	0	0	0	0	0	0	0	0	0	0	1
Center Right	3	1	0	0	3	4	7	3	4	3	5	1	2	3	2	0
Liberal/Centrist	2	1	0	0	0	0	3	0	0	1	2	3	0	1	0	0
Center Left (Social Democratic)	6	2	4	3	4	5	5	9	10	8	8	9	8	8	4	6
Leftist Coalition	14	19	19	20	14	15	13	11	12	14	11	15	18	16	22	21
Far Left	2	3	2	1	4	1	1	0	0	0	0	0	0	0	0	0

SOURCE: "Übersicht über die Ergebnisse der Wahlen zu den Studentenvertretungen," *Westdeutsche Rektorenkonferenz* (Bonn: Westdeutsche Rektorenkonferenz), 1968–1984.

NOTES: The universities are: Berlin (Free University), Bochum, Bonn, Erlangen-Nurnberg, Frankfurt-am-Main, Freiberg im Breisgau, Giessen, Göttingen, Hamburg, Heidelberg, Kiel, Köln, Mainz, Mannheim, Marburg an der Lahn, Munich, Münster, Saarbrücken, Tübingen, and Würzburg. Among the largest universities are the following seven technical universities: Aachen, Berlin Technical University, Braunschweig Technical University, Hannover Technical University, Karlsruhe, Munich Technical University, Stuttgart. *Statistisches Jahrbuch der Bundesrepublik Deutschland, 1970,* p. 76.

NOTES *continued*:

On the order of the city of Berlin, the student government was abolished and elections were not held at either the Free University of Berlin or the Technical University of Berlin from 1970 to 1979. No elections were held at the Technical University in Braunschweig from 1971 to 1973.

The political coalitions referred to are as follows: *Conservative* = Youth organization of CDU/CSU, the RCDS [Ring of Christian Democratic Students]. *Center Right* = Coalition of youth organization of liberals, *Liberaler Hochschulband* (LHV) [Liberal University Association] and *Sozial-liberal Hochschulband* (SLH) [Social Liberal University Association] with RCDS. *Center* = Young liberals only. *Center Left* = Young liberals + youth organization of SPD, *JUSO-Hochschulband* (JUSO-HSG) [Young Socialists-University Association]. *Social Democratic* = JUSO-HSG only [Young Socialist-University Association]. *Leftist Coalition* = JUSO-HSG + new left, alternative, Green, "basis" groups, left-wing socialists, and groups with ties to DKP, the *Sozialistidher Hochschulband* (SHB) [Socialist University Association] and *MSB Spartakus* [Marxist Students Association-Spartacist]. *Far Left* = *MSB Spartakus* and other communist and Marxist-Leninist groups only.

Each of the twenty-eight universities had at least 4,000 students in summer 1969. (This criteria excluded politically and intellectually significant new expansion universities such as Bielefeld, Bremen, and Konstanz. In the period from 1968 to 1984, these three universities grew rapidly: Bielefeld, 933 students in summer 1968 to 7,112 in 1984; Bremen, 430 to 4,686; Konstanz, 696 to 3,160. New expansion universities would be more subject to the immediate political climate because of the absence of institutional traditions). The universities listed came from all the states of West Germany, with the exception of Bremen. In 1968, 98% of all West German students attended these 28 schools. Because of the advent of the new universities and the growth of others, this figure declined to 88% by 1984. The University of Mannheim is a school of economics and business, with the rank of university.

Table 11. Election Results for the Student Governments (AStA) at the University of Bonn, 1969–1984

	Winter Semester															
	69	70	71	72	73	74	75	76	77	78	79	80	81	82	83	84
Voter turnout (%)	54	56	58	54	50	53	—	54	—	—	52	46	44	40	44	—
							Seats Gained									
Political group:																
SDS	3															
Basis Groups					3	3		1								
ML/Red Cells		2	2	4												
Communist Groups				1	1	1		1	1	2	2					
MSB Spartacist	1	8*	9*	10*	6*	8*	5	6	4	3	4	3	4*	2	2	2*
Sozialistischer																
Hochschulband (SHB)	6	8*	12*	14*	14*	13*	12	15	9	9	5	8	9*	6	6	4*
Education and Science Union (GEW)							13*									
JUSOS-HSG									10	10	10	8	6	5	8	9*
Socialist Fraktion																
Evangelical																

Student (ESG)																
Humanistic Student Union (HSU)																
Catholic Students																
Liberaler Studenten Verband (LHV)	2	1				4	3	3	3	12*					4*	1
New Liberal Grouping		5	17	14	9	14*	9*	10*	14*	12*	10	7*			9*	9
Sozial-Liberal Hochschulband (SLH)	9*	5	–	2	2	3*	6*	6*	3*	3*	3	4*			2*	1
RCDS	9*	8	8	10		16*	16*	16*	14*	13*	10*	12	16*		14*	14
Fraternities																
Independent Left															7	8
Independent Liberals	23*	22*	18	7	6	4	1									
Alternative/Green											4	3*	3	3	3	3*
Independent Right											2			3*		
Local groups	8*						1								2*	7
Total # Seats	61	53	60	60	56	36	67	60	59	63	52	50	51	51	54	49

NOTE: The asterisk (*) indicates that this political group was part of the student government or AStA, in addition to gaining the indicated number of seats in the university student parliament.

247

Table 12. Election Results for the Student Governments (AStA) at the University of Frankfurt, 1969–1984

	Winter Semester															
	69	70	71	72	73	74	75	76	77	78	79	80	81	82	83	84
Voter turnout (%)	40	34	48	37	41	30	24	30	32	32	–	43	33	–	28	26
Seats Gained																
Political group:																
SDS	5*	5														
Undogmatic Left†										11*	11*	10*	7*	8*	10*	8*
Basis Groups																
ML/Red Cells				6*	2*	2	2	1								
Communist Groups					1	1	2	2	1							1
MSB Spartacist		2								1	1	1	1	1		
Sozialistischer																
Hochschulband (SHB)	3*	5*	11		5	7*										
Education and Science																
Union (GEW)									2	2	2	2				
JUSOS-HSG						4*	4*	5*	3*	2		3	5*	3*	2	3
Socialist Fraktion				6*	6*	7*	–	7*	9*	3*						
Evangelical																

248

Students (ESG)							
Humanistic Student Union (HSU)							
Catholic Students							
Liberaler Studenten Verband (LHV)	3*	1				1	1*
New Liberal Grouping Sozial-Liberal			2	2			2
			2	1			2
Hochschulband (SLH)	10	9*	9*	7	6	1	
RCDS				2	2	4	5
Independent Liberals		9	9			2	4
Alternative/Green†						2	
Independent Right						3	
Local groups	1	3	3	2	3	4	3
Total # Seats	22	29	29	22	22	22	22

NOTE: The asterisk (*) indicates that this political group was part of the student government or AStA, in addition to gaining the indicated number of seats in the university student parliament.

† In Frankfurt, the "undogmatic left" referred to a coalition of the Sozialistischer Hochschul-Initiative (SHI), the Sozialistisches Büro (SB), and Spontis, who espoused varieties of "anti-authoritarian" successors to new left cultural-political radicalism as opposed to more orthodox Marxist-Leninism and Social Democracy. In the late seventies, "the undogmatic left" evolved into the Greens in Frankfurt.

Table 13. Election Results for the Student Governments (AStA) at the University of Hamburg, 1969–1984

								Winter Semester								
	69	70	71	72	73	74	75	76	77	78	79	80	81	82	83	84
Voter turnout (%)	46	41	39	38	38	52	34	—	—	34	33	25	23	—	25	17
Seats Gained																
Political group:																
SDS	2	3*	2													
Basis Groups			34*													
ML/Red Cells																
Communist Groups				15	4						7					
MSB Spartacist Sozialistischer				30*	28*	24*	21*	16*	14*	18*	18*	19*	21*	21*	22*	25*
Hochschulband-SHB	18*	13*	13*	23*	37*	40*	36*	32*	22*	17*	9*	16*	18*	17*	15*	15*
Education and Science Union (GEW)																
JUSOS-HSG								12*	29*	32*	26*	28*	25*	26*	24*	24*
Socialist Fraktion																
Evangelical																

Student (ESG)	9*	13*	16*											
Humanistic Student Union (HSU)														
Catholic Students														
Liberaler Studenten Verband (LHV)	2	1								10	8	5	4	2
New Liberal Grouping	11	23						13	10					
Sozial-Liberal														
Hochschulband (SLH)	9	3						7	1	1				
RCDS	13	9	3			2	2	8	7	11	12	10	9	
Fraternities			12*											
Independent Left	29	31	6	3	1	7	1	7	1	20	2			
Independent Liberals														
Alternative/Green								4	3*	3	3*			
Independent Right								2						
Local groups	6		8	4	1	1	1							2
Total # Seats	79	80	78	80	80	80	80	80	78	85	94	94	94	94

NOTE: The asterisk (*) indicates that this political group was part of the student government or AStA, in addition to gaining the indicated number of seats in the university student parliament.

Table 14. Politics and West German University Students, 1978

	Total (%)	Voter (%)	Non-Voter (%)	Stud. Gov. (%)	Gen. Pol. AStA (%)	AStA Univ. (%)	High Political Interest (%)	Low Political Interest (%)
Very left	8.5	10.2	6.3	24.5	14.0	3.6	21.7	1.1
Moderate left	39.4	47.0	30.1	44.9	53.1	23.7	46.1	29.7
Middle	35.1	27.8	45.6	16.3	25.9	40.8	19.1	50.3
Moderate right	13.1	11.3	15.5	9.2	3.7	26.6	8.7	17.7
Very right	1.2	1.9	0.5	2.0	1.2	1.8	2.6	0.6
No answer	2.3	1.9	1.9	3.1	2.1	3.6	1.7	0.6

SOURCE: Allensbach Institute, *Studenten 78* (Allensbach: Institut für Demoskopie Allensbach, 1978). Reprinted by permission.

Column head abbreviations: Stud. Gov., Student government; *Gen. Pol. AStA*, Student government should concern itself with general political issues; *AStA Univ.*, Student government should concern itself first with university issues.

Table 15. West German University Student Opinion on Coalition Decisions of the JUSOS, 1978

"When, in student governments in (West) German universities, student (political groups) oriented to the SPD or FDP cooperate with Communist students, do you approve or reject such cooperation with communists?"

	Total (%)	Voter (%)	Non-Voter (%)	Gov. (%)	Stud. Gen. Pol. AStA (%)	AStA Univ. (%)	Political Interest High (%)	Political Interest Low (%)	Right (%)	Center (%)	Mod. Left (%)	Far Left (%)
Approve	30.0	33.8	25.7	49.0	45.7	14.2	42.6	21.1	5.8	11.8	43.9	80.5
Reject	35.6	36.1	35.4	27.6	21.8	55.6	27.8	41.7	71.0	45.9	20.6	7.3
Undecided	28.3	26.3	31.1	21.4	28.4	25.4	27.8	29.1	17.4	31.8	31.7	12.2
No answer	6.2	3.8	8.3	3.1	4.1	5.3	1.7	8.6	5.8	11.2	3.7	0.0

SOURCE: Allensbach Institute, Studenten 78 (Allensbach: Institut für Demoskopie Allensbach, 1978). Reprinted by permission.

Table 16. West German University Student Opinion on Refusal of JUSOS to Coalesce with Young Conservatives, 1978

"When SPD-oriented student groups at the university refuse under any circumstances to enter a coalition with the RCDS, the Ring Christlich Demokratischer Studenten, do you approve or reject this stance?"

	Total (%)	Voter (%)	Non-Voter (%)	Stud. Gov. (%)	Gen. Pol. AStA (%)	AStA Univ. (%)	Political Interest High (%)	Political Interest Low (%)	Right (%)	Center (%)	Mod. Left (%)	Far Left (%)
Approve	33.3	39.8	25.7	60.2	48.6	15.4	57.4	14.3	13.0	16.5	48.1	75.6
Reject	44.2	47.0	41.7	32.7	32.5	62.1	33.0	53.7	66.7	55.3	34.4	9.8
Undecided	22.5	13.2	32.5	7.1	18.9	22.5	9.6	32.0	20.3	28.2	17.5	14.6
No answer	—	—	—	—	—	—	—	—	—	—	—	—

SOURCE: Allensbach Institute, *Studenten 78* (Allensbach: Institut für Demoskopie Allensbach, 1978). Reprinted by permission.

Table 17. West German University Student Opinion on Communism, 1978

"Which of the following three statements about communism is closest to what you think? Communism is a fundamentally mistaken idea. Communism is a good idea which has been perverted in practice. Communism is a good idea and existing communist states are certainly superior to capitalism."

	Total (%)	Voter (%)	Non-Voter (%)	Stud. Gov. (%)	Gen. Pol. AStA (%)	AStA Univ. (%)	Political Interest High (%)	Political Interest Low (%)	Right (%)	Center (%)	Mod. Left (%)	Far Left (%)
Bad idea	27.1	26.7	28.2	16.3	14.0	43.8	20.0	33.1	65.3	21.6	17.1	4.5
Perverted practice	60.6	63.2	56.8	67.3	72.0	50.3	65.2	56.6	30.5	72.5	72.1	66.7
Good idea	6.0	6.8	5.3	15.3	9.9	3.0	16.5	0.0	0.0	0.0	5.5	25.8
Undecided	6.2	3.4	9.7	1.0	4.1	3.0	3.5	10.3	4.2	5.9	4.7	3.0

SOURCE: Allensbach Institute, *Studenten 78* (Allensbach: Institut für Demoskopie Allensbach, 1978). Reprinted by permission.

Table 18. Political Views of Students at Five West German
Universities, 1979

	Total (%)	Hamburg (%)	Heidelberg (%)	Bonn (%)	Berlin (%)	Frankfurt (%)
Communists	9.1	10.0	2.0	2.0	11.5	17.5
Socialists	22.1	25.0	24.0	26.7	23.1	15.1
New Left	23.2	24.0	19.0	6.9	27.9	34.1
Liberals	32.5	30.0	42.0	39.6	26.9	26.2
Conservatives	12.9	11.0	13.0	24.8	10.6	7.1

SOURCE: Klaus Scherer and Detlef Lehnert, *Zwischen Revolution und Resignation* (Bonn: Verlag Neue Gesellschaft, 1980).

Table 19. Political Views by Field of Study at Five West German
Universities, 1978

	Total (%)	Economics (%)	Humanities (%)	Social Science (%)	Natural Science (%)	Medicine (%)	Law (%)
Communists	9.1	5.4	26.1	6.2	6.2	5.2	3.7
Socialists	22.1	23.3	22.5	19.9	25.9	18.4	24.7
New Left	23.2	9.6	25.1	33.1	20.4	24.8	13.2
Liberals	32.5	46.9	36.3	19.7	34.4	27.7	35.9
Conservatives	12.9	14.9	10.3	2.1	12.3	21.4	22.5

SOURCE: Klaus Scherer and Detlef Lehnert, *Zwischen Revolution und Resignation* (Bonn: Verlag Neue Gesellschaft, 1980).

A NOTE ON "NON-ATTITUDES," "PUBLIC OPINION," AND PUBLIC OPINIONS

DURING THE BATTLE OVER the euromissiles dozens, perhaps hundreds, of polls of West European "public opinion" were conducted on the issue. Following defeat in the March elections of 1983, missile opponents claimed that a majority of West Germans were opposed to deployments.

As Wilhelm Hennis, a West German political theorist, has written, what we call public opinion is quite different from what liberal thinkers of the nineteenth century had in mind.[1] For them, a public opinon was one that could be traced to a particular source; it was a public argument directed towards others, in contrast to opinions that remained in the private sphere of friends and family; "public opinion" was a result of the interchange of individual public opinions by well-informed citizens with the courage, ability, and freedom to express their views to one another. Clearly, responses to the questions of public opinion pollsters fit none of these criteria. Private responses to precast questions and answers, given with the promise of anonymity and based on no necessary knowledge, could not be more remote from the public opinions that Hennis thought so important for the definition of a free, liberal democratic polity.

The American survey researcher Phillip Converse introduced another caveat about polls on political issues. Much, and in foreign affairs a very great deal indeed, of what public opinion polls measure is what he called "non-attitudes."[2] Non-attitudes are opinions on subjects about which the mass public may know or care very little in comparison to more proximate issues; however slight the knowledge of respondents may be, their responses are tallied as "attitudes" and "opinions."[3]

West German public opinion polls confirm these images of a relatively uninformed and uninterested public. After looking at the results of polls on these issues from 1970 to 1984, Hans Rattinger, a West German political scientist, concluded that the percentage of West Germans responding that preservation of peace was a political problem never exceeded 20 percent and was often less than 10 percent, with only a slight increase during the battle over the euromissiles. It declined shortly thereafter.[4] In this state of relative apathy, politics is a contest among organized minorities. Rattinger found that seven of eight surveys of information about the euromissiles done between January 1981 and October 1983 show a high percentage (between 27 and 34) of "don't konw" and "undecided" responses. With different wording—mentioning or not mentioning NATO, the SS-20s, arms control—different surveys arrived at very different results. Rattinger concluded that "depending on one's predilections one could claim either that only one fourth or that more than half of the West German population agree with the December 1979 decision and its implications." If don't knows and undecided's were excluded, one could claim that 70 percent were either in favor or opposed.[5]

For example, in July 1983, on a West German television program devoted to political polls, the commentator asked the following two questions.[6] The first question was, "The Soviet Union and the US are currently conducting disarmament negotiations about medium-range missiles in Geneva. If these negotiations do not produce an agreement by the fall, what should happen next?" Given three choices, 72 percent favored "Continue to negotiate about disarmament and do not deploy any new missiles in the Federal Republic," 22 percent supported "Continue to negotiate about disarmament but at the same time deploy new missiles in the Federal Republic," and 2 percent favored "Break off negotiations and deploy new missiles in the Federal Republic." The second question was, "Assuming that new missiles were to be deployed in this area. Would you agree with this or would you not agree with it?" Twenty-one percent said, "would agree"; 79 percent said, "would not agree."[7] The commentator concluded that there the figures made it evident that there was "a discrepancy between official German national security policy and the majority opinion of the population."[8]

One month later, Elizabeth Nölle-Neumann's own Institute für Demoskopie posed the question of deployment presented in Table 1, with the results indicated there.

In the Table 1 findings, the 72 percent antimissile majority disappears. In August 1983, 40 percent opposed deployments, 37 percent supported them, and 28 percent were undecided. A clear majority (59 percent) of

Table 1. Deployment Survey Results from the Federal Republic and West Berlin, aged 16 and over, Aug. 1983

Question: "A question about the Geneva negotiations: If the negotiations have not yielded any results by the time they end in October and the Soviet Union keeps its SS-20 missiles pointed at Europe: Should the new American Pershing II medium-range missiles be deployed in the Federal Republic then, as is provided for by the NATO two-track decision or should they not be deployed?"

	Total Population (%)	CDU Voters (%)	SPD Voters (%)	FDP Voters (%)	Green Voters (%)
Should not be deployed	40	23	51	36	83
Should be deployed	37	59	25	45	6
Undecided	23	18	24	19	11

SOURCE: Allensbach Institute, IfD Survey 4031.

CDU voters favored deployment, while 45 percent of FDP voters and only 25 percent of SPD voters, and 6 percent of Green supporters did. The considerable differences among respondents adhering to different parties is also evident. In fact, party preference was a stronger predictor of views on the euromissile issue than demographic variables such as age, sex, class, education, or religion.[9]

In four surveys (see Table 2) done from July 1981 to April 1982 in Great Britain, West Germany, Italy, Netherlands, and Belgium, the United States International Communication Agency (USICA) polled people about

Table 2. Awareness of INF Capabilities, USSR and NATO

	Responses from West Germany			
	7/81	10/81	1/82	4/82
Unaware of Soviet lead:				
Both USSR, NATO have INF.	53%	51%	58%	60%
NATO has INF, USSR does not (NATO leads).	26%	25%	22%	16%
Neither USSR nor NATO has INF.	5%	3%	3%	3%
Total unaware	84%	79%	83%	79%
Aware of Soviet lead:				
USSR has INF, NATO does not.	16%	20%	18%	20%

SOURCE: "West European Public Opinion on Key Security Issues, 1981–1982," USICA, Table 40.

their knowledge of the intermediate-force nuclear weapons (INF) capabilities of NATO and the USSR.

In April 1982, almost two and one-half years after the NATO two-track decision of December 1979, only 20 percent of respondents were "aware of the Soviet lead," that is, that the Soviet Union had SS-20s at all, while 60 percent thought both the USSR and NATO had such weapons and 16 percent (down from 26 percent) thought only NATO had medium-range nuclear missiles. According to the USICA data, circulated mostly to officials in Washington and Western Europe, 80 percent of the West European public was not accurately informed concerning the existence of the Soviet Union's SS-20 arsenal and the nonexistence of any American land-based intermediate-range nuclear weapons in Western Europe. Such confusion and lack of knowledge about an elementary fact of the entire dispute supports the hypothesis that the polls were measuring non-attitudes.

In March 1981, the Institute für Demoskopie asked West Germans, "If you hear or read the word 'NATO-Nachrüstung' (i.e., INF-deployment according to the two-track decision), can you tell me what this means?"[10] Only 15 percent were able to give the correct answer, while 46 percent gave a wrong answer and 39 percent said they didn't know. Several months later in May 1981, another West German polling firm, *INFAS*, asked "In your opinion, what is NATO's double-track decision about?" Here, only 10 percent gave the correct answer, while 46 percent gave a wrong or uninformed answer and 44 percent gave no answer or didn't know.[11] Such low levels of knowledge of the issue at that time make clear the vanguard role of opinion makers in defining the issue (coupling or limited nuclear war) that we examined in this period. In February 1983, in the midst of the "missile election," the Institute für Demoskopie asked, "Do you happen to know who proposed the zero option, the Germans, the Americans, or the Russians?" Only 27 percent correctly answered that it was the United States, while 28 percent said the Soviet Union and 45 percent didn't know or gave no answer. Given that the zero option was announced by Reagan fourteen months earlier, in November 1981, and was repeatedly stressed by the West German government, such results do not confirm assertions of a rapid increase in knowledge of foreign and defense policy in the mass public.[12] Instead, the polls underscored the importance of articulate elites in shaping the "non-attitudes" which "public opinion" polls measure. There is a difference between public opinion as the result of the public arguments of identifiable public figures and the private and anonymous non-attitudes delivered by public opinion polls.

NOTES

Chapter 1
WAR BY OTHER MEANS

1. See my *Reactionary Modernism: Technology, Culture and Politics in Weimar and the Third Reich* (New York: Cambridge University Press, 1984). Gertrude Himmelfarb's essays make a powerful case for attention to ideas, individuals, and contingency in history. See *The New History and the Old* (Cambridge: Harvard University Press, 1987). On the "turn to interpretation" which, however, largely avoids political history, see Paul Rabinow and William M. Sullivan, eds., *Interpretive Social Science: A Second Look* (Berkeley and Los Angeles: University of California Press, 1987).

2. See Henry Ashby Turner, Jr., *The Two Germanies Since 1945* (New Haven: Yale University Press, 1987). Also see the very comprehensive history of postwar West Germany, Hans-Peter Schwarz, et al., *Geschichte der Bundesrepublik Deutschland*, 6 vols. (Stuttgart: Deutsche Verlags-Anstalt, 1983).

3. On this see Arnulf Baring, *Unser neuer Grössenwahn: Deutschland zwischen Ost und West*, 2nd ed. (Stuttgart: Deutsche Verlags-Anstalt, 1989).

4. Edward Shils, "Center and Periphery," in *The Constitution of Society* (Chicago: University of Chicago Press, 1982), 93–109.

5. Jeffrey Herf, "Center, Periphery and Dissensus: West German Intellectuals and the Euromissiles," in Liah Greenfeld and Michel Martin, eds., *Center: Ideas and Institutions* (Chicago: University of Chicago Press, 1988), 110–129.

6. Turner, *Two Germanies*, 38–39.

7. Jeffrey Herf, "Neutralism and Moral Order in West Germany," in Walter Laqueur and Robert E. Hunter, eds., *European Peace Movements and the Future of the Atlantic Alliance* (New Brunswick, N.J.: Transaction Books, 1985), 356–401. For a discussion of the formation of the postwar consensus, see Richard Lowenthal and Hans-Peter Schwarz, *Die Zweite Republik* (Stuttgart: Seewald Verlag, 1974).

8. Karl Dietrich Bracher, *Europa und Entspannung* (Frankfurt/Main: Ullstein,

1979), 29–30. Also see Hans-Peter Schwarz and Boris Meissner, eds., *Entspannungspolitik in Ost und West* (Cologne & Heymann, 1979).

9. On the political history of *Ostpolitik*, see William Griffith, *The Ostpolitik of the Federal Republic of Germany* (Cambridge: MIT Press, 1978); and for its economic dimensions see Angela Stent, *From Embargo to Ostpolitik* (Cambridge: Cambridge University Press, 1981).

10. Peter Bender, *Das Ende des Ideologischen Zeitalters. Die Europäisierung Europas* (West Berlin: Siedler Verlag, 1981).

11. Daniel Bell, *The Coming of Post-Industrial Society* (New York: Basic Books, 1973) and *The Cultural Contradictions of Capitalism* (New York: Basic Books, 1976). Also see Irving Kristol, "The Adversary Culture of Intellectuals," in *Reflections of a Neoconservative* (New York: Basic Books, 1983), 27–42. For survey-based studies on the leftism of humanistic, social-scientific Western university-educated strata in this period see Everett Ladd and Seymour M. Lipset, *The Divided Academy: Professors and Politics* (New York: McGraw-Hill, 1975); and Ronald Inglehart, *The Silent Revolution: Changing Values and Political Styles Among Western Publics* (Princeton: Princeton University Press, 1977); and Stephen Brint, "Liberal Attitudes of Professionals," *American Journal of Sociology* 90, no. 1 (July 1984): 30–71.

12. Richard Lowenthal, "Why German Security Is So Insecure," *Encounter*, January, 1982, 31–37; *Kulturkrise und Gesellschaftswandel: Zukunftsprobleme der westlichen Demokratien* (Franfurt am Main: Fischer Taschenbuch, 1979).

13. See, for example, Peter Brandt and Herbert Ammon, eds., *Die Linke und die nationale Frage* (Reinbek bei Hamburg: Rowohlt Verlag, 1981).

14. Edward Thompson, the British social historian and a leading voice of the neutralist left in Great Britain in the 1980s, referred to the combined foreign policies of the United States and the Soviet Union as "exterminism." "Exterminism simply confronts itself. It does not exploit a victim: it confronts an equal." "Notes on Exterminism, the Last Stage of Civilization," in Edward Thompson, et al., *Exterminism and Cold War* (London: Verso Editions, 1982), 24.

15. Günter Grass, *On Writing and Politics, 1967–1983*, trans. Ralph Mannheim (New York: Harcourt, Brace, Jovanovich, 1985); Egon Bahr, *Was wird aus den Deutschen?* (Reinbek bei Hamburg: Rowohlt Verlag, 1982).

16. See Wolfgang Pohrt, *Endstation: Über die Wiedergeburt der Nation* (Berlin: Rotbuch Verlag, 1982) and *Kreisverkehr, Wendepunkt: Über die Wechseljahre der Nation und die Linke im Widerstreit der Gefühle* (Berlin: Tiamat, 1984).

17. See Clemens Graf Podewils, ed., *Tendenzwende? Zur geistigen Situation der Bundesrepublik* (Stuttgart: Ernst Klett Verlag, 1975); Helmut Kohl, *Zwischen Ideologie und Pragmatismus* (Stuttgart: Verlag Bonn Aktuell, 1973). An important recent effort that examines "deradicalization" and the emergence of postwar West German conservatism is Jerry Z. Muller, *The Other God That Failed:*

Hans Freyer and the Deradicalization of West German Conservatism (Princeton, N.J.: Princeton University Press, 1987), esp. chs. 9 and 10. For a critical view of the *Tendenzwende* as an authoritarian threat to modernity and rationality in West Germany, see Jürgen Habermas, "Introduction," in Jürgen Habermas, ed., *Observations on the Spiritual Situation of the Age*, trans. Andrew Buchwalter (Cambridge: MIT Press, 1984), 10–15.

18. Alexander Hamilton, James Madison, and John Jay, *The Federalist Papers* (New York: Mentor Books, 1961). Alexander Hamilton supported a strong presidency, with "energy in the executive" to balance power politics and republican principles, Federalist No. 70, pp. 423–424. On the American founding fathers and foreign policy see Nathan Tarcov, "Principle and prudence in foreign policy: the founders' perspective," *The Public Interest*, no. 76 (1984): 45–60.

19. Edward Hallett Carr, *The Twenty Years' Crisis* (New York: Harper and Row, 1964), 132–145; and Hans Morgenthau, *Politics Among Nations*, 3d ed. (New York: Alfred A. Knopf, 1963). Morgenthau blamed the weakness and irresolution of France in the 1930s on unresolved class, religious, and ideological divisions, not on the vulnerabilities of democracies.

20. Kenneth Waltz, *Foreign Policy and Democratic Politics: The American and British Experience* (Boston: Little, Brown and Co., 1967), 308.

21. Kenneth Waltz, *Man, the State, and War* (New York: Columbia University Press, 1959). Waltz criticized liberal internationalists, behavioral scientists, and heirs of the Marxist and socialist tradition who believed that a change in regime or in human nature would eliminate war.

22. Kenneth Waltz, *Theory of International Politics* (1979; reprint, Reading, Mass: Addison-Wesley, 1983), 99.

23. An American tradition of realism sensitive to the impact of forms of government in international politics began in *The Federalist Papers* but has remained largely outside American academic theories of international politics. See *Federalist Papers*, esp. Nos. 3, 4, and 70. Also see Tarcov, "Principle and Prudence in Foreign Policy," 45–60.

24. See Aaron Friedberg, *Weary Titan: Britain and the Experience of Relative Decline, 1895–1905* (Princeton: Princeton University Press, 1988), 4–8.

25. On this, see the important essay by the West German historian of Nazism, Karl Dietrich Bracher, "The Role of Hitler: Problems of Interpretation," in Walter Laqueur, ed., *Fascism: A Reader's Guide* (Berkeley and Los Angeles: University of California, 1976). For a more recent example of similar projection of rationality to ideologically driven adversaries see Elie Kedourie, "How Not to Make a Mess of Foreign Policy," *Encounter*, November 1984, 15–29.

26. See my arguments on this issue in Herf, *Reactionary Modernism*, 4.

27. Stanley Hoffman has written that it was precisely Aron's concern for history,

context, and the nature of actors that contributed to the weakness of reception of his work by American political scientists who were drawn to the apparently more scientific form of Morgenthau and Waltz's parsimonious hypotheses about power and the national interest. Stanley Hoffman, "Raymond Aron and International Relations," in his *Janus and Minerva: Essays in the Theory and Practice of International Politics* (Boulder: Westview Press, 1987), 53–59.

28. Raymond Aron, *Peace and War: A Theory of International Relations*, trans. Richard Howard and Annette Baker Fox (New York: Doubleday, 1966; Malabar, Fla.: Robert E. Krieger, 1981), 148.

29. Ibid.

30. Ibid., 149. For a recent account of the interaction of international and domestic politics in the Peloponnesian War, see Donald Kagan, *The Fall of the Athenian Empire* (Ithaca: Cornell University Press, 1987).

31. As Clausewitz put it, "it is true that war itself has undergone significant changes in character and methods, changes that have brought it closer to its absolute form. But these changes did not come about because the French government freed itself, so to speak, from the harness of policy; they were caused by the new political conditions which the French Revolution created both in France and in Europe as a whole, conditions that set in motion new means and new forces, and have made possible a degree of energy in war that otherwise would have been inconceivable." Carl von Clausewitz, *On War*, ed. and trans. Michael Howard and Peter Paret (Princeton: Princeton University Press, 1976), 610.

32. Ibid., 67.

33. Aron's interest in the interaction of democracy and dictatorship should also be understood in light of the fall of France and his involvement with de Gaulle and the Free French in London. See Raymond Aron, *Memoires* (Paris: Julliard, 1983), chs. VI and VII.

34. Winston Churchill, *The Gathering Storm* (Boston: Houghton Mifflin, 1948), 17–18.

35. Ibid., 89. For an account that includes Churchill's speeches, correspondence, and articles of the period, see Martin Gilbert, *Winston S. Churchill: The Prophet of Truth, 1922–1939* (Boston: Houghton-Mifflin, 1977). Also see Martin Gilbert, *The Roots of Appeasement* (London: 1967); and Paul Kennedy, *The Realities Behind Diplomacy* (London: George Allen and Unwin, 1981).

36. Churchill, *The Gathering Storm*, 102–3.

37. Henry Kissinger analyzed such asymmetric pressures in his discussion of the Paris negotiations over the war in Vietnam. See Henry Kissinger, *White House Years* (Boston: Little, Brown, 1979), 292–93.

38. It was not, Howard continued, "moral deficiencies in our societies" but "precisely those characteristics in them we wish to defend and that our adversaries wish to eliminate" that contributed to difficulties in sustaining an effective

military policy. "Nothing would bring the Alliance more quickly into disarray than if it could convincingly be depicted as the creature of the Right, a new Holy Alliance directed not at maintaining the political and territorial sovereignty of its members but at preserving a particular structure of society about whose merits there was deep disagreement." Michael Howard, "Social Change and the Defence of the West," in *The Causes of Wars* (Cambridge, Mass: Harvard University Press, 1983), 70, 72.

39. Lothar Rühl, "Soviet Policy and the Domestic Politics of Western Europe," in Richard Pipes, ed., *Soviet Strategy in Europe* (New York: Crane, Russak: 1976), 95. Aron himself wrote that the Soviet Union held a "Clausewitzian-Leninist formula" in which war and military force still constituted the pursuit of politics by other means. "George Kennan's Isolationism," *Washington Quarterly* (Fall 1979), 8.

40. Ibid., 96.

41. Hans Ruhle, director of the Christian Democrats' research institute, the Adenauer Foundation, and then director of the planning staff in the West German defense ministry, made a similiar assessment in "Warum Nachrüstung," *Aus Politik und Zeitgeschichte* (September 24, 1983), 23.

42. Rühl, "Soviet Policy and Domestic Politics of Western Europe," 91.

43. Ibid., 92. Also see similar comments of Richard Pipes on the vulnerability of democracies to a strategy of divide and conquer in his *Survival Is Not Enough* (New York: Simon and Schuster, 1984).

44. K. Peter Stratmann, *NATO Strategie in der Krise* (Baden-Baden: Nomos Verlag, 1981), 242. Also see Uwe Nerlich, "Alliance Strategy in the 1980s and the Political Approach to Soviet Power," in Uwe Nerlich, ed., *Soviet Power and Western Negotiating Policies, vol. 1, The Soviet Asset: Military Power in the Competition Over Europe* (Cambridge, Mass.: Ballinger, 1983), 331–342; "Theatre Nuclear Forces in Europe: Is NATO Running out of Options?" *Washington Quarterly* (Winter 1980), 100–125; and, with Falk Bomsdorf, "Rustungskontrolle als ein Prozess der Selbstbindung: Wirkungsweisen westlicher Verhandlungspolitik," in *Soviet Power and Western Negotiating Policies*, 389–443.

45. Jean-Francois Revel, *How Democracies Perish*, trans. William Byron (New York: Doubleday and Co., 1984).

46. Ibid., 147–48.

47. Michel Tatu, "Public Opinion as Both Means and Ends for Policy-Makers: I," *Adelphi Papers* 191 (Summer 1984): 29. Also see Tatu, *La bataille des euromissiles* (Paris: Editions du Seuil, 1983). Falk Bomsdorf, one of Nerlich's associates at Ebenhausen, referred to a "process of self-binding" linked to arms control negotiations. See Uwe Nerlich and Falk Bomsdorf, eds., *Sowjetische Macht und westliche Verhandlungspolitik in Wandel militarischer Kraftverhältnisse* (Baden-Baden: Nomos Verlag, 1982).

48. Ibid.

49. Nerlich, *The Soviet Asset: Military Power in Competition over Europe.*

50. Uwe Nerlich, "Western Europe's Relations with the United States," in *Daedalus* 108, no. 1, (Winter 1979): 87–112. Also see Karl Kaiser, "Prioritäten Sozialdemokratischer Aussen- und Sicherheitspolitik," and Gesine Schwan, "Die SPD und die westliche Freiheit," in Jürgen Maruhn and Manfred Wilke, eds., *Wohin treibt die SPD?: Wende oder Kontinuität sozialdemokratischer Sicherheitspolitik* (Munich: Günter Olzog Verlag, 1984), 9–27 and 38–52.

51. Max Weber, "Politics as a Vocation," in Hans Gerth and C. Wright Mills, eds., *From Max Weber: Essays in Sociology* (New York: Oxford University Press, 1948), 77–128; Clifford Geertz, *The Interpretation of Cultures* (New York: Basic Books, 1973); and Helmut Schelsky, *Die Arbeit Tun die Anderen* (Munich: Deutscher Taschenbuch Verlag, 1977); J. P. Nettl, "Ideas, Intellectuals, and Structures of Dissent," in Phillip Rieff, ed., *On Intellectuals* (New York: Anchor Books, 1970), 57–136.

52. Gabriel Almond, "Public Opinion and National Security Policy," *Public Opinion Quarterly* 20, no. 2 (Summer 1956): 371–378. Also see Richard Converse, "Attitudes and Non-Attitudes: Continuation of a Dialogue," in E. R. Tufte, ed., *The Quantitative Analysis of Social Problems* (Reading, Mass.: Addison-Wesley, 1970), 168–190. On "spirals of speech" and "spirals of silence" see Elizabeth Nölle-Neumann, *The Spiral of Silence* (Chicago: University of Chicago Press, 1984). On "cognitive mobilization" and the university educated see Inglehart, *The Silent Revolution,* 293–321.

53. Alexis de Tocqueville, *The Old Regime and the French Revolution* (Garden City, N.J.: Doubleday Anchor, 1960); and Max Weber, "Politics as a Vocation."

54. Hans-Peter Schwarz, *Die gezähmten Deutschen: Von der Machtbesessenheit zur Machtvergessenheit* (Stuttgart: Deutsche Verlags-Anstalt, 1985).

55. Ibid., 124. Jürgen Habermas, commonly thought of as a leading voice of dissent in West German political culture, actually stands much closer to the center of this internationalist mood. His focus on "communicative competence," "domination free discussion," and a "theory of communicative competence" made him the philosopher of the social-liberal era in both its central dimensions—détente in foreign affairs and "daring more democracy" at home. See Jürgen Habermas, *Theorie des kommunikativen Handelns,* 2 vols. (Frankfurt/Main: Suhrkamp Verlag, 1981).

56. Schelsky, *Die Arbeit Tun die Anderen;* idem, "Wider Setting of Disorder in the West German Universities," *Minerva* 10, no. 4 (October 1972): 617.

57. Martin Kriele, "Das 'Recht der Macht': Die normative Kraft des Faktischen und der Friede" [The Right of might: peace and the normative power of facts], *kontinent* 3 (1983): 13–15; cited in Baring, *Unser neuer Grössenwahn,* 115–118.

58. Ibid.

Chapter 2
THE ORIGINAL BOUNDARIES OF MILITANT DEMOCRACY

1. On the intellectual and political prehistory of the West German republic, see Hans-Peter Schwarz, *Vom Reich zur Bundesrepublik: Deutschland im Widerstreit der aussenpolitischen Konzeptionen in den Jahren der Besatzungsherrschaft, 1945– 1949,* 2d ed. (Stuttgart: Klett, 1980).

2. On the German conservatism and the animus against the West see Klaus Epstein, *The Genesis of German Conservatism* (Princeton: Princeton University Press, 1966); Leonard Krieger, *The German Idea of Freedom* (Chicago: University of Chicago Press, 1957); George Mosse, *The Crisis of German Ideology* (New York: Grosset and Dunlap, 1964); and Fritz Stern, *The Politics of Cultural Despair* (Berkeley and Los Angeles: University of California Press, 1974).

3. On the deradicalization of German conservatism in these years, see Jerry Z. Muller's important study, *The Other God That Failed: Hans Freyer and the Deradicalization of German Conservatism* (Princeton: Princeton University Press, 1987).

4. On the concept of "militant democracy" and "antitotalitarian consensus," see Richard Lowenthal and Hans-Peter Schwarz, eds., *Die Zweite Republik* (Stuttgart: Seewald, 1975).

5. On this see David Gress, *Peace and Survival: West Germany, the Peace Movement, and European Security* (Stanford, Calif.: Hoover Institution Press, 1985), 3–45.

6. See Hans-Peter Schwarz, *Adenauer, Der Aufsteig: 1876–1952* (Stuttgart: Deutsche Verlags-Anstalt, 1986).

7. "24 Marz 1946: Grundsatzrede des 1. Vorsitzenden der Christlich-Demokratischen Union für die Britische Zone in der Aula der Kölner Universität," in Konrad Adenauer, *Reden 1917–1967: Eine Auswahe,* ed. Hans-Peter Schwarz (Stuttgart: Deutsche Verlagsanstalt, 1975), 84.

8. Ibid., 85. Adenauer continued: "As a result of the spirit of the people [*Volksgeist*] discovered by Herder and the romantics, and above all due to Hegel's conception of the state as the embodiment of reason and morality, the state became an almost divine being in the consciousness of the people. This exaggerated celebration of the state was inevitably linked to a sinking in the evaluation of the individual person. Power is inseparably bound to the essence of the state. The organization in which state power is most impressively and manifestly evident is the army. So, militarism became the dominant factor in the thinking and feeling of the broadest sectors of the population."

9. Ibid., 86. "National Socialism was nothing other than the consequence taken to the criminal plane of this idolatry of power and the contempt, yes, contempt for the individual human being that grows from the materialistic world view."

10. Ibid.

11. Ibid., 89–90.

12. Konrad Adenauer, "Juli. 21 1949, Wahlrede bei einer CDU/CSU-Kundgebung im Heidelberger Schloss," in Adenauer, *Reden*, 140.

13. Ibid., 148.

14. Konrad Adenauer, "21 October 1949, "Regierungserklarung vor dem Deutschen Bundestag zur Gründung der DDR," in Adenauer, *Reden*, 172.

15. "In times such as those in which we are living it will be decided whether freedom, human dignity, Christian-Western thought of humanity will survive or if the spirit of darkness and of slavery, of anti-Christian spirit will force its chains on humanity lying helplessly on the ground." Konrad Adenauer, "'20 October 1950, Deutschlands Stellung und Aufgabe in der Welt,' Rede auf dem 1. Bundesparteitag der CDU in Goslar," in Adenauer, *Reden*, 182.

16. Ibid., 184.

17. Konrad Adenauer, "8 November 1950, Regierungserklärung vor dem Deutschen Bundestag," in Adenauer, *Reden*, 197.

18. Ibid., 191.

19. See Konrad Adenauer, *Erinnerungen 1945–1953* (Stuttgart: Deutsche Verlagsanstalt, 1965); idem, *Erinnerungen 1953–1955* (Stuttgart: Deutsche Verlagsanstalt, 1966); and idem, *Erinnerungen 1955–1959* (Stuttgart: Deutsche Verlagsanstalt, 1967).

20. Adenauer, *Erinnerungen 1953–1955*, 301.

21. Ibid., 64. Cited by Baring, *Unser neuer Grössenwahn*.

22. Ibid., 26.

23. Ibid., 30.

24. Ibid.

25. Ibid., 31.

26. At the first party congress of the SPD in Hannover on May 9, 1946, he said, "in Germany today, democracy is not much stronger than the Social Democratic Party. All the others needed the war potential and supremacy of Anglo-Saxon weapons for their hearts to discover democracy. We didn't need them. We would be democrats even if the English and Americans were fascists. If the situation among the bourgeois parties is bad, democracy is a phrase completely without substance for the Communists." Kurt Schumacher, "September 9, 1945: Sozialismus als integrierende Kraft der Europaischen Demokratie," in *Türmwachter der Demokratie* (Berlin: Arani Verlag, 1953), 148.

27. Ibid., 31–32. Schumacher urged frank discussion of the Nazi's war against the Jews and called for punishment of the perpetrators and for moral and financial reparations to Jewish survivors and their families. See Kurt Schumacher, "Von der Freiheit zur sozialen Gerechtigkeit" (June 23, 1947) ibid., 130; idem, "Die Kluft kann überbrückt werden," (November 1950), ibid., 313–316.

28. Kurt Schumacher, "Demokratie und Sozialismus zwischen Osten und Westen," ibid., 52.

29. Ibid., 56.

30. Ibid., 57.

31. Ibid.

32. Ibid., 64. Schumacher made a similar argument in "Kontinentale Demokratie," Die Zeit, no. 7 (April 4, 1946); reprinted in Türmwachter der Demokratie, 419–423.

33. Kurt Schumacher, "September 9, 1949: Sozialismus als Integrierende Kraft der Europaischen Demokratie," in ibid., 148.

34. Kurt Schumacher, "Wie kann die Ostzone Befreit Werden?" (August 7, 1951), ibid., 521. In 1949, at the first party conference of the SED, the Communists issued a statement describing the Western zone as "a colonial sphere of Anglo-American imperialism" that was a launching point for military and economic aggression. The Americans and the British were instituting a "colonial policy of enslavement" by domestic and foreign "monopoly capital" over the Germans that was directed against German sovereignty, democratization, and independence. Junkers, monopoly capitalists, and reactionary civil servants were handmaidens of this policy as well as "West German politicians, Adenauer, Schumacher and Co, who also supported the policy of the enslavement of the German people. . . . They carry out the oppression and further enslavement of the working class and laboring people under the leadership of German monopoly capital, under the protectorate of English, American and French imperialists and with the active support of the leader of Social Democracy," "Die nächsten Aufgaben der SED: Der Kampf um die Einheit Deutschlands und für einen gerechten Frieden. Entschliessung der I. Parteikonferenz der SED vom 25. bis 28. 1. 1949," in Peter Brandt and Herbert Ammon, Die Linke und die nationale Frage (Reinbek bei Hamburg: Rowohlt, 1981), 94.

35. Kurt Schumacher, "June 1, 1947: Europa—Demokratisch und Sozialistisch," in Türmwachter der Demokratie, 425.

36. Ibid., 434.

37. For further comments on Soviet strategy and the Social Democratic resistance in the postwar years, see Kurt Schumacher, "Aufstand Gegen die Sowjetdeutsche Diktatur," (March 1, 1951), ibid., 493–95.

38. Ibid., 495.

39. Ibid., 496.

40. Kurt Schumacher, "Die Deutsche Einheit—Eine Zentrale Aufgabe," (March 9, 1951), ibid., 525.

41. Ibid.

42. Ibid., 526.

43. Kurt Schumacher, "Wie Kann die Ostzone Befreit Werden?" [How can the Eastern Zone be liberated?] (August 7, 1951), ibid., 517.

44. For his criticisms of Soviet policy against ethnic Germans after the war see Kurt Schumacher, "Politik Macht Man Nicht Mit Den Beinen, Sondern Mit Dem Kopf" (August 17, 1951), in ibid., 504.

45. See Erich Ollenhauer, "Rede vor dem Bundestag am 15.12.1954" in Brandt and Ammon, *Die Linke und die nationale Frage*, 126–28. "In practical terms, the *integration of the Federal Republic in the West* has always had *priority over reunification.*" On this see Gress, *Peace and Survival.*

46. "Entschließsung des SPD-Parteitags in München zur deutschen Wiedervereinigungspolitik vom 14.7.1956," in Brandt and Ammon, *Die Linke und die nationale Frage*, 134.

47. "Deutschlandplan der SPD," March 18, 1959, ibid., 169–74.

48. Ibid., 170–71.

49. "Schreiben des Zentralkomitees der SED an die SPD vom 2.3.1959," ibid., 174–75.

50. Starting in 1951, the ENMID institute has repeatedly asked a representative sample of the population, "Which do you personally think important: that we as Germans get on good terms with the Americans—that we get on good terms with the Russians—or that we should act neutrally towards both?" The responses are given in Table 1. Neutralist sentiment in West Germany long preceded the crises of the 1980s. Such polls are extremely sensitive to events of the moment, but it was not until 1961 that a stable majority for siding with the Americans, compared to remaining neutral, persisted. In the 1950s, when the crucial decisions were taken concerning West integration, both elections and polling data indicated that the West German conservatives were far more supportive of an Atlanticist policy than were Social Democratic voters.

51. A look at one United States Information Agency (USIA) poll from 1957 allows us to disaggregate support for West integration and neutralism among demographic categories and between political party identification. In 1957, equipping the West German armed forces with nuclear weapons was becoming a burning political question, while Soviet proposals for neutralization or collective security in Europe had been the topic of much public discussion. The results, presented in Table 2, suggest that Konrad Adenauer, far from responding to a wave of popular enthusiasm for West integration, was pursuing a policy preferred by only 22% of this representative sample in 1957. The strong support for option C (34%), a general security system that would include the United States, Russia, and other European nations could suggest sympathy for Soviety proposals for collective security or a more ambiguous desire for superpower cooperation in Europe. Those with high school and/or university degrees, still in 1957 a small elite in West German society, were least supportive of neutrality (7%) compared to 19% of those without schooling or only elementary school. Compared to the general population, the most educated were both more supportive of "present arrangements" (30% compared to 22%) and a general security system (55% compared to 34%).

Table 1. West German Attitudes on Foreign Policy, 1951–1980

	Year											
Goal	1951	1952	1953	1955	1956	1957	1959	1960	1961	1964	1967	1980
Good terms with Americans	39	41	46	48	31	39	41	45	55	49	35	52
Good terms with Russians	1	1	1	3	2	2	2	2	1	2	6	4
Remain neutral	48	44	42	45	62	55	54	48	34	42	57	43
Not clear/no opinion	12	14	11	4	5	4	3	5	10	7	4	1

Table 2. USIA International Survey, May 1957: West Germany

"Under present circumstances, which do you think is the most practical way for West Germany to insure its security?"

A. To continue present arrangements for Western defense based on alliance with West European countries and the United States.

B. To form an alliance of West European countries.

C. To arrange a general security system which would include the United States, Russia and other European nations.

D. To withdraw from all alliances and take a position of neutrality.

	A (%)	B (%)	C (%)	D (%)	Other (%)	Don't Know (%)	Cases (N)
All West Germans	22	7	34	18	—	19	611
Education:							
No school/elementary	21	7	31	19	1	21	506
Secondary/trade school	28	7	45	10	—	10	78
High school/university	30	4	55	7	—	4	27
Party Preference:							
SPD	14	8	41	24	1	12	169
CDU/CSU	36	8	29	14	—	13	206
FDP	17	6	68	9	—	—	35

The differences between the political parties are apparent. The CDU/CSU emerged as by far the strongest supporter of "present arrangements," while the SPD was the least supportive, and the Free Democratic party was not much more supportive. Conversely, while 24% of respondents identified with the SPD-supported neutrality, 14% of CDU/CSU and 9% of FDP respondents did. The survey also asked respondents if they thought West Germany was treated as a equal partner by the United States. Of the SPD respondents, 36% said West Germany was so treated and 50% disagreed, while 62% of respondents who identified with the CDU/CSU agreed and 25% disagreed; 43% of FDP respondents agreed and 52% disagreed.

52. Herbert Wehner, "Rede vor der Arbeitsgemeinschaft Außen-Wiedervereinigungs- und Sicherheitspolitik des SPD-Parteitages in Hannover am 22.11.1960," in Brandt and Ammon, *Die Linke und die Nationale Frage*, 189–91.

53. Willy Brandt, "Erklärung vor dem Berliner Abgeordnetenhaus," August 13, 1961, ibid., 199.

54. Richard Lowenthal, "Vom kalten Krieg zur Ostpolitik," in Lowenthal and Schwarz, *Die Zweite Republik*, 659.

Chapter 3
BOUNDARY EROSION

1. On this development, see Hans-Peter Schwarz, *Die gezähmten Deutschen: Von der Machtbesessenheit zur Machtvergessenheit* (Stuttgart: Deutsche Verlags-Anstalt, 1985).

2. Willy Brandt, "Mein Standort," in *Plädoyer für die Zukunft: Beiträge zur deutschen Politik,* expanded ed. (Frankfurt-am-Main: Europäische Verlagsanstalt, 1971), 15–16.

3. Willy Brandt, "Entschlossener Neubeginn," in *Wille zum Frieden* (Hamburg: Hoffmann und Campe, 1971), 37.

4. Ibid., 39–40.

5. Willy Brandt, "Die weltpolitische Lage und die Aufgaben der SPD," ibid., 44.

6. Willy Brandt, "Um den besten Weg zur deutschen Einheit," ibid., 56.

7. Ibid., 59–60.

8. Willy Brandt, "Zwischen den Gipfelkonferenzen" (Juli 6, 1960), ibid., 61–62.

9. Willy Brandt, "Politik für Deutschland: Rede vom 25. November 1960," in *Willy Brandt . . . Auf der Zinne der Partei . . .: Parteitagsreden 1960–1983,* ed. Werner Krause and Wolfgang Gröf (Berlin and Bonn: Dietz, 1984), 31–32.

10. Ibid., 38. Brandt here was responding to political attacks on him for having been an emigrant during the Nazi era.

11. Ibid., 39.

12. Willy Brandt, "Wehrhafte Demokratie," in *Plädoyer für die Zukunft,* 45.

13. Ibid., 46.

14. Willy Brandt, "Berlin und die Einheit der Nation," in *Plädoyer für die Zukunft,* 58.

15. Ibid., 59.

16. Willy Brandt, *"Geistige Aufrustung,"* in *Plädoyer für die Zukunft,* 76.

17. Willy Brandt, "Unsere Stellung in der Welt," *Plädoyer für die Zukunft,* 33.

18. Ibid., 37.

19. Ibid.

20. Ibid., 41.

21. In particular, Helmut Kohl and Alois Mertes argued for the application of universal human rights to Eastern Europe. Also see Ludger Kühnhardt, *Die Universalität der Menschenrechte* (Munich: Günter Olzog Verlag, 1987).

22. Willy Brandt, "Eine nüchterne Bestandsaufnahme der Lage der Nation," *Wille zum Frieden,* 68–69.

23. Willy Brandt, "Eine politische Strategie für die Herausforderung dieser Zeit," ibid., 81.

24. Willy Brandt, "Wagnis und Chance der Koexistenz," ibid., 85.

25. Willy Brandt, "Denk ich an Deutschland . . . ," ibid., 89–112.

26. Ibid., 89.

27. Ibid., 94–95.

28. Ibid., 95.

29. Egon Bahr, "Vortrag in der Evangelischen Akademie in Tutzing am 15.7.1963," in Peter Brandt and Herbert Ammon, *Die Linke und die nationale Frage* (Hamburg: Rowohlt, 1981), p. 235.

30. Ibid., 236–7.

31. Ibid., 236.

32. Ibid., 237.

33. Ibid., 240.

34. A good overall discussion of détente and its impact is Karl Bracher, *Europa in der Krise* (Frankfurt/Main: Ullstein, 1979).

35. Willy Brandt, "Die Lage der Nation: Rede vom 1. Juni 1966," in *Auf der Zinne der Partei*, 127.

36. Ibid., 136.

37. "The Future Tasks of the Alliance," *NATO Final Communiques: 1949–1974* (Brussels: NATO Information Service, 1974), 198–99.

38. Ibid., 199.

39. Ibid., 200.

40. Willy Brandt, "SPD—die vorwärtstrebende politischer Kraft: Rede vom 18. Marz 1968," in *Auf der Zinne der Partei*, 152.

41. Willy Brandt, *A Peace Policy for Europe*, trans. Joel Carmichael (New York: Holt, Rinehart and Winston, Inc., 1969).

42. Ibid., 23.

43. Ibid., 24.

44. Ibid., 27.

45. Ibid.

46. Ibid., 29.

47. Ibid., 18.

48. Ibid., 117.

49. Ibid., 120.

50. Ibid., 124.

51. Ibid., 141.

52. Ibid., 190.

53. WIlly Brandt, "Erste Regierungserklärung Willy Brandts," in Helmut Schmidt, ed., *Willy Brandt: Bundestagsreden* (Bonn: az studio, 1972), 111.

54. Ibid., 134–35.

55. Ibid., 136–37.

56. Willi Stroph, "Erklärung in Erfurt am 19.3.1970," in Brandt and Ammon, *Die Linke und die nationale Frage,* 308–10.

57. Willy Brandt, "Erklärung nach dem Treffen in Erfurt," 244–48, and "Erklärung nach dem Treffen in Kassel," in *Wille zum Frieden,* 249–51.

58. Willy Brandt, "Erklärung in Erfurt am 19.3.1970," *Brandt and Ammon, Die Linke und die nationale Frage,* 310–14.

59. Willy Brandt, "Fernsehansprache aus Moskau," in *Wille zum Frieden,* 251.

60. Ibid., 252–53.

61. Willy Brandt, "Friedenspolitik in unserer Zeit," ibid., 353.

62. Ibid., 354.

63. Brandt's Oslo speech was an example of the "forgetting of power" and moralizing internationalism described as the distinctive West German style in foreign policy by Schwarz in *Die gezähmten Deutschen.* On the relationship between Hitler's ideology and his strategy, and how both diverged from traditional power politics, see the still untranslated classic by Andreas Hillgrüber, *Hitler's Strategie: Politik und Kriegführung, 1940–1941,* 2d ed. (Munich: Bernard and Graefe Verlag, 1982).

64. Ibid., 358–9.

65. Ibid., 365.

66. Kissinger and others thought Bahr was at heart "an old-fashioned German nationalist," who, like Bismarck, sought to exploit Germany's central position for its national goals, that is, reunification. See Henry Kissinger, *The White House Years* (Boston: Houghton Mifflin, 1979), 147. For a sampling of suspicions that Bahr's long-term strategy was the dissolution of the alliances see Walter Hahn, "West Germany's Ostpolitik: The Grand Design of Egon Bahr," *Orbis* (1973), 859–80. Also see Martin Döhren, "Die gleichen Ziele wie Moskau: "NATO-Auflösung als Konsequenz von Brandts bisheriger Politik," *Bayern Kurier,* April 7, 1973; and "Die Opposition dringt auf Klärung der Äusserungen Bundesminister Bahrs," *Die Welt,* April 9, 1973; "Gibt es einen Plan Bahrs zur Auflösung der NATO?" *Die Welt,* March 31, 1973; and Bruno Bandulet, "Ostpolitik: Ausgleich oder tödliche Bedrohung?" *Die Welt,* March 31, 1973.

67. "Statt Annäherung 'Koexistenz auf deutsch,'" *Die Welt,* July 12, 1973.

68. Dieter Cycon, "Permanenter 'Wandel' oder Einigung Westeuropas?" *Die Welt,* July 18, 1973.

69. Ibid.

70. Egon Bahr, "Ist die Bundesrepublik auf dem Weg in den Neutralismus: Contra, Kein Raum für Neutralismus," *Deutsche Zeitung,* November 11, 1973.

71. "Bahr: Neutralisierung Deutschlands undenkbar," *Frankfurter Allgemeine Zeitung,* November 27, 1973.

72. Quoted in "Egon Bahr bekam Friedenspries," *Bonner Rundeschau* January 24, 1973.

73. "Keine Menschenrechte ohne Frieden," *Vorwärts*, July 14, 1977, 8.

74. Ibid. Peter Bender, an early advocate of détente, pointed out in *Vorwärts* in June 1977 that relations between Moscow and Bonn improved as relations between Moscow and Washington deteriorated in the wake of Carter's human rights campaign because Moscow appreciated the reservations of the French and West Germans concerning the new American crusade. Peter Bender, "Es ist Zeit für das Chefgespräch," *Vorwärts*, June 16, 1977, 11.

75. In a debate in the Bundestag in September 1977, Manfred Wörner, the leading conservative speaker on defense matters, said that "if we in the West concern ourselves with the fate of a few freedom fighters imprisoned in mental institutions then we hear: No intervention in internal affairs!" Manfred Wörner in *Verhandlungen des Deutschen Bundestages*, Band 102, September 8, 1977, p. 2996. The parliamentary interventions of Alois Mertes and Helmut Kohl in this period also took up the issue of the relationship between détente and human rights in Eastern Europe.

76. Willy Brandt, "Nachwort: SPD Parteibeschlusses, 1980," cited by Gasine Schwan, "Die SPD und die westliche Freiheit," in Jürgen Maruhn and Manfred Wilke, eds., *Wohin treibt die SPD? Wende oder Kontinuität sozialdemokratischer Sicherheitspolitik* (Munich: Gunter Olzog, 1984), 46–47.

77. Willy Brandt, *Theorie und Grundwerte: Freiheit und Sozialismus: Rede zum 30. Jahrestag der Eröffnung des Karl-Marx-Hauses, Trier, 4 Mai 1977* (Bonn: Vorstand der SPD, 1977).

78. "Sozialdemokratie und Kommunismus," SPD Parteirat, February 26, 1971. Cited by Horst Nieggemeier in "Wie stellt sich die SPD ihre Abgrenzung gegenüber Kommunisten vor," in Maruhn and Wilke, eds., *Wohin treibt die SPD?* 93.

Chapter 4
HELMUT SCHMIDT

1. See Jonathan Carr, *Helmut Schmidt* (Düsseldorf: Econ Verlag, 1985), 17.

2. On "deradicalization," see Muller's insightful and balanced study, *The Other God That Failed: Hans Freyer and the Deradicalization of German Conservatism* (Princeton: Princeton University Press, 1987).

3. Author's interview with Kurt Becker, Hamburg (June 21, 1984).

4. Helmut Schmidt, *Defense or Retaliation* (New York: Praeger, 1962), 1–3.

5. Ibid., 90.

6. Ibid., 112.

7. Ibid., 113.

8. Ibid., 116.

9. Ibid., 117.

10. Ibid., 121.

11. Ibid., 51.

12. Ibid., 53–54.

13. Ibid., 138.

14. Ibid., 179.

15. Ibid., 246.

16. Ibid., 318.

17. Bundesminister der Verteidigung, *Weissbuch 1970: Zur Sicherheit der Bundesrepublik Deutschland und zur Lage der Bundeswehr* (Bonn: Presse- und Informationsamt der Bundesregierung, 1970).

18. Ibid., 20.

19. Ibid.

20. Ibid., 20.

21. Ibid.

22. Ibid., 21.

23. *Livre Blanc 1973/1974* (Bonn: Presse- und Informationsamt der Bundesregierung, 1974), 12–17. According to the White Book of 1973/74, the Warsaw Pact had a 2-to-1 advantage over NATO in tanks (15,500 to 6,200), 140,000 more troops in Central Europe (920,000 to 802,000), about twice as many divisions (60 to 29) and tactical aircraft (7,400 to 2,900). It noted the growth of the Soviet Navy based on the Kola peninsula and in the Baltic and North Seas. The report stressed the existence of nuclear parity between the United States and the Soviet Union.

24. *Weissbuch 1975/1976* (Bonn: Presse- und Informationsamt der Bundesregierung, 1976).

25. Ibid., 17.

26. Ibid., 22.

27. Ibid., 23.

28. Ibid., 31.

29. Ibid.

30. Ibid., 31–33.

31. Ibid., 39–44.

32. "Alliance Defense for the Seventies: Annex to the Communique of December 3–4, 1970, Brussels," *NATO Communiques: 1949–1974*, 250–51. Also see Helga Haftendorn, "Zur Vorgeschichte des NATO-Doppelbeschlusses von 1979," Vierteljahreshefte für Zeitgeschichte, no. 2 (1985), esp. 246–54.

33. "Alliance Defense for the Seventies: Annex to the Communique of December 3–4, 1970, Brussels," *NATO Communiques: 1949–1974*, 250–51.

34. "Defense Planning Committee, June 14, 1974," ibid., 311.

35. "Defense Planning Committee, Brussels, December 10–11, 1974," ibid., 323.

36. "Defense Planning Committee, May 23, 1975," *NATO Communiques: 1975–1980* (Brussels: NATO Information Service, 1980), 25–26.

37. "Nuclear Planning Group, Hamburg, January 21–22, 1976," ibid., 42. Also see "Nuclear Planning Group, Brussels, June 14–15, 1976," ibid., 52–53.

38. "Defense Planning Committee, Brussels, December 7–8, 1976," ibid., 56–57.

39. "Nuclear Planning Group, Ottowa, June 8–9, 1977" and "Nuclear Planning Group, Bari, Italy, October 10–11, 1977," ibid., 74–76 and 76–77.

40. Helmut Schmidt, interview with the author, New York, September 30, 1985.

41. Ibid.

42. Ibid.

43. Helmut Schmidt, *Perspectives on Politics*, ed. Wolfram Hanrieder (Boulder, Colo.: Westview Press, 1982), 26.

44. Michel Tatu, *La bataille des euromissiles*, (Paris, Seuil, 1983), 9–27.

45. Ibid., 26.

46. Ibid., 27.

47. Lothar Rühl, "Der Nutzen der Militärischer Macht in Europa," in Karl Kaiser and Karl Markus Kreis, eds., *Sicherheitspolitik vor neuen Aufgaben* (Frankfurt/Main: Metzger Verlag, 1977), 223. Also see Lothar Rühl, "Soviet Policy and the Domestic Politics of Western Europe," in Richard Pipes, ed., *Soviet Strategy in Europe* (New York: Crane, Russak, 1976), 65–103; and "Das Verhandlungsangebot der NATO an die Sowjetunion," *Europa Archiv* 35, no. 7 (1980): 215–226; "Der Beschluss der NATO zur Einführung nuklearer Mittelstreckenwaffen," *Europa Archiv* 35, no. 4 (1980): 98–110.

48. Rühl, "Der Nutzen der Militärischer Macht in Europa," 232.

49. Ibid.

50. Ibid., 238.

51. Ibid., 239.

52. Ibid., 252.

53. Ibid., 256.

54. Ibid., 223. Rühl placed much greater emphasis than did Chancellor Schmidt on NATO's ability to strike Soviet territory with nuclear weapons. These considerations entered into NATO's assessments during the Euromissile dispute. In 1983, one NATO statement said that the combination of American-Soviet parity and European disparities in theater nuclear forces "could give rise to the risk that the Soviets might believe—however incorrectly—that they could use long-range forces to make or threaten limited strikes against Western Europe from a 'sanctuary' in the Soviet Union. There could be a misperception that without adequate theater-based systems of its own capable of reaching Soviet territory, and in the era of parity at the nuclear level, NATO

lacked credible and appropriate means of response." See *Progress Report on Intermediate-Range Nuclear Forces (INF) 1983*, Special Consultative Group (SCG) (Brussels: NATO Information Service, 1983), 7. At the time, Rühl was *Staatssekretär* in the West German Defense Ministry in charge of International Security Affairs.

55. For Rühl, as for Raymond Aron and American critics of the doctrine of mutually assured destruction, or MAD, the appearance of the SS-20 was an additional piece of evidence supporting the belief that the Soviet Union did ascribe to the view that nuclear weapons were of great political utility. On the criticism of the "technocratic" and "apolitical" nature of MAD see Jeffrey Herf, "Western Strategy and Public Discussion," *Telos*, no. 52 (Summer 1982): 114–128; Lawrence Freedman, *The Evolution of Nuclear Strategy* (New York and London: St. Martin's Press, 1981), esp. chs. 22–26; and Edward Luttwak, "Nuclear Strategy: The New Debate," in *Strategy and Politics* (New Brunswick, N.J.: Transaction Press, 1980), 37–50.

56. *Progress Report on Intermediate-Range Nuclear Forces*, 6.

57. See Raymond Aron, "Hope and Despair in the Western Camp," *Encounter* 58, no. 6 (June–July 1982): 121–129. Aron believed that because of their political regime, the Soviets held "a major trump card, that of being able to hit first." With the SS-20s, they could "dismantle the Western defense system." In Europe, the Soviets retained the choice of means in Europe because they possessed "superiority at every level" except at the level of strategic nuclear weapons, where they were "at the very least on an equal footing."

58. On Kantian, Hobbesian, and Grotian principles in the construction of an "international society," see Hedley Bull, *The Anarchical Society: A Study of Order in World Politics* (New York: Columbia University Press, 1977).

59. *Livre Blanc 1979* (Bonn: Bundesminister der Verteidigung, 1979), 133.

60. Ibid., 132–33. The White Book of 1979 also noted expansion of the Soviet submarine fleet, air and amphibious forces capable of action far from the Soviet Union, to an extent "which is no longer justified" by the needs of defense. "The Warsaw Pact aspires to mastery of the North Atlantic and the Norwegian sea. It threatens not only the maritime lanes which link America to Northern Europe and which are vital to NATO but also the long coast of NATO members in Northern Europe," ibid., 115.

61. There are a number of accounts: Haftendorn, "Zur Vorgeschichte des NATO-Doppelbeschlusses von 1979," 244–87; Josef Joffe, *The Limited Partnership: Europe, the United States, and the Burdens of Alliance* (Cambridge, Mass.: Ballinger, 1987), 60–92; James A. Thomson, "The LRTNF decision: evolution of US theatre nuclear policy, 1975–1979," *International Affairs* 60, no. 4 (1984): 601–15; David Schwartz, *NATO's Nuclear Dilemmas* (Washington, D.C.: Brookings Institutions, 1983).

62. For this view, see Thomson, "The LRTNF decision: evolution of US theatre nuclear policy, 1975–1979."

63. See Uwe Nerlich, ed., *Soviet Power and Western Negotiating Policies*, vol. 1, *The Soviet Asset: Military Power in the Competition over Europe*; vol. 2, *The Western Panacea: Constraining Soviet Power Through Negotiation* (Cambridge, Mass.: Ballinger, 1983).

64. Tatu, *La Bataille des euromissiles*, 35–36.

65. Ibid., 38.

66. Jan Reifenberg, "Vor dramatischer Debatte im Kongress über Amerikas Atomstrategie," *Frankfurter Allgemeine Zeitung*, July 7, 1977.

67. See "Neutronenbombe schon getestet," *Frankfurter Allgemeine Zeitung*, July 9, 1977; and "Neutronenbombe ist Angriff gegen die Menschenrechte," *Neues Deutschland*, July 8, 1977.

68. Egon Bahr, "Ist die Menscheit dabei, verrückt zu werden? Die Neutronenbombe ist ein Symbol der Perversion des Denkens," *Vorwärts*, no. 29, July 21, 1977, p. 4.

69. Egon Bahr, "Ist die Menscheit dabei, verruckt zu werden? Die Neutronenbombe ist ein Symbol der Perversion des Denkens," *Vorwärts*, no. 29, July 21, 1977, p. 4. Reprinted in *Foreign Broadcast Information Service (FBIS): Western Europe*, July 19, 1977, J 4.

70. "Development of Neutron Bomb, FRG Position Discussed: Comment by Schmidt, Others," *FBIS Western Europe*, July 19, 1977, J 2–4.

71. "Neutron-Bombe: Amerikas Wunderwaffe für Europa," *Der Spiegel*, July 18, 1977, pp. 19–27.

72. Ibid., 26.

73. "Wir wissen nun, was auf uns zukommt," *Der Spiegel*, July 25, 1977, pp. 21–22.

74. Manfred Wörner in *Verhandlungen des Deutschen Bundestages*, Band 102, September 8, 1977, p. 2993.

75. Ibid.

76. Ibid.

77. Ibid.

78. Georg Leber, *Verhandlungen des Deutschen Bundestages*, 39 Sitzung, September 8, 1977, p. 3009.

79. Local branches of the SPD passed resolutions opposing the neutron bomb in the fall. See "Die SPD bleibt bei ihren Vorbehalten gegen die Neutronenbombe," *Frankfurter Allgemeine Zeitung*, November 18, 1977, p. 3.

80. See Karl Feldmeyer, "Angst vor der atomaren Apokalypse: Warum die Diskussion über die Neutronenbombe so schwierig zu führen ist," *Frankfurter Allgemeine Zeitung*, August 9, 1977, p. 8. Feldmeyer was one of the few West German journalists or politicians who made the argument that deterrence would be more stable if NATO had more options with which to strike directly at the Soviet Union, thus precluding the Soviet effort to limit a conventional or nuclear war to Central Europe.

81. On the center and conservative response to Carter's decision also see Thomas Kielinger, "Das Atom-Rätsel des Präsidenten. Nach langem Hin und Her um die Neutronenwaffe hinterläst Carter nur Konfusion," *Die Welt*, April 13, 1978, p. 5; W. Hertz-Eichenrode, "Bilanz eines Scherbenhaufens. Die Neutronenwaffe und die neue SPD-Doppelstrategie," *Die Welt*, April 13, 1978, p. 6; Adalbert Weinstein, "Neutronenwaffe und Bundnis," *Frankfurter Allgemeine Zeitung*, April 10, 1978, p. 1.

82. Lothar Rühl, writing in *Die Zeit*, called the neutron bomb affair a "lesson in confusion . . . in the mismanagement of an alliance." "Ein Lehrstück der Verworrenheit: Mit seiner einsamen Entscheidung über die Neutronenwaffe hat Jimmy Carter die Verbündeten abermals in tiefe Unruhe versetzt," *Die Zeit*, April 14, 1978, p. 3. Kurt Becker, "Jimmy Carter's neuer Umfall: Entscheidung gegen die Neutronenbombe: Ein Schlag für die NATO," *Die Zeit*, April 7, 1978, p. 1.

83. Rolf Zundel, "Carter hat nichts preisgegeben: ZEIT-Interview mit dem SPD-Bundesgeschäftsführer," *Die Zeit*, April 21, 1978, pp. 5–6.

84. Ibid.

85. Helmut Schmidt, "Die Verständigung vertiefen," *Vorwärts*, Nr. 19 (May 11, 1978), pp. II–III.

86. Interview by author with Helmut Schmidt, New York, September 30, 1985; also see Jonathan Carr, *Helmut Schmidt: Helmsman of Germany* (London: Weidenfeld and Nicolson, 1985).

87. "Leonid Breschnew und Willy Brandt zum Besuch des Generalsekretärs der KPdSU in Bonn: Entspannungspolitik muss sich bewähren," *Vorwärts*, Nr. 18, May 4, 1978, pp. 15–16.

88. Dieter Lutz, "Kommt der dritte Weltkrieg 1983?" *Vorwärts*, Nr. 46 (November 16, 1978), pp. 16–17.

89. Ibid., p. 17.

90. Tatu, *La Bataille des euromissiles*, 42–46.

91. "Aussen und Deutschland politik, Antrag 1," *Parteitag der Sozialdemokratischen Partei Deutschlands von 3. bis 7. Dezember 1979: Band II*, "Sicherheitspolitik im Rahmen der Friedenspolitik," SPD resolution from Berlin Parteitag, p. 1228.

92. Ibid., 1229.

93. Ibid., 1233.

94. Ibid., 1243–44.

Chapter 5
THE POPULAR FRONT OF THE 1970s

1. Figures taken from *Statistisches Jahrbuch des Bundesrepublik Deutschland.*

2. See Michel Levy, "Singularities allemandes," *Population et Societes*, no. 118

(November 1978): 1–3; Karl Ulrich Mayer, "Strukturwandel im Beschäftigungssystem und berüfliche Mobilität zwischen Generationen," in *Zeitschrift für Bevolkerungswissenschaft* 5, no. 3 (1979): 267–298.

3. Ralf Dahrendorf notes the ironic, job-securing consequences of the expansion of government employment combined with leftist radicalism in "Die Revolution, die nie stattfand," *Die Zeit*, May 13, 1988, p. 3.

4. *Statistisches Jahrbuch der Bundesrepublik Deutschland, 1964–1983.*

5. *Arbeitsdaten* (Hamburg: *Spiegel Verlag*). In all cases "readership" is larger than "circulation," the assumption being that individual copies of magazines are read by more than one person. From 1973 to 1985 both magazines lost readership, *Stern* about 22%, *Spiegel*, 17%. But the number of readers of other prestige newspapers and magazines generally declined from 20 million in 1973 to 17 million in 1985. *Capital* lost 15% of its readership; *Die Zeit*, 43%; *Welt am Sonntag*, 50%. Only the *Süddeutsche Zeitung*, which gained 25% in readership, and the *FAZ*, unchanged between 1975 and 1985, did not lose readership. The changes in market share are not major. *Stern* decline from a high of 50% (about 9 million readers) in 1974 to 44% (8.5 million) from 1981 to 1985, while *Der Spiegel* moved from 29% (5.75 million) in 1973, to a low of 25% (5 million) in 1979 and back to 28% of the market in 1985 (5 million).

6. West Germany's leading national newspaper remains the *Frankfurter Allgemeine Zeitung*. Only 23% of its readership live in the state of Hesse in which Frankfurt is located. By contrast, 78% of the readers of the *Süddeutsche Zeitung* live in Bavaria. Among the regional West German newspapers, the *FAZ* most closely approaches being a national institution and the counterpart to *The New York Times*, Le Monde, or *The Times of London*. The readership of *Stern*, *Der Spiegel*, *Die Zeit*, and *Capital* are more evenly distributed across the country.

7. The continued domination of *Stern* and *Spiegel* is all the more striking in view of two events. First, one of *Stern*'s editors was jailed for participating in a forgery of what were purported to be Hitler's diaries. Second, the intellectual climate was supposed to have turned toward the right in the 1970s, the so-called *Tendenzwende*, and the social-liberal coalition fell in 1982. Despite this, West German conservatism was unable to establish a successful competitor for *Stern* and *Spiegel*.

8. Of the 4.68 million readers of *Der Spiegel*, 7% read the *FAZ*, 4% read *Die Welt*, 7% read *Welt am Sonntag*, 10% read *Capital*, and 47% read *Stern*. The table presents a pattern of a largely non-cross-pressured readership. Conversely, 32% of the readers of *Die Welt*, 33% of the readers of the *FAZ*, 49% of the readers of *Die Zeit*, 43% of the readers of *Capital*, 54% of the readers of *Wirtschaftswoche*, and 31% of the readers of the *Süddeutsche Zeitung* also read *Der Spiegel*. See *Arbeitsdaten MA'82* (Hamburg: Spiegel Verlag, 1982), p. 44.

9. *Arbeitsdaten MA 1980* (Hamburg: *Spiegel Verlag*, 1980), p. 5.

10. The figures for this group were: *Der Spiegel* (32%), *Stern* (32%), *Capital* (14%),

Die Zeit (13%), *FAZ* (9%), *Süddeutsche Zeitung* (8%), *Die Welt* (7%), and *Welt am Sonntag* (6%). *Ibid.*, "Tabelle 36 a," p. 46. The annual reports from 1975 to 1985 indicate that these relative market shares remained stable over the decade.

11. The numbers of graduates in various fields in West Germany in 1979 was 1,733,000. Of these, 123,000 had studied engineering, 152,000 humanities, 110,000 law, 129,000 natural science, 134,000 social science, and 534,000 education for teaching in primary and secondary school; and 551,000 were graduates of vocational and technical colleges. E. Witte, *Akademiker in Deutschland: Eine Analyse ihrer beruflichen Situation und ihrer gesellschaftpolitischen Einstellung* [Academics in Germany: An Analysis of Their Career Situation and Their Social-Political Outlook] (Hamburg: *Spiegel* Verlag, 1980), 427–432.

12. Ibid., 70.

13. Ibid., 18. The proportions by disciplines were the following: teachers, 27.5% (542,000), humanities, 7.9% (156,000), natural sciences 6.7% (132,000), medicine/pharmacy, 10.5% (206,000), law, 5.7% (112,000), engineering 6.3% (125,000), economics and social science, 7.0% (137,000), and graduates of lower-level colleges 28.5% (561,000). In the postwar period, the student body at the elite universities and technical universities ceased to be an exclusively upper-class and upper-middle-class group. In 1953, 4% of students came from working-class backgrounds, 22% from white-collar families, and 29% from professional families, and 38% were children of civil servants. In 1967, for the first time, children from white-collar families equaled those from the upper- and upper-middle classes. By 1982 the percentages were as follows: 15% came from working-class backgrounds, 37% white-collar, 20% professional, and 23% civil servant. These figures are taken from Bundesminister für Bildung und Wissenschaft, *Das Soziale Bild der Studentenschaft in der Bundesrepublik Deutschland: Ergebnisse der 10. Sozialerhebung des Deutschen Studentenwerks im Sommersemester 1982* (Bonn: Schriftenreihe Hochschule 46, 1983), 30–31.

14. In spite of the great interest in sociology of intellectuals in West Germany, this is, as far as I know, the only survey that contained data allowing correlations between disciplines and political views comparable to the study of American professors by Everett Ladd and Seymour Martin Lipset in the 1970s, *The Divided Academy: Professors and Politics* (New York: McGraw-Hill, 1975). Also see Steven Brint, "Cumulative Trends or New Class," *American Journal of Sociology* 90, no. 1 (July 1984): 30–71. On the need to disaggregate the term "intelligentsia" into component parts, and into different historical contexts, see Daniel Bell "The New Class: A Muddled Concept," in *The Winding Passage* (New York: Basic Books, 1980), 144–64; and Irving Kristol, "The Adversary Culture of the Intellectuals," in *Reflections of a Neoconservative* (New York: Basic Books, 1983), pp. 27–42. The advantage of *Akademiker in Deutschland* and the Lipset and Ladd studies over other surveys of "youth"

or "students" lies in their size and detail, which permit disaggregation of the notoriously vague "intelligentsia" into discrete disciplinary (history, physics, law, etc.) and career (professor, journalist, doctor, etc.) categories, in addition to standard demographic variables.

15. Ibid., 53.

16. Ibid., 54.

17. Those asserting a "strong interest" were 35% of university graduates and 17% of the general public, respectively; those with "medium interest" were 37% of the graduates and 47% of the general public; only 6% of the college educated indicated "little interest" compared to 18% of the general employed population; and while 1% of the graduates had "no interest at all" in politics, 10% of the public did. Ibid., p. 47.

18. Ibid.

19. Lipset and Ladd, *The Divided Academy,* 55–92. The measure of leftism in both surveys rests on self-placement on left-right scales, as well as on answers to questions about political issues.

20. Rudolf Wildenmann, *Eliten in der Bundesrepublik 1968* (Mannheim: Universtät Mannheim, 1969); Rudolf Wildenmann and Werner Kaltefleiter, *Westdeutsche Führungsschicht 1972* (Mannheim: Universtät Mannheim, 1973); and Rudolf Wildermann et al., *Führungsschicht in der Bundesrepublik Deutschland 1981* (Mannheim: Universtät Mannheim, 1982). For publications based on the surveys, see Wildenmann et al., *Führungsschicht in der Bundesrepublik Deutschland 1981,* 23–25.

21. For a detailed listing of the institutions included and for a description of the methodology of the Mannheim elite studies see Wildenmann et al., *Führungsschicht in der Bundesrepublik Deutschland 1981,* 1–20.

22. Rudolf Wildenmann, "Die Elite wünscht den Wechsel. Unsere obere Dreitausend, II: Mehr 'rechts' als 'links'," *Die Zeit* 11 (March 12, 1982), 6–7.

23. See Wildenmann, *Führungsschicht in der Bundesrepublik Deutschland,* p. 54, for responses to the statement that "the greatest danger for the Western democracies is now, as before, aggressive world communism which can only be met with firmness."

24. The results of the biannual elections and the character of the political coalitions that emerged from them have been collected by the *Westdeutsche Rektorenkonferenz* (West German Conference of University Rectors). The data are taken from the biannual reports, *Westdeutsche Rektorenkonferenz: Mitteilungen. Dokumentation, Übersicht: Über die Ergebnisse der Wahlen zu den Studentenvertretungen* [West German Conference of University Rectors: Communications, Documentation, and Overview: On the Results of Elections to Student Governments] (Bonn: Westdeutsche Rektorenkonferenz, 1968–1983).

25. This account draws heavily on the *Report on German Universities,* German

Universities Commission (New York: International Council on the Future of the Universities, 1977).

26. Walter Rüegg, "The Intellectual Situation in German Higher Education," *Minerva* 12, no. 1 (Spring 1975): 110–11. Rüegg was the Rektor of the University of Frankfurt am Main and president of the national West German Rectors Conference. He offered the following letter as an example of student attempts to influence appointments: "Dear Comrades, Professor X of your university has had his name put forward for a professorship in Marburg in the field of chemistry. For this reason we would like to ask certain questions about him: Has he taken up a position on behalf of the privileges of the ordinary professors? Has he made proposals for the equal status of all university teachers? Is he in contact with the *Bund Freiheit der Wissenschaft*? Does he actively boycott student demands for co-determination? Does he have good relations with industry? What is his reputation as an examiner? Is his general attitude reactionary? Conservative? Liberal? Progressive?"

27. Author's interview with Friedbert Pfluger, Bonn, June 26, 1985.

28. *Übersicht* (Bonn: Westdeutsche Rektorenkonferenz), July 1979, p. 40.

29. According to the 1971 report of the interior ministry, then led by Hans Dietrich Genscher, there were 250 left-wing radical groups in West Germany, with 84,300 members. According to the report, orthodox Communist groups close to the DKP had 81,000 members. Some 420 newspapers of left-wing radicalism with a circulation of 2 million appeared, among which were 320 papers of orthodox communist orientation reaching, 1,650,000.

30. As one of its leaders put it in the founding congress, "the battle for the anchoring of Marxism in the bourgeois universities will be an instrument for the repression of all forms of destructive knowledge (*Vernichtungs-wissenschaft*) for there can be no peaceful coexistence between Marxist and bourgeois scholarship in the university." Christoph Stawe, cited by Gerd Langguth, *Protestbewegung* (Cologne: Verlag Wissenschaft und Politik, 1983), 176. For a description of an *MSB* attack on the historian of Hitler's strategy, Andreas Hillgrüber, see Kurt Reumann, "Spartakus und Hillgrüber," in *Blicke ins Innere: Berichete von der akademischen Front* (Zürich: Edition Interfrom, 1975), 95–100. In 1969, the Verband Deutscher Studentenschaften (VDS) placed Hillgrüber, author of a major 1965 study of Hitler's strategy, in fifth place on a list of twenty-four West German *Vernichtungswissenschaftlern* (annihilation-scholars) because he had been the director of the Office of Military History in Freiburg for several months.

31. Langguth, *Protestbewegung,* 183–187.

32. *Juso-Hochschulgruppen Materialen,* p. 41, in ibid., 190.

33. *Rote Blätter,* No. 15, 1973, in ibid., 193.

34. *6. Bundeskongress des MSB Spartakus, Protokoll,* p. 49, in ibid., 194.

35. See *Übersicht über die Erbebnisse der Wahlen zu den Studentenvertretungen* for

Wintersemester from 1968/69 to 1983/84 (Bad Godesberg: Westdeutsche Rektorenkonferenz-Dokumentationsabteilung, Bibliothek und Pressestelle).

36. These figures are taken from the yearly *Übersicht* of student elections published by the *Westdeutsche Rektorenkonferenz*. Figures for absolute numbers of students are taken from the West German *Statistisches Jahrbuch* for 1984, pp. 354– 355.

37. On Marxism in France and the background to the French election of 1981, see Tony Judt, *Marxism and the French Left* (New York and Oxford: Oxford University Press, 1986), chapters 4 and 5.

38. According to a survey conducted by Rudolf Wildenmann, in the decade 1968 to 1979, 80% of university students did not belong to any political, religious, or social group. "The student body as a whole," he concluded, "is undifferentiated, unstructured, amorphous, individualistic." Wildenmann, *Studenten 79*, 19. Wildenmann found that about 8% of university professors and students adopted a stance of aggressive political behavior, that is, a willingness to attack persons and things based on an ideological world view. This compared to 5% in the general population. In large universities such as Hamburg, Heidelberg, Munich, Frankfurt, Münster, Mannheim, Free University in Berlin, Mainz, Tubingen, Göttingen, Hannover, and Bonn, this meant that a radical left willing to adopt aggressive political action amounted to a critical mass of 1,500 to 2,000 people; ibid., 26.

39. Elizabeth Nölle-Neumann, "Wie demokratisch sind unsere Studenten," *Frankfurter Allgemeine Zeitung*, October 2, 1978.

40. The following data are taken from *Studenten: Ergebnisse einer Repräsentativebefragung an Universitäten, Technischen Universitäten und Technischen Hochschulen in Wintersemester 1977/78: Computerband I and II* (Allensbach: Institut für Demoskopie Allensbach, 1989), Band II, Tabelle, 102.

41. Christian Krause, Detlef Lehnert, and Klaus-Jürgen Scherer, *Zwischen Revolution und Resignation: Alternativkultur, politische Grundströmungen und Hochschulaktivitäten in der Studentenschaft: Eine empirische Untersuchung über die politischen Einstellungen von Studenten* (Bonn: Verlag Neue Gesselschaft, 1980).

42. Ibid. See Appendix.

43. Ibid., 222–227.

44. Ibid., 225–226.

Chapter 6
DARING MORE DEMOCRACY MEETS THE LONG MARCH

1. See Rudi Dutschke, *Mein Langer Marsch: Reden, Schriften und Tagebücher aus zwanzig Jahren* (Reinbek bei Hamburg: Rowohlt Verlag, 1980). Dutschke was born in 1940 in what became East Germany. In 1960 he moved to West Berlin. In 1961 he began to study sociology at the Free University. A leader

of the West Berlin student left, he joined SDS in 1965 and became its most prominent spokesman and leader in anti-Vietnam war protests. In April 1968, he was critically wounded as a result of an assassination attempt and moved to England to recuperate. He welcomed the emergence of the ecology movements of the 1970s and encouraged the formation of the Green Party in Bremen in 1977. He died in December 1979 of complications originating in the assassination attempt of 1968.

2. For his criticism of West German terrorism, see "Kritik an Terror muss klarer Werden," *Die Zeit*, September 16, 1977; "Toward Clarifying Criticism of Terrorism," *New German Critique*, no. 12 (Fall, 1977): 9–10.

3. Dutschke, *Mein Langer Marsch*, 22–23.

4. Rudi Dutschke, "Stern-Interview vom 26.November 1967," in *Mein Langer Marsch*, 63–64.

5. The West German sociologist Helmut Schelsky noted at the time that Dutschke's strategy was a far more realistic strategy of revolution in an advanced industrial society than previous fantasies of armed rebellion. See Helmut Schelsky, "The Wider Setting of Disorder in the West German Universities," *Minerva* 10, no. 4 (October 1972), 614–626.

6. On the "proletarian public sphere" see Oskar Negt and Alexander Kluge, *Öffentlichkeit und Erfahrung: Zur Organisationsanalyse von bürgerlicher und proletarischer Öffentlichkeit* (Frankfurt am Main: Suhrkamp Verlag, 1974), 12; Discussion of the "public sphere" in West Germany in the 1970s drew on Jürgen Habermas, *Strukturwandel der Öffentlichkeit* (Neuwied and Berlin: Luchterhand, 1971, orig. 1962). See Jürgen Habermas, *The Structural Transformation of the Public Sphere*, trans. Thomas Burger with the assistance of Frederick Lawrence (Cambridge: MIT Press, 1989).

7. Franz Brüseke and Hans-Martin Grosse-Oetringhaus, *Blätter von Unten: Alternativzeitung in der Bundesrepublik* (Offenbach: Verlag 2000, 1981).

8. Two examples are Klaus Theweleit's *Männerphantasien* (Frankfurt/Main: Roter Stern Verlag, 1978); and Wolfgang Pohrt, *Endstation: Über die Wiedergeburt der Nation* (Berlin: Rotbuch Verlag, 1982).

9. On the emergence and development of peace research in West Germany see Karl Heinz Koppe, "Zur Entwicklung der Deutschen Gesellschaft für Friedens- und Konfliktforschung (DGFK) und der Friedensforschung in der Bundesrepublik Deutschland," in *DGFK Jahrbuch 1979/80* (Baden-Baden: Nomos Verlagsgesellschaft, 1980); Gertrud Kühnlein, *Die Entwicklung der kritischen Friedensforschung in der Bundesrepublic Deutschland* (Frankfurt/Main, 1978); Hans Joachim Arndt, *Die Staatliche geforderte Friedens- und Konfliktforschung in der Bundesrepublik Deutschland von 1970 bis 1979* (Munich: Bayerische Staatskanzlei, 1980); Karl Kaiser, *Friedensforschung in der Bundesrepublik: Studie im Auftrag der Stiftung Volkswagenwerk* (Göttingen, 1970); Ekkehard Krippendorf, *Friedensforschung* (Cologne/Berlin: 1968): and Klaus Hornung, ed., *Frieden ohne Utopie* (Krefeld: Sinus Verlag, 1983). Also see my article

"War, Peace, and the Intellectuals," *International Security* 10, no. 4 (Spring 1986): 172–200.

10. Interview with Anton Andreas-Guha, Frankfurt-am-Main, June 17, 1984. See his *Die Nachrüstung: Der Holocaust Europas* (Freiburg: Dreisam Verlag, 1981).

11. See Herf, "War, Peace, and the Intellectuals," 172–200.

12. Reiner Steinweg, *Das kontrollierte Chaos: Die Krise der Abrüstung* (Frankfurt am Main: Suhrkamp Verlag, 1980), 262.

13. See Karsten Voigt, *Wege zur Abrüstung* (Frankfurt am Main: Eichborn Verlag, 1981); Oskar Lafontaine, *Angst vor den Freunden* (Reinbek bei Hamburg: Rowohlt Verlag, 1983); and Erhard Eppler, *Wege aus der Gefahr* (Reinbek bei Hamburg: Rowohlt Verlag, 1981).

14. Roland Vogt, "Vitalismus als erste Antwort auf den Drang zur Auslöschung (Exterminismus)" [Vitalism as the First Answer to the Push towards Extinction (Exterminism)] in *Entrüstet Auch: Analysen zur Atomaren Bedröhung, Wege zum Frieden* (Bonn: Bundesvorstand der Grünen, 1981), 80.

15. Franz Alt, *Frieden ist Möglich: Die Politik der Bergpredigt* (Munich: Piper Verlag, 1983).

16. Hans Gunter Brauch, *Entwicklung und Ergebnisse der Friedensforschung (1969–1978)*, (Frankfurt am Main: HSFK, 1979), 41.

17. Hans-Peter Schwarz, *Die gezähmten Deutschen: Von der Machtbesessenheit zur Machtvergessenheit* (Stuttgart: Deutsche Verlags-Anstalt, 1985), 136–37.

18. The term comes from the French sociologist Raymond Boudon. See his *L'idéologie: L'origine des idees recues* (Paris: Fayard, 1986).

19. Karl Kaiser, director of the Society for Foreign Policy in Bonn, wrote that "an optimistic assumption lies at the root of all serious peace research, namely that man is master of himself and his environment. This science assumes that the world, the future and also peace can be made and planned and that a new scientific and technical potential now stands ready to accomplish this task." Kaiser, *Friedensforschung in der Bundesrepublik*, 21 and 34–51.

20. For a West German conservative criticism of the Enlightenment optimism and utopianism of peace research, see Frederick Tenbruck, "Friede durch Friedensforschung? Ein Heilsglaube unserer Zeit," *Frankfürter Allgemeine Zeitung*, December 22, 1973; reprinted in Hornung, ed., *Frieden ohne Utopie*, 91–112. For a criticism of the tendency of American peace researchers in the 1950s and 1960s to neglect the elements of power in international politics see Kenneth Waltz, *Man, the State, and War* (New York: Columbia University Press, 1959).

21. Gertud Kuhnlein, *Die Entwicklung der kritischen Friedensforschung in der Bundesrepublik Deutschland* (Frankfurt am Main, 1978).

22. For the West German conservative-realist criticism of peace research on the grounds that it displaced a historically and philosophically inclined German social science with a positivistic search for a scientific politics see Arndt, *Die*

Staatliche geforderte Friedens- und Konfliktforschung in der bundesrepublik Deutschland von 1970 bis 1979, 18–19; Frederick Tenbruck, "Frieden durch Friedensforschung"; Helmut Schelsky, *Die Arbeit tun die Anderen: Klassenkampf und Priesterherrschaft der Intellektuellen* (Munich: Deutscher Taschenbuch Verlag, 1977), 389–98; and Schwarz, *Die gezähmten Deutschen*.

23. Koppe, "Zur Entwicklung der Deutschen Gesellschaft," 893.

24. Johan Galtung, *Strukturelle Gewalt* (Reinbek bei Hamburg: Rowohlt Verlag, 1975), 44, 49, 54–55.

25. Günter Gillesson, "Nicht pfuschen mit der Friedens-forschung," *Frankfürter Allgemeine Zeitung*, February 2, 1971; also see "Selbstbedienungladen der Wissenschaftler," *Der Spiegel*, June 1, 1972.

26. Hans-Joachim Arndt, in his report to the Bavarian government in which he recommended cutting off public funding for peace research, wrote that only nine of 130 projects dealt with the Soviet Union at all and that none of those examined Soviet "imperialism" and/or Soviet control over Eastern Europe and East Germany. See his *Die staatliche gefordete Friedens- und Konfliktforschung*, 33.

27. Dieter Senghaas, *Abschreckung und Frieden: Studien zur kritik organisierter Friedlosigkeit* (Frankfurt am Main: Europäische Verlagsanstalt, 1969; rev. ed., 1981), 28.

28. See Dieter Senghaas, ed., *Kritische Friedensforschung* (Frankfurt am Main: Suhrkamp Verlag, 1972); same, ed., *Imperialismus und strukturelle Gewalt* (Frankfurt am Main: Suhrkamp Verlag, 1973); see also his *Gewalt, Konflikt, Frieden* (Hamburg: Hoffmann und Campe, 1974). Senghaas published frequently in English on peace research, arms control, and dependency. For example, see "The Specific Contributions of Peace Research to the Analysis of the Causes of Social Violence: Transdisciplinarity," in *Bulletin of Peace Proposals* 7, no. 1 (1976): 64–68; and with the American political scientist Karl Deutsch, "The Fragile Sanity of States: A Theoretical Analysis," in Martin Kilson, ed., *New States in the Modern World* (Cambridge and New York: Cambridge University Press, 1975), 200–44.

29. Senghaas, *Abschreckung und Frieden*, 29–30.

30. Ibid., 31.

31. Ibid., 33.

32. Ibid., 37.

33. Ibid.

34. Ibid., 56.

35. Ibid., 68. See Herbert Marcuse, "The Struggle Against Liberalism in the Totalitarian View of the State," in *Negations*, trans. Jeremy Shapiro (Boston: Beacon Press, 1968), 3–42. On the issue of change and continuity in German strategy in World War I and II, see Andreas Hillgrüber's now-classic work,

Hitler's Strategie: Politik und Kriegführung, 1940–1941 (Munich: Bernard and Graefe, 1965, revised edition, 1982).

36. Ibid., 93.

37. Ibid., 95.

38. Ibid., 99–102.

39. Ibid., 102.

40. Ibid., 103 and 105.

41. Ibid., 160.

42. Ibid., 266.

43. Also see Senghaas, *Gewalt, Konflikt, Frieden.*

44. Galtung, *Strukturelle Gewalt.* By 1982, *Strukturelle Gewalt* had sold 27,000 copies. The series in which Galtung's collection appeared was called "rororo aktuell." The series was edited by Freimut Duve, a Social Democratic member of the Bundestag.

45. See "Gewalt, Frieden und Friedensforschung," "Friedensforschung: Vergangenheitserfahrungen und Zukunftsperspektiven," and "Probleme der Friedenserziehung," in Galtung, *Strukturelle Gewalt,* 7–36, 37–59, and 92–107. Also see the following, all by the same author: "Violence, peace, and peace research," *Journal of Peace Research* 6 (1969): 167–191; "Gewalt, Frieden und Friedensforschung," in Senghaas, ed., *Kritische Friedensforschung*; and "Probleme der Friedenerziehung," in Christoph Wulf, ed., *Kritische Friedenserziehung* (Frankfurt am Main: Suhrkamp Verlag, 1973). In "Probleme der Friedenserziehung," Galtung discusses curricula of peace education and how it could be linked to peace action.

46. See Johan Galtung, "Institutionalisierte Konfliktlösung: Ein theoretische Paradigma," in *Anders Verteidigen* (Reinbek bei Hamburg: Rowohlt, 1982), 153–216. The essay was first published in English in 1965 and in West Germany in 1972. See Walter L. Bühl, ed., *Konflikt und Konfliktstrategie* (Munich: Nymphenburger Verlagshandlung, 1972).

47. Galtung, "Friedensforschung: Vergangenheits-erfahrungen und Zukunftperspektiven," in *Strukturelle Gewalt,* 37–59.

48. Johan Galtung, "Gewalt, Frieden, und Friedensforschung," 9.

49. Ibid.

50. Ibid., 10.

51. Ibid., 11. For contemporary criticisms see Pierre Hassner, "On ne badine pas avec la paix," *Revue francaise de science politique* 23 (1973), 1268–1303; and Tenbruck, "Friede durch Friedenforschung?"

52. Ibid., 12.

53. Ibid., 13.

54. Ibid., 30–31.

55. Ibid., 36.

56. The statement appears in Senghaas, ed., *Kritische Friedensforschung*, 416–419.

57. Ibid., 32.

58. Galtung, "Friedensforschung: Vergangenheits-erfahrungen und Zukunftsperspektiven," 48.

59. Johan Galtung, "Das Kriegssystem," in *Anders Verteidigen*; reprint from Klaus Jürgen Gantzel, *Herrschaft und Befreiung in der Weltgesellschaft* (Frankfurt am Main: Campus Verlag, 1975).

60. Johan Galtung, "Zwei Konzepte der Verteidigung," in *Anders Verteidigung*, 139.

61. Ibid., 152.

62. A revised version of the talk appears as "Rüstungswettlauf und Kriegsgefahr," in Dieter S. Lutz, ed., *Sicherheitspolitik am Scheideweg?* (Baden-Baden: Nomos Verlag, 1982), 231–256.

63. Author's interview with Dieter Lutz, Reinbek bei Hamburg, June 22, 1984.

64. Dieter S. Lutz, *Weltkrieg wider Willen?* (Reinbek bei Hamburg: Rowohlt, 1981).

65. Ibid., 314.

66. Carl Friedrich von Weizsäcker, "Erforschung der Lebensbedingung," in *Der bedrohte Friede* (Munich: Deutscher Taschenbuch, 1983), 452.

67. Weizsäcker, "Gedanken zum Arbeitsplan," in *Der bedrohte Friede*, 197.

68. Ibid., 201–02.

69. Ibid., 181.

70. Weizsäcker, "Erforschung der Lebensbedingung," 449–85.

71. Ibid., 451.

72. Weizsäcker, "Erforschung der Lebensbedingung," 459.

73. Weizsäcker, "Kriegsfolgen und Kriegsverhütung," in *Der bedrohte Friede*, 221.

74. Ibid., 224.

75. Ibid., 229.

76. Carl Friedrich von Weizsäcker, *Wege in der Gefahr* (Munich: Hanser Verlag, 1976; reprint, Munich: DTV, 1981).

77. Weizsäcker, "Fünf Thesen zum Dritten Weltkrieg," in *Wege in der Gefahr*, 109–139.

78. Ibid., 118.

79. Ibid., 124.

80. Ibid., 136–37.

81. Ibid., 138.

82. Horst Ahfeldt, *Verteidigung und Frieden* (Munich: Hanser Verlag, 1977).

83. Ibid., 235.

84. Weizsäcker, "Moskaus Rüstung: defensive und bedrohlich," in *Der bedrohte Friede*, 491–97.

85. Weizsäcker, "Europäische Rüstungsgefahr der Achtzigerjahre," in *Der bedrohte Friede*, 498–499. Originally in *Die Zeit*, November 16, 1979.

86. Weizsäcker, "Hintergrund zur europäischen Rüstungsgefahr," in *Der bedrohte Friede*, 513–517.

87. Ibid., 514–515.

88. Dutschke, *Mein langer Marsch*, 190–192.

89. Ibid., 191.

90. Also see Heinz Brüggemann, et al., *Über den Mangel an politischen Kultur in Deutschland* (West Berlin: Wagenbach Verlag, 1978), 93–116. Thomas Schmid, a Frankfurt leftist, attacked the West German self-denigration that stood "in the tradition of imperialist de-Nazification by the God-damned Yankees, who decreed democracy here in Germany. Of course, I will not forget the German horror—but I also will no longer forget or pass over my German being (*Deutschsein*). . . . I want a left that is not only 'cosmopolitan' but also 'German.' The lack of political culture in Germany will not be overcome by seeking models from other countries but by developing a specifically German political culture," ibid., 112–113.

Chapter 7
CONSERVATISM, *TENDENZWENDE*, AND MILITANT DEMOCRACY

1. Figures taken from David Conradt, *The German Polity*, 3d ed. (New York and London: Longman, 1986), 128. In the 1972 election, the CDU received 45% and the SPD, 46%. In 1976, the figures were CDU/CSU 49% and the SPD, 42%. In 1980, with Strauss running, the CDU/CSU dropped to 44%, a point more than the SPD's 43%.

2. Brandt's election was aided by a decade-long effort by intellectuals to argue for a government of a left. See the contributions by Martin Walser, Carl Amery, Hans Magnus Enzensberger, Günter Grass, Hans Werner Richter, Siegfried Lenz, and Fritz Raddatz in Martin Walser, eds., *Die Alternative oder Brauchen Wir Eine Neue Regierung* (Reinbek bei Hamburg: Rowohlt Verlag, 1961); and Günter Gaus, "Die Intellektuellen," *Süddeutsche Zeitung*, no. 107, May 3/4, 1963.

3. On the Brandt circle see Arnulf Baring, *Machtwechsel: Die Ära Brandt-Scheel* (Munich: Deutsche Taschenbuch Verlag, 1984).

4. For Grass's political essays, see the following, all by Günter Grass: *Über das Selbsverständliche: Politische Schriften* (Munich: Deutscher Taschenbuch Verlag, 1969), especially "Loblied auf Willy," 21–31; *Der Bürger und seine Stimme: Reden, Aufsätze, Kommentare* (Berlin and Neuwied: Luchterhand, 1974); *Denkzettel: Politische Reden und Aufsätze* (Berlin and Neuwied: Luchterhand,

1978); and *Widerstand Lernen: Politische Gegenreden, 1980–1983* (Berlin and Neuwied, Luchterhand, 1984). For a bibliography, see Franz Josef Görtz, ed., *Günter Grass: Auskunft für Leser* (Berlin and Neuwied: Luchterhand, 1984).

5. Willy Brandt, "Braucht die Politik den Schriftsteller?" in Dieter Lattmann, ed., *Einigkeit oder Einzelgänger: Dokumentation des Ersten Schriftstellerkongresses des Verbands Deutscher Schriftsteller (VS)*, (Munich: Kindler Verlag, 1971), 9–18. Also see Heinrich Böll, "Das Ende der Bescheidenheit," in Bernd Balzer, ed., *Henrich Böll Werke: Essayistische Schriften und Reden 2, 1964–1972* (Cologne: Kiepenheuer and Witsch, 1979–80), p. 385. For Böll's political essays, speeches, and interviews see the following by Heinrich Böll: *Vermintes Gelände: Essayistische Schriften, 1977–1981* (Cologne: Kiepenheuer and Witsch, 1982); *Ein- und Zusprüche: Schriften, Reden und Prosa, 1981–1983* (Cologne: Kiepenheuer and Witsch, 1984); *Die Fähigkeit zu trauern: Schriften und Reden, 1983–1985* (Cologne: Kiepenheuer and Witsch, 1986).

6. For example, see the following by Wolfgang Bergsdorf: "Intellektuelle und Politik," *Aus Politik und Zeitgeschichte*, 24 (June 15, 1974); "Ohnmacht und Anmassung," *Die Politische Meinung* 23, no. 178 (May–June 1978): 53–66; and *Politik und Sprache* (Munich, 1978); also see Wolfgang Bergsdorf, ed., *Die Intellektuellen: Geist und Macht* (Pfullingen: Verlag Günter Neske, 1982).

7. "Rede von Dr. Helmut Kohl nach der Wahl zum Bundesvorsitzenden der CDU am 12. Juni 1973 in Bonn," in Helmut Kohl, *Zwischen Ideologie und Pragmatismus* (Bonn: Bonn Aktuell, 1973), 105–114.

8. Ibid., 110–111.

9. Ibid., 111.

10. Kohl, *Zwischen Ideologie und Pragmatismus.*

11. Ibid., 11–12.

12. Ibid., 30–31.

13. Ibid., 32.

14. Ibid., 33–34.

15. Ibid., p. 34.

16. Ibid., p. 35.

17. Ibid., p. 36.

18. Ibid.

19. Bergsdorf, "Ohnmacht und Anmassung," 65.

20. Thomas Nipperdey, "Wem dienen unsere Universitäten," in Thomas Nipperdey, ed., *Hochschulen zwischen Politik und Wahrheit* (Zurich: Edition Interfrom, 1981), 12. The founders included: Richard Lowenthal (Berlin), Herman Lübbe (Munich), Hans Maier (Munich), Thomas Nipperdey (Munich), Elisabeth Nölle-Neumann (Mainz and Allensbach), Ernst Nolte (Berlin), Walter Rüegg (Frankfurt/Main), Erwin Scheuch (Cologne), Helmut Schelsky (Bielefeld), Frederick Tenbruck (Tübingen), and Ernst Topitsch (Graz). Beginning in

1970 the *Bund* published *Hochschulpoltische Information* and, later, *Freibeit der Wissenschaft.*

21. Also see the collection of reports on the West German academic scene by Kurt Reumann, published in the *Frankfurter Allgemeine Zeitung* from 1971 to 1974: *Blick ins Innere: Berichte von der akademischen Front* (Zurich: Edition Interfrom, 1975).

22. *Freibeit der Wissenschaft*, no. 4 (1974), 7.

23. These episodes were reported in the "Krawall-Kalender Wintersemestter 1973/74–2. Hälfte," *Freibeit der Wissenschaft*, no. 3 (1974), 5–7; "Krawallkalender für das Sommersemester 1974," *Freibeit der Wissenschaft* nos. 8/9 (1974), 5.

24. These examples are taken from *Freibeit der Wissenschaft* and *Hochschulpolitische Information*, published by the *Bund Freibeit der Wissenschaft.*

25. For example, "SPD und Kommunisten: Bundnisse an deutschen Hochschulen," *Freibeit der Wissenschaft*, no. 2 (1976), 10.

26. Elisabeth Nölle-Neumann, "Universität und Öffentlichkeit," *Freibeit der Wissenschaft*, nos. 11 and 12 (1980), 142–148.

27. See the epilogue to Helmut Schelsky, *Die Arbeit tun die Anderen: Klassenkampf und Priesterberrschaft der Intellektuellen* (Munich: Deutscher Taschenbuch Verlag, 1977), 512–514. Schelsky noted that among those who said he exaggerated the degree of radical leftist threat to academic freedom were many who had left the universities in the 1970s including Ralf Dahrendorf, Jürgen Habermas, and Carl F. von Weizsäcker. "Those who leave teaching in the universities cannot so easily mock the 'embitterment' of the others who stayed," ibid., 514.

28. See Hartmut Hentschel, "Trügerische Ruhe an den Universitäten," *Freibeit der Wissenschaft*, no. 4 (1975), 1–4.

29. Thomas Nipperdey, "Die bildungspolitische Lage und der Bund Freiheit der Wissenschaft," *Freibeit der Wissenschaft*, no. 11 (1974), 3.

30. Ibid. On the University of Bremen, see Guenther Lewy, "Emancipatory Consciousness in the Federal Republic of Germany," in *False Consciousness* (New Brunswick: Transaction Books, 1982).

31. Thomas Nipperdey, "Ponto und die Hochschulereform," *Freibeit der Wissenschaft*, no. 9 (1977), 5.

32. Ibid.

33. Thomas Nipperdey, "Schule und Hochschule: Politische Lagebericht des Bundes Freiheit der Wissenschaft," *Freibeit der Wissenschaft*, no. 12 (1978), 3–11.

34. Ibid., 7–8.

35. Thomas Nipperdey, "Wem dienen unsere Universitäten," 9.

36. Erwing Scheuch, "Die Allianz zwischen Systemveränderern und Bürokraten," *Freibeit der Wissenschaft*, nos. 1 and 2 (1981), 2–10.

37. Rudolf Wildenmann, *Studenten 79: Studentische Beteiligung an den universitären Wahlen* (Bonn: Forum des Hochschulverbandes, 1980), 37. Also see "Praxis und Techniken der 'Vollversaammlungsdemokratie,'" in *HPI—Hochschulpolitische Information* 2, no. 8 (May 6, 1971), 1–6. The HPI was a precursor to *Freiheit der Wissenschaft.*

38. On this point see Richard Lowenthal, "Der Kampf um die Hochschule und die Zukunft unserer Demokratie," *HPI—Hochschulpolitische Information*, nos. 23 and 24 (1971), 21–25.

39. Thomas Nipperdey, "Schule and Hochschule," *Freiheit der Wissenschaft*, 11.

40. Wilhelm Hennis, *Die missverstandene Demokratie* (Freiburg im Breisgau: Verlag Herder, 1973). For his analysis and criticism of the erosion of the *Abgrenzung* between "democratic socialism" and the Communists in the 1970s, see his *Organisierter Sozialismus* (Stuttgart: Ernst Klett Verlag, 1977).

41. Hennis, *Die missverstandene Demokratie.*

42. See Hermann Lübbe, "Aufklärung und Gegenaufklärung," in Michael Zöller, ed., *Aufklärung Heute: Bedingungen unserer Freiheit* (Zurich: Edition Interfrom, 1980), 11–27; Herman Lübbe, *Zwischen Trend und Tradition* (Zurich: Edition Interfrom, 1981).

43. Hermann Lübbe, "Zur Philosophie des Liberalismus und seines Gegenteils," in Hermann Lübbe, *Fortschrittsreaktionen: Über konservative und destruktive Modernität* (Graz, Vienna, and Cologne: Styria Verlag, 1987), 41–55.

44. Ibid., 615.

45. Ibid., 616.

46. Ibid., 617.

47. Erwin K. Scheuch, *Kulturintelligenz als Machtfaktor* (Zurich: Edition Interfrom, 1974). Other themes in this series include ecology, Marxism, the counterculture, foreign policy, education, the media, and the intellectuals.

48. Ibid., 8.

49. Helmut Schelsky, "Mehr Demokratie oder Mehr Freiheit? Der Grundsatzkonflikt der 'Polarisierung' in der Bundesrepublik Deutschland," in *Systemüberwindung, Demokratisierung und Gewaltenteilung: Grundsatzkonflikte der Bundesrepublik* (Munich: C.H. Beck, 1973), 47–82. It was first printed in *Frankfürter Allgemeine Zeitung* of January 20, 1973. For a critique of the *Tendenzwende* as an authoritarian threat to liberal democracy see Habermas, "Einleitung," in Jürgen Habermas, ed., *Stichworte zur "Geistigen Situation der Zeit,"* vol. 1, *Nation und Republik* (Frankfurt/Main: Suhrkamp Verlag, 1979), pp. 7–35; translated by Andrew Buchwalter as *The Spiritual Situation of the Age* (Cambridge: MIT Press, 1984).

50. Ibid., 47–48.

51. Ibid., 57.

52. Ibid., 70.

53. Ibid., 72.

54. Ibid., 76–77.

55. Ibid., 78.

56. Ibid., 80–81.

57. On this, see Jerry Z. Muller's important study, *The Other God That Failed: Hans Freyer and the Deradicalization of German Conservatism* (Princeton: Princeton University Press, 1988).

58. Hans-Peter Schwarz, "Finnlandisierung? Ein Reizwort: Wirklichkeit und Aktualität," *Politische Meinung* 23 (November–December 1978): 14–23.

59. Alois Mertes, *Verhandlungen des deutschen Bundestages*, 39 Sitzung (September 8, 1977), 3046.

60. Ibid.

61. Alois Mertes, *Verhandlungen des deutschen Bundestages* (March 9, 1979), 11261.

62. Alois Mertes, *Verhandlungen des deutschen Bundestages* (September 21, 1978), 8268.

63. Ibid., 8271.

64. Alois Mertes, *Verhandlungen des deutschen Bundestages* (June 21, 1978), 7820.

65. Leszek Kolakowski, Speech in Cologne, March 17, 1977, cited by Mertes, *Verhandlungen des deutschen Bundestages*, ibid., 7821.

66. Ibid.

67. Ibid., 7822.

68. Ibid., 7823.

69. Ibid.

70. For example, see Dr. Egon Klepsch, "Sicherheit ja—Neutralisierung nein," *Protokoll 27 Bundespareitag 25–27 Marz 1979. Kiel* (Christlich Demokratische Union Deutschlands: Bonn, 1979), 230.

71. "Beschluss: Sicherheit ja—neutralisierung nein," *Protokoll 27 Bundesparteitag 25.–27. Marz 1979. Kiel*, 263–266.

72. Ibid., 264.

73. Ibid.

74. "Für den Frieden und Freiheit in dere Bundesrepublik Deutschland und in der Welt: Wahlprogram dere CDU/CSU für die Bundestagswahl 1980," *Protolkoll 28. Bundesparteitag 19–20 Mai 1980. Berlin* (Bonn: Christlich Demokratische Union, 1980), 199–228.

75. Ibid., 206–207.

76. Helmut Kohl, "Bericht des Parteivorsitzenden," *Protokoll 28 Bundesparteitag 19–20 Mai 1980. Berlin* 28–29.

77. Ibid., 29–30.

78. Ibid., 32.

79. "Rede des Kanzlerkandidaten der CDU/CSU," *Protokoll 28 Bundesparteitag 19–20 Mai 1980. Berlin* 159–187.

80. Ibid., 180–181.

Chapter 8
THE WAR OF WORDS BEGINS

1. On the Greens see Gerd Langguth, *The Green Factor in German Politics: From Protest Movement to Political Party* (Boulder, Co.: Westview Press, 1986), 1–21.

2. "Aussen und Deutschland politik, Antrag 1," *Parteitag der Sozialdemokratischen Partei Deutschlands von 3. bis. 7. Dezember 1979: Band II*, SPD Parteitag Protokoll, 1243.

3. See Alfred Mechtersheimer, ed., *Nachrüsten? Dokumente und Positionen zum Nato-Doppelbeschluss* (Reinbek bei Hamburg: Rowohlt Verlag, 1981), 267–271.

4. INF stands for "intermediate nuclear forces." INF replaced the initial acronym of "LRTNF" or "long-range theatre nuclear forces." In the semantics of strategy, some West Europeans thought "LRTNF" evoked images of a separate European "theatre" in contrast to the desired coupling effect of the decision.

5. "12 December 1979: Special Meeting of Foreign and Defence Ministers, Brussels," *NATO Final Communiques 1975–1980*, (Brussels: NATO Information Service, 1980), 123.

6. *Deutscher Bundestag—8 Wahlperiode—194 Sitzung* (December 14, 1979), pp. 15465–15477.

7. Hans-Dietrich Genscher, *Deutscher Bundestag—8 Wahlperiode—194 Sitzung* (December 14, 1979), p. 15465.

8. Manfred Wörner, *Deutscher Bundestag—8 Wahlperiode—194 Sitzung* (December 14, 1979), p. 15469.

9. Ibid.

10. Ibid., 15471.

11. Alfons Pawelczyk, *Deutscher Bundestag—8 Wahlperiode—194 Sitzung* (December 14, 1979), p. 15472.

12. Jürgen Möllemann, *Deutscher Bundestag—8 Wahlperiode—194 Sitzung* (December 14, 1979), p. 15474.

13. Helmut Kohl, *Deutscher Bundestag—8 Wahlperiode—196 Sitzung* (January 17, 1980), p. 15590.

14. Franz Josef Strauss, *Deutscher Bundestag—8 Wahlperiode—196 Sitzung* (January 17, 1980), pp. 15602–07.

15. Ibid., 15613.

16. *Der Spiegel* had criticized American foreign policy for many years. For a quantitative content analysis of its reporting on international politics from 1960 to 1980 see Hans Mathias Kepplinger of the University of Mainz, *Die Berichterstattung des Spiegel über die Politik der USA und der UdSSR sowie über die Situation von NATO und Warschauer Pakt im Zusammenhang mit Fragen der Auf- und Abrüstung: 1960–1981* [The Reporting of *Spiegel* on the United States and the Soviet Union Regarding NATO and the Warsaw Pact in Connection with Armament and Disarmament Questions] (Mainz: Universität Mainz, 1983), unpublished manuscript.

17. Rudolf Augstein, "Krieg in Sicht?" *Der Spiegel* no. 5, January 28, 1980, 18.

18. Ibid.

19. Ibid.

20. Ibid.

21. Wolf Perdelwitz, *Wollen die Russen Krieg?* [Do the Russians Want War?] (Hamburg: Stern Bucher, 1980). Also see Wolf Perdelwitz and Heiner Bremer, *Geisel Europa* [Hostage Europe] (Hamburg: Stern Bucher, 1981).

22. Ibid., 178.

23. Ibid., 265.

24. Ibid., 266–67.

25. Ibid., 274, 275–76.

26. For Bastian's criticism see Gert Bastian, *Frieden Schaffen! Gedanken zur Sicherheitspolitik* (Munich: Kindler Verlag, 1983). Bastian joined the Green Party and served in its parliamentary faction.

27. "Aufruf der Berliner Initiative für Frieden, International Ausgleich und Sicherheit," reprinted in Anton-Andreas Guha, *Die Nachrüstung: Die Holocaust Europas* (Freiberg: Dreisam Verlag, 1981), 122–23.

28. Ibid., 123–24.

29. Thomas Brasch, Günter Grass, Sarah Kirsch, Peter Schneider, "Vier deutsche Schriftsteller, die in Berlin leben, rufen zum Frieden auf," in *Günter Grass: Widerstand lernen. Politische Gegenreden, 1980–1983,* (Darmstadt and Neuwied: Luchterhand, 1984), 13–14.

30. Ibid., 14.

31. Mechtersheimer, *Nachrüsten?* 269.

32. For Schmidt's account, see Helmut Schmidt, *Menschen und Mächte* (West Berlin: Siedler Verlag, 1987), 99–125.

33. "Krefelder Appell," in Mechtersheimer, *Nachrüsten?* 249–50.

34. *Der Krefelder Appell,* in Guha, *Die Nachüstung,* 134.

35. Ibid., 134–35.

36. "Bielefelder Erklärung," in Guha, *Die Nachrüstung,* 124–25.

37. Ibid., 125–26. The *Deutscher Gewerkschaftsbund,* the umbrella organization of West German trade unions, also issued a "call for peace," though it was more moderate in tone, urging the United States and the USSR to begin

negotiations whose goal would be the rejection of new deployments of medium-range weapons. See "Aufruf des Deutschen Gewerkschaftsbundes," in Guha, *Die Nachrüstung*, 126–29.

38. Peter Bender, *Das Ende des Ideologischen Zeitalters* (Berlin: Severin and Siedler, 1981).

39. See Daniel Bell, *The End of Ideology* (Cambridge: Harvard University Press, 1988).

40. Bender, *Das Ende*, 116.

41. Ibid., 117.

42. Ibid., 171–172.

43. Ibid., 180.

44. Ibid., 185.

45. Ibid., 260–261.

46. Wilhelm Bittorf, "Euroshima, mon futur," *Der Spiegel*, no. 7, (February 9, 1981), pp. 110–111.

47. Ibid., 111.

48. "Die Bundesrepublik will kein 'Ja aber' Verbündeter sein: Genscher aussert sich zur Sicherheits- und Bundnispolitik," *FAZ*, March 4, 1981, p. 4.

49. "Schmidt: "Verwirklichung des Doppelbeschlusses ist Voraussetzung für Verhandlungsergebnisse," *FAZ*, April 2, 1981, p. 1.

50. "Der Doppelbeschluss der NATO strebt nicht nach Uberlegenheit," *FAZ*, March 28, 1981, p. 1.

51. "Bahr fordert Einbeziehung aller Atomwaffen," *Frankfurter Allgemeine Zeitung*, April 22, 1981.

52. Erhard Eppler, *Wege aus der Gefahr* (Reinbek bei Hamburg: Rowohlt Verlag, 1981). By June, 1981, 40,000 copies were sold. Also see the following by Erhard Eppler: *Spannungsfelder: Beiträge zur Politik unserer Zeit* (Stuttgart: Seewald Verlag, 1968); *Ende oder Wende: Von der Machbarkeit des Notwendigen*, 2d ed. (Berlin: Kohlhammer, 1975); and *Weichen stellen . . . Rede, 1973–1980* (Tübingen: Widerspruch Verlag, 1981).

53. Eppler, *Wege aus der Gefahr*, 80.

54. Eppler's arguments were popularizations of the "critique of instrumental reason" of the Frankfurt School's critical theorists. The classic text for the 1970s was Jürgen Habermas, "Science and Technology as Ideology," in his *Toward a Rational Society*, trans. Jeremy Shapiro (Boston: Beacon Press, 1970). Also see Herbert Marcuse, *One-Dimensional Man* (Boston: Beacon Press, 1964); and Max Horkheimer and Theodor Adorno, *Dialectic of Englightenment*, trans. John Cumming (New York: Herder and Herder, 1974).

55. *Denkschrift*, Deutsche Gesellschaft für Friedens- und Konfliktforschung, DGFK-PP, Nr. 26, p. 3, cited by Eppler, *Wege aus der Gefahr*, 85.

56. Ibid., 90–95.

57. Ibid., 207–208.

58. Ibid., 216.

59. "Der Kanzler kämpft für die Nachrüstung, Warnungen an die Partei vor Selbstzerstörung," *FAZ*, May 18, 1981, p. 1–2.

60. Helmut Schmidt, "Damit stehe und falle ich," *Vorwärts*, no. 22, May 21, 1981, p. 5.

61. "Schläge für die SPD aus dem Südwesten, Der Nachrüstungsbeschluss in Frage gestellt," *FAZ*, May 4, 1981, p. 1.

62. "Genscher warnt seine Partei vor 'politischen Bocksprüngen,'" *FAZ*, May 30, 1981, p. 1–2.

63. "Der Bundeskanzler zu umstrittenen Themen in der SPD: Einseitige Abrüstung kann für uns nicht in Betracht kommen," *FAZ*, February 2, 1981, p. 2.

64. "Entschliesungsantrag der Fraktionen der SPD und FDP zu der Erklärung der Bundesregierung vom 26. Mai 1981," *Deutscher Bundestag, 9 Wahlperiode, Drucksache 9/505*. The key passage read as follows: "The German Bundestag supports the West German Government in the consistent and timely implementation of NATO's decision of December 12, 1979 in both of its parts. It underscores in this connection the statement of the double-decision that the West will examine NATO's need for medium range missile in light of the concrete results of the negotiations."

65. "Der Bundestag einmütig für die Nachrüstung, Nur die SPD-Linke widersetzt sich," *FAZ*, May 27, 1981, p. 1.

66. Willy Brandt, *Deutscher Bundestag—9 Wahlperiode—38 Sitzung*, May 26, 1981, pp. 1981–1982.

67. Helmut Kohl, *Deutscher Bundestag—9 Wahlperiode—38 Sitzung*, May 26, 1981, pp. 1973–1974. Kohl welcomed the leadership of the new Reagan administration, whose firmness in foreign policy was, he thought, a welcome contrast to West Germany where there was a "dangerous obliviousness and the willingness of left-wing public opinion to put wishful thinking in place of reality," ibid., p. 1976.

68. Jürgen Möllemann, *Deutscher Bundestag—9 Wahlperiode—38 Sitzung*, May 26, 1981, pp. 1985–1986.

69. *Erklärung der Gustav-Heinemann-Initiative vom 13. Juni 1981*, in Guha, *Die Nachrüstung*, 129–30.

70. Ibid.

71. Rudolf Augstein, "'Raketen zu Lande ausgesprochen bedenklich': Rudolf Augstein über Bonn und die sogenannte Nachrüstung" [Missiles on land are decidedly risky: Rudolf Augstein on Bonn and the so-called *Nachrüstung*], *Der Spiegel*, no. 21, May 25, 1981, pp. 30–32.

72. Ibid., 30.

73. Ibid.

74. Ibid.

75. Ibid., 31.

76. Ibid., 31–32.

77. Alois Mertes, "Moskaus Kampagne der Desinformation und Einschüchter-ung," *Deutschland-Union-Dienst,* June 24, 1981, p. 1.

78. Wilhelm Bittorf, "Schiessplatz der Supermächte," *Der Spiegel,* nos. 28–30, 1981.

79. Wilhelm Bittorf, "Schiessplatz der Supermächte," Part 1, *Der Spiegel,* no. 28, July 13, 1981, p. 138.

80. Ibid., 112. The text reads in German as follows: "durch eine krude Manipu-lation also, die der bundesdeutschen Öffentlichenkeit gleichwohl so verbor-gen geblieben ist wie nur irgendein Statistikschwindel der Sowjet-Presse dem Sowjet-Volk."

81. Ibid., 116.

82. Ibid.

83. Wilhelm Bittorf, "Schiessplatz der Supermächte," Part 2, *Der Spiegel,* no. 29, July 13, 1981, p. 121.

84. Ibid., 125.

85. "Appell der Schriftsteller Europas," in Guha, *Die Nachrüstung,* 135.

86. Helmut Schmidt, "Political Action Aimed at Fostering Understanding: Speech to the Congress on 'Kant in Our Time,'" in Wolfram Hanrieder, ed., *Helmut Schmidt: Perspectives on Politics* (Boulder, Co.: Westview Press, 1982), 181–82.

87. Hans Apel et al., *Sicherheitspolitik contra Frieden? Ein Forum zur Friedensbeweg-ung* (Berlin/Bonn: Verlag Dietz, 1981).

88. Egon Bahr, "Zehn Thesen über Frieden und Abrüstung," in *Sicherheitspolitik contra Frieden?* 10–11.

89. Ibid., 12.

90. Ibid.

91. Ibid., 13.

92. Ibid., 14.

93. For a good summary of the negotiating record, see Special Consultative Group, *Progress Report on Intermediate-Range Nuclear Forces (INF)* (Brussels: NATO Information Service, 1983). On the initial American and Soviet pro-posals, see pp. 11–14.

94. Guha, *Die Nachrüstung.*

95. Anton-Andreas Guha, "Thesen zur Kritik der Sicherheitspolitik und des Brüsseler Beschlusses," in Apel et al., *Sicherheitspolitik contra Frieden,* 19. Guha stressed the impossibility of a nonsuicidal defense of West Germany in an interview with the author in Frankfurt/Main, June 17, 1984.

96. For his vivid description of the consequences of a nuclear war in Europe,

see Anton-Andreas Guha, *Ende: Tagebuch aus dem 3. Weltkrieg* (Königstein, Ts.: Athenäum Verlag, 1983).

97. Guha, "Thesen zur Kritik der Sicherheitspolitik und des Brüsseler Beschlusses," 19.

98. Ibid., 20.

99. Ibid., 27.

100. Ibid.

101. Karl Kaiser, *Sicherheitspolitik contra Frieden*, 39–41.

102. Apel, *Sicherheitspolitik contra Frieden*, 59.

103. Apel, *Sicherheitspolitik contra Frieden*, 55–61, 61–63. Apel found it ironic that he was a defender of the NATO decision, given his participation in the antinuclear movements of the late 1950s. Author's interview with Hans Apel, Bonn, June 28, 1984.

104. Author's interviews with: Hans Apel, Bonn (June 28, 1984); Kurt Becker, Grashütten bei Hamburg (June 21, 1984); Peter Cortierer, Cambridge, Mass. (April 24, 1984); Klaus Dieter Leister, Dusseldorf (June 20, 1984); Wilfried Penner, Bonn (June 27, 1984); Jürgen Ruhrfus, Bonn (July 3, 1984); Bernd von Staden, Bonn (July 2, 1984); Walter Stützle, Bonn (June 28, 1984). Stützle, the director of the planning staff in the defense ministry, and Ruhrfus, a career diplomat and close adviser to Schmidt on defense matters, both worked on Schmidt's London 1977 speech. Stützle was critical of the American conduct of the Geneva negotiations.

105. "Geissler wirft der SPD Verwischung der Bundnisunterschiede vor," *FAZ*, August 29, 1981, pp. 1–2.

106. "Neue Rüge Schmidts für den 'Krefelder Appell'," *FAZ*, August 31, 1981, p. 1.

107. Alois Mertes, *ZDF Hearing*, August 26, 1980, p. 5 (Bundes-Presse-Archiv).

108. Alois Mertes, *Deutschland Union Dienst*, August 28, 1980, p. 3. For his comments on a trip to Moscow by Willy Brandt in summer 1981 see Alois Mertes, "Ein Versuch, Brandt's Moscow-Reise mit sowjetischen Augen zu sehen," *Die Welt*, July 15, 1981.

109. "Haig: Die Demokratie kann nicht überleben ohne die Bereitschaft zu ihrer Verteidigung," *FAZ*, September 14, 1981, p. 1.

110. "Haig: Die Nachrüstung hängt ab von Erbegnissen der Verhandlungen mit Moskau," *FAZ*, September 15, 1981, pp. 1–2.

111. Karsten Voigt, *Wege zur Abrüstung* (Frankfurt/Main: Eichborn Verlag, 1981).

112. Ibid., 46.

113. Ibid., 47 and 140.

114. Ibid., 52–55, 19–133.

115. Ibid., 142. Author's interview with Karsten Voigt, Frankfurt/Main, June

15, 1984. For Voigt's discussion of the historical traditions of "Social Democratic peace policy," see his *Wege zur Abrüstung,* 115–129.

116. For the *JUSOS* rejection of the rationale of the dual-track decision, see "Wie aus 'Argumenten' 'klägliche Legitimationsversuche' werden," *Frankfurter Rundschau,* September 25 and 26, 1981.

117. "Zeitungsanzeige gegen den Nato-Beschluss: Der SPD- Vorsitzende des Saarlandes begründet seine Ablehnung," *FAZ,* October 1, 1981, p. 2. Also see Oskar Lafontaine, "Angst ist die Grundlage unseres Sicherheitssystems," *Frankfurter Rundschau,* October 2, 1981, p. 10.

118. Rudolf Augstein, "Lieber rot als tot"? *Der Spiegel,* no. 8, February 22, 1982, p. 18.

119. Ibid., 18. The weakness of the Soviet Union, its fears of encirclement, and its economic backwardness in the face of the dynamic West was also a theme pursued by *Der Spiegel'*s defense correspondent, Wilhelm Bittorf. See "Mitleid mit dem Kreml?" *Der Spiegel,* no. 6, February 4, 1980, pp. 120–21.

120. Ibid., 18.

121. "Schmidt: Die Jugend soll auch die Sorgen unserer Generation ernst nehmen," *FAZ,* October 10, 1981, pp. 1–2; *Verhandlungen des Deutschen Bundestag—9 Wahlperiode—57 Sitzung* (October 9, 1981), p. 3325.

122. Ibid., 3326.

123. Ibid., 3328.

124. Willy Brandt, *Verhandlungen der Deutscher Bundestag,* October 9, 1981, p. 3320.

125. Helmut Kohl, *Verhandlungen der Deutscher Bundestag—9 Wahlperiode—57 Sitzung* (October 9, 1981), p. 3330.

126. "Die Situation Bonns vor der 'Friedenkundgebung' immer heikler," *FAZ,* October 2, 1981, p. 1; and "Weitere SPD-Abgeordnete unsterstützen 'Friedensdemonstration,'" *FAZ,* October 3, 1981, p. 4.

127. "Biedenkopf gegen Kohls 'Volksfront'—These," *FAZ,* October 17, 1981, p. 3.

128. "Bonn befasst sich mit Reagans Äusserungen zum begrenzten Atomkrieg," *FAZ,* October 20, 1981, pp. 1–2. Also see Adalbert Weinstein, "Der Mythos der begrenzten Krieg," *FAZ,* October 22, 1981, p. 1.

129. Rudolf Augstein, "Reagan, Weinberger, Haig," *Der Spiegel,* no. 44, October 26, 1981, p. 22.

130. Ibid.

131. Ibid.

132. Rudolf Augstein, "Der zuckersüsse Breschnew," *Der Spiegel,* no. 46, November 9, 1981, p. 27.

133. Günter Gaus, "Die Berliner Rede," in *Deutschland und die Nato,* (Reinbek bei Hamburg: Rowohlt Verlag, 1984), pp. 75–121.

134. Author's interview with Günter Gaus, Reinbek bei Hamburg (June 22, 1984).

135. Ibid., 77.

136. Ibid., 87.

137. Ibid., 103–104. For an excellent discussion of nationalism, the peace movement, and its response to the developments in Poland, see Sigrid Meuschel, "Neo-nationalism and the Peace Movement," *Telos* 56 (Summer 1983): 119–130.

138. Ibid., 107.

139. Ibid., 107–108.

140. Ibid., 111.

141. Ibid., 110.

142. Ibid., 121.

143. Another manifestation of Social Democratic opposition to the missiles came three days later when the Social Democratic Party in the Saarland, led by Oskar Lafontaine, voted 299 to 64 to reject the deployments of American missiles. "Die SPD im Saarland lehnt die Nachrüstung moch vor Beginn von Verhandlungen ab," *FAZ*, November 11, 1981, p. 2.

144. Jürgen Habermas, *Stichworte zur 'Geistigen Situation der Zeit,'* vol. 1, *Nation and Republik* (Frankfurt/Main: Suhrkamp Verlag, 1979). See in particular the essays by Martin Walser, Dieter Wellershoff, and Iring Fetscher.

145. Wolfgang Pohrt, *Endstation: Über die Wiedergeburt der Nation* (Berlin: Rotbuch Verlag, 1982); also see his *Stammesbewusstsein, Kulturnation* (West Berlin: Edition Tiamat, 1984); and *Kreisverkehr, Wendepunkt* (West Berlin: Edition Tiamat, 1984).

146. Pohrt, *Endstation,* 94.

147. Pohrt, "Endstation: Über die Widergeburt der Nation" [Last Stop: On the Rebirth of the Nation], in *Endstation,* 95–128.

148. Ibid., 116.

149. Ibid., 117.

150. "Schmidt und Frau Thatcher begrüssen die Initiative Reagans," *FAZ*, November 19, 1981, p. 1.

151. "Der Kreml nennt Reagans Vorschläge zur Abrüstung, 'reine Propaganda,'" *FAZ*, November 20, 1981, p. 1.

152. Robert Held, "Dilemma in Genf," *Frankfurter Allgemeine Zeitung*, November 19, 1981, p. 1. Held, an editor of the *FAZ*, argued that any zero option should stop short of inclusion of British and French missiles in the INF calculations. He defended French "nuclear Gaullism" as a response to the nuclear primacy of the two great powers. There was "no prospect" of arriving at a zero option at the cost of nuclear powers of the "second class"— Britain and France. German ideas along those lines were "at best provincial wishful thinking."

153. Fritz Ullrich Fack, "'Annähernade Parität—ein Märchen," *FAZ*, November 23, 1981, p. 1.

154. "Brezhnev droht in Bonn mit 'ernsten Gegenmassnahmen," *FAZ*, November 24, 1983, pp. 1–2. For comments by Brezhnev and Schmidt, see "Breschnew: Wir könnten Hunderte von Waffen zurückziehen—ich widerhole, Hunderte," *FAZ*, November 25, 1981, p. 2; and Helmut Schmidt, "Schmidt: Das Deutsche Volk will den Frieden, aber Moskaus Verhalten machte uns Sorgen," *FAZ*, November 25, 1981, p. 2.

155. "Brandt und Wehner: Verzögerung der Nachrüstung möglich," *FAZ*, December 1, 1981, pp. 1–2.

156. Ibid., 2.

157. Bundeskanzler Schmidt, *Deutscher Bundestag—9 Wahlperiode—70 Sitzung* (December 3, 1981), p. 4053; also see "Der Bundeskanzler sieht 'Anlass zur Hoffnung', Kohl lobt feste Haltung Schmidts und Genschers," *FAZ*, December 4, 1981, pp. 1–2.

158. Helmut Kohl, *Deutscher Bundestag—9 Wahlperiode—70 Sitzung* (December 3, 1981), p. 4059.

159. Ibid., 4064.

160. Ibid.

Chapter 9
SCHMIDT'S FALL, KOHL'S RISE

1. For a transcript of the two meetings see: Ingrid Krüger, ed., *Berliner Begegnung zur Friedensförderung: Protokolle des Schriftstellertreffens am 13./14. Dezember 1981* (Neuwied und Darmstadt: Luchterhand, 1982); and Ingrid Krüger, ed., *Zweite Berliner Begegnung: Den Frieden erklären, Protokolle des zweiten Berliner Schriftstellertreffens am 22./23. April 1983* (Neuwied und Darmstadt: Luchterhand, 1983).

2. On press reports in West Germany on the 1981 conference, see the following: "Literaten in Ost-Berlin: Der Frieden aus unterschiedlicher Sicht: Polen warf seine Schatten auch über den Schriftsteller-Kongress," *Die Welt*, December 16, 1981, p. 3; "Ich habe mir einen Traum erfüllt: Aus den Reden der Schriftsteller aus Ost und West, die sich am 13. und 14. Dezember zur 'Berliner Begegnung' trafen," *Die Zeit*, no. 53, December 25, 1981, p. 29–30; "Zwischen Ohnmacht und Aufbruch: Der Frieden, Polen und windelweiche Westlichkeiten: Das Berliner Gespräch der Schriftsteller," *Frankfurter Allgemeine Zeitung*, December 16, 1981, p. 23.

3. Krüger, ed., *Berliner Begegnung*, 44.

4. Ibid., 45–46.

5. Ibid., 48.

6. Ibid., 56–8.

7. Ibid., 133–34.

8. "Literaten in Ost-Berlin, 3; "Ich habe mir einen Traum erfüllt," 29–30.

9. Günter de Bruyn, cited in "Ich habe mir einen Traum erfüllt, 29.

10. Also see Günter Grass, "Haager Treffen (24–26. Mai 1982 in Gravenhage-Scheveningen), in Günter Grass, *Widerstand Lernen. Politische Gegenreden, 1980–1983* (Darmstadt and Neuwied: Luchterhand, 1984), 28–29.

11. Egon Bahr, *Was wird aus den Deutschen?* (Reinbek bei Hamburg: Rowohlt, 1982).

12. Ibid., 12.

13. Ibid., 15.

14. Ibid., 22.

15. Ibid., 23.

16. Ibid., 24.

17. Ibid., 27.

18. Ibid., 136.

19. Ibid., 101.

20. Ibid., 151.

21. Ibid., 173.

22. Ibid., 211–212.

23. Ibid., 234.

24. "Bahr greif Kritik von Gaus auf," *FAZ*, January 19, 1982, p. 3.

25. "Hamburger Kompromiss: Die SPD stimmt in der Sicherheitspolitik gegen Schmidt und Apel," *FAZ*, January 25, 1982, pp. 1–2.

26. "SPD-Vorstand: Rüstungskontrolle und Abrüstung sind notwendig und erreichbar," *FAZ*, January 28, 1981, pp. 1–2.; "Gleichgewicht zwischen den Bündnissen: Leitantrag des SPD-Vorstands zur Sicherheitspolitik," *Frankfurter Rundschau*, January 28, 1982, p. 15.

27. "Vor dem SPD-Parteitag: Was wird aus dem Raketen-Moratorium?," *FAZ*, February 2, 1982, p. 3.

28. "Wie es mit dem Frieden weitergeht," *Frankfurter Rundschau*, February 4, 1982, p. 4. Signers of *Friedensmanifest 82* included Heinrich Albertz, Ulrich Albrecht, Gert Bastian, Heinrich Böll, Volkmar Deile, Walter Dirks, Ingeborg Drewitz, Berndt Engelmann, Erhard Eppler, Helmut Gollwitzer, Walter Jens, Robert Jungk, Petra Kelly, Oskar Lafontaine, Josef Leinen, Alfred Mechtersheimer, Wolf-Dieter Narr, Martin Niemöller, Horst-Eberhard Richter, Dorothee Sölle, Kurt Scharf, and Klaus Vack. They represented *Aktion Sühnezeichen*, the *Heinemann Initiative*, and the *Kommittee für Grundrechte und Demokratie*.

29. Rudolf Bahro, "The SPD and the Peace Movement," *New Left Review* (January–February 1982), pp. 20–31. Also see Rudolf Bahro, *Elemente einer neuen*

Politik (West Berlin: Verlag Olle and Wolter, 1980); and Rudolf Bahro, *Socialism and Survival: (Articles, Essays, Talks, 1979–1982)*, trans. David Fernbach (London: Heretic Books, 1980).

30. Ibid., 22.

31. Robert Held, "Angst," *Frankfurter Allgemeine Zeitung,* March 9, 1982, p. 1.

32. See Karl Feldmeyer, "Schmidts taktischer Erfolg mit der Nachrüstung," *Frankfurter Allgemeine Zeitung,* December 7, 1979, p. 12; and author's interview with Karl Feldmeyer, Bonn, June 27, 1984; author's interview with Robert Held, Frankfurt/Main, June 14, 1985.

33. "Breschnew lockt mit Stationierungs-Stopp für das Gebiet westlich des Ural," *FAZ,* March 17, 1982, pp. 1–2.

34. "Bonn: Versuch, den Nachrüstungsgegnern Anknüpfungspunkte zu liefern," *FAZ,* March 17, 1982, p. 2.

35. "Schmidt: Breschnews Vorschlag kein wichtiger Schritt," *FAZ,* March 30, 1982, p. 2.

36. "Bonn: Versuch, den Nachrüstungsgegnern Anknüpfungspunkte zu liefern," 2.

37. "Die Union bietet sich als Stütze der Aussenpolitik Genschers dar," *FAZ,* March 19, 1982, pp. 1–2.

38. "Genscher: Bonn steht zum NATO-Beschluss, Moskau vor 'folgenschwerem Irrtum' gewarnt," *FAZ,* March 20, 1982, pp. 1–2.

39. Egon Bahr, "Der Vorrang militärischen Denkens schwächt die NATO," *Vorwärts,* March 11, 1982, p. 3; Egon Bahr, "Eine erste Diagnose: Der Krieg wird vorbereitet," *Vorwärts,* March 18, 1982, p. 11.

40. Alois Mertes, *Saarland Rundfunk: Journal* (March 30, 1982), pp. 11–12 (in the BPA Nachrichtenabt) Mertes 0330-5. Mertes returned to this theme often in the euromissile debate. See "Verteidigung und Verständigung garantieren gemeinsam Sicherheit: Nicht die Soldaten schaffen das Risiko, sondern die politischen Führer, die ihnen Befehlen," *Frankfurter Allgemeine Zeitung,* November 8, 1983, p. 11. Raymond Aron was making similar arguments about the political significance of the SS-20s in the Soviet Union's attempt to split the Atlantic Alliance. See Aron, "Hope and Despair in the Western Camp," *Encounter* (June–July 1982), pp. 121–129. Aron added that the Soviets "thanks to their kind of political regime hold a major trump, that of being ready to hit first. . . ."

41. "Ich lade die jungen DDR-Bürger ein, uns zu besuchen: SPD-Vorstandsmitgleich Oskar Lafontaine forderte in Ost-Berlin einseitige atomare Abrüstung und Jugenaustausch zwischen beiden deutschen Staaten," *Frankfurter Rundschau,* March 24, 1982; and "Die Gleichgewichtsformel ist sinnlos: Lafontaine in Ost-Berlin—Auszüge aus einer Rede," *FAZ,* March 17, 1982, p. 2.

42. Ibid.

43. Ibid.

44. "Bahr: Moratoriums-Diskussion gefährlich," *FAZ*, April 3, 1981, p. 5. Along these lines, also see Karsten Voigt, "Gemeinsam schnell abrüsten," *Vorwärts*, April 8, 1982, p. 17.

45. "Drei Wochen vor dem SPD-Parteitag mancherlei Bemühungen zur Mässigung der Linken," *FAZ*, March 27, 1982, p. 4.

46. "Die Gegner einer Nachrüstung sorgen sich nicht um die Regierungsfähigkeit der SPD," *FAZ*, March 25, 1982, p. 3.

47. Helmut Schmidt, Speech at the Munich SPD Party Congress, reprinted in *Vorwärts*, April 15, 1982.

48. Ibid., 2.

49. "Die Friedens- und Sicherheitspolitik der SPD: Beschluss der SPD-Parteitages, Munchen, 19–23. April 1982," *Politik: Aktuelle Informationen der Sozialdemokratischen Partei Deutschlands Nr. 3*, pp. 1–2.

50. Ibid., 3–4. It also established a commission to examine alternatives to nuclear deterrence.

51. Egon Bahr, "Neuer Ansatz der gemeinsamen Sicherheit," *Die Neue Gesellschaft* (July 1982): 660; also see, "Bahr für Abzug der Atomwaffen aus den Nicht-Atomwaffen-Staaten," *FAZ*, May 24, 1982, pp. 1–2.

52. Ibid., 662.

53. Ibid., 654–55.

54. Ibid., 668.

55. Egon Bahr, "Sicherheitspartnershaft," *Die Neue Gesellschaft* (November 1982): 1041–1053.

56. "Die Rede des Amerikanischen Präsidenten im Bundestag: Deutschland, wir stehen auf deiner Seite! Du stehst nicht allein," *FAZ*, June 11, 1982, p. 6.

57. "Piecyk nennt die Politik der Bundesregierung verheerend," *FAZ*, June 12, 1982, p. 3.

58. Bernt Engelmann et al., eds., *Es geht, es geht. . . : Zeitgenössische Schriftsteller und ihr Beitrag zum Frieden—Grenzen und Möglichkeiten* (Munich: Wilhelm Goldmann Verlag, 1982).

59. Sergei Michalkov, in Englemann, ed., *Es geht, es geht . . .* , 75.

60. Ibid., 79, 82–83, 84–85, and 94.

61. "Gemeinsame Erklärung der Teilnehmer am Haager Treffen vom 26. Mai 1982," in Engelmann, ed., *Es geht, es geht*, 133–134.

62. "Moskaus Kampf um die westliche Öffentlichkeit," *FAZ*, August 21, 1982, p. 3.

63. Special Consultative Group, *Intermediate Range Nuclear Forces (INF): Progress Report to Ministers by the Social Consultative Group* (Brussels: NATO Information Service, December 8, 1983), p. 16.

64. Ibid., 17.

65. For the American version of this view, see Strobe Talbott, *Deadly Gambits* (New York: Alfred A. Knopf, 1984).

66. "Linksliberale verstehen sich als Teil der Friedensbewegung," *FAZ*, September 6, 1982, p. 4.

67. "FDP-Forderung: Atomwaffenfreies Europa," *Süddeutsche Zeitung*, September 13, 1982, p. 6.

68. Ibid.

69. "Die Bonner Koalition zerbrach auch an der Aussenpolitik," *FAZ*, September 20, 1982, p. 3.

70. Hans-Dietrich Genscher, "Unsere Kinder und Enkelen die Schrecken des Kreiges ersparen," *Frankfurter Rundschau*, September 8, 1982, p. 14.

71. Hans-Dietrich Genscher, *Brief an die Mitglieder der Führungsgremien und an die Mandatsträger der Freien Demokratischen Partei*, August 20, 1981 (Bonn: Pressedienst der Freien Demokratischen Partei, 1981).

72. Hans-Dietrich Genscher, *Brief an die Mitglieder der Führungsgremien und an die Mandatsträger der Freien Demokratischen Partei*, October 4, 1982 (Bonn: Pressedienst der Freien Demokratischen Partei, 1982), 3.

73. "Die Bonner Koalition ist zerbrochen," *FAZ*, September 18, 1982, pp. 1–2. See the speeches by Schmidt, Kohl, and Genscher to the Bundestag: "Der Erklärung des Bundeskanzlers vor dem Parlament," *FAZ*, September 18, 1982, p. 4: "Kohl: Unser Erfolg braucht einen neuen Anfang, und wir sind dazu bereit," *FAZ*, September 18, 1982, p. 5; "Genscher: Der Weg ist offen für alle Möglichkeiten, die das Grundgesetz bietet," *FAZ*, September 18, 1982, p. 5.

74. Helmut Schmidt, *Deutscher Bundestag—9 Wahlperiode—111 Sitzung* (September 9, 1982), p. 6746.

75. Willy Brandt, *Deutscher Bundestag—9 Wahlperiode—111 Sitzung* (September 9, 1982), p. 6776.

76. Horst Ehmke, *Deutscher Bundestag—9 Wahlperiode—111 Sitzung* (September 9, 1982), p. 6804.

77. Alois Mertes, *Deutscher Bundestag—9 Wahlperiode—111 Sitzung* (September 9, 1982), p. 6805.

78. Horst Ehmke, *Deutscher Bundestag* (September 9, 1982), p. 6805.

79. Helmut Kohl, *Deutscher Bundestag—9 Wahlperiode—111 Sitzung* (September 9, 1982), p. 6765.

80. Ibid., p. 6766.

81. Karsten Voigt, *Deutscher Bundestag—9 Wahlperiode—114 Sitzung* (September 16, 1982), p. 7044.

82. Volker Rühe, *Deutscher Bundestag—9 Wahlperiode—114 Sitzung* (September 16, 1982), p. 7038.

83. Volker Rühe, *Deutscher Bundestag* (September 16, 1982), p. 7038.

84. Manfred Wörner, *Deutscher Bundestag—9 Wahlperiode—114 Sitzung* (September 16, 1982), p. 7055.

85. Manfred Wörner, *Deutscher Bundestag* (September 16, 1982), p. 7057.

86. "Wechsel in Bonn—Helmut Kohl ist Bundeskanzler," *FAZ,* October 1, 1982), pp. 1–2.

87. Helmut Kohl, *Deutscher Bundestag—9 Wahlperiode—121 Sitzung* (October 13, 1982), p. 7220.

88. Helmut Kohl, *Deutscher Bundestag* (October 13, 1982), pp. 7220–21.

89. Helmut Kohl, *Deutscher Bundestag—9 Wahlperiode—130 Sitzung* (November 25, 1982), p. 8014.

90. Hans-Dietrich Genscher, *Deutscher Bundestag—9 Wahlperiode—121 Sitzung* (October 13, 1982), p. 7280.

91. Hans-Dietrich Genscher, *Deutscher Bundestag* (October 13, 1982), p. 7261. Manfred Wörner also stressed the importance of clarity about West Germany's partnership with the United States.

92. Ernst-Otto Maetzke, "Wort-Raketen," *FAZ,* November 12, 1982, p. 1.

93. Ibid.

94. Ibid.

Chapter 10
HISTORY, LANGUAGE, AND STRATEGY

1. Egon Bahr, "Neokonservatismus und Sicherheitspolitik: Sicherheitspartnershaft," *Die Neue Gesellschaft* (November 1982): 1041–1045. Also see comments by Rudiger Moniac, Dieter Senghaas, and Peter Stratmann, pp. 1045–1054.

2. Ibid., 1041.

3. Ibid., 1043.

4. Ibid., 1044–1045.

5. "Die SPD befindet sich von heute an im 'akuten Vorwahlkampf,'" *FAZ,* November 19, 1982, p. 1.

6. "Vogel erläutert Schultz die sicherheitspolitische Position der SPD," *FAZ,* December 9, 1982), pp. 1–2.

7. "SPD: Bundnis ja, Fesseln nein," *Frankfurter Rundschau,* December 21, 1982, p. 1.

8. "Andropow lockt und droht Raketenabbau bei Verzicht auf die Nachrüstung," *FAZ,* December 22, 1982, pp. 1–2. For the text of Andropov's speech, see "Die Sowjetunion ist bereit, sehr weit zu gehen: Die Rede des Generalsekretärs des ZK der KPdSU, Jurij Andropow, zum 60 Jahrestag der UdSSR," *Frankfurter Rundschau,* January 6, 1983, p. 10; also see "The enticement of Europe," *The Economist,* January 15, 1983, pp. 43–44. Andro-

pov repeated the offer on January 12, 1983. See "Moskau erwägt Zerstörung eines Teils der SS-20 Raketen," *FAZ*, January 13, 1983, pp. 1–2.

9. "Vogel: Die Sowjetunion bewegt sich auf eine realistischere Haltung zu," *FAZ*, December 24, 1982, p. 2.

10. "Kohl rechnet mit 'konkret Ergebnis' der Genfer Verhandlungen," *FAZ*, December 29, 1982, pp. 1–2.

11. "Die SPD sieht in Andropows Vorstoss verhandlungsfähige Zugeständnisse," *FAZ*, December 30, 1982, p. 1.

12. "Vogel glaubt an Änderung der amerikanischen Position in Genf," *FAZ*, January 8, 1983, pp. 1–2.

13. "The da and the nyet on the West German ballot," *The Economist*, January 22, 1983, pp. 37–38.

14. "Bahr: Andropows Wort testen," *FAZ*, January 5, 1983, p. 2.

15. *FBIS, USSR International Affairs, Western Europe* (January 12, 1983), G1–G5.

16. *FBIS*, ibid., G1.

17. "Vogel TV Interview: Hamburg ARD Television Network," *FBIS*, ibid., G2; and "Moscow TV Report," *FBIS* (January 13, 1983), p. G2–G3. Vogel said he was "greatly impressed" with Andropov's arguments, G3. For an interview with Egon Bahr see *FBIS*, "Literaturnaya Gazeta Interviews SPD Member Bahr" (January 12, 1983), G4.

18. *FBIS*, "Izvestiya Delineates New Soviet Missile Proposal" January 12, 1983), AA5.

19. *FBIS, USSR International Affairs* (January 12, 1983), "FRG Reaction to Soviet Missiles Offer Viewed," AA6–AA7.

20. Ibid., AA7.

21. "Die SPD stellt eine 'linken patriotism' in den Vordergrund," *FAZ*, January 22, 1983, pp. 1–2.

22. "Vogel sieht nach dem Gespräch mit Andropow mehr Hoffnungen für die Genfer Verhandlungen," *FAZ*, January 12, 1983, p. 1.

23. "Die Bundesregierung an einer Null-Lösung 'brennend interressiert,'" *FAZ*, January 11, 1983, p. 1.

24. "Die Bundesregierung klärt ihre Haltung zum Doppelbeschluss," *FAZ*, January 13, 1983, pp. 1–2.

25. Ibid., 2.

26. "Friedensforscher optimistisch: Wissenschaftler rechnen mit Zwischenlösung in Raketenfrage," *Frankfurter Rundschau*, January 13, 1983, pp. 1–2.

27. Ibid., 2.

28. Author's interview with Egbert Jahn, Frankfurt/Main (June 14, 1984).

29. "Vogel: Das letzte Wort über Mittelstreckenwaffen ist noch nicht gesprochen," *FAZ*, January 14, 1983, pp. 1–2.

30. *FBIS, USSR International Affairs, Western Europe,* "Gromyko Dinner Speech" (January 18, 1983), G5.

31. *FBIS, USSR International Affairs, Western Europe,* "Moscow Radio Assesses Visit" (January 19, 1983), G7.

32. "Der sowjetische Aussenminister in Bonn, Genscher spricht von der Überlebensfrage Europas," *FAZ,* January 17, 1983, pp. 1–2.

33. "Genscher zu Gromyko: Niemand darf ein Raketen-Monopol wollen," *FAZ,* January 18, 1983, p. 1.

34. "Gromyko in Bonn dieses Mal gemässigt und ruhig, Kohl erläutert die Null-Lösung," *FAZ,* January 19, 1983, pp. 1–2.

35. See Cornelius Castoriadis, *Devant la Guerre* (Paris: Fayard, 1981); Andre Glucksmann, *La Force du Vertige* (Paris: Bernard Grasset, 1983).

36. Pierre Hassner, "Zwei deutsche Staaten in Europa: Gibt es gemeinsame Interesse in internationalen Politik?" in Werner Weidenfeld, ed., *Die Identität der Deutschen* (Munich: Hanser Verlag, 1983), 294–323; and Joseph Rovan, *L'Allemagne du changement* (Paris: Calmann-Levy, 1983).

37. See Andre Gorz, "On the German Non-Response to the Polish Crisis: An Interview with Andre Gorz," *Telos,* no. 51 (Spring 1982): 121; and Günter Gaus, "Polen und die westliche Allianz, oder ein Plädoyer für die Entspannungspolitik," in Heinrich Böll, ed., *Verantwortlich für Polen?* (Reinbek bei Hamburg: Rowohlt Verlag, 1982), 111; and Egon Bahr, "Fürchtet Euch nicht mes chers, amis francais!" *Vorwärts,* November 12, 1981, p. 12.

38. Raymond Aron, *In Defense of Decadent Europe* (South Bend: Regency/Gateway, 1977); Renata Fritsch-Bournazel, *L'Union Sovietique et les deux Allemagnes* (Paris, 1979); Pierre Hassner, "Western European Perceptions of the USSR," *Daedalus* 108 (Winter, 1979): 145; also see Josef Joffe, "Detente Versus Alliance," in *The Limited Partnership: Europe, the United States and the Burdens of Alliance* (Cambridge, MA: Ballinger, 1987), 1–44.

39. See Pierre Lellouche, "Does NATO Have a Future?" in Robert W. Tucker and Linda Wrigley, eds., *The Atlantic Alliance and Its Critics* (New York: Praeger, 1983), 129–154.

40. "Mitterand fordert ein wehrhaftes Westeuropa, Friedenssicherung durch Gleichgewicht," *FAZ,* January 21, 1983, pp. 1–2.

41. Francois Mitterand, *Deutscher Bundestag—9 Wahlperiode—142 Sitzung* (January 20, 1983), pp. 8987–8988.

42. "Kohl in Paris: Wir haben die gleichen Sorge und die gleichen Einschätzungen," *FAZ,* January 22, 1983, pp. 1–2.

43. *FBIS, USSR International Affairs, Western Europe,* "Literaturnaya Gazeta, Vogel's Washington, Moscow Trips Compared" (January 31, 1983), G1.

44. *FBIS, USSR International Affairs, Western Europe* (January 24, 1983), "TASS: SPD Position on Nuclear Arms," G2.

45. "Kohl sieht die SPD auf dem 'gefährlichen Weg der Isolation,'" *FAZ*, January 24, 1983, p. 4.

46. Günter Grass, "On the Right to Resist," in Grass, *On Writing and Politics, 1967–1983*, trans. Ralph Mannheim (New York: Harcourt, Brace, Jovanovich, 1985), 141–148; and Günther Grass, "Vom Recht auf Widerstand," in his *Widerstand Lernen. Politische Gegenreden*, 1980–1983 (Darmstadt and Neuwied: Luchterhand, 1984), 58–67.

47. Ibid., 141–142.

48. Ibid., 146.

49. Ibid., 147–48.

50. "Bush spricht von einer Politik der ausgestreckten Hand," *FAZ*, February 2, 1983, pp. 1–2.

51. *FBIS, USSR International Affairs*, "TASS, 'Zero Option' Will Eliminate Military Balance" (February 3, 1983), AA6.

52. "Genscher warnt vor 'Hang zur Äquidistanz,'" *FAZ*, February 10, 1983, p. 4; Hans-Dietrich Genscher, "Liberal-Sein ist kein Zuckerlecken," *Die Zeit*, no. 7, February 11, 1983, "Politik," p. 3.

53. Ibid.

54. Ibid.

55. Ibid.

56. Alois Mertes, "Hans Joachim Vogel kapituliert vor Egon Bahr: Zur Gefahr eines National-Neutralismus," *Deutschland Union Dienst*, February 11, 1983, p. 3.

57. Ibid.

58. Ibid.

59. Egon Bahr, "Gefahr für das Bündnis, *Vorwärts*, February 17, 1983), p. 5.

60. "Gromyko ruft Europa zum Widerstand gegen 'NATO-Raketen' auf," *FAZ*, February 25, 1983, p. 1.

61. "Bundestagswahlen seit 1949," *FAZ*, March 8, 1983, p. 3.

62. Actually, it went from a four-party to a five-party system because the Christian Social Union, led by Franz Josef Strauss, was an independent party, though in practical terms it comprised a part of a national conservative party in coalition with the CDU.

63. "Für Washington der Auftake zu ernsthaften Verhandlungen in Genf," *FAZ*, March 7, 1983, p. 1.

64. *FBIS, USSR International Affairs, Western Europe* (March 8, 1983), "Vremya newscast, Results of FRG Election Is Assessed," G1.

65. "Lafontaine stellt die deutsche Nato-Mitgliedschaft in Frage," *FAZ*, March 28, 1983, p. 2. For Karsten Voigt's criticism of Lafontaine, see "Voigt widerspricht Lafontaine," *FAZ*, March 29, 1983, p. 3. For a sample of discussions

about a possible SPD-Green alliance see Wolfram Bickerich, ed., *SPD und Grüne: Das neue Bündnis?* (Reinbek bei Hamburg: Spiegel Verlag, 1985).

66. See Appendix 2, "Public Opinion, 'Public Opinions,' and the War of Words."

67. Robert Held, "Mut zu Mehr Wahrheit," *FAZ*, March 22, 1982, p. 1.

68. *Weissbuch 1983* (Bonn: Bundesminister der Verteidigung, 1983), 207.

69. "Sicherheitspolitischer Zick-Zack der SPD," *FAZ*, April 16, 1983, p. 2.

70. Rudolf Augstein, "Der vielleicht nicht wünschenswerte Zufall," *Der Spiegel*, April 19, 1982, p. 20.

71. Ibid., 21.

72. "Friede und Menschenrechte," *FAZ*, April 25, 1983; Ingrid Krüger, ed., *Zweite Berliner Begegnung: Den Frieden erklären: Protokolle des zweiten Berliner Schriftstellertreffens am 22/23. April 1983* (Darmstadt and Neuwied: Luchterhand, 1983).

73. Günter Grass, in Krüger, ed., *Zweite Berliner Begegnung*, 48.

74. Ibid., 48–50.

75. Ibid., 49–50. On Auschwitz and the nuclear issue during the Euromissile dispute in West Germany, see the following, by Wolfgang Pohrt: *Endstation: Über die Wiedergeburt der Nation* (Berlin: Rotbuch, 1982); *Kreisverkehr, Wendepunkt: Über die Wechseljahre der Nation und die Linke im Widerstreit der Gefühle* (Berlin: Tiamat, 1984); *Stammesbewusstsein, Kulturnation: Pamphlete, Glossen, Feuilleton* (Berlin: Tiamat, 1984).

76. On this see Wolfgang Minaty, "Wie Schriftsteller aus Ost und West den Frieden erklären," *Die Welt*, April 25, 1983, p. 3. The dissenting East Germans were Günter de Bruyn and Rolf Schneider.

77. Sergei Baruzdin, in Krüger, ed., *Zweite Berliner Begegnung*, 56.

78. Ibid., 56–57.

79. Ibid., 58.

80. Ibid., 143.

81. Ibid., 167.

82. Ibid., 172–173. Edward Thompson developed a similar position. See "Notes on Exterminism, the Last Stage of Civilization," in Edward Thompson, et al., *Exterminism and Cold War* (London: Verso Editions, 1982), 1–34.

83. Wladimir Bukowski, *Dieser stechende Schmerz der Freiheit: Russicher Traum und westliche Realität* (Stuttgart: Seewald Verlag, 1983); and *Pazifisten gegen den Frieden: Friedensbewegung und Sowjetunion* (Bern: Verlag SOI, 1983).

84. Erhard Eppler, *Die tödliche Utopie der Sicherheit* (Reinbek bei Hamburg: Rowohlt Verlag, 1983).

85. Ibid., 81.

86. Ibid., 82.

87. Ibid., 85.

88. Ibid., 86.

89. Ibid.

90. Ibid., 92.

91. Eppler was also an important figure in the Evangelical Church in West Germany. For a discussion of West German Protestantism and the peace movement in general, see Siegfried Scharrer, "War and Peace and the German Church," in Laqueur and Hunter, eds., *European Peace Movements and the Atlantic Alliance*, 273–317; see also Alice Holmes Cooper, "The West German Peace Movement and the Christian Churches: An Institutional Approach," *Review of Politics* 50, no. 1 (Winter 1988).

92. Franz Alt, *Frieden ist Möglich: Die Politik der Bergpredigt* (Munich: Piper Verlag, 1983). Alt's book sold over 600,000 copies in hard cover within a few months. See Walter Laqueur, *Germany Today: A Personal Report* (Boston: Little, Brown, and Co., 1985), 208.

93. "Zehn Professoren beenden den Burgfrieden in der SPD," *FAZ*, May 25, 1983, pp. 1–2. The signers were Helmut Berding, Helmut Coper, Hartmut Jäckel, Karl Kaiser, Thomas Nipperdey, Gasine Schwan, Kurt Sontheimer, Werner Skuhr, and Peter Steinbach, and Heinrich August Winkler.

94. Ibid.

95. Ibid.

96. "Zur Lage und Zukunft der Sozialdemokratie," *FAZ*, May 28, 1983, p. 5.

97. See Helmut Kohl, *Deutscher Bundestag—10 Wahlperiode—4 Sitzung* (May 4, 1983), p. 71; and Hans-Joachim Vogel, *Deutscher Bundestag—10 Wahlperiode—4 Sitzung* (May 4, 1983), p. 82; Hans-Dietrich Genscher, *Deutscher Bundestag—10—Wahlperiode—4 Sitzung* (May 4, 1983), pp. 108–09.

98. Alfred Dregger, *Deutscher Bundestag—10 Wahlperiode—6 Sitzung* (May 6, 1983), p. 264.

99. Ibid.

100. Ibid., 264–65.

101. Ibid., 267.

102. On the development of the SS-20 arsenal see *Bericht zur Rüstungskontrolle und Abrüstung 1983* (Bonn: Presse- und Informationsamt der Bundesregierung, 1983), 18.

103. "Bekenntnis zum Doppelbeschluss in Williamsburg, Das Treffen harmonisch und zuversichtlich," *FAZ*, May 30, 1983, pp. 1–2.

104. "Washington doppelte Warnung an die Sowjetunion: Raketendrohung ist Griff nach Überlegenheit—Schluss mit einer Ermutigung Syriens," *FAZ*, May 30, 1983, p. 3.

105. Ibid.

106. Helmut Kohl, *Deutscher Bundestag—10 Wahlperiode—11 Sitzung* (June 9, 1983), p. 528.

107. "Kohl: Beim dem Raketenmonopol Moskaus kann es nicht bleiben," *FAZ*, June 10, 1983, p. 3.

108. Hans-Dietrich Genscher, *Deutscher Bundestag—10 Wahlperiode—13 Sitzung* (June 15, 1983), pp. 696–697.

109. Ibid., 696–97.

110. Egon Bahr, *Deutscher Bundestag—10 Wahlperiode—13 Sitzung* (June 15, 1983), p. 701.

111. Ibid., 702.

112. Ibid., 698–699.

113. Gert Bastian, *Deutscher Bundestag—10 Wahlperiode—13 Sitzung* (June 15, 1983), pp. 712–15. For a full presentation of his views, also see Bastian, *Frieden Schaffen: Gedanken zur Sicherheitspolitik* (Munich: Kindler Verlag, 1983).

114. Bastian, *Deutscher Bundestag* (June 15, 1983), p. 714.

115. Ibid., 715.

116. Manfred Wörner, *Deutscher Bundestag—10 Wahlperiode—13 Sitzung* (June 15, 1983), p. 720.

117. Ibid., 720.

118. Ibid.

119. Ibid., 721–722.

120. Ibid., 722.

121. Ibid.

122. Ibid., 724–725.

123. Ibid., 725.

124. Ibid., 726.

125. Ibid., 727–728.

126. Ibid., 727. Ustinov was quoted in the East German newspaper *Neues Deutschland* of April 17, 1983, as saying: "The United States would not be unpunished in this case. If people in Washington think that our answer to the use of missiles like Pershing 2 and Cruise missiles will only be directed against targets in Western Europe, they are very mistaken. Retaliation would unavoidably also affect the United States itself."

127. Ibid., 727.

128. *Deutscher Bundestag—10. Wahlperiode, Drucksache 10/155* (June 15, 1983), "Entschliessungsantrag der Fraktionen der CDU/CSU und FDP," pp. 1–3. The parliament defeated an SPD resolution calling on both world powers to seek an agreement and which reserved a decision on deployments until fall 1983, and a Green resolution explicitly calling for incorporation of the British and French missiles in the Geneva talks and for an immediate beginning to negotiations on all nuclear weapons already in or for Europe. See

Deutscher Bundestag—10 Wahlperiode—Drucksache 10/152, "Entschliessungsantrag der SPD" (June 15, 1983), p. 1; and *Deutscher Bundestag—10 Wahlperiode—Drucksache 10/150*, "Entschliessungsantrag der Fraktion Die Grunen" (June 15, 1983), pp. 1–2.

129. Quoted by Joschka Fischer, *Deutscher Bundestag—10 Wahlperiode—16 Sitzung* (June 15, 1983), p. 1048.

130. "Geissler gibt eine ethische Begründung für die Verteidigungspolitik" *FAZ*, May 26, 1983, p. 2.

131. Heiner Geissler, *Deutscher Bundestag—10 Wahlperiode—13 Sitzung* (June 15, 1983), pp. 752–53.

132. Ibid., 755.

133. Ibid.

134. Ibid., 756.

135. Ibid., 756–57.

136. See Winston Churchill, *The Gathering Storm* (Boston: Houghton Mifflin, 1948); Martin Gilbert, *Winston S. Churchill: The Prophet of Truth, 1922–1939* (Boston: Houghton Mifflin, 1977); Gerhard L. Weinberg, *The Foreign Policy of Hitler's Germany*, 2 vols. (Chicago: University of Chicago Press, 1970, 1980); and Williamson Murray, *The Change in the European Balance of Power in Europe, 1938–1939* (Princeton: Princeton University Press, 1984).

137. See Chapter 1.

138. Ibid., 761.

139. Horst Ehmke, *Deutscher Bundestag—10 Wahlperiode—13 Sitzung* (June 15, 1983), p. 772. Also see the remarks of the Free Democrat Hildegaard Hamm-Brucher, *Deutscher Bundestag—10 Wahlperiode—13 Sitzung* (June 15, 1983), p. 772, who stressed that Britain and France did arm in the 1930s but that Hitler had armed earlier and in greater quantity.

140. See Jürgen Schmude, *Deutscher Bundestag—10 Wahlperiode—16 Sitzung* (June 23, 1983), p. 1043.

141. Hans-Joachim Vogel, *Deutscher Bundestag—10 Wahlperiode—16 Sitzung* (June 23, 1983), pp. 1001–02.

142. Ibid., 1002–1003.

143. Helmut Kohl, *Deutscher Bundestag—10 Wahlperiode—16 Sitzung* (June 23, 1983), 1004–05.

144. Ibid., 1007. Also see Alfred Dregger, *Deutscher Bundestag—10 Wahlperiode—16 Sitzung* (June 23, 1983), p. 1010–16.

145. Otto Schilly, *Deutscher Bundestag—10 Wahlperiode—16 Sitzung* (June 23, 1983), p. 1019.

146. Ibid.

147. Schmude, *Deutscher Bundestag* (June 23, 1983), p. 1043–44.

148. Joschka Fischer, *Deutscher Bundestag—10 Wahlperiode—16 Sitzung* (June 23, 1983), p. 1049.

149. Ibid., 1050.

150. Ibid., 1050.

151. Heiner Geissler, *Deutscher Bundestag—10 Wahlperiode—16 Sitzung* (June 23, 1983), 1051.

152. Ibid., 1052.

153. Ibid.

154. Ibid., 1052–53.

155. See "Die Koalition lehnt die Entlassung Bundesminister Geisslers ab," *FAZ*, June 24, 1983, p. 1.

156. "Südwest-SPD will die Stationierung ablehnen," *FAZ*, June 27, 1983, p. 3. The committee said that the United States had abandoned the negotiating position of 1979, that British and French missiles should be included, and that more time was needed.

157. "Abrüstungsvorschläge der SPD mit unterschiedlichen Zielvorstellungen," *FAZ*, June 30, 1983, p. 4. For the text of the report see, "Egon Bahr: Bericht der Arbeitsgruppe 'Neue Strategien,' beim SPD-Parteivorstand vom Juli 1983," in Hans Günter Brauch, ed., *Sicherheitspolitik am Ende?* (Gerlingen: Bleicher Verlag, 1984), 275–90. Members of the working group on new strategies included: Hans Apel, Wolf Graf von Baudissin, Wilhelm Bruns, Andreas von Bülow, Horst Ehmke, Katrin Fuchs, Erwin Horn, Gerhard Heimann, Christian Krause, Oskar Lafontaine, Ulrich Mackensen, Alfons Pawelczyk, Hermann Scheer, Klaus von Schubert, and Karsten Voigt.

158. Ibid., 276–79.

159. Ibid., 282–83.

160. Ibid., 289–90.

161. "Harte und klare Aussprache in Moskau, Vage Drohungen Andropows mit Gegenmassnahmen," *FAZ*, July 6, 1983, pp. 1–2.

162. Ibid.

163. "Münchener SPD sagt 'klat und uneingeschränkt nein' zu Raketen," *Frankfurter Rundschau*, July 21, 1983, p. 4.

164. "Lafontaine für kernwaffenfrei Bundesrepublik," *Die Welt*, July 28, 1983, p. 8.

165. "Andropows Angebot belebt Hoffnung auf ein Ergebnis in Genf," *FAZ*, August 29, 1983, pp. 1–2.

166. "Bonn: Die Sowjetunion beharrt auf ihrer Uberlegenheit," *FAZ*, August 30, 1983, pp. 1–2.

167. "Andropow wirbt, droht, und verschickt Briefe an die Europäer," *FAZ*, August 31, 1983, pp. 1–2.

168. Oskar Lafontaine, *Angst vor den Freunden: Die Atomwaffen-Strategie der Supermächte zerstört die Bündnisse* (Reinbek bei Hamburg: Spiegel Verlag, 1983).

169. Ibid., 8–9.

170. Ibid., 12–14.

171. Ibid., 91.

172. Ibid., 105.

173. Ibid., 130.

174. Ibid., 37.

175. "Bonn: Im Ergebnis begünstigt Bahr die Politik der Sowjetunion," *FAZ*, October 20, 1983, p. 1. Also see Alois Mertes, "SPD-Wende zur sicherheitspolitischen Konfrontation: Eine Ära geht zu Ende," *Deutschland Union Dienst*, September 9, 1983, p. 2.

176. Alois Mertes, "Hans Joachim Vogel kapituliert vor Egon Bahr," p. 3.

177. Alois Mertes, "Friedenserhaltung—Friedensgestaltung," *Europa Archiv 35* (1983): 190; and Alois Mertes, "Egon Bahrs Manöver bedrohen unsere Sicherheit," *Deutschland Union Dienst*, July 19, 1983, p. 2.

178. Ibid., 183.

179. Ibid., 196.

Chapter 11
DEMOCRATIC RESILIENCE

1. "Baden-Würtembergs SPD sagt 'endgültig' nein zur Nachrüstung," *FAZ*, September 12, 1983, pp. 1–2.

2. Hans-Dietrich Genscher, *Deutscher Bundestag—10 Wahlperiode—23 Sitzung* (September 16, 1983), p. 1578.

3. Horst Ehmke, *Deutscher Bundestag—10 Wahlperiode—23 Sitzung* (September 16, 1983), p. 1583–85; Gert Bastian, *Deutscher Bundestag—10 Wahlperiode—23 Sitzung* (September 16, 1983), p. 1595.

4. Manfred Wörner, *Deutscher Bundestag—10 Wahlperiode—23 Sitzung* (September 16, 1983), p. 1600.

5. "Geissler: Die SPD übernimmt Moskaus Arguments," *FAZ*, September 19, 1983, p. 1.

6. Ibid.

7. "Geissler bekraftigt Vorwurf an die SPD," *FAZ*, September 23, 1983, p. 2.

8. "Die SPD zwischen 'Jetz schon nein' und 'Noch nicht nein,'" *FAZ*, September 26, 1983, pp. 1–2; and "Das Nein der SPD zur Nachrüstung gilt jetzt als sicher," *FAZ*, October 3, 1983, pp. 1–2; and "Die SPD vervollständigt ihr Nein zur Nachrüstung, Untertöne einer Abkehr von Washington," *FAZ*, October 10, 1983, p. 1. The twelve were Baden-Wurtenberg, Berlin, Bre-

men, Hamburg, Hessen, and Schleswig-Holstein, Rhineland-Pfalz, Hannover, East and South Bavaria, Franken, and Central Rhine.

9. Karl Kaiser, "Prioritäten sozialdemokratischer Aussen- und Sicherheitspolitik," in Jürgen Maruhn and Manfred Wilke, eds., *Wohin treibt die SPD? Wende oder Kontinuität sozialdemokratischer Sicherheitspolitik* (Munich: Günter Olzog Verlag, 1984), 9–27. It first appeared in the *FAZ* on October 6, 1983. It was reprinted in *Vorwärts* (October 6 and 13, 1983) and the *Frankfurter Rundschau* (October 11, 1983).

10. Ibid., 12.

11. Ibid.

12. Ibid., 18.

13. Ibid., 19–20.

14. Egon Bahr, "Unangenehme Wahrheiten für die SPD," *Vorwärts*, October 13, 1983, 14.

15. Ibid., 15.

16. Ibid.

17. Gesine Schwan, "Die SPD und die westliche Freiheit," in Maruhn and Wilke, eds., *Wohin treibt die SPD?* 38–52.

18. Ibid., 38.

19. Ibid., 39.

20. Ibid., 43.

21. Ibid., 44.

22. Ibid., 47.

23. Ibid., 48–49.

24. Ibid., 50. For a discussion of "leftist patriotism" with a more moderate tone see Peter Glotz, "Linker Patriotism," in his *Die Arbeit der Zuspitzung: Über die Organisation einer regierungsfähigen Linken* (West Berlin: Siedler Verlag, 1984), 41–101.

25. Ibid., 51. For a collection that brought together leftist and rightist German nationalists see Wolfgang Venohr, ed., *Die deutsche Einheit kommt bestimmt* (Bergisch Gladbach: Gustav Lübbe Verlag, 1982). In fact, though not much discussed at the time, right-wing, anti-Western nationalism also emerged during the euromissile dispute and eventually developed into the anti-immigrant, radical right-wing party, *Die Republikaner.*

26. Manes Sperber, "Rede anlässlich der Verleihung des Friedenspreises des Deutschen Buchhandels am 16. Oktober 1983," in Maruhn and Wilke, eds., *Wohin treibt die SPD?*, 171–185.

27. Ibid., 181.

28. Ibid., 181–182.

29. Ibid., 183.

30. Ibid., 184.

31. On this development, see Karl Dietrich Bracher, *Zeitgeschichtliche Kontroversen: Um Faschismus, Totalitärismus, Demokratie* (Munich: Piper Verlag, 1984).

32. "Bahr empfiehlt die Annahme der sowjetischen Vorschlage in Genf," *FAZ*, October 19, 1983, pp. 1–2. Andropov's statement that a new "ice age" in East-West relations would follow from deployments did not escape his attention. See Egon Bahr, "Andropows Einstimmung," *Vorwärts*, October 6, 1983, p. 1.

33. "Bonn: Im Ergebnis begünstigt Bahr die Politik der Sowjetunion," *FAZ*, October 20, 1983, pp. 1–2.

34. Author's interview with Dr. Hans Ruhle, West German Defense Ministry, June 26, 1984.

35. *Weissbuch 1983: Zur Sicherheit der Bundesrepublik Deutschland* (Bonn: Defense Ministry, 1983), pp. 192–223 and 33–117.

36. Ibid., 159–66.

37. Ibid., 168.

38. Ibid., 114.

39. "SPD-Präsidium stellt sich hinter Brandt," *Süddeutsche Zeitung*, October 26, 1983, p. 5.

40. "Hunderttausende demonstrieren auf den Strassen für Frieden," *FAZ*, October 24, 1983, pp. 1–2.

41. "Brandt kritisiert die Vereinigten Staaten und die Sowjetunion," *FAZ*, November 18, 1983, pp. 1–2.

42. Helmut Schmidt, "Zur Lage der Sicherheitspolitik," in Maruhn and Wilke, eds., *Wohin treibt die SPD?*, 132.

43. Ibid., 142.

44. Ibid., 143.

45. Ibid., 145.

46. Ibid., 153–154.

47. Ibid., 159.

48. Ibid.

49. Ibid., 161.

50. Ibid., 163.

51. Ibid., 164.

52. "Vor Bundestagsdebatte und Raketenstationierung gibt der SPD Schmidts Politik auf," *FAZ*, November 21, 1983, pp. 1–2.

53. Willy Brandt, "SPD: Partei für Europa, Rede vom 18. November 1983," in *Willy Brandt . . . Auf der Zinne der Partei . . . Parteitagsreden 1960 bis 1983*, edited by Werner Krause and Wolfgang Gröf (Berlin and Bonn: Dietz, 1984), 344; also see excerpts in the *FAZ,*, November 21, 1983, p. 2.

54. Ibid., 347–348.

55. Ibid., 349.

56. "Ja zu einer europäischen Friedenspolik. NEIN zu immer mehr Atomwaffen: Beschluss des Kölner Parteitages der SPD vom 19.11.1983," *Politik: Aktuelle Information der Sozialdemokratischen Partei Deutschlands,* Nr. 16 (November, 1983), p. 3.

57. Ibid.

58. Ibid.

59. See Günter Grass' open letter to the West German parliament in which he returned to his arguments about the responsibility of the Germans for peace in view of the country's "history of guilt." Günter Grass, "Offener Brief an die Abgeordneten des Deutschen Bundestages," in Günter Grass, *Widerstand Leisten, Politische Gegenreden 1980–1983* (Darmstadt and Neuwied: Luchterhand, 1984), 84–90.

60. "Kohl: Die Stationeierung ist geboten, Vogel begründet das Nein der SPD," *FAZ,* November 22, 1983, pp. 1–2, 6–7.

61. Helmut Kohl, *Deutscher Bundestag—10 Wahlperiode—35 Sitzung* (November 21, 1983), pp. 2321–322.

62. Ibid., 2322.

63. Ibid., 2323.

64. Ibid.

65. Ibid., 2325.

66. Ibid., 2328–329.

67. Ibid., 2329.

68. Ibid. The German reads: "Wir sind keine Wanderer zwischen Ost und West . . . Zwischen Demokratie und Diktatur gibt es keinen Mittelweg. Wir stehen auf der Seite der Freiheit."

69. Ibid., 2331.

70. Alfred Dregger, *Deutscher Bundestag—10 Wahlperiode—35 Sitzung,* (November 21, 1983), p. 2346. At this point, Joschka Fischer, of the Greens, called Dregger "a dinosaur of the Cold War."

71. Ibid., 2347.

72. Ibid., 2353. At this point, one of the Greens called out, "New stab-in-the-back legends!"

73. Dregger, *Deutscher Bundestag* (November 21, 1983), p. 2354. Also see Jürgen Tödenhofer, *Deutscher Bundestag—10 Wahlperiode—35 Sitzung* (November 21, 1983), p. 2407–09, who asked why the Soviet Union didn't "openly discuss" the SS-20 decision with Willy Brandt when he was West German chancellor in 1974.

74. Manfred Wörner, *Deutscher Bundestag—10 Wahlperiode—36 Sitzung* November 22, 1983), p. 2461.

75. Ibid., 2464.

76. Ibid., 2465.

77. Hans-Dietrich Genscher, *Deutscher Bundestag—10 Wahlperiode—35 Sitzung* (November 21, 1983), p. 2356.

78. Ibid., 2359.

79. Ibid., 2362.

80. Hans-Joachim Vogel, *Deutscher Bundestag—10 Wahlperiode—35 Sitzung* (November 21, 1983), 2334–335.

81. Ibid.

82. Ibid., 2338.

83. Ibid., 2339.

84. Ibid., 2343–344.

85. Ibid., 2340–341.

86. Egon Bahr, *Deutscher Bundestag—10 Wahlperiode—35 Sitzung* (November 21, 1983), 2401.

87. Ibid., 2402.

88. Ibid., 2405.

89. Willy Brandt, *Deutscher Bundestag—10 Wahlperiode—36 Sitzung* (November 22, 1983), p. 2500.

90. Ibid., 2501.

91. Ibid., 2509.

92. Ibid., 2510–511.

93. Helmut Schmidt, *Deutscher Bundestag—10 Wahlperiode—35 Sitzung* (November 21, 1983), pp. 2376–377.

94. Ibid., 2378.

95. Ibid., 2384.

96. "Der Antrag der Grünen," in *Die Nachrüstungsdebatte im Deutschen Bundestag* (Reinbek bei Hamburg: Rowohlt, 1984), 264–266.

97. Otto Schily, *Deutscher Bundestag—10 Wahlperiode—35 Sitzung* (November 21, 1983), p. 2364.

98. Ibid., 2366.

99. Ibid., 2368.

100. Petra Kelly, *Deutscher Bundestag—10 Wahlperiode—36 Sitzung* (November 22, 1983), pp. 2520–2521.

101. Ibid., 2522.

102. Ibid., 2523.

103. Beck-Oberdorf, *Deutscher Bundestag—10 Wahlperiode—36 Sitzung* (November 22, 1983), pp. 2562–2563.

104. Alois Mertes, *Deutscher Bundestag—10 Wahlperiode—36 Sitzung* (November 22, 1983), pp. 2565–2566.

105. "Der Antrag der Koalition von CDU/CSU und FDP," in *Die Nachrüstungsdebatte in Deutschen Bundestag*, 272–274.

106. "Der Bundestag billigt die Stationierung, 'Das Bündnis bedroht niemanden,'" *FAZ*, November 23, 1983, pp. 1–2.

107. Moskau unterbricht die Genfer Verhandlungen, Bonn: 'Einige Initiativen' zur Wiederaufnahme," *FAZ*, November 24, 1983, p. 1.

108. "Moskau droht mit 'beschleunigter' Stationierung taktischer Atomwaffen," *FAZ*, November 25, 1983, p. 1.

109. *FBIS, USSR International Affairs, Western Europe*, "Pravda, Kohl's CDU Report Denounced as 'Fabrications'" (November 22, 1983), pp. G4–G6.

110. Ibid., G6.

111. *FBIS, USSR International Affairs, Western Europe*, "TASS, Bundestag Assent to Missiles 'Dubious, Sinister,'" (November 23, 1983), p. G1.

112. Ibid.

113. Karl Feldmeyer, "Signal der Ratlosigkeit," *Frankfurter Allgemeine Zeitung*, November 29, 1983, p. 1.

114. Ibid.

Chapter 12
AFTERMATH AND THE INF TREATY, 1983–1987

1. "Beschlüsse des Essener Parteitages der SPD zur Friedenspolitik," *Politik: Aktuelle Informationen der Sozialdemokratischen Partei Deutschlands* Nr. 5 (June) (Bonn: Vorstand der SPD, 1984), p. 2. Hearings in the Bundestag were held in 1984 on "alternative strategies." Some contributions are collected in Diethelm Schröder, ed., *Krieg oder was sonst? NATO Strategie der Unsicherheit* (Reinbek bei Hamburg: Rowohlt Verlag, 1984).

2. Ibid., 2.

3. Ibid.

4. Ibid., 3. For the response of American government officials to this resolution, see the assessment offered by Richard Perle at a conference held in Bonn in June 1984. See Richard Perle, "Excerpts: Speech by Assistant Secretary of Defense Richard N. Perle Before the Friedrich Ebert Stiftung in Bonn, June 28," *Wireless Bulletin from Washington*, no. 121 (June 29, 1984), pp. 13–17; Richard Burt, an Assistant Secretary of State, also spoke to the conference. See Robert Held, "Die Freiheit als Herzenssache—Amerika warnt die SPD," *FAZ*, July 4, 1984, p. 7.

5. Horst Ehmke, *"Konzept für die Selbstbehauptung Europas,"* April 11, 1984 (Bonn: SPD Vorstand), p. 4.

6. The articles and speeches of the Bitburg controversy are collected in Geoffrey H. Hartman, ed., *Bitburg in Moral and Political Perspective* (Bloomington: Indiana University Press, 1986).

7. Josef Joffe cogently analyzed the relationship between domestic politics of the euromissile battle and the Bitburg episode in "The Battle of the Historians: A Report from Germany," *Encounter* 69 (June 1987): 72–77.

8. Michael Stürmer, "Abkoppelung: Thema mit Variationen," *FAZ*, May 13, 1986; reprinted in Michael Stürmer, *Deutsche Fragen: Oder die Suche nach der Staatsräson* (Munich: Piper Verlag, 1988), 122–24. Also see his "Die Deutschen und Genf," *FAZ*, May 7, 1985, pp. 108–10; and "Frieden im ideologischen Zeitalter," *FAZ*, October 7, 1985, pp. 113–116.

9. Michael Stürmer, "Abkoppelung: Thema mit Variationen," 124.

10. Ibid.

11. Mikhail Gorbachev, "The 27th Party Congress: The Political Report of the Central Committee of the CPSU to the Party Congress of the CPSU, Moscow, February 25, 1986," in Gorbachev, *Toward a Better World* (New York: Richardson and Steirman, 1987), 83–202.

12. Ibid., 91.

13. Ibid., 95.

14. Ibid., 96–99.

15. Ibid., 99.

16. Ibid., 171–172.

17. On the Soviet program see U.S. Department of Defense, *Soviet Military Power 1987* (Washington, D.C.: U.S. Government Printing Office, 1987), 45–62.

18. Mikhail Gorbachev, "Televised Speech: On the Resumption of U.S. Nuclear Testing, Moscow, March 29, 1986," in Gorbachev, *Toward a Better World*, 213–220. As the Soviet Union had just completed a set of tests, it was an opportune moment to criticize the United States.

19. Mikhail Gorbachev, *Perestroika: New Thinking for Our Country and the World* (New York: Harper and Row, 1987), 194–195.

20. Ibid., 192–193.

21. Ibid., 201–204.

22. "Die Streit der Ideologien und die gemeinsame Sicherheit. Das gemeinsame Papier der Grundwertkomission der SPD und der Akademie für Gesellschaftswisssenschaften beim ZK der SED," *FAZ*, August 28, 1987, p. 7.

23. Ibid.

24. Egon Bahr, *Zum europäischen Frieden: Eine Antwort auf Gorbatschow* (West Berlin: Corso bei Siedler, 1988).

25. Ibid., 23–24.

26. Ibid., 28.

27. Ibid., 36–37.

28. Ibid., 85.

29. Ibid., 91.

30. Ibid., 101.

31. Michael Stürmer, "Lehren einer langen Krise," *FAZ*, October 14, 1987; reprinted in Stürmer, *Deutsche Fragen*, 141–142.

Appendix 2
"NON-ATTITUDES" AND PUBLIC OPINIONS

1. Wilhelm Hennis, "Meinungsforschung und Representative Demokratie," in *Politik als praktische Wissenschaft* (Munich: Piper Verlag, 1968).
2. Phillip Converse, "Attitudes and Non-Attitudes: Continuation of a Dialogue," in E.R. Tufte, ed., *The Quantitative Analysis of Social Problems* (Reading, Mass.: Addison-Wesley, 1970), 168–189. Also see Gabriel Almond, "Public Opinion and National Security Policy," *Public Opinion Quarterly* 20, no. 2 (Summer 1956): 371–378.
3. The expertise of the mass public is evident in response to the question, "Are you happy?"
4. Hans Rattinger, "National Security and the Missile Controversy in the West German Public," 1986 Annual Meeting of the American Political Science Association, August 28–31, 1986, pp. 2–3. In the same period West German perceptions of an increased Soviet threat increased from below 30 percent to about 50 percent, and approval of membership in NATO has shown a continuous upward trend for three decades, ibid., pp. 3–4. Also see Gregory Flynn and Hans Rattinger, eds., *The Public and Atlantic Defense* (Totowa, N.J.: Rowman and Allanheld, 1985); and Hans Rattinger, "Change and Continuity in Public Attitudes on National Security and Nuclear Weapons," *Public Opinion Quarterly* (Fall 1987).
5. Hans Rattinger, "Table 2: Attitudes on INF-deployment and the double-track decision, 1981–1983," ibid., p. 9.
6. Elizabeth Nölle-Neumann, "Are Three-Quarters of the Germans Opposed to Deployment? The Situation Is Actually More Complex," *FAZ*, September 16, 1983.
7. Ibid., p. 2.
8. Horst Schättle, cited by Nölle-Neumann, in ibid.
9. See Josef Joffe's perceptive analysis of public opinion data in *The Limited Partnership* (Cambridge, Mass: Ballinger, 1987), pp. 95–110; also see Richard Eichenberg, *Public Opinion and National Security in Western Europe* (Ithaca: Cornell University Press, 1989).
10. Rattinger, "National Security," 17.
11. Ibid.
12. Ibid., 13.

BIBLIOGRAPHY

DOCUMENTS AND GOVERNMENT REPORTS

Arbeitsdaten. Reichweite und Affinität für alle überregionalen Zeitschriften und Zeitungen. Hamburg: Spiegel Verlag, 1973–1984.

Auswartiges Amt. *Abrüstung und Rüstungskontrolle: Dokumentation zur Haltung der Bundesrepublik Deutschland.* Bonn: 1981.

Bundesministerium des Innern. *betrifft: Verfassungsschutz* for years 1969–1983. Bonn.

——. *Linksextremistische Einflusse auf die Kampagne gegen die NATO-Nachrüstung.* Bonn: 1983.

Bundesminister der Verteidigung. *Weissbuch 1970. Zur Sicherheit der Bundesrepublik Deutschland und zur Lage der Bundeswehr.* Bonn, 1970. 1971/1972. 1973/1974. 1975/1976. 1979. 1983. 1985.

Bundesminister der Verteidigung. Planungsstab. *Die nukearen Mittelstreckenwaffen: Modernisierung und Rüstungskontrolle. Texte, Materialien und Argumente zum Beschluss der NATO vom 12. Dezember 1979.* Bonn: 1980.

Bundesregierung, Presse- und Informationsamt. *Bericht zur Rüstungskontrolle und Abrüstung 1983.* Bonn: 1983.

Christlichen Demokratischen Union Deutschlands. *Bundesparteitag.* 1979–1983.

Deutscher Bundestag. *Verhandlungen des Deutschen Bundestages.* 1977–1983.

——. *Verteidigungsausschuss. Stenographisches Protokoll: Anhörung von sachverständigen zum Thema 'Alternative Strategien.'* Bonn: 10. Wahlperiode, 1983/84.

Federal Ministry of Defense. *Force Comparison 1987. NATO and the WARSAW PACT.* Bonn: Press and Information Office of the Federal Republic of Germany, 1988.

Foreign Broadcast Information Service (FBIS) Daily Reports. Soviet Union. Western Europe. 1977–1987. Washington, D.C. National Technical Information Service.

*Die Nachrüstungsdebatte im Deutschen Bundestag: Protokolle einer historischen Entschei-
dung.* Reinbek bei Hamburg: Rowohlt, 1984.

Friedrich Nauman Stiftung. *Für eine Politik der Friedenssicherung.* 2 vols. Bonn:
Liberal, 1983.

NATO Information Service. *NATO Final Communiques: 1949–1974.* Brussels:
1974.

————. *NATO Final Communiques: 1975–1980.* Brussels: 1980. 1981. 1982. 1983.

————. *Progress Report on Intermediate-Range Nuclear Forces (INF)* Brussels: Special
Consultative Group, 1983.

NATO Information Service. *NATO and the Warsaw Pact: Force Comparisons 1982.*
Brussels: 1982.

Office of Research. International Communication Agency. United States of America. "West European Public Opinion on Key Security Issues, 1981–82." (June
1982).

Report of Secretary of Defense Caspar Weinberger. *Annual Report to the Congress,
Fiscal Year 1983.* Washington, D.C.: U.S. Government Printing Office, 1983.

Sozial Demokratischen Partei. *SPD Parteitag Protokoll.* 1976–1984.

SPD Parteivorstand. "Kriegsverhinderung im atomzeitalter: Bericht der Arbeitsgruppe 'Neue Strategien' beim SPD Parteivorstand." Bonn: 1983.

Special Consultative Group (SCG). *Progress Report on Intermediate-Range Nuclear
Forces (INF) 1983.* Brussels: NATO Information Service, 1983.

Statistisches Jahrbuch des Bundesrepublik Deutschland. 1950–1985.

U.S. Department of Defense. *Soviet Military Power.* Washington, D.C.: U.S. Government Printing Office, 1983. 1985. 1987. 1988.

Westdeutsche Rektorenkonferenz. *Übersicht über die Ergebnisse der Wahlen zu den
Studentenvertretungen.* Bonn-Bad Godesberg: Dokumentations-absteilung, Bibliothek und Pressestelle: 1968–1983.

ARCHIVES

Bonn. Abteilung Wissenschaftliche Dokumentation des Deutschen Bundestages—
Parlamentsarchiv; Pressearchiv des Deutschen Bundestages; Pressearchiv des Sozial
Demokratischen Partei, Erich Ollenhauer Haus; Westdeutsche Rektorenkonferenz

Ebenhausen. Pressearchiv Stiftung Wissenschaft und Politik

Frankfurt/Main. Pressearchiv. *Frankfurter Allgemeine Zeitung*

Cambridge, Mass. Government Documents Division, Widener Library, Harvard
University.

NEWSPAPERS AND JOURNALS

The Economist

Europa Archiv

Foreign Affairs

Frankfurter Allgemeine Zeitung

Frankfurter Rundschau

Freiheit der Wissenschaft: Materialien zur Schul- und Hochschulpolitik (1969–1981)

HPI—Hochschulpolitische Informationen (1969–1980)

Die Neue Gesellschaft

The New York Times

Die Politische Meinung

Die Süddeutsche Zeitung

Vorwärts

Die Welt

Die Zeit

SURVEYS

The extent of polling on all topics in the Federal Republic is vast. Those interested in examining these sources further should consult *Umfragen aus der empirischen Sozialforschung, 1945–1982: Datenbestandskatalog des Zentralarchivs für empirische Sozialforschung.* Beiträge zur empirischen Sozialforschung. Zentralarchiv für empirische Sozialforschung. Frankfurt/Main: Campus, 1982. The United States Information Agency has conducted polls on international affairs in West Germany, as well as worldwide, in the entire postwar period. Printouts and computer tapes are available at the Roper Center for Public Opinion Research at the University of Connecticut and at the National Archives in Washington, D.C.

Institut für Demoskopie, Allensbach. *Studenten: Ergebnisse einer Repräsentativbefragung an Universitäten, Technischen Universitäten und Technischen Hochschulen im Winter Semester 1977–78.* 2 vols.

——. *Pazifismus und Antiamerikanismus 1981.*

——. *Das Politische Klima, Mai 1981.*

——. *Die Deutsch-Amerikanischen Beziehungen und die Öffentliche Meinung. Dokumentation des Artikels in der Frankfurter Allgemeine Zeitung Nr. 146 vom 28. Juni 1985.*

Enmid Institute, Bielefeld. *Einstellungen zur Sicherheitspolitik, September 1983.*

——. *Meinungsbild zur Wehrpolitischen Lage, Herbst 1983.*

——. *Meinungsbild zur Wehrpolitischen Lage, Herbst 1984.*

Infratest Wirtschaftsforschung, Munich and Prof. Eberhard Witte. *Akademiker in*

Deutschland: Eine Analyse ihrer beruflichen Situation und ihrer gesellschaftpolitischen Enstellung. Hamburg: Spiegel Verlag, 1980.

West German Defense Ministry: Informations-u. Pressestab 3. *Jugendumfragen im Trend: Ergebnisse der Representativbefragungen bei Jugendlichen 1977 bis 1984.* Munich: 1984.

Wildenmann, Rudolf. *Eliten in der Bundesrepublik 1968.* Mannheim: Universität, 1969.

Wildenmann, Rudolf, and Werner Kaltefleiter. *Westdeutsche Führungsschicht 1972.* Mannheim: Universität Mannheim, 1973.

Wildenmann, Rudolf et al. *Führungsschicht in der Bundesrepublik Deutschland 1981.* Mannheim: Universität Mannheim, 1982.

INTERVIEWS

Apel, Hans. West German Defense Minister, 1979–1982. Bonn. June 28, 1984.

Bartolomai, Reinhold. SPD politician in Hesse. Mainz. June 18, 1984.

Bastian, Gert. Former Bundeswehr General. Member of the Green Parliamentary Fraction, 1983–. Bonn. July 3, 1984.

Baudissen, Wolf. Former West German General in the Bundeswehr. Director of the Institute for Peace Research at the University of Hamburg. Reinbek bei Hamburg. June 22, 1984.

Becker, Kurt. Journalist and West German government spokesman from October 1980 to April 1982. Grashütten bei Hamburg. June 21, 1984, and Hamburg July 1, 1985.

Bertram, Christoph. Foreign affairs journalist at *Die Zeit.* Hamburg. July 1, 1985.

Bittorf, Wilhelm. Security and foreign affairs correspondent at *Der Spiegel.* Hamburg. July 1, 1985.

Bomsdorf, Falk. Strategic analyst. Ebenhausen. July 3, 1985.

Bulow, Andreas von. Former Minister for Science and Technology in the Schmidt government. SPD member of the Bundestag. Bonn. June 28, 1984.

Busche, Jürgen. Cultural affairs correspondent for the *FAZ.* Frankfurt/Main. June 18, 1985.

Corterier, Peter. SPD member of the Bundestag. *Staatsminister* in the West German Foreign Ministry, June 1981 to October 1982. Cambridge, Mass. April 25, 1984.

Falenski, Hans-Joachim. Staff member of the CDU/CSU delegation in the Bundestag. Bonn. June 27, 1984.

Feldmeyer, Karl. Security correspondent for the *FAZ.* Bonn. July 5, 1984.

Fetscher, Iring. Professor of political science, University of Frankfurt. Frankfurt/Main. June 18, 1984.

Gaus, Günter. Author, journalist. *Staatssekretär* and first Director of the West German representation in East Germany, 1974 to January 1981. Reinbek bei Hamburg. June 22, 1984.

Gillessen, Günter. Journalist at the *FAZ*. Frankfurt/Main. June 18, 1984.

Grüber, Edmund. Official at ARD Aktuell television in Hamburg. June 28, 1985.

Guha, Anton-Andreas. Security correspondent at the *Frankfurter Rundschau*. Frankfurt/Main. June 17, 1984.

Heise, Dr. Hans Heinrich. Member of the planning staff, West German defense ministry. Bonn. June 26, 1984.

Held, Robert. Editor, *FAZ*. Frankfurt/Main. June 14, 1985.

Hoffmann, Günter. Political correspondent at *Die Zeit*. Bonn. June 1984 and June 1985

Horn, Erwin. SPD member of the Bundestag. Member of the Defense Committee. Bonn. June 27, 1984.

Ischinger, Wolfgang. Assistant to West Germany Foreign Minister Hans-Dietrich Genscher. Bonn. July 4, 1984.

Jahn, Egbert. Professor of Political Science, University of Frankfurt. Frankfurt/Main. June 14, 1984.

Kaiser, Karl. Director of the West German Society for Foreign Policy. Cambridge, Mass. Spring 1986.

Koppe, Karl-Heinz. Director of the Deutsche Gesellschaft für Friedens- und Konfliktforschung. Bad-Godesberg. June 26, 1985.

Kubbig, Dr. Bernd. W. Research Fellow, *Hessische Stiftung für Friedens- und Konfliktforschung*. Frankfurt. June 17, 1984.

Leister, Klaus-Dieter. State Secretary in the West German Defense Ministry, January 1981 to October 1982. Dusseldorf. June 20, 1984.

Lowenthal, Richard. Professor of political science and member of the Social Democratic Party. Cambridge, Mass. January 6, 1985.

Lutz, Dieter S. Assistant Director of the Institute for Peace Research at the University of Hamburg. Reinbek bei Hamburg. June 22, 1984.

Naumann, Michael. Journalist at *Der Spiegel* and editor at *Rowohlt*. Hamburg. June 21, 1984.

Nerlich, Uwe. Strategic analyst and director of research at Foundation for Science and Politics at Ebenhausen. Ebenhausen. July 3, 1985.

Penner, Wilfried. SPD member of the Bundestag. Bonn. June 27, 1984.

Pflüger, Friedbert. Former national chairman of the RCDS and press secretary for Bundespresident Richard von Weizäcker. Bonn. June 26, 1985.

Pohrt, Wolfgang. Freelance journalist and commentator. Hannover. July 2, 1985.

Rühl, Lothar. Assistant Secretary of Defense for International Security Affairs, West German Defense Ministry. Bonn. June 26, 1984.

Ruhle, Hans. Director of the planning staff in the West German Defense Ministry, 1982–. Bonn. June 26, 1984.

Ruhrfus, Jürgen. Career diplomat, director of foreign policy in the West German Defense Ministry (1976–1979), and adviser to Chancellor Helmut Schmidt, 1976–1982. Bonn. July 3, 1984.

Ruth, Frederick. Ambassador for Disarmament and Arms Control in the West German Foreign Ministry. Bonn. June 26, 1984.

Scheuch, Erwin. Director of the Institute of Applied Social Research at the University of Cologne. Cologne. June 20, 1985.

Schilly, Otto. Member of the Green delegation in the Bundestag. Bonn. July 3, 1984.

Schmidt, Helmut. West German Chancellor, 1974–1981. New York. September 30, 1985.

Sommer, Theo. Editor of *Die Zeit.* Hamburg. July 1, 1985.

Stratmann, K. Peter. Strategic analyst at the Foundation for Science and Politics at Ebenhausen. Ebenhausen. July 3, 1985.

Stützle, Walter. Director of the planning staff in the West German Defense Ministry, 1974–1982. Bonn. June 29, 1984.

Staden, Bernd von. Career diplomat in the West German Foreign Ministry. Bonn. National security adviser to Chancellor Helmut Schmidt. *Staatsekretär* in the Foreign Ministry from June 1981. July 2, 1984.

Voigt, Karsten. Speaker on foreign policy of the SPD delegation in the Bundestag. Frankfurt/Main. June 15, 1984.

Weisser, Capt. Ulrich. Assistant for National Security, West German Chancellor's Office. Bonn. June 25, 1984.

Zundel, Rolf. Political correspondent at *Die Zeit.* June 26, 1984.

BOOKS AND ARTICLES

Adenauer, Konrad. *Erinnerungen 1945–1953.* Stuttgart: Deutsche Verlagsanstalt, 1965.

——. *Erinnerungen 1953–1955.* Stuttgart: Deutsche Verlagsanstalt, 1966.

——. *Erinnerungen 1955–1959.* Stuttgart: Deutsche Verlagsanstalt, 1967.

——. *Reden 1917–1967: Eine Auswahl.* Edited by Hans-Peter Schwarz. Stuttgart: Deutsche Verlagsanstalt, 1975.

Konrad Adenauer Stiftung. *Bildungssystem und Berufsaussichten von Hochschulabsolventen.* Stuttgart: Bonn Aktuell, 1978.

Adler, Kenneth P., and Douglas A. Wertman. "West European Security Concerns for the Eighties: Is NATO in Trouble?" Washington, D.C.: U.S. International Communication Agency, 1981.

Ahfeldt, Horst. *Eine Andere Verteidigung: Alternativen zur Atomaren Abschreckung.* Munich: Hanser, 1973.

———. *Verteidigung und Frieden.* Munich: Hanser, 1976.

———. *Defensive Verteidigung.* Reinbek bei Hamburg: Rowohlt, 1983.

Adomeit, Hannes. *Soviet Risk-Taking and Crisis Behavior: A Theoretical and Empirical Analysis.* London: George Allen & Unwin, 1982.

Aktion Sühnezeichnen/Friedensdienste. *Keine neue Waffen in der Bundesrepublik.* Bornheim: Vamus, 1982.

Albrecht, Ulrich. *Kündigt den Nachrüstungsbeschluss!* Frankfurt/Main: Fischer, 1982.

Alexander, Jeffrey. *Theoretical Logic in Sociology.* Vol. 1, *Positivism, Presuppositions, and Current Controversies.* Berkeley: University of California Press, 1983.

Allerbeck, Klaus. *Demokratisierung und soziale Wandel in der Bundesrepublik Deutschland: Sekundaranalyse von Umfragedaten, 1953–1974.* Opladen: Westdeutscher, 1976.

Almond, Gabriel A. "Public Opinion and National Security Policy." *Public Opinion Quarterly* 20 (Summer 1956):371–78.

Almond, Gabriel A., and Sidney Verba, eds. *The Civic Culture Revisited.* Boston: Little, Brown, 1980.

Alt, Franz. *Frieden ist Möglich. Die Politik der Bergpredigt.* Munich: Piper, 1983.

Apel, Hans et al. *Sicherheitspolitik contra Frieden? Ein Forum zur Friedensbewegung.* Berlin and Bonn: J. H. W. Dietz, 1981.

Arend, Peter. *Die innerparteilische Entwicklung der SPD, 1966–1975.* Konard Adenauer Stiftung Sozialwissenschaftliches Forschungsinstitut. Sozialwissenschaftliche Studien zur Politik, Band 7. Bonn: Eicholz Verlag, 1975.

Arndt, Hans-Joachim. *Die staatliche geforderte Friedens- und Konfliktforschung in der Bundesrepublik Deutschland von 1970 bis 1979.* Munich: Bayerische Staatskanzlei, 1980.

———. "Betrachtungen zur Geschichte, Wesen und Kritik der Friedensforschung." In Klaus Hornung, ed., *Frieden ohne Utopie,* 52–90. Krefeld: Sinus, 1983.

Aron, Raymond. *Peace and War: A Theory of International Relations.* Translated by Richard Howard and Annette Baker Fox. Malabar, Florida: Robert E. Krieger Publishing Company, 1981.

———. *In Defense of Decadent Europe.* South Bend: Regency/Gateway, 1977.

———. "George Kennan's Isolationism." *Washington Quarterly* (Fall 1979).

———. "Hope and Despair in the Western Camp." *Encounter* 58, no. 6 (June–July 1982): 121–129.

———. *Memoires. 50 ans de reflexion politique.* Paris: Julliard, 1983.

———. *Politics and History.* Translated and edited by Miriam Bernheim Conant. New York: The Free Press, 1978. Reprint. New Brunswick: Transaction, 1984.

——. *History, Truth, Liberty: Selected Writings of Raymond Aron.* Edited by Franciszek Draus. Chicago: University of Chicago Press, 1985.

——. *Clausewitz: Philosopher of War.* Translated by Christine Booker and Norman Stone. Englewood Cliffs, N.J.: Prentice-Hall, 1985.

Augstein, Rudolf. *Meinungen zu Deutschland.* Frankfurt/Main: Suhrkamp, 1967.

Bahr, Egon. "Vortrag in der Evangelischen Akademie in Tutzing am 15.7.1963." In Peter Brandt and Herbert Ammon, eds., *Die Linke und die nationale Frage,* 235–40. Reinbek bei Hamburg: Rowohlt, 1981.

——. *SPD. Portrait einer Partie.* Munich: Gunter Olzog, 1980.

——. "Zehn Thesen über Frieden und Abrüstung." In *Sicherheitspolitik contra Frieden? Ein Forum zur Friedensbewegung,* 10–17. Berlin and Bonn: J. H. W. Dietz, 1981.

——. *Was wird aus den Deutschen?* Reinbek bei Hamburg: Rowohlt, 1982.

——. "Sicherheitspartnerschaft." *Neue Gesellschaft* (November 1982):1041–53.

——. "Neokonservatismus und Sicherheitspolitik." *Neue Gesellschaft* (November 1982):1041–45.

——. *Zum europäischen Frieden. Eine Antwort auf Gorbatschow.* Berlin: Siedler, 1988.

Bahro, Rudolf. *Die Alternative—Zur Kritik des real existierenden Sozialismus.* Reinbek bei Hamburg: Rowohlt, 1980.

——. *Elemente einer neuen Politik.* Berlin: Olle and Wolter, 1980. Translated by David Fernbach under the title *Socialism and Survival.* London: Heretic Books, 1982.

——. *Wahnsinn mit Methode. Über die Logik der Blockkonfrontation, die Friedensbewegung, die Sowjet Union und die DKP.* Berlin: Olle und Wolter, 1982.

——. "The SPD and the Peace Movement." *New Left Review* (January–February 1982):20–31.

Baker, Kendall, Dalton, Russel J., and Hildebrandt, Kai. *Germany Transformed: Political Culture and the New Politics.* Cambridge, Mass: Harvard University Press, 1981.

Baring, Arnulf. *Machtwechsel: Die Ära Brandt-Scheel.* Munich: Deutscher Taschenbuch Verlag, 1984.

——. *Unser neuer Grössenwahn: Deutschland zwischen Ost und West.* 2d ed. Stuttgart: Deutsche Verlagsanstalt, 1989.

Bark, Dennis L., and David Gress, *A History of West Germany.* Oxford, UK, and Cambridge, Mass.: Blackwell, 1989.

Bastian, Gert. *Frieden Schaffen! Gedanken zur Sicherheitspolitik.* Munich: Kindler, 1983.

Baudissin, Wolf Graf von, and Dieter S. Lutz. "Kooperative Rüstungssteuerung in Europa." *IFSH-Forschungsberichte* 11 (1979).

Bell, Daniel. *The Coming of Post-Industrial Society.* New York: Basic Books, 1973.

———. *The Cultural Contradictions of Capitalism.* New York: Basic Books, 1976.

———. *The Winding Passage: Essays and Sociological Journeys, 1960–1980.* New York: Basic Books, 1980.

———. *The End of Ideology.* New York: The Free Press, 1965. Reprint. With a new Afterword. Cambridge: Harvard University Press, 1988.

Bender, Peter. *Das Ende des ideologischen Zeitalters.* Berlin: Severin und Siedler, 1981.

Bergsdorf, Wolfgang. "Intellektuelle und Politik." *Aus Politik und Zeitgeschichte* 24 (June 15, 1974): 15–25.

———. "Ohnmacht und Anmassung: Das Verhältnis von Intellektuellen zur Politik." *Die Politische Meinung* 23 (May–June 1978): 53–66.

———. *Herrschaft und Sprache. Studien zur politischen Terminologie der Bundesrepublik Deutschland.* Pfullingen: Neske, 1983.

———, ed. *Die Intellektuellen: Geist und Macht.* Pfüllingen: Neske, 1982.

———, ed. *Worter als Waffen.* Stuttgart: Bonn Aktuell, 1979.

Bering, Dietz. *Die Intellektuellen. Geschichte eines Schimpfwortes.* Frankfurt/Main: Ullstein, 1982.

Berman, Russell A. "The Peace Movement Debate: Provisional Conclusions" *Telos,* no. 57 (Fall 1983): 129–44.

Bickerich, Wolfram, ed. *SPD und Grüne: Das neue Bündnis?* Reinbek bei Hamburg: Rowohlt, 1985.

Bittorf, Wilhelm. "Schiessplatz der Supermächte." *Der Spiegel,* nos. 28–30 (1981).

Bloch, Ernst. *Erbschaft dieser Zeit.* Frankfurt/Main: Suhrkamp, 1962.

Bloch, Marc. *Strange Defeat.* New York: Norton, 1968.

Böll, Heinrich. *Heinrich Böll Werke: Essayistische Schriften und Reden 2, 1964–1972.* Edited by Bernd Balzer. Cologne: Kiepenheuer and Witsch, 1979–80.

———. *Vermintes Gelände: Essayistische Schriften, 1977–1981.* Cologne: Kiepenheuer and Witsch, 1982.

———. *Ein- und Zusprüche: Schriften, Reden und Prosa, 1981–1983.* Cologne: Kiepenheuer and Witsch, 1984.

———. *Die Fähigkeit zu trauern: Schriften und Reden, 1983–1985.* Colonge: Kiepenheuer and Witsch, 1986.

Böll, Heinrich, ed. *Verantwortlich für Polen?* Reinbek bei Hamburg: Rowohlt, 1982.

Bölling, Klaus. *Die letzten 30 Tage des Kanzlers Helmut Schmidt. Ein Tagebuch.* Reinbek bei Hamburg: Rowohlt, 1982.

Bomsdorf, Falk. "Arms Control as a Process of Self-Restraint: The Workings of Western Negotiating Policy." In Uwe Nerlich, ed., *Soviet Power and Western Negotiating Policies,* vol. 2, 67–116. Cambridge, Mass.: Ballinger, 1983.

Bossle, Lothar, ed. *Konservative Bilanz der Reformjahre. Kompendium des mondernen christlich-freiheitlichen Konservatismus.* Würzburg: Naumann, 1981.

Boudon, Raymond. *L'Ideologie: L'origine des idees recues.* Paris: Fayard, 1986.

Bracher, Karl Dietrich. *The German Dictatorship.* Translated by Jean Steinberg. New York: Praeger, 1970.

———. "The Role of Hitler: Problems of Interpretation." In Walter Laqueur, ed., *Fascism: A Reader's Guide.* Berkeley: University of California, 1976.

———. *Europa in der Krise.* Frankfurt/Main: Ullstein, 1979.

———. *Europa und Entspannung.* Frankfurt/Main: Ullstein, 1979.

———. *Zeitgeschichtliche Kontroversen.* 4th ed. Munich: Piper, 1980.

———. *Geschichte und Gewalt. Zur Politik im 20. Jahrhundert.* Berlin: Severin und Siedler, 1981.

———. *Zeit der Ideologien.* Stuttgart. Deutsche Verlags-Anstalt, 1982. Translated by Ewald Osers under the title *Age of Ideologies.* London: Weidenfeld and Nicolson, 1984.

Bracher, Karl, Wolfgang Jäger, and Werner Link. *Republik im Wandel, 1969–1974: Die Ära Brandt.* Vol. 5 of *Geschichte der Bundesrepublik Deutschland.* Stuttgart: Deutsche Verlags-Anstalt, 1985.

Brandt, Peter, and Herbert Ammon, eds. *Die Linke und die nationale Frage.* Reinbek bei Hamburg: Rowohlt, 1981.

Brandt, Willy. *A Peace Policy for Europe.* Translated by Joel Carmichael. New York: Holt, Rinehart and Winston, 1969.

———. *Plädoyer für die Zukunft. Beiträge zur deutschen Politik.* Rev. ed. Frankfurt/Main: Europäische Verlagsanstalt, 1971.

———. *Bundeskanzler Brandt. Reden und Interviews.* Hamburg: Hoffman und Campe, 1971.

———. *Wille zum Frieden: Perspektiven der Politik.* Hamburg: Hoffman und Campe, 1971. 2d ed. 1972.

———. *Plädoyer für die Zukunft. Beiträge zur deutschen Politik.* Frankfurt/Main: Europäische Verlagsanstalt, 1972.

———. *Bendestagsreden.* Bonn: Verlag as studio, 1972.

———. *Freiheit oder Sozialismus?* Bonn: Vorstand der SPD, 1976.

———. *Freiheit und Sozialismus.* Bonn: Vorstand der SPD, 1977.

———. *Godesberg nicht verspielen!* Bonn: Vorstand der SPD, 1979.

———. *Willy Brandt . . . Auf der Zinne der Partei . . . : Parteitagsreden 1960–1983.* Edited by Werner Krause and Wolfgang Gröf. Berlin and Bonn: Dietz, 1984.

———. *Die Abschiedsrede.* Berlin: Siedler, 1987.

Brauch, Hans Günter, *Entwicklung und Ergebnisse der Friedensforschung (1969–1978).* Frankfurt am Main: Hessische Stiftung für Friedens- und Konfliktforschung, 1979.

Brauch, Hans Günter, ed. *Sicherheitspolitik am Ende?* Gerlingen: Bleicher, 1984.

Brint, Stephen. "Liberal Attitudes of Professionals." *American Journal of Sociology* 90, no. 1 (July 1984):30–71.

Brüggemann, H., et al. *Über den Mangel an politischen Kultur in Deutschland.* Berlin: Klaus Wagenbach, 1978.

Brüseke, Franz, and Hans-Martin Grosse-Oetringhaus. *Blätter von Unten. Alternativzeitungen in der Bundesrepublik.* Offenbach: Verlag 2000, 1981.

Bruce-Briggs, B. *The New Class.* New Brunswick, N.J.: Transaction Books, 1979.

Bukowski, Vladimir. *Dieser stechende Schmerz der Freiheit: Russischer Traum und westliche Realität.* Translated by Anton Manzella. Stuttgart: Seewald, 1983.

———. *Pazifisten gegen den Frieden.* Translated by Hanni Tarsis. Bern: SOI Verlag, 1983.

———. "The Peace Movement and the Soviet Union." *Commentary* (June 1982).

Bull, Hedley. *The Anarchical Society.* New York: Columbia University Press, 1977.

Bundesminister für Bildung und Wissenschaft. *Thema: Student und Gesellschaft: Ergebnisse einer repräsentativen Befragung an wissenschaftlichen Hochschulen und Fachschulen in der Bundesrepublik.* Bonn: 1982.

———. "Studiensitutation und studentische Orientierungen. Eine repräsentative Untersuchung im Wintersemester 1982/83." In *Bildung Wissenschaft Aktuell,* no. 7 (October 4, 1984). Bonn: 1984.

Bundesvorstand der Grünen. *Entrüstet Auch: Analysen zur Atomaren Bedröhung, Wege zum Frieden.* Bonn: 1981.

Bundy, McGeorge, Kennan, George, McNamara, Robert, and Smith, Gerard. "Nuclear Weapons and the Atlantic Alliance." *Foreign Affairs* 60 (1981–1982):753–768.

Brzezinski, Zbigniew. *Power and Principle: Memoirs of the National Security Adviser, 1977–1981.* Rev. ed. New York: Farrar, Straus, Giroux, 1985.

Carr, Edward Hallett. *The Twenty Years' Crisis, 1919–1939.* New York: Harper and Row, 1964.

Carr, Jonathan. *Helmut Schmidt.* Düsseldorf: Econ, 1985. [Translated into English as *Helmut Schmidt: Helmsman of Germany.* New York: St. Martin's Press, 1985.].

Castoriadis, Cornelius. *Devant la Guerre.* Paris. Fayard, 1981.

CDU-Bundesgeschaftsstelle, ed. *Frieden und Freiheit. Die Argumente der CDU zur aktuellen Friedensdiskussion.* Bonn, 1981.

Childs, David. *From Schumacher to Brandt: The Story of German Socialism, 1945–1965.* New York and London: Oxford University Press, 1966.

Churchill, Winston. *The Second World War.* Vol. 1: *The Gathering Storm.* Boston: Houghton Mifflin, 1948.

———. *The Second World War.* Vol. 2: *Their Finest Hour.* Boston: Houghton Mifflin, 1948.

Clausewitz, Carl von. *On War.* Edited and translated by Michael Howard and Peter Paret. Princeton: Princeton University Press, 1976.

Cohen, Eliot. "Guessing Game: A Reappraisal of Systems Analysis." In Samuel P. Huntington, ed., *The Strategic Imperative: New Policies for American Security*, 163–92. Cambridge, Mass.: Ballinger, 1982.

Conradt, David P. *The German Polity*. 3d ed. White Plains, N.Y.: Longman, 1986.

Converse, Phillip E. "The Nature of Belief Systems in Mass Publics." In David E. Apter, ed., *Ideology and Discontent*, 202–61. New York: Free Press, 1964.

———. "Attitudes and Non-Attitudes: Continuation of a Dialogue." In Edward R. Tufte, ed., *The Quantitative Analysis of Social Problems*, 168–90. Reading, Mass.: Addison-Wesley, 1970.

Coppik, Manfred, and Jürgen Roth. *Am Tor der Hölle: Strategien der Verführung zum Atomkrieg*. Cologne: Kiepenheuer and Witsch, 1982.

Cox, Caroline, and Roger Scruten. *Peace Studies. A Critical Survey*. London: Alliance Publishers, 1983.

Craig, Gordon. *The Germans*. New York: G. P. Putnam's Sons, 1982.

Craig, Gordon, and Alexander George. *Force and Statecraft*. New York: Oxford University Press, 1983.

Crozier, Michel J., Samuel P. Huntington, and Joji Watanuki. *The Crisis of Democracy: Report on the Governability of Democracies to the Trilateral Commission*. New York: New York University Press, 1975.

Cziempiel, Ernst-Otto. "Kritik des Gutachten von Herrn Professor Hans-Joachim Arndt zur Lage der DGFK." *Beiträge zur Konflikforschung* 1 (1982):169–72.

Dahrendorf, Ralf. "Die Revolution, die nie stattfand." *Die Zeit*, no. 20 (May 13, 1988): 3.

Dallek, Robert. *Franklin D. Roosevelt and American Foreign Policy: 1932–1945*. New York: Oxford University Press, 1980.

Deile, Volkmar, ed. *Zumutungen des Friedens*. Reinbek bei Hamburg: Rowholt, 1982.

Deutscher Gesellschaft für Friedens- und Konfliktforschung. *Dokumentation zur Tätigkeit der Deutschen Gesellschaft für Fridens- und Konfliktforschung, 1970–1983*. Bonn-Bad Godesberg: Deutsche Gesellschaft für Friedens und Konfliktforschung, 1983.

Dickhoener, Ericka, ed. *Bildungssystem und Berufsaussichten von Hochschulabsolventen*. Bonn: Konrad Adenauer Stiftung, 1978.

Does, Karl-Josef. "Abschied vom Protest oder Ruhe vor dem Sturm?" *Aus Politik und Zeitgeschichte* 12, no. 72 (March 26, 1977).

Dohnanyi, Klaus von. *Education and Youth Employment in the Federal Republic of Germany*. Berkeley: Carnegie Council on Policy Studies in Higher Education, 1978.

Draper, Theodore. "The Western Misalliance." In *Present History*, 51–114. New York: Random House, 1983.

Dutschke, Rudi. *Mein langer Marsch. Reden, Schiften und Tagebücher aus zwanzig Jahren.* Reinbek bei Hamburg. Rowohlt, 1980.

———. "Zur nationalen Frage." In Peter Brandt and Herbert Ammon, eds., *Die Linke und die nationale Frage. Dokumente zur deutschen Einheit seit 1945,* 334–335. Reinbek bei Hamburg: Rowholt, 1981.

Duve, Freimut, ed. *Die Nachrüstungsdebatte im Deutschen Bundestag.* Reinbek bei Hamburg: Rowohlt, 1984.

Easterlin, Richard. *Birth and Fortune.* 2d ed. Chicago: University of Chicago Press, 1987.

Eichberg, Henning. *Nationale Identität: Entfremdung und nationale Frage in der Industriegesellschaft.* Munich: Langen-Muller, 1978.

Eichenberg, Richard. *Public Opinion and National Security in Western Europe.* Ithaca: Cornell University Press, 1989.

Engelmann, Bernt. *Weissbuch: Frieden.* Cologne: Keupenheuer and Witsch, 1982.

Engelmann, Bernt, et al., eds. *Es geht, es geht . . : Zeitgenössische Schriftsteller und ihr Beitrag zum Frieden—Grenzen und Möglichkeiten.* Munich: W. Goldmann, 1982.

Eppler, Erhard. *Spannungsfelder. Beiträge zur Politik unserer Zeit.* Stuttgart: Seewald, 1968.

———. *Ende oder Wende: Von der Machbarkeit des Notwendigen.* 2d ed. Berlin: Kohlhammer, 1975.

———. *Wege aus der Gefahr.* Reinbek bei Hamburg: Rowohlt, 1981.

———. *Weichen Stellen . . . Rede, 1973–1980.* Tübingen: Widerspruch, 1981.

———. *Die tödliche Utopie der Sicherheit.* Reinbek bei Hamburg: Rowohlt, 1983.

———. *Wie Feuer und Wasser: Sind Ost und West friedensfähig?* Reinbek bei Hamburg: Rowohlt, 1988.

———, ed. *Grundwerte für ein neues Godesberger Programm. Die Texte der Grundwerte-Kommission der SPD.* Reinbek bei Hamburg: Rowohlt, 1984.

Erler, Hans. *Fritz Erler contra Willy Brandt.* Stuttgart: Seewald, 1976.

European Security Study. *Strengthening Conventional Deterrence in Europe.* New York: St. Martin's Press, 1983.

Flynn, Gregory A., and Hans Rattinger, eds. *The Public and Atlantic Defense.* Totowa, N.J.: Rowman and Allanheld, 1984.

Freedman, Lawrence. *The Evolution of Nuclear Strategy.* New York and London: St. Martin's Press, 1981.

Friedberg, Aaron L. *The Weary Titan: Britain and the Experience of Relative Decline, 1895–1905.* Princeton, N.J.: Princeton University Press, 1988.

Friedrich Ebert Stiftung, ed. *Programme der deutschen Sozial-demokratie.* Bonn: Friedrich Ebert Stiftung, 1978.

Fritsch-Bournazel, Renata. *L'Union Sovietique et les deux Allemagnes.* Paris: Presses de la Fondatrion National des Sciences Politiques, 1979.

Funke, Manfred. ed. *Friedensforschung—Entscheidungshilfe gegen Gewalt.* Munich: Paul List, 1975.

Galtung, Johan. *Strukturelle Gewalt.* Reinbek bei Hamburg: Rowohlt, 1975.

———. *Anders Verteidigen.* Reinbek bei Hamburg: Rowohlt, 1982.

Gaus, Günter. "Opposition in der Bundesrepublik: Die Intellektuellen." In *Die Süddeutsche Zeitung,* no. 107, May 3/4, 1963, p. 71.

———. *Texte zur deutschen Frage.* Darmstadt und Neuwied: Luchterhand, 1981.

———. *Wo Deutschland Liegt.* Hamburg: Hoffmann und Campe. 1983.

———. "Günter Gaus." In *Reden über das eigene Land: Deutschland.* Munich: C. Bertelsmann, 1983.

———. "Schöner ist der Friede nicht zu haben: Zur Aussen- und Deutschlandpolitik." *Kursbuch* 71 (March 1983).

———. *Deutschland und die NATO. Drei Reden.* Reinbek bei Hamburg: Rowohlt, 1984.

Geertz, Clifford. *The Interpretation of Cultures.* New York: Basic Books, 1973.

Gella, Aleksander, ed. *The Intelligentsia and the Intellectuals.* London and Beverly Hills: Sage, 1976.

Gelman, Harry. *The Brezhnev Politburo and the Decline of Detente.* Ithaca: Cornell University Press, 1984.

Giddens, Anthony. *Social Theory and Modern Sociology.* Stanford: Stanford University Press, 1987.

———. *The Nation-State and Violence.* Berkeley: University of California Press, 1987.

Gilbert, Martin. *The Roots of Appeasement.* London: Weidenfeld and Nicolson, 1967.

———. *Winston S. Churchill: The Prophet of Truth, 1922–1939.* Boston: Houghton Mifflin, 1977.

Gilpin, Robert G. *War and Change in World Politics.* New York: Cambridge University Press, 1981.

Glotz, Peter. *Die Arbeit der Zuzpitzung. Über die Organisation einer regierungsfähigen Linken.* Berlin: Siedler, 1984.

———, ed., *Ziviler Ungehorsam im Rechtsstaat.* Frankfurt/Main: Suhrkamp, 1983.

Glucksmann, Andre. *La Force du Vertige.* Paris: Grasset, 1983.

Göbel, Ulrich, and W. Schlaffke, eds. *Berichte zur Bildungspolitik 1978 des Instituts der deutschen Wirtschaft.* Cologne: Deutscher Instituts Verlag, 1978.

Gorbachev, Mikhail. *Perestroika. New Thinking for Our Country and the World.* New York: Harper and Row, 1987.

———. *Toward a Better World.* New York: Richardson and Steirman, 1987.

Gortz, Franz Josef, ed. *Günter Grass: Auskunft für Leser.* Berlin and Neuwied: Luchterhand, 1984.

Gourevitch, Peter. "The Second Image Reversed: The International Sources of Domestic Politics." *International Organization* 32 (Autumn 1978).

Grass, Günter. *Über das Selbstverständliche. Politische Schriften.* Berlin: Luchterhand, 1968. Reprint. Munich: Deutscher Taschenbuch Verlag, 1969.

——. *Der Bürger und seine Stimme: Reden, Aufsätze, Kommentare.* Darmstadt und Neuwied: Luchterhand, 1974.

——. *Denkzettel: Politische Reden und Aufsätze.* Darmstadt und Neuwied: Luchterhand, 1978.

——. *Widerstand Lernen. Politische Gegenreden, 1980–1983.* Darmstadt und Neuwied: Luchterhand, 1984.

——. *On Writing and Politics, 1967–1983.* Translated by Ralph Mannheim. New York: Harcourt, Brace, Jovanovich, 1985.

Griffith, William E. *The Ostpolitik of the Federal Republic of Germany.* Cambridge: MIT Press, 1978.

Grosser, Alfred. *The Western Alliance.* New York: Viking, 1980.

Bundesvorstand der Grünen. *Entrüstet Euch. Analysen zur Atomaren Bedrohung. Wege zum Frieden. Wir Wollen Leben.* Bonn: 1981.

Guha, Anton-Andreas. *Die Neutronenbombe oder Die Perversion menschlichen Denkens.* Frankfurt/Main: Fischer Taschenbuch, 1977.

——. *Die Nachrüstung. Der Holocaust Europas.* Freiburg i. Br.: Dreisam, 1981.

——. *Ende: Tagebuch aus dem 3. Weltkrieg.* Königstein, Ts.: Athenäum, 1983.

Habermas, Jürgen. *Strukturwandel der Öffentlichkeit.* Neuwied and Berlin: Luchterhand, 1962. Translated by Thomas Burger with the assistance of Frederick Lawrence under the title *The Structural Transformation of the Public Sphere: An Inquiry into a Category of Bourgeois Society.* Cambridge: MIT Press, 1989.

——. *Toward a Rational Society.* Translated by Jeremy Shapiro. Boston: Beacon Press, 1970.

——. "Ziviler Ungehorsam—Testfall für den demokratischen Rechtsstaat. Wider den autoritären Legalismus in der Bundesrepublik." In Peter Glotz, ed., *Ziviler Ungehorsam im Rechtsstaat,* 29–53. Frankfurt/Main: Suhrkamp, 1983.

——. *Theorie des kommunikativen Handelns.* 2 vols. Frankfurt/Main: Suhrkamp, 1981.

——, ed. *Stichworte zur "Geistigen Situation der Zeit."* Frankfurt/Main: Suhrkamp, 1979. Translated by Andrew Buchwalter under the title *Observations on the "Spiritual Situation of the Age."* Cambridge: MIT Press, 1984.

Habermas, Jürgen, and Niklas Luhmann. *Theorie der Gesellschaft oder Sozialtechnologie.* Frankfurt/Main: Suhrkamp, 1971.

Haftendorn, Helga. *Sicherheit und Entspannung. Zur Aussenpolitik der Bundesrepublik Deutschland 1955–1982.* Baden-Baden: Nomos, 1983.

——. "Zur Vorgeschichte des NATO Doppelbeschlusses von 1979." *Vierteljahreshefte,* no. 2 (1985):244–87.

Hahn, Walter. "West Germany's Ostpolitik. The Grand Design of Egon Bahr." *Orbis* 26, no. 4 (Winter 1973):859–80.

Hall, John A. *Liberalism.* London: Paladin, 1988.

Hamilton, Alexander, James Madison, and John Jay. *The Federalist Papers.* New York: Mentor Books, 1961.

Hassner, Pierre. "On ne badine pas avec la paix." *Revue Francaise de Science Politique* 23, no. 6 (1973):1268–1303.

———. "Western European Perceptions of the USSR." *Daedalus* 108, no. 1 (Winter 1979):113–50.

———. "Arms Control and the Politics of Pacifism in Protestant Europe." In Uwe Nerlich, ed., *Soviet Power and Western Negotiating Policies,* vol. 2, 117–50. Cambridge, Mass.: Ballinger, 1983.

———. "Moscow and the Western Alliance." *Problems of Communism* (May–June 1981):37–54.

———. "Pacifisme et terreur." In Pierre Lellouche, ed., *Pacifisme et Dissuasion,* 155–76. Paris: Institut Francais des Relations Internationales, 1983.

———. "Recurrent Stresses, Resilient Structures." In Robert W. Tucker and Linda Wrigley, eds., *The Atlantic Alliance and Its Critics,* 61–94. New York: Praeger, 1983.

———. "Was geht in Deutschland vor?" *Europa Archiv* 37 (1982):517–26; English version, "The Shifting Foundation" *Foreign Policy,* no. 48 (Fall 1982):3–20, without notes.

———. Zwei deutsche Staaten in Europa: Gibt es gemeinsame Interessen in der internationalen Politik?" In Werner Weidenfeld, ed., *Die Identität der Deutschen,* 294–323. Munich: Hanser 1983.

Hättich, Manfred. *Weltfrieden durch Friedfertigkeit? Ein Antwort an Franz Alt.* Munich: Olzog, 1983.

Heller, Mikhail, and Alexander Nekrich. *Utopia in Power: The History of the Soviet Union from 1917 to the Present.* Translated by Phyllis B. Carlos. New York: Summit Books, 1986.

Hennis, Wilhelm. "Meinungsforschung und repräsentative Demokratie." In *Politik als praktische Wissenschaft,* 125–61. Munich: Piper, 1968.

———. *Die deutsche Unruhe: Studien zur Hochschulpolitik.* Hamburg: Christian Wagner, 1969.

———. *Demokratisierung: Zur Problematik eines Begriffs.* 2d ed. Opladen: Westdeutscher, 1972.

———. *Die missverstandene Demokratie.* Freiburg in Br.: Herder, 1973.

———. *Organisierter Sozialismus.* Stuttgart: Klett, 1977.

———. *Politik und praktische Philosophie.* Stuttgart: Keltt, 1977.

Hennis, Wilhelm, P. Graf Kielmansegg, and Ulrich Matz, eds. *Regierbarkeit.* Stuttgart, 1979.

Herf, Jeffrey, "Western Strategy and Public Discussion: The Double Decision Makes Sense" *Telos*, no. 52 (Summer 1982): 114–128.

———. "Illusions of European Neutralism" *Partisan Review* 50, no. 2 (1983):227–243.

———. "The Double Decision Still Makes Sense" *Telos*, no. 56 (Summer 1983):156–71.

———. *Reactionary Modernism: Technology, Culture and Politics in Weimar and the Third Reich*. New York: Cambridge University Press, 1984.

———. "Neutralism and Moral Order in West Germany." In Walter Laqueur and Robert E. Hunter, eds., *European Peace Movements and the Future of the Atlantic Alliance*, 356–401. New Brunswick, New Jersey: Transaction Books, 1985.

———. "War, Peace and the Intellectuals: The West German Peace Movement." *International Security* 10, no. 4 (Spring 1986):172–200.

———. "Center, Periphery, and Dissensus: West German Intellectuals and the Euromissiles." In Liah Greenfeld, ed., *Center: Ideas and Institutions*. Chicago: University of Chicago Press, 1988.

———. "West German Political Culture." *The National Interest*, no. 17 (Fall 1989).

Hertel, Peter and Alfred Paffenholz. *Für eine politische Kirche. Schwerter zu Pflugscharen.* Hannover. Fackelträger, 1982.

Hessische Stiftung für Friedens- und Konfliktforschung. *Publikationenen 1971–1979: Gesamtverzeichnis.* Frankfurt/Main: Hessische Stiftung für Friedens- und Konfliktforschung, 1980.

———. "Bericht über Organisation und Laufende Forschung." *Mitteilungen Nr. 17/1983.* Frankfurt/Main: Hessische Stiftung für Friedens- und Konfliktforschung, 1983.

Hessische Stiftung für Friedens- und Konfliktforschung. *Publikationenen 1971–1986: Gesamtverzeichnis.* Frankfurt/Main: Hessische Stiftung für Friedens- und Konfliktforschung, 1986.

Hillgrüber, Andreas. *Germany and the Two World Wars*. Translated by William C. Kirby. Cambridge: Harvard University Press, 1981.

———. *Hitler's Strategie: Politik und Kriegführung, 1940–1941.* 1965. 2d ed. Munich: Bernard and Graefe, 1982.

Himmelfarb, Gertrude. *The New History and the Old: Critical Essays and Reappraisals.* Cambridge: Harvard University Press, 1987.

Hochschule Information System (HIS). *Studenten zwischen Hochschule und Arbeitswelt.* Munich: K. G. Sauer, 1980.

Hoffmann, Stanley. *Dead Ends: American Foreign Policy in the New Cold War.* Cambridge, Mass.: Ballinger, 1983.

———. *Janus and Minerva: Essays in the Theory and Practice of International Politics.* Boulder: Westview Press, 1987.

Hoffmann-Lange, Ursula, et al. *Konsens und Konflikt zwischen Führungsgruppen in der Bundesrepublik Deutschland.* Frankfurt/Main: Peter D. Lang, 1980.

Hollander, Paul. *Political Pilgrims. Travels of Western Intellectuals to the Soviet Union, China, and Cuba.* New York: Oxford University Press, 1981.

——. *The Survival of the Adversary Culture. Cultural Criticism and Political Escapism in American Society.* New Brunswick, N.J.: Transaction, 1988.

Horkheimer, Max, and Theodor Adorno. *The Dialectic of Enlightenment.* Translated by John Cumming. New York: Herder and Herder, 1974.

Hornung, Klaus, ed. *Frieden ohne Utopie.* Krefeld: Sinus, 1983.

Howard, Michael. *The Causes of Wars.* Cambridge: Harvard University Press, 1983.

Huntington, Samuel P. "Post-Industrial Politics: How Benign Will It Be?" *Comparative Politics* 6, no. 2 (January 1974):174–187.

——. *American Politics: The Promise of Disharmony.* Cambridge: Harvard University Press, 1981.

Huntington, Samuel P., ed. *The Strategic Imperative. New Policies for American Security.* Cambridge, Mass.: Ballinger, 1982.

Inglehart, Ronald. *The Silent Revolution. Changing Values and Political Styles Among Western Publics.* Princeton: Princeton University Press, 1977.

Ikle, Fred C. "Can Nuclear Deterrence Last Out our Century," *Foreign Affairs* 51, no. 2 (1973): 267–285.

International Council on the Future of the University. *German Universities.* New York, 1977.

International Institute for Strategic Studies. *Strategic Survey 1981–1982.* London: 1982.

Jaspers, Karl. *Wohin treibt die Bundesrepublik?* Munich, 1966.

Jenkins, Craig. "Resource Mobilization Theory and the Study of Social Movements." *Annual Review of Sociology: 1983:* 532–33.

Jens, Walter, ed. *In letzter Stunde: Aufruf zum Frieden.* Munich: Kindler, 1982.

Joffe, Josef. "Von der Nachrüstung zur Null-Rüstung. Die Geschichte des 'Doppelbeschlusses.' Innenpolitik war wichtiger als Militärstrategie." *Die Zeit,* no. 27 (November 1981).

——. *The Limited Partnership: Europe, the United States, and the Burdens of Alliance.* Cambridge, Mass.: Ballinger, 1987.

Kagan, Donald. *The Fall of the Athenian Empire.* Ithaca: Cornell University Press, 1987.

Kaiser, Karl. *Friedensforschung in der Bundesrepublik.* Göttingen, 1970.

——. "Prioritäten sozialdemokratischer Aussen- und Sicherheitspolitik." In Jürgen Maruhn and Manfred Wilke, eds., *Wohin treibt die SPD?* 9–27. Munich: Günter Olzog, 1984.

——. "Der Zerfall des Sicherheitspolitischen Konsensus in der Bundesrepublik

Deutschland." In Manfred Funke et al., eds., *Demokratie und Diktatur: Geist und Gestalt politischer Herrschaft in Deutschland und Europa*, 476–92. Bonn: Bundeszentrale für politische Bildung, 1987.

Kaiser, Karl, and Karl Markus Kreis, eds. *Sicherheitspolitik vor neuen Aufgaben.* Frankfurt/Main: Metzer, 1977.

Kaltebrunner, Gerd-Klaus, ed. *Die Herausforderung der Konservativen.* Freiburg i. Br: Herder, 1974.

Katzenstein, Peter J., ed. *Between Power and Plenty: Foreign Economic Policies of Advanced Industrial Societies.* Madison: University of Wisconsin Press, 1978.

Kennedy, Paul. *The Realities Behind Diplomacy. Background Influences on British External Policy, 1865–1980.* London: George Allen and Unwin, 1981.

Keohane, Robert, ed. *Neorealism and Its Critics.* Ithaca: Cornell University Press, 1986.

Kepplinger, Hans Mathias, ed. *Angepasste Aussenseiter. Was Journalisten denken und wie sie arbeiten.* Freiburg i. Br.: Karl Alber, 1979.

——. *Die aktuelle Berichterstattung des Hörfunks: Ein Inhaltsanalyse der Abendnachrichten und politischen Magazine.* Freiburg i. Br.: Karl Alber, 1985.

Kielmansegg, Peter Graf. *Nachdenken über Demokratie.* Stuttgart: Klett-Cotta, 1980.

Kirkpatrick, Jeane J. *Dictatorships and Double Standards. Rationalism and Reason in Politics.* New York: Simon and Schuster, 1982.

Kissinger, Henry. *A World Restored. Metternich, Castlereagh and the Problems of Peace, 1812–1822.* Boston: Houghton Mifflin, 1957. Reprint. Boston: Houghton Mifflin, 1973.

——. "The Future of NATO." *The Atlantic Quarterly* 17, no. 4 (Winter 1979/80): 464–475.

——. *The White House Years.* Boston: Houghton Mifflin, 1979.

Kohl, Helmut. *Zwischen Ideologie und Pragmatismus.* Bonn: Verlag Bonn Aktuell, 1973.

——, ed. *Konrad Adenauer, 1876–1976.* Stuttgart: Belser, 1976.

Komitee für Grundrechte und Demokratie. *Frieden mit anderen Waffen. Fünf Vorschläge zu einer alternativen Sicherheitspolitik.* Reinbek bei Hamburg: Rowohlt, 1983.

Koppe, Karl-Heinz. "Zur Entwickling der Deutschen Gesellschaft für Friedens und Konfliktforschung (DGFK) und der Friedensforschung in der Bundesrepublik Deutschland." in *DGFK Jahrbuch 1979/80.* Baden-Baden: Nomos, 1980.

Krause, Christian, Detlef Lehnert, and Klaus Jürgen Scherer. *Zwischen Revolution und Resignation. Alternative Kultur, politische Grundstrommungen und Hochschuleaktivitäten in der Studentenschaft.* Bonn: Verlag Neue Gesellschaft, 1980.

Kraushaar, Wolfgang. *Was Sollen die Grünen im Parlament?* Frankfurt/Main: Verlag Neue Kritik, 1983.

Kriele, Martin. *Befreiung und politische Aufklärung.* Freiburg i. Br: Herder, 1980.

——. "Das 'Recht der Macht'. Die Normative Kraft des Faktischen und der Friede" *kontinent* 3 (1983): 13–15.

Krippendorf, Ekkehart. *Friedensforschung* (Cologne: Kiepenheuer and Witsch, 1968)

Kristol, Irving. *Reflections of a Neoconservative.* New York: Basic Books, 1983.

Krüger, Horst, ed. *Was ist heute links? Thesen und Theorien zu einer politischen Position.* Munich: 1963.

Krüger, Ingrid, ed. *Mut zue Angst—Schriftsteller für den Frieden.* Darmstadt und Neuwied: Luchterhand, 1981.

——. *Berliner Begegnung zur Friedensförderung. Protokolle des Schriftstellertreffens am 13/14 Dezember 1981.* Darmstadt und Neuwied: Luchterhand, 1981.

——. *Zweite Berliner Begegnung. Den Frieden erklären. Protokolle des zweiten Berliner Schriftstellertreffens am 22/23. April 1983.* Darmstadt und Neuwied: Luchterhand, 1983.

Kühnhardt, Ludger. *Die Universalität der Menschenrechte.* Munich: Günter Olzog, 1987.

Kühnlein, Gertrud. *Die Entwicklung der kritischen Friedensforschung in der Bundesrepublik Deutschland.* Frankfurt/Main, 1978.

Ladd, Everett Carll, Jr., and Seymour Martin Lipset. *The Divided Academy: Professors and Politics.* New York: McGraw-Hill, 1975.

Lafontaine, Oskar. *Angst vor den Freunden. Die Atomwaffen Strategie der Supermächte zerstört die Bundnisse.* Reinbek bei Hamburg: Rowohlt, 1983.

Langguth, Gerd. *Protestbewegung. Entwicklung, Niedergang, Renaissance. Die Neue Linke seit 1968.* Cologne: Verlag Wissenschaft und Politik, 1983.

——. *The Green Factor in German Politics: From Protest Movement to Political Party.* Translated by Richard Strauss. Boulder and London: Westview Press, 1986.

Laqueur, Walter. *Germany Today: A Personal Report.* Boston: Little, Brown, 1985.

Laqueur, Walter, and Robert E. Hunter. *European Peace Movements and the Future of the Atlantic Alliance.* New Brunswick, N.J.: Transaction Books, 1985.

Lattmann, Dieter, ed. *Einigkeit oder Einzelgänger: Dokumentation des Ersten Schriftstellerkongresses des Verbands Deutscher Schriftsteller (VS).* Munich: Kindler Verlag, 1971.

Leinemann, Jürgen. *Die Angst der Deutschen.* Reinbek bei Hamburg: Rowohlt, 1982.

Lellouche, Pierre, ed. *Pacifisme et dissuasion.* Paris: Institut Francais des Relations Internationales, 1983.

Levy, Michel. "Singularites allemandes." *Population et Societes,* no. 118 (November 1978): 1–3.

Lewy, Guenther. "Emancipatory Consciousness in the Federal Republic of Germany." In *False Consciousness.* New Brunswick, N.J.: Transaction Books, 1982.

Linz, Juan J. *The Breakdown of Democratic Regimes. Crisis, Breakdown, and Reequilibration.* Baltimore: Johns Hopkins University Press, 1978.

Lowenthal, Richard. "Der Kampf um die Hochschule und die Zukunft unserer Demokratie." *Hochschulpolitische Information,* no. 23–24 (1971):21–25.

———. *Gesellschaftswandel und Kulturkrise. Zukunftsprobleme der westlichen Demokratien.* Frankfurt/Main: Fischer Taschenbuch, 1979. Translated under the title *Social Change and Cultural Crisis.* New York: Columbia University Press, 1984.

———. "Vom kalten Krieg zur Ostpolitik." In Richard Lowenthal and Hans Peter Schwarz, eds. *Die zweite Republik,* 604–99. Stuttgart: Seewald, 1974.

Lowenthal, Richard, and Hans-Peter Schwarz. *Die Zweite Republik.* Stuttgart: Seewald, 1975.

Lübbe, Hermann. *Unsere stille Kulturrevolution.* Zurich: Edition Interfrom, 1976.

———. *Endstation Terror.* Stuttgart: Seewald, 1978.

———. *Zwischen Trend und Tradition: Überfordert uns die Gegenwart?* Zurich: Edition Interfrom, 1981.

———. *Politischer Moralismus: Der Triumph der Gesinnung über die Urteilskraft.* Berlin: Siedler, 1987.

Lübbe, Hermann, et al. *Tendenzwende? Zur geistigen Situation der Bundesrepublik.* Stuttgart: 1975.

Luhmann, Niklas. *The Differentiation of Society.* Translated by Stephen Holmes and Charles Larmore. New York: Columbia University Press, 1982.

Luttwak, Edward. "Nuclear Strategy: The New Debate." In *Strategy and Politics,* 37–50. New Brunswick, N.J.: Transaction, 1980.

Lutz, Dieter S. *Weltkrieg wider Willen? Die Nuklearwaffen in und für Europa.* Reinbek bei Hamburg: Rowohlt, 1981.

———. "Rüstungswettlauf und Kriegsgefähr." In Dieter S. Lutz, ed., *Sicherheitspolitik am Scheideweg?* 231–56. Baden-Baden: Nomos Verlag, 1982.

———. *Lexikon: Rüstung, Frieden, Sicherheit.* Munich: Beck, 1987.

———, ed. *Die Rüstung der Sowjetunion: Rüstungsdynamik und bürokratische Strukturen.* Baden-Baden: Nomos, 1979.

Lutz, Dieter S., and Egon Bahr. *Gemeinsame Sicherheit. Idee und Konzept.* Vol. 1. Baden-Baden: Nomos, 1986.

Lutz, Ernst. *Lexikon zur Sicherheitspolitik.* Munich. C. H. Beck, 1980.

Marcuse, Herbert. *One-Dimensional Man.* Boston: Beacon Press, 1964.

Maruhn, Jürgen, and Manfred Wilke, eds. *Wohin treibt die SPD? Wende oder Kontinuität sozialdemokratischer Sicherheitspolitik.* Munich: Gunter Olzog, 1984.

Mayer, Karl Ulrich. "Strukturwandel im Beschäftigungssystem und berüfliche Mobilität zwischen Generationen." In *Zeitschrift für Bevolkerungswissenschaft 5,* no. 3 (1979): 267–298.

McAdams, James. A. *East Germany and Detente.* New York: Cambridge University Press, 1985.

Mearsheimer, John. *Conventional Deterrence.* Ithaca, N.Y.: Cornell University Press, 1983.

Mechtersheimer, Alfred. *Rüstung und Frieden: Argumente für eine neue Sicherheitspolitik.* Reinbek bei Hamburg: Rowohlt, 1984.

———, ed. *Nachrüsten? Dokumente und Positionen zum Nato-Doppelbeschluss.* Reinbek bei Hamburg: Rowohlt, 1981.

Mechtersheimer, Alfred, and Peter Barth, eds. *Den Atomkrieg führbar und gewinnbar machen? Dokumente zur Nachrüstung Band 2.* Reinbek bei Hamburg: Rowohlt, 1983.

Merritt, Anna J., and Richard L. *Politics, Economies and Society in the Two Germanies, 1945-1975.* Champaign-Urbana, Illinois, 1978.

Merritt, Richard, and Donald Puchala. *Western European Perspectives on International Affairs.* New York: Praeger, 1968.

Mertes, Alois. "Friedenserhaltung—Friedensgestaltung: Zur Diskussion über 'Sicherheitspartnershaft.'" *Europa Archiv* 35 (1983):187–96.

Meuschel, Sigrid. "Neo-Nationalism and the West German Peace Movement's Reaction to the Polish Military Coup." *Telos,* no. 56 (Summer 1983): 119–30.

———. "Für Menscheit und Volk. Kritik fundamentaler und nationaler Aspekte in der deutschen Friedensbewegung." In Wolf Schäfer, ed., *Neue Soziale Bewegungen. Konservativer Aufbruch in buntem Gewand?* 37–46. Frankfurt/Main: Fischer Taschenbuch, 1983.

Meyer, Stephen M. *Soviet Theatre Nuclear Forces.* Part 1: *Development of Doctrine and Objectives.* Part 2. *Capabilities and Implications.* Adelphi Papers 187–188. London: International Institute for Strategic Studies, 1983, 1984.

Molnar, Thomas. "Der Konservatismus und die Intellektuellen." *Die Welt,* May 13, 1972.

Moreton, Edwina, and George Segal, eds. *Soviet Strategy Toward Western Europe.* London: George Allen and Unwin, 1984.

Morgenthau, Hans J. *Politics Among Nations: The Struggle for Power and Peace.* 3d ed. New York: Knopf, 1963.

———. *Scientific Man Versus Power Politics.* Chicago: University of Chicago Press, 1946; Chicago: University of Chicago, Phoenix Books, 1965.

Mosse, George. *The Crisis of German Ideology.* New York: Grosset and Dunlap, 1964.

Muller, Jerry Z. *The Other God That Failed: Hans Freyer and the Deradicalization of West German Conservatism.* Princeton, N.J.: Princeton University Press, 1987.

Murray, Williamson. *The Change in the European Balance of Power, 1938-1939,* Princeton: Princeton University Press, 1984.

Mushaben, Joyce Marie. "Anti-Politics and Successor Generations: The Role of

Youth in the West and East German Peace Movements." *The Journal of Political and Military Sociology* 12, no. 1 (Spring 1984):171–190.

Myrdal, Alva. *The Game of Disarmament.* New York: Pantheon Press, 1982.

Negt, Oskar, and Alexander Kluge. *Öffentlichkeit und Erfahrung Zur Organisationsanalyse von bürgerliche und proletarischer Öffentlichkeit.* Frankfurt/Main: Suhrkamp, 1974.

Nerlich, Uwe. "Western Europe's Relations with the United States" *Daedalus* 108, no. 1 (Winter 1979):87–112.

——. "Theatre Nuclear Forces in Europe: Is NATO Running Out of Options?" *The Washington Quarterly* 1, no. 1 (Winter 1980): 100–25.

——, ed. *Soviet Power and Western Negotiating Policies.* Vol. 1: *The Soviet Asset: Military Power in Competition over Europe.* Vol. 2: *The Western Panacea: Constraining Soviet Power Through Negotiations.* Cambridge, Mass.: Ballinger, 1983.

Nerlich, Uwe, and Falk Bomsdorf, eds. *Sowjetische Macht und westliche Verhandlungspolitik in Wandel militarischer Kraftverhältnisse* (Baden-Baden: Nomos Verlag, 1982).

Nettl, J. P. "Ideas, Intellectuals, and Structures of Dissent." In Phillip Rieff, ed., *On Intellectuals,* 57–136. New York: Anchor, 1970.

Nipperdey, Thomas, ed. *Hochschulen zwischen Politik und Wahrheit: Sind die Reformen zu verkraften?* Zurich: Edition Interfrom, 1981.

——. "Die bildungspolitische Lage an den Universitäten." *Freiheit der Wissenschaft,* no. 11 (1974):3.

——. "Schule und Hochschule." *Freiheit der Wissenschaft* (1978):3–11.

Nitze, Paul. "Deterring Our Deterrent." *Foreign Affairs* 25 (Winter 1976–77).

Nölle-Neumann, Elizabeth. *The Germans: Public Opinion Polls, 1967–1980.* London: Greenwood Press, 1981.

——. *The Spiral of Silence.* Chicago: University of Chicago Press, 1984.

——. "Are Three-Quarters of the Germans Opposed to Deployment? The Situation Is Actually More Complex." Allensbach: Institut für Demoskopie, 1983.

Nordlinger, Eric A. *On The Autonomy of the Democratic State.* Cambridge: Harvard University Press, 1981.

Paret, Peter. *Clausewitz and the State.* Princeton: Princeton University Press, 1985.

Perdelwitz, Wolf. *Wollen die Russen Krieg?* Hamburg: Stern, 1980.

Perdelwitz, Wolf, and Heiner Bremer. *Geisel Europa.* Berlin: Olle und Wolter, 1981.

Perle, Richard. "Excerpts: Speech by Assistant Secretary of Defense Richard N. Perle Before the Friedrich Ebert Foundation in Bonn, June 28." In *Wireless Bulletin from Washington,* 13–17. Bonn: United States Information Service (June 29, 1984).

Pestalozzi, Hans A. *Frieden in Deutschland.* Munich: Goldmann, 1982.

Pfaltzgraff, Robert, Jr., et al. *The Greens of West Germany: Origins, Strategies and Transatlantic Implications.* Cambridge, Mass.: Institute for Foreign Policy Analysis, 1983.

Pipes, Richard. *Soviet Strategy in Europe.* New York: Crane, Russak, 1976.

——. "Why the Soviet Union thinks it could fight and win a nuclear war." *Commentary* 64, no. 1 (July 1977).

——. *Survival Is Not Enough.* New York: Simon and Schuster, 1984.

——. "'Intelligentsia' from the German 'Intelligenz.'" *Slavic Review* 30 (September 1971): 615–618.

Pohrt, Wolfgang. *Ausverkauf: Von der Endlösung zu ihrer Alternative, Pamphlete und Essays.* Berlin: Rotbuch Verlag, 1980.

——. *Endstation: Über die Wiedergeburt der Nation.* Berlin: Rotbuch, 1982.

——. *Kreisverkehr, Wendepunkt: Über die Wechseljahre der Nation und die Linke im Widerstreit der Gefühle.* Berlin: Tiamat, 1984.

——. *Stammesbewusstsein, Kulturnation: Pamphlete, Glossen, Feuilleton.* Berlin: Tiamat, 1984.

Putnam, Robert. "Two Level Games." Paper delivered at the meeting of the American Political Science Association, Washington, D.C. August 28–31, 1986.

Rabinow, Paul, and William M. Sullivan, eds. *Interpretive Social Science: A Second Look.* Berkeley and Los Angeles: University of California Press, 1987.

Rattinger, Hans. "The Federal Republic of Germany: Much Ado About (Almost) Nothing." In Gregory Flynn and Hans Rattinger, eds., *The Public and Atlantic Defense,* 101–74. Totowa, N.J.: Rowman and Allenheld, 1985.

——. "National Security and the Missile Controversy in the West German Public." Paper delivered at the American Political Science Association Meetings, Washington, D.C. August 28–31, 1986.

Reumann, Kurt. *Blick ins Innere: Berichte von der akademischen Front.* Zurich: Edition Interfrom, 1975.

Revel, Jean-Francois. *How Democracies Perish.* Translated by William Byron. New York: Doubleday, 1984.

Roth, Roland. *Parlamentarisches Ritual und politisiche Alternativen.* Frankfurt/Main: Campus, 1980.

Rovan, Joseph. *l'Allemagne du changement.* Paris: Calmann-Levy, 1983.

Rudzio, Wolfgang. *Das politische System der Bundesrepublik Deutschland.* Opladen: Leske, 1983.

Ruegg, Walter. "The Intellectual Situation in German Higher Education." *Minerva* 12, no. 1 (Spring 1975):103–20.

Rühl, Lothar. *Machtpolitik und Friedensstrategie.* Hamburg. 1974.

——. "Soviet Policy and the Domestic Politics of Western Europe." In Richard Pipes, ed., *Soviet Strategy in Europe,* 65–103. New York: Crane, Russak: 1976.

——. "Der Nutzen militärischer Macht in Europa." In Karl Kaiser and K. Markus

Kreis, eds., *Sicberbeitspolitik vor neuen Aufgaben*, 220–272. Frankfurt/Main. Metzger, 1977.

——."Die Auswirkungen von SALT–2 auf Europa." *Eüropäische Webrkunde* 27, no. 12 (December 1978): 618–623.

——. "Der Beschluss der NATO zur Einführung nuklearer Mittlestreckenwaffen." *Europa-Archiv* 35, no. 4 (February 1980): 99–110.

——. "Das Verhandlungsangebot der NATO an der Sowjetunion: Suche nach einem Gleichgewicht bei den 'euro-strategischen' Waffen." *Europa Archiv* 35, no. 7 (April 1980): 215–226.

——. "The Media and the Image of Defence Policy." In *Defence and Consensus. The Domestic Aspect of Western Security. Part I. Adelpbi Paper No. 182.* London: International Institute for Strategic Studies, 1983.

——. "The Threat Perceived? Leverage of Soviet Military Power in Western Europe." In Uwe Nerlich, ed., *Soviet Power and Western Negotiating Policies*, vol. 1, 195–205. Cambridge, Mass.: Ballinger, 1983.

——. *Mittelstreckenwaffen in Europa: Ibre Bedeutung in Strategie, Rüstungskontrolle, und Bündnispolitik.* Baden-Baden: Nomos, 1987.

Rühle, Hans. "Warum Nachrüstung." *Aus Politik und Zeitgeschichte*, no. 38 (September 24, 1983): 20–27.

——. "The Theater Nuclear Issue in German Politics." *Strategic Review* (Spring 1981): 54–60.

——. *Angriff auf die Volkseele: Über Pazifismus zum Weltfrieden.* Zurich: Edition Interfrom, 1984.

Schäfer, Wolf, ed. *Neue Soziale Bewegungen: Konservativer Aufbruch in buntem Gewand?* Frankfurt/Main: Fischer, 1983.

Scharpf, Fritz, W. *Arbeitsmarktpolitik für Akademiker?* Meisenheim an Glan: Anton Heim, 1979.

Schelsky, Helmut. *Abschied von der Hochschulpolitik: die Universität im Fadenkreuz des Versagens.* Dusseldorf: Bertelsmann, 1969.

——. *Einsamkeit und Freiheit: Idee und Gestalt der deutshen Universität und ibrer Reformen.* Dusseldorf: Bertelsmann Universitätsverlag, 1971.

——. "The Wider Setting of Disorder in the West German Universities." *Minerva* 10, no. 4 (October 1972):614–26.

——. *Systemüberwindung, Demokratisierung, und Gewaltenteilung: Grundsatzkonflikte der Bundesrepublik.* Munich: C. H. Beck, 1973.

——. *Die Arbeit Tun die Anderen: Klassenkampf und Priesterberrschaft der Intelektuellen.* Munich: Deutscher Taschenbuch Verlag, 1977.

——. *Politik und Publizität.* Stuttgart: Seewald, 1983.

Scheuch, Erwin. *Kulturintelligenz als Machtfaktor?* Zurich: Edition Interfrom, 1974.

——. "Die Allianz zwischen Systemveränderen und Bürokraten," *Freiheit der Wissenschraft*, nos. 1 and 2 (1981), 2–10.

Schmid, Günther. *Sicherheitspolitik und Friedensbewegung: Der Konflikt um die 'Nachrüstung'*. Munich: Günter Olzog, 1982.

Schmidt, Helmut. *Defense or Retaliation*. New York: Praeger, 1962.

——. *Strategie des Gleichgewichts*. Stuttgart: Seewald, 1969.

——. *Bundestagsreden*. Edited by Peter Corterier. Bonn: AZ studio, 1975.

——. *Der Kurs heisst Frieden*. Dusseldorf: Econ, 1979.

——. *Helmut Schmidt: Perspectives on Politics*. Edited by Wolfram Hanreider. Boulder: Westview, 1982.

——. "Zur Lage der Sicherheitspolitik." In Jürgen Maruhn and Manfred Wilke, eds., *Wohin treibt die SPD?* 129–64. Munich: Günter Olzog, 1984.

——. *Freiheit Verantworten*. Dusseldorf: Econ, 1983.

——. *Pflicht zur Menschlichkeit*. Dusseldorf: Econ, 1984.

——. *Menschen und Mächte*. Berlin: Siedler, 1987.

Schnitzer, Klaus, et al. *Das soziale Bild der Studentenschaft in der Bundesrepublik Deutschland. 10. Sozialerhebung des Deutschen Studentenwerks*. Schriftenreihe Hochschule 46. Bonn: Bundesminister für Bildung und Wissenschaft, 1983.

Schössler, Dietmar. *West German Elite Views on National Security and Foreign Policy Issues*. Konigstein, Ts.: Athenauem, 1978.

Schröder, Diethelm, ed. *Krieg oder was sonst? NATO Strategie der Unsicherheit*. Reinbek bei Hamburg: Rowohlt, 1984.

Schubert, Klaus v., ed. *Heidelberger Friedensmemorandum*. Reinbek bei Hamburg: Rowohlt, 1983.

Schumacher, Kurt. *Türmwachter der Demokratie. Reden und Schriften*. Edited by Arno Schulz and Walther G. Oschilweski. Berlin: Arani Verlag, 1953.

Schwan, Alexander, and Gasine Schwan. *Socialdemokratie und Marxismus. Zum Spannungsverhältnis von Godesberger Programm und marxistischer Theorie*. Hamburg: Hoffmann und Campe, 1974.

Schwan, Gasine. "Die SPD und die westliche Freiheit." In Jürgen Maruhn and Manfred Wilke, eds., *Wohin treibt die SPD?* 38–52. Munich: Günter Olzog, 1984.

Schwartz, David. *NATO's Nuclear Dilemmas*. Washington, D.C.: Brookings Institution, 1983.

Schwarz, Hans-Peter. "Die aussenpolitische Grundlagen des westdeutschen Staates." In Richard Lowenthal and Hans-Peter Schwarz, eds., *Die zweite Republik*, 27–63. Stuttgart: Seewald, 1974.

——. "Das europäische Konzert der gelähmten Leviathane: Variationen zum Thema Unregierbarkeit und Aussenpolitik." In Wilhelm Hennis et al., eds., *Regierbarkeit: Studien zu ihrer Problematisierung*, vol. 1, 296–312. Stuttgart: Klett-Cotta, 1977.

——. "Finnlandisierung Ein Reizwort: Wirklichkeit und Aktualität." *Politische Meinung* 23 (November–December 1978):14–23.

——. *Vom Reich zur Bundesrepublik: Deutschland in Widerstreit der aussenpolitischen Konzeptionen in den Jahren der Besatzungsherrschaft, 1945–1949.* 2d ed. Stuttgart: Klett, 1980.

——. *Die Ära Adenauer, 1949–1957.* Vol. 2 of *Geschichte der Bundesrepublik Deutschland.* Stuttgart: Deutsche Verlags-Anstalt, 1981.

——. *Die Ära Adenauer, 1957–1963.* Vol. 3 of *Geschichte der Bundesrepublik Deutschland.* Stuttgart: Deutsche, Verlags-Anstalt, 1983.

——. "The West Germans, Western Democracy, and Western Ties in Light of Public Opinion Research." Paper delivered at a conference on German-American Relations and the Federal Republic of Germany at the Wilson Center, Washington, D.C. September 22–23, 1983.

——. *Die gezähmten Deutschen: Von der Machtbesessenheit zur Machtvergessenheit.* Stuttgart: Deutsche Verlags-Anstalt, 1985.

Schwarz, Hans-Peter, and Boris Meissner, eds. *Entspannungspolitik in Ost und West.* Cologne: Heymann, 1979.

Schwarz, Klaus-Deiter, ed. *Sicherheitspolitik.* 3d ed. Bad Honnef-Erpel: Osang, 1981.

Seidel, Peter. *Die Diskussion um den Doppelbeschluss: Eine Zwischenbilanz.* Munich: Bernard & Graefe, 1982.

Senghaas, Dieter. *Gewalt, Konflikt, Frieden.* Hamburg: Hoffman und Campe, 1974.

——. *Abschreckung und Frieden: Studien zur Kritik organisierter Friedlosigkeit 1969.* Rev. ed. Frankfurt/Main: Europäische Verlagsanstalt, 1981.

——. "Auch ohne die drohende SS-20 hätte die NATO umgerüstet." In *Frankfurter Rundschau,* July 21, 1981.

——, ed. *Imperialismus und strukturelle Gewalt.* Frankfurt/Main: Suhrkamp, 1973.

Shils, Edward. *The Intellectuals and the Powers and Other Essays.* Chicago: University of Chicago Press, 1972.

——. *Tradition.* Chicago: University of Chicago Press, 1981.

Shils, Edward. "Center and Periphery." In *The Constitution of Society,* 93–109. Chicago: University of Chicago Press, 1982.

Sontheimer, Kurt. *Der Überdruss an Demokratie: Neue Linke, Alte Rechte.* Cologne: Markus, 1970.

——. *Das Elend unserer Intellektuellen: Linke Theorie in der Bundesrepublik Deutschland.* Hamburg: Hoffman und Campe, 1976.

——. *Die verunsicherte Republik.* Munich: Piper, 1979.

——. "Zwei deutsche Republiken und ihre Intellektuellen." *Merkur* (November 1982):1062–71.

——. *Zeitenwende? Die Bundesrepublik Deutschland zwischen alter und alternativer Politik.* Hamburg: Hoffman und Campe, 1983.

Sperber, Mannes. "Rede anlässlich der Verleihung des Friedenpreises des Deutschen Buchhandels am 16. Oktober 1983." In Jürgen Maruhn and Manfred Wilke, eds., *Wohin treibt die SPD?* 171–86. Munich: Günter Olzog, 1984.

Spiegel-Untersuchungen, -Dokumentation, -Beratungsservice. *Arbeitsdaten. Reichweite und Affinität für alle überregionalen Zeitschriften und Zeitungen.* Hamburg: Spiegel Verlag, for years 1973–84.

Statistisches Bundesamt. *Statistische Jahrbücher für die Bundesrepublik Deutschland.* 1950–1984.

Steinweg, Reiner, ed. *Friedensanalysen: Für Theorie und Praxis 2. Schwerpunkt: Rüstung.* Frankfurt/Main: Suhrkamp, 1976.

———. *Das kontrollierte Chaos: Die Krise der Abrüstung.* Frankfurt/Main: Suhrkamp, 1980.

———. *Die neue Friedensbewegung. Analysen aus der Friedensforschung.* Frankfurt/Main: Suhrkamp, 1982.

Stent, Angela. *From Embargo to Ostpolitik.* London: Cambridge University Press, 1981.

———. "The USSR and Germany." *Problems of Communism* (September–October 1981):1–24.

Stern, Fritz. *The Politics of Cultural Despair.* New York: Anchor, 1965. Reprint Berkeley and Los Angeles: University of California Press, 1974.

Stratmann, K. Peter. "Entspannung contra Sicherheit? Zur Notwendigkeit einer offensiven Rüstungskontrollpolitik der NATO für Europa." In Stiftung Wissenschaft und Politik, ed., *Polarität und Interdependenz. Beiträge zu Fragen der Internationalen Politik,* 167–185. Baden-Baden: Nomos, 1978.

———. *NATO Strategie in der Krise.* Baden-Baden: Nomos, 1981.

———. "Vorlage zur öffentlichen Anhörung im Verteidigungsausschus des Deutschen Bundestages zum Thema 'Alternativen Strategien.'" *Verteidigungsausschuss. Stenographisches Protokoll: Anhörung von sachverständigen zum Thema 'Alternative Strategien.'* Bonn: 10. Wahlperiode (November 28, 1983).

Strauss, Franz-Josef. *Gebote der Freiheit.* Munich: Grünewald, 1980.

Stürmer, Michael. *Deutsche Fragen: Oder die Suche nach der Staatsräson.* Munich: Piper, 1988.

Stützle, Walter. *Politik und Kräftverhältnis.* Herford: Mittler, 1983.

Szabo, Stephen F. *The Successor Generation: International Perspectives of Postwar Europeans.* London: Butterworths, 1983.

———. "Brandt's Children: The West German Successor Generation." *Washington Quarterly* 7, no. 1 (Winter 1984):50–59.

Talbott, Strobe. *Deadly Gambits.* New York: Knopf, 1984.

Tarcov, Nathan. "Principle and Prudence in Foreign Policy: The Founders' Perspective." *The Public Interest,* no. 76 (1984):45–60.

Tatu, Michel. "Public Opinion as Both Means and Ends for Policy-Makers." *Adelphi Papers* 191 (Summer 1984):26–33.

———. *La bataille des euromissiles.* Paris: Editions du Seuil, 1983.

Tatz, Jürgen, ed. *Alternativen zur Abschreckungspolitik.* Freiburg i. Br.: Dreisam, 1983.

Teichler, Ulrich. *Higher Education and the Needs of Society.* Oxford: International Labor Organization, 1980.

———. *Der Arbeitsmarkt für Hochschulabsolventen.* Munich: K. G. Saur, 1981.

Telos, no. 51 (Spring 1982). Special issue on the European Peace Movements.

Tenbruck, Friedrich H. "Frieden durch Friedensforschung? Ein Heilsglaube unserer Zeit." *Frankfurter Allgemeine Zeitung* (December 22, 1973). Reprinted in Klaus Hornung, ed., *Frieden ohne Utopie,* 91–112. Krefeld: Sinus, 1983.

———. *Die unbewältigten Sozialwissenschaften oder Die Abschaffung des Menschen.* Vienna and Cologne: Verlag Styria, 1984.

Tessaring, Manfred and Heinz Werner. *Beschäftigungsprobleme und Hochschulabsolventen im internationalen Vergleich.* Göttingen: Otto Schwartz, 1975.

———. *Beschäftigung und Arbeitsmarkt für Hochschulabsolventen in den Ländern der Europäischen Gemeinschaft.* Beiträge zur Arbeitsmarkt und Berufsforschung No. 46. Nürnberg: Institut für Arbeitsmarkt und Berufsforschung der Bundesanstalt für Arbeit: 1981.

Thompson, Edward, et al. *Exterminism and Cold War.* London: Verso, 1982.

Thomson, James A. "The LRTNF decision: evolution of US theatre nuclear policy." *International Affairs* 60, no. 4 (1984):601–15.

Thucydides. *The Peloponnesian War.* Translated by Rex Warner. Baltimore: Penguin, 1954. Reprint 1965.

Tocqueville, Alexis de. *The Old Regime and the French Revolution.* Translated by Stuart Gilbert. Garden City, N.J.: Anchor, 1960.

Treverton, Gregory F. "Nuclear Weapons and the 'Grey Area.'" *Foreign Affairs* 57, no. 5 (Summer 1979): 1075–1089.

Tucker, Robert W., and Linda Wrigley, eds. *The Atlantic Alliance and Its Critics.* New York: Praeger, 1983.

Turner, Henry Ashby, Jr. *The Two Germanies Since 1945.* New Haven and London: Yale University Press, 1987.

Ulam, Adam. *Dangerous Relations. The Soviet Union and the World, 1970–1982,* New York: Oxford University Press, 1983.

———. "Europe in Soviet Eyes." *Problems of Communism* (May–June 1983): 22–30.

Venohr, Wolfgang, ed. *Die deutsche Einheit kommt bestimmt.* Bergische Gladbach: Lübbe, 1982.

Verband Deutscher Schriftsteller. *Ende der Bescheidenheit. Die Texte der Grundungssammlung des Verbands Deutscher Schriftsteller (VS).* Munich: 1969.

Vinocur, John. "New German Worry: Nationalism on the Left." *The New York Times Magazine,* November 12, 1981.

Vogt, Wolfgang R., ed. *Sicherheitspolitik und Streitkräfte in der Legitimitätskrise: Analysen zum Prozess der Delegitimierung des Militärischen im Kernwaffenzeitalter.* Baden-Baden: Nomos, 1983.

Voigt, Karsten. *Wege zur Abrüstung.* Frankfurt/Main: Eichborn, 1981.

Walser, Martin, ed. *Die Alternative oder Brauchen Wir Eine Neue Regierung?* Reinbek bei Hamburg: Rowohlt, 1961.

Waltz, Kenneth. *Man, the State, and War.* New York: Columbia University Press, 1959.

———. *Foreign Policy and Democratic Politics: The American and British Experience.* Boston: Little, Brown, 1967.

———. *Theory of International Politics.* 1979. Reprint. Reading, Mass.: Addison-Wesley, 1983.

Weber, Max. *From Max Weber: Essays in Sociology.* Translated, edited and with an introduction by H. H. Gerth and C. Wright Mills. New York: Oxford University Press, 1948.

Weidenfeld, Werner, ed. *Die Identität der Deutschen.* Munich: Hanser, 1983.

Weinberg, Gerhard. *The Foreign Policy of Hitler's Germany.* 2 vols. Chicago: University of Chicago Press, 1970, 1980.

Weizsäcker, Carl Friedrich von. *Wege in der Gefahr.* Munich: Hanser Verlag, 1976; reprint, Munich: DTV, 1981.

———. *Der bedrohte Friede. Politische Aufsätze, 1945–1981.* Munich: Deutscher Taschenbuch, 1983.

Wettig, Gerhard. "Die Sowjetunion und die eurostrategische Problematik." In *Politische Vierteljahresschrift* 21, no. 4 (1980):346–62.

———. *Die Funktion der westeuropäischen Friedensbewegung in sowjetischer Sicht.* Berichte des Bundesinstituts für ostwissenschaftliche und internationale Studien, no. 49, 1983.

Wieseltier, Leon. *Nuclear War, Nuclear Peace.* New York: Holt, Rinehart and Winston, 1983.

Wight, Martin. "The balance of power." In H. Butterfield and Martin Wight, eds., *Diplomatic Investigations: Essays in the Theory of International Politics.* London: Allen and Unwin.

———. *Systems of States.* Atlantic Heights, N.J.: Humanities Press, 1977.

———. *Power Politics.* Leicester: Leicester University Press, 1978.

Wildenmann, Rudolf. "Praxis und Techniken der 'Vollversammlungs-demokratie." *Hochschulpolitische Information* 2, no. 8 (May 6, 1971):1–6.

———. *Studenten 79. Studentische Beteiligung an den universitären Wahlen.* Bonn: Forum des Hochschulverbandes, 1980.

——. "Die Elite wünscht den Wechsel. Unsere Oberen Dreitausend (II): Mehr 'Rechts' als 'Links.'" *Die Zeit*, no. 11 (1982).

——. "Public Opinion and the Defence Effort: Trends and Lessons. Europe." In *Defence and Consensus: The Domestic Aspects of Western Security*, Part i, 24–28. Adelphi Paper 182. London: International Institute for Strategic Studies, 1983.

Wohlstetter, Albert. "Is There a Strategic Arms Race?" *Foreign Policy*, no. 15 (Summer 1974):3–20.

Wolfers, Arnold. *Discord and Collaboration: Essays on International Politics*. Baltimore: Johns Hopkins, 1962.

Zöller, Michael, ed. *Aufklärung heute: Bedingungen unserer Freiheit*. Zurich: Edition Interfrom, 1980.

INDEX